PROGRAMMING
PERL
in the
.NET
ENVIRONMENT

D1258546

ISBN 0-13-065206-7

90000

9 790130 6 2064

The Integrated .NET Series from Object Innovations and Prentice Hall PTR

C#

Introduction to C# Using .NET
Oberg

Application Development Using C# and .NET
Stiefel/Oberg

VISUAL BASIC

Introduction to Visual Basic Using .NET
Wyatt/Oberg

Application Development Using Visual Basic and .NET
Oberg/Thorsteinson/Wyatt

VISUAL C++

.NET Architecture and Programming Using Visual C++
Thorsteinson/Oberg

WEB APPLICATIONS

Fundamentals of Web Applications Using .NET and XML
Bell/Feng/Soong/Zhang/Zhu

PERL

Programming Perl in the .NET Environment
Menaker/Saltzman/Oberg

PROGRAMMING
PERL
in the .NET
ENVIRONMENT

YEVGENY MENAKER
MICHAEL SALTZMAN
ROBERT J. OBERG

PH
PTR

Prentice Hall PTR, Upper Saddle River, NJ 07458
www.phptr.com

Library of Congress Cataloging-in-Publication Data

Menaker, Yevgeny.
  Programming Perl in the .NET Environment / Yevgeny Menaker, Michael Saltzman,
  Robert J. Oberg
        p. cm.—(Integrated .NET series from Object Innovations and Prentice Hall PTR)
  Includes index.
  ISBN 0-13-065206-7
  1. Perl (Computer program language). 2. Microsoft .NET. I. Saltzman, Michael. II.
  Oberg, Robert J. III. Title. IV. Series.

  QA76.73.P22 M47 2002
  005.2'762—dc21   2002030774

Editorial/production supervision: *Jane Bonnell*
Composition: *Argosy Publishing*
Cover design director: *Jerry Votta*
Cover design: *Anthony Gemmellaro*
Interior series design: *Gail Cocker-Bogusz*
Manufacturing buyer: *Maura Zaldivar*
Executive editor: *Jill Harry*
Editorial assistant: *Kate Wolf*
Marketing manager: *Dan DePasquale*

© 2003 Pearson Education, Inc.
Publishing as Prentice Hall PTR
Upper Saddle River, New Jersey 07458

Prentice Hall books are widely used by corporations and government agencies for training, marketing, and resale.
For information regarding corporate and government bulk discounts please contact:
Corporate and Government Sales (800) 382-3419 or corpsales@pearsontechgroup.com

Company and product names mentioned herein are the trademarks or registered trademarks
of their respective owners.

Printed in the United States of America
10 9 8 7 6 5 4 3 2

ISBN 0-13-065206-7

Pearson Education LTD.
Pearson Education Australia PTY, Limited
Pearson Education Singapore, Pte. Ltd.
Pearson Education North Asia Ltd.
Pearson Education Canada, Ltd.
Pearson Educación de Mexico, S.A. de C.V.
Pearson Education—Japan
Pearson Education Malaysia, Pte. Ltd.

CONTENTS

FOREWORD

I've been working with Perl and Microsoft technologies since 1994, when I helped port Perl 5 to the Windows platform. Microsoft funded this effort and subsequent projects: Perl for ISAPI which allows Perl to run in-process to IIS; and PerlScript, an ActiveScripting engine for Perl.

These projects paved the way for over a million programmers to easily use Perl on the Windows platform. Growing interest in Perl led to ActiveState's founding in 1997, with the goal of creating solutions that enable customers to leverage their Perl expertise.

With ActiveState, I feel fortunate to have had the opportunity to make it easier for programmers to use Perl with new technologies and to bridge the gap between the open source community and Microsoft technologies.

This connection became even stronger when ActiveState was one of the first firms Microsoft approached to work with the .NET Framework, a significant advancement in platform architectures. This platform is still young and how languages such as Perl work with it are still evolving. This is an exciting time!

Books are an important part of how a new technology is adopted. With the knowledge contained in this book, you will be able to tap into the power that Perl offers you when working with the .NET Framework.

Enjoy!

Dick Hardt
Founder and CEO of ActiveState

Microsoft .NET is an advance in programming technology that greatly simplifies application development both for traditional, proprietary applications and for the emerging paradigm of Web services. The technology was designed to grow and evolve by providing us an option to add third-party products, such as plug-ins for Visual Studio and compilers for different languages. As part of an effort to integrate the popular Perl language into the Microsoft development environment in general and into the .NET family specifically, ActiveState has recently released a new product, PerlNET, which is part of the Perl Development Kit. With PerlNET it is now possible to use and create .NET components and to wrap existing Perl modules so that they are available to all .NET-compliant languages. PerlNET enables you to enjoy both worlds—.NET and Perl. By combining their features you'll have an ability to develop powerful robust components that may be reused in other .NET applications.

Audience

This book is intended for both .NET and Perl programmers to help bring these two rich worlds together. In Perl there is a saying: "There is always more than one way to do it." That is even more true now, as you can add "the .NET way." If you are a Perl programmer, this book will help you understand .NET and the vast array of services available to you. You will learn how, through Web services, you can connect to a wide variety of heterogeneous systems using standard Internet protocols. If you are a .NET programmer, you will learn why Perl has become one of the most popular languages in the world and how to access the vast CPAN archive of Perl modules.

Overview and Organization

The book has been designed to make it easy for you to navigate to what you need to know. Part 1 is an introduction to .NET and Perl and should be at least skimmed by everyone, with different emphasis depending on your background. Chapter 1 introduces .NET and covers the fundamentals of the .NET Framework. It also guides you to setting up a testbed consisting of .NET, Perl, and the special tools provided by ActiveState. If you are an experienced Perl programmer, you can skip directly to Part 2.

If you are new to Perl, you can quickly come up to speed with the tutorial on Core Perl in Chapters 2 to 8. It includes an in-depth treatment of objects in

Perl and introduces the CPAN Perl archive. The treatment of Core Perl is very generic, and you will easily be able to apply what you have learned to any system that supports Perl. You can read much more about Perl in the book *Modern Perl Programming* by Michael Saltzman (Prentice Hall PTR, 2002). In that book you can also learn how to program Perl in a UNIX environment. In this book we focus on programming Perl in Windows. Part of the joy of programming Perl in Windows is Visual Perl, which is an add-on to Visual Studio .NET. We cover Visual Studio and Visual Perl in Appendix A.

Part 2 covers in detail the use of PerlNET to bring together the worlds of .NET and Perl. We show you how to use .NET classes in Perl programs and how to create .NET components using Perl. Important .NET classes are surveyed, and there is coverage of using .NET in specific areas, including graphical user interfaces, database programming, and using ADO.NET, ASP.NET, and Web services.

You can learn much more about .NET from other books in The Integrated .NET Series. Also, Appendix B, "C# Survival Guide for PerlNET Programmers," will help you get started with C#, and you can see how Perl interoperates with .NET languages, using C#, the language designed for .NET, as an example.

Sample Programs

The only way to really learn a programming language is to read and write many, many programs. This book provides many programs that illustrate features of Perl and .NET. The sample programs are provided in a self-extracting file on the book's Web site. When expanded, a directory structure is created whose default root is **c:\OI\NetPerl**. The sample programs are in directories **Chap01**, **Chap02**, and so on. All the samples for a given chapter are in individual folders within the chapter directories. The names of the folders are clearly identified in the text. An icon in the margin alerts you to a code example. Visual Perl projects are provided for the sample programs, and they can also be built at the command line. There is also a stock management case study that illustrates many features of Perl and .NET working together in combination, as they would in a practical application. A special point is made of demonstrating the object-oriented features of Perl and .NET. If you are new to object orientation, studying the case study is a must!

Code
Example

Web Site

The Web site for the book series is *www.objectinnovations.com/dotnet.htm*. A link is provided at that Web site for downloading the sample programs for this book.

Acknowledgments

We are indebted to Mike Meehan for helping to launch not only this book project but also the entire Integrated .NET Series, of which this volume is the seventh. We would also like to thank Jill Harry, our editor at Prentice Hall, for her ongoing support of this ambitious project.

A technical book always depends on reviewers, and on this book we were particularly fortunate to have very conscientious reviews by Srini Manickam and Avi Ruzhinsky. Jan Dubois of ActiveState, the author of PerlNET, was kind enough to review several chapters, helping to keep us on the right path. Despite being busy, Jan always was there to answer the authors' questions concerning PerlNET and did it in the best way. Naturally, the responsibility for any remaining mistakes or missteps remains with the authors.

We would also like to thank Eric Promislow and Dick Hardt of ActiveState for their support and encouragement and for the software they provided to us.

Yevgeny thanks his parents, Arkady and Nina, for creating the inspiring atmosphere at home and for their encouragement along the way. Many thanks to all my friends for taking a keen interest in the book; this always cheered me up.

Robert would like to thank his wife, Marianne, for all her support of his long .NET book writing project. This one is the last for a while, and you will see a little bit more of me!

Michael would like to thank his wife, Susan, and his coworkers Alan Baumgarten, Dave Flanagan, Erin Flanagan, Maria Gonzales, and Patti Ordonez. Also belated thanks go to Stan McFarland for his assistance in many Perl endeavors.

About this Series
Robert J. Oberg, Series Editor

Introduction

The Integrated .NET Book Series from Object Innovations and Prentice Hall PTR is a unique series of introductory and intermediate books on Microsoft's important .NET technology. These books are based on proven industrial-strength course development experience. The authors are expert practitioners, teachers, and writers who combine subject-matter expertise with years of experience in presenting complex programming technologies such as C++, MFC, OLE, and COM/COM+. These books *teach* in a systematic, step-by-step manner and are not merely summaries of the documentation. All the books come with a rich set of programming examples, and a thematic case study is woven through several of the books.

From the beginning, these books have been conceived as an *integrated whole*, and not as independent efforts by a diverse group of authors. The initial set of books consists of three introductory books on .NET languages and four intermediate books on the .NET Framework. Each book in the series is targeted at a specific part of the important .NET technology, as illustrated by the diagram below.

		C# Learning Pathway	VB.NET Learning Pathway		
.NET Language Introductions	**Programming Perl in the .NET Environment**	Introduction to C# Using .NET	Introduction to Visual Basic Using .NET		
Intermediate .NET Framework Titles		Application Development Using C# and .NET	Application Development Using Visual Basic and .NET	.NET Architecture and Programming Using Visual C++	Fundamentals of Web Applications Using .NET and XML

Introductory .NET Language Books

The first set of books teaches several of the important .NET languages. These books cover their language from the ground up and have no prerequisite other than programming experience in some language. Unlike many .NET language books, which are a mixture of the language and topics in the .NET Framework, these books are focused on the languages, with attention to important interactions between the language and the framework. By concentrating on the languages, these books have much more detail and many more practical examples than similar books.

The languages selected are the new language C#, the greatly changed VB.NET, and PerlNET, the open source language ported to the .NET environment. Visual C++ .NET is covered in a targeted, intermediate book, and JScript.NET is covered in the intermediate level .NET Web-programming book.

Introduction to C# Using .NET

This book provides thorough coverage of the C# language from the ground up. It is organized with a specific section covering the parts of C# common to other C-like languages. This section can be cleanly skipped by programmers with C experience or the equivalent, making for a good reading path for a diverse group of readers. The book gives thorough attention to the object-oriented aspects of C# and thus serves as an excellent book for programmers migrating to C# from Visual Basic or COBOL. Its gradual pace and many examples make the book an excellent candidate as a college textbook for adventurous professors looking to teach C# early in the language's life-cycle.

Introduction to Visual Basic Using .NET

Learn the VB.NET language from the ground up. Like the companion book on C#, this book gives thorough attention to the object-oriented aspects of VB.NET. Thus the book is excellent for VB programmers migrating to the more sophisticated VB.NET, as well as for programmers experienced in languages such as COBOL. This book would also be suitable as a college textbook.

Programming Perl in the .NET Environment

A very important part of the vision behind Microsoft® .NET is that the platform is designed from the ground up to support multiple programming languages from many sources, and not just Microsoft languages. This book, like other books in the series, is rooted in long experience in industrial teaching. It covers the Perl language from the ground up. Although oriented toward the ActiveState PerlNET compiler, the book also provides excellent coverage of the Perl language suitable for other versions as well.

Intermediate .NET Framework Books

The second set of books is focused on topics in the .NET Framework, rather than on programming languages. Three parallel books cover the .NET Framework using the important languages C#, VB.NET, and Visual C++. The C# and VB.NET books include self-contained introductions to the languages suitable for experienced programmers, allowing them to rapidly come up to speed on these languages without having to plow through the introductory books. The fourth book covers the important topic of Web programming in .NET, with substantial coverage of XML, which is so important in the .NET Framework.

The design of the series makes these intermediate books much more suitable to a wider audience than many similar books. The introductory books' focus on languages frees up the intermediate books to cover the important topics of the .NET Framework in greater depth. The series design also makes for flexible reading paths. Less experienced readers can read the introductory language books followed by the intermediate framework books, while more experienced readers can go directly to the intermediate framework books.

Application Development Using C# and .NET

This book does not require prior experience in C#. However, the reader should have experience in some object-oriented language such as C++ or Java™. The book could also be read by seasoned Visual Basic programmers who have experience working with objects and components in VB. Seasoned programmers and also a less experienced reader coming from the introductory C# book can skip the first few chapters on C# and proceed directly to a study of the framework. The book is practical, with many examples and a major case study. The goal is to equip the reader with the knowledge necessary to begin building significant applications using the .NET Framework.

Application Development Using Visual Basic and .NET

This book is for the experienced VB programmer who wishes to learn the new VB.NET version of VB quickly and then move on to learning the .NET Framework. It is also suitable for experienced enterprise programmers in other languages who wish to learn the powerful RAD-oriented Visual Basic language in its .NET incarnation and go on to building applications. Like the companion C# book, this book is very practical, with many examples, and includes the same case study implemented in VB.NET.

.NET Architecture and Programming Using Visual C++

This parallel book is for the experienced Visual C++ programmer who wishes to learn the .NET Framework to build high-performing applications. Unlike the C# and VB.NET book, there is no coverage of the C++ language itself, because C++ is too complex to cover in a brief space. This book is specifically for experienced C++ programmers. Like the companion C# and VB.NET books, this book is very practical, with many examples, and includes the same case study implemented in Visual C++.

Fundamentals of Web Applications Using .NET and XML

The final book in the series provides thorough coverage of building Web applications using .NET. Unlike other books about ASP.NET, this book gives attention to the whole process of Web application development. The book incorporates a review tutorial on classical Web programming, making the book accessible to the experienced programmer new to the Web world. The book contains significant coverage on ASP.NET, Web Forms, Web services, SOAP, and XML.

INTRODUCTION TO .NET AND PERL

INTRODUCTION TO .NET AND PERL

Part 1 is an introduction to .NET and Perl and should be at least skimmed by everyone, with different emphasis depending on your background. Chapter 1 introduces .NET and covers the fundamentals of the .NET Framework. It also guides you to setting up a testbed consisting of .NET, Perl, and the special tools provided by ActiveState. If you are an experienced Perl programmer, you can now skip directly to Part 2.

If you are new to Perl, you can quickly come up to speed with the tutorial on Core Perl in Chapters 2 to 8. It includes an in-depth treatment of objects in Perl and introduces the CPAN Perl archive. The treatment of Core Perl is very generic, and you will easily be able to apply what you have learned to any system that supports Perl. In this book we focus on programming Perl in Windows. Part of the joy of programming Perl in Windows is Visual Perl, which is an add-on to Visual Studio .NET. We cover Visual Studio and Visual Perl in Appendix A.

.NET Framework

*T*he open source language Perl has become one of the most popular languages in the world, widely used as a scripting language in Web applications. Microsoft .NET is a new framework in the Windows environment that allows multiple languages to compile down to the Common Language Runtime (CLR) and to make use of the vast array of functionality provided by the .NET Framework class library. Microsoft itself provides support for the languages C#, Visual Basic .NET, Visual C++ .NET, and JScript .NET. Third parties are providing support for many other programming languages in the .NET environment. ActiveState supports Perl through the PerlNET tool. In this chapter, we introduce the .NET Framework in sufficient detail so that you can immediately begin Perl programming in the .NET environment. For more in-depth information about .NET, you can refer to Part 2 of this book and to other books in The Integrated .NET Series from Object Innovations and Prentice Hall PTR.

.NET: What You Need to Know

A beautiful thing about .NET is that, from a programmer's perspective, you scarcely need to know anything about it to write programs for the .NET environment. You write a program in a high-level language, a compiler creates an executable (.EXE) file, and you run that EXE file. We show you exactly how to do that in just a few pages. Naturally, as the scope of what you want to do expands, you will need to know more, but to get started you need to know very little.

Even very simple programs, if they perform any input or output, generally require the use of the services found in *library* code. A large library, called the

.NET Framework Class Library, comes with .NET, and you can use all of the services of this library in your programs.

What is *really* happening in a .NET program is somewhat elaborate. The EXE file that is created does not contain executable code, but rather *Intermediate Language,* or IL, code (sometimes called Microsoft Intermediate Language, or MSIL). In the Windows environment, this IL code is packaged up in a standard portable executable (PE) file format, so you will see the familiar EXE extension (or, if you are building a component, the DLL extension). When you run the EXE, a special runtime environment (the CLR) is launched, and the IL instructions are executed by the CLR. Unlike some runtimes, where the IL would be interpreted each time it is executed, the CLR comes with a just-in-time (JIT) compiler, which translates the IL to native machine code the first time it is encountered. Then, on subsequent calls, the code segment runs as native code.

Thus, in a nutshell, the process of programming in the .NET environment is:

1. Write your program in a high-level .NET language.
2. Compile your program into IL.
3. Run your IL program, which will launch the CLR to execute your IL, using its JIT to translate your program to native code as it executes.

A Testbed for PerlNET

If you're like most programmers, you don't want to start a programming book with a lot of theory, but would like to get your feet wet with a little programming right away. This section is intended to get you up and running using the .NET Framework SDK and PerlNET. If you want to continue in hands-on mode, you can then proceed directly to Chapter 2. If you would like to get some .NET theory under your belt, you could read the rest of this chapter.

Installing the .NET SDK

The first tool you need to compile and run the programs in this book is the .NET Framework SDK. This SDK is available on CD or can be downloaded for free from the Microsoft .NET Web site, *http://msdn.microsoft.com/net/*. Follow the installation directions for the SDK, and make sure that your computer meets the hardware requirements. (A rule of thumb for the SDK is that you need a fast Pentium processor and at least 128M of RAM.) The recommended software requirements include Windows 2000 or Windows XP. Part of the installation is a Windows Component Update, which updates your system, if necessary, to recent versions of programs such as Internet Explorer. The SDK installs tools such as compilers, documentation, sample programs, and the CLR.

The starting place for the SDK documentation is the .NET Framework SDK Overview (see Figure 1-1).

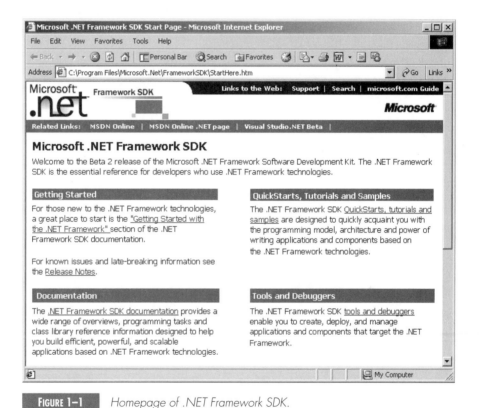

FIGURE 1-1   *Homepage of .NET Framework SDK.*

Installing the Perl Dev Kit (PDK)

The second tool you need is the Perl Dev Kit, or PDK, from ActiveState. The PDK can be downloaded from the ActiveState Web site, *www.ActiveState.com*. Follow the installation directions for the PDK. If your system meets the hardware and software requirements for the .NET Framework SDK, you will automatically meet the requirements of the PDK, which are less stringent. The PDK installs tools such as PerlApp, PerlCOM, PerlNET, and HTML documentation. Figure 1-2 illustrates the home page of the PDK documentation.

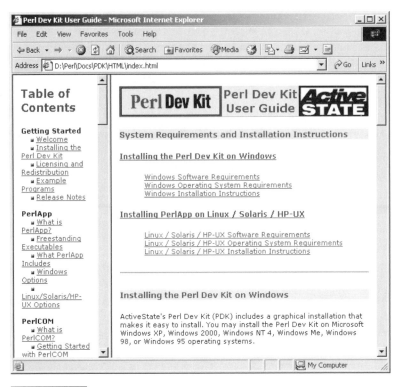

FIGURE 1–2   *Homepage of the PDK documentation.*

Installing the Book Software

The example programs found in this book are available on the Web site *http://www.objectinnovations.com/dotnet/*. Download the file **Install_NetPerl.exe**. Then, run this self-extracting file. If you accept the suggested installation directory, the software will be installed in the directory **OI\NetPerl** on your C: drive. There are subdirectories for each chapter of the book. The directory for Chapter 1 is **Chap01**. Sample programs are in named subdirectories of the chapter directory, and we refer to these sample programs simply by name, such as **Hello**.

Your First PerlNET Program

Code
Example

Although we won't actually start to examine the structure of PerlNET programs until Chapter 9, you don't have to wait to compile and run your first PerlNET program. Start the command prompt and navigate to the **HelloPerlNET** directory for this chapter (if you accepted the default installation, the directory is

c:\OI\PerlNet\Chap01\HelloPerlNET). The source file is **Hello.pl**. To compile this program, enter the following command:

```
>plc hello.pl
```

The file **Hello.exe** will be created, which you can now run.

```
>hello
Hello World!
```

Perl and PerlNET

If you have previously worked with Perl, you may be a bit confused by the concept of "compiling" a Perl source file into an "executable" file such as **Hello.exe**. After all, Perl is an interpreted language. The normal way you program with Perl is to run the Perl interpreter against a Perl script file. As an illustration, go to the folder **Chap01\HelloPerl**. You can then run the Perl script **HelloPerl.pl** by the command perl helloperl.pl, which invokes the Perl interpreter.

What is happening when you use the PerlNET compiler to create an executable? Ordinary, IL code is generated. The IL code calls the Perl interpreter to execute Perl statements.

Also, if you compare the files in **HelloPerlNET** and **HelloPerl**, you will see that the first file uses the .NET class **Console** to perform output, while the second file uses the Perl **print** statement. These concepts are described in more detail in Part 2 of this book.

Visual Studio .NET and Visual Perl

Although the PDK and .NET Framework SDK are all you need to compile and run PerlNET programs, the process is much easier and more pleasant if you use the Visual Studio .NET integrated development environment (IDE). The IDE provides an easy-to-use editor, access to the compiler and debugger, and access to online help. Visual Perl is an add-on, which allows you to work with Perl projects quite seamlessly with the Visual Studio environment. We discuss Visual Studio .NET and Visual Perl in Appendix A.

Understanding .NET

If you are eager to start learning about PerlNET programming right away, and you already know Perl, by all means proceed directly to Chapter 9. The nice thing about a high-level programming language is that, for the most part, you do not need to be concerned with the platform on which the program executes (unless you are making use of services provided by the platform). You can work with the abstractions provided by the language and with functions provided by libraries.

However, you will appreciate PerlNET and its potential for creating sophisticated applications better if you have a general understanding of .NET.

The rest of this chapter is concerned with helping you to achieve such an understanding. We address three broad topics:

- What Is Microsoft .NET?
- .NET Framework
- Common Language Runtime

What Is Microsoft .NET?

In this section, we answer the high-level question "What is .NET?" In brief, .NET represents Microsoft's vision of the future of applications in the Internet age. .NET provides enhanced interoperability features based upon open Internet standards.

The classic Windows desktop has been plagued by robustness issues. .NET represents a great improvement. For developers, .NET offers a new programming platform and superb tools.

XML plays a fundamental role in .NET. It is used in Web services, in database access, in configuration files, and in many other ways. Enterprise servers, such as SQL Server 2000, expose .NET features through XML.

Microsoft .NET is a new platform at a higher level than the operating system. Three years in the making before public announcement, .NET is a major investment by Microsoft. .NET draws on many important ideas, including XML, the concepts underlying Java, and Microsoft's Component Object Model (COM). Microsoft .NET provides the following:

- A robust runtime platform, the CLR
- Multiple language development
- An extensible programming model, the .NET Framework, which provides a large class library of reusable code available from multiple languages
- A networking infrastructure built on top of Internet standards that supports a high level of communication among applications
- A new mechanism of application delivery, the Web service, that supports the concept of an application as a service
- Powerful development tools

Microsoft and the Web

The World Wide Web has been a big challenge to Microsoft. It did not embrace it early. But the Web actually coexists quite well with Microsoft's traditional strength, the PC. Using the PC's browser application, a user can gain access to a whole world of information. The Web relies on standards such as HTML, HTTP, and XML, which are essential for communication among diverse users on a variety of computer systems and devices.

The Windows PC and the Internet, although complex, are quite standardized. However, a Tower of Babel exists with respect to the applications that try to build on top of them: multiple languages, databases, and development environments. The rapid introduction of new technologies has created a gap in the knowledge of workers who must build systems using these technologies. This provides an opening for Microsoft, and some of the most talked about parts of .NET are indeed directed toward the Internet.

.NET provides many features to greatly enhance our ability to program Web applications. We touch on Web application development in Part 2. For more information, please consult the following three books in The Integrated .NET Series:

- *Application Development Using C# and .NET*
- *Application Development Using Visual Basic and .NET*
- *Fundamentals of Web Applications Using .NET and XML*

Windows on the Desktop

Microsoft began with the desktop, and the company has achieved much. The modern Windows environment has become ubiquitous. Countless applications are available, and most computer users are at least somewhat at home with Windows. There is quite a rich user interface experience, and applications can work together. But there are also significant problems.

PROBLEMS WITH WINDOWS

One of the most troublesome problems is the maintenance of applications on the Windows PC. Applications consist of many files, registry entries, shortcuts, and so on. Different applications can share certain DLLs. Installing a new application can overwrite a DLL that an existing application depends on, possibly breaking the older application (which is known as "DLL hell"). Removing an application is complex and often is imperfectly done. Over time, a PC can become less stable, and the cure eventually becomes reformatting the hard disk and starting from scratch.

There is tremendous economic benefit to using PCs, because standard applications are inexpensive and powerful, the hardware is cheap, and so on. But the savings are reduced by the cost of maintenance.

A ROBUST WINDOWS ENVIRONMENT

.NET has many features that result in a much more robust Windows operating system. Applications no longer rely on storing extensive configuration data in the registry. In .NET, applications are self-describing, containing *metadata* within the program executable files themselves. Different versions of an application can be deployed *side by side*.

Applications run *managed code*. Managed code is not executed directly by the operating system, but rather by the special runtime—the CLR. The CLR can perform checks for type safety, such as for array out-of-bounds and memory overwrites. The CLR performs memory management, including automatic garbage collection, resulting in sharp reduction of memory leaks and similar problems.

Languages such as VB.NET and C# (pronounced "C sharp"), but not C++, can produce managed code that is verifiable as secure. Managed code that is not verifiable can run if the security policy allows the code to ignore the verification process.

A New Programming Platform

.NET provides a new programming platform at a higher level than the operating system. This level of abstraction has many advantages:

- Code can be validated to prevent unauthorized actions.
- It is much easier to program than the Win32 API or COM.
- All or parts of the platform can be implemented on many different kinds of computers (as has been done with Java).
- All the languages use one class library.
- Languages can interoperate with each other.

We outline the features of this new platform, the *.NET Framework*, in the next section.

.NET Framework Overview

The .NET Framework consists of the CLR, the .NET Framework Class Library, the Common Language Specification (CLS), a number of .NET languages, and Visual Studio.NET. The overall architecture of the .NET Framework is depicted in Figure 1-3.

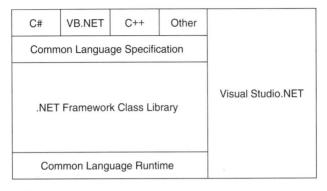

C#	VB.NET	C++	Other	
Common Language Specification				Visual Studio.NET
.NET Framework Class Library				
Common Language Runtime				

FIGURE 1–3   *Overall block diagram of .NET Framework.*

Common Language Runtime

A runtime provides services to executing programs. Traditionally, different programming environments have different runtimes. Examples of runtimes include the standard C library, MFC, the Visual Basic runtime, and the Java Virtual Machine (JVM).

The runtime environment provided by .NET, the CLR, manages the execution of code and provides useful services. The services of the CLR are exposed through programming languages. The syntax for these services varies from language to language, but the underlying execution engine providing the services is the same.

Not all languages expose all the features of the CLR. The language with the best mapping to the CLR is the new language C#. VB.NET, however, does an admirable job of exposing the functionality.

.NET Framework Class Library

The .NET Framework class library is huge, comprising more than 2,500 classes. All this functionality is available to all the .NET languages. The library (see Figure 1–4) consists of four main parts:

- Base class library (which includes networking, security, diagnostics, I/O, and other types of operating system services)
- Data and XML classes
- Windows UI
- Web services and Web UI

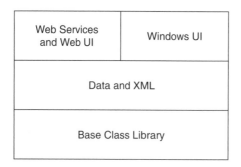

Web Services and Web UI	Windows UI
Data and XML	
Base Class Library	

FIGURE 1–4   *Block diagram of .NET Framework class library.*

Common Language Specification

An important goal of the .NET Framework is to support multiple languages. But all languages are not created equal, so it is important to agree upon a common subset that all languages will support. The CLS is an agreement among language designers and class library designers about those features and usage conventions that can be relied upon.

CLS rules apply to public features that are visible outside the assembly where they are defined. (An assembly can be thought of as a logical EXE or DLL and will be discussed later in this chapter.) For example, the CLS requires that public names do not rely on case for uniqueness, because some languages are not case sensitive. For more information, see "Cross Language Interoperability" in "Inside the .NET Framework" in the .NET Framework SDK Documentation.

Languages in .NET

A language is a CLS-compliant *consumer* if it can use any CLS-compliant type— that is, if it can call methods, create instances of types, and so on. (A type is basically a class in most object-oriented languages, providing an abstraction of data and behavior, grouped together.) A language is a CLS-compliant *extender* if it is a consumer and can also extend any CLS-compliant base class, implement any CLS-compliant interface, and so on.

Microsoft itself is providing four CLS-compliant languages. VB.NET, C#, and C++ with Managed Extensions are extenders. JScript.NET is a consumer.

Third parties are providing additional languages (more than two dozen so far). ActiveState is implementing Perl and Python. Fujitsu is implementing COBOL. It should be noted that at present some of these languages are not .NET languages in the strict sense. For example, PerlNET creates a .NET component from a Perl class. This facility enables .NET applications to call the wealth of Perl modules, but it does not make Perl into either a consumer or an extender. We discuss PerlNET in detail in Part 2.

Common Language Runtime

In this section, we delve more deeply into the structure of .NET by examining the CLR. We look at the design goals of the CLR and discuss the rationale for using managed code and a runtime. We outline the design of the CLR, including the concepts of MSIL, metadata, and JIT compilation. We compare the CLR with the JVM. We discuss the key concept in .NET of assembly, which is a logical grouping of code. We explore the central role of types in .NET and look at the Common Type System (CTS). We explain the role of managed data and garbage collection. Finally, we use the Intermediate Language Disassembler (ILDASM) tool to gain some insight into the structure of assemblies.

Design Goals of the CLR

The CLR has the following design goals:

- Simplify application development.
- Support multiple programming languages.
- Provide a safe and reliable execution environment.
- Simplify deployment and administration.
- Provide good performance and scalability.

SIMPLE APPLICATION DEVELOPMENT

With more than 2,500 classes, the .NET Framework class library provides enormous functionality that the programmer can reuse. The object-oriented and component features of .NET enable organizations to create their own reusable code. Unlike COM, the programmer does not have to implement any plumbing code to gain the advantages of components. Automatic garbage collection greatly simplifies memory management in applications. The CLR facilitates powerful tools such as Visual Studio.NET that can provide common functionality and the same UI for multiple languages.

MULTIPLE LANGUAGES

The CLR was designed from the ground up to support multiple languages. This feature is the most significant difference between .NET and Java, which share a great deal in philosophy.

The CTS makes interoperability between languages virtually seamless. The same built-in data types can be used in multiple languages. Classes defined in one language can be used in another language. A class in one language can even inherit from a class in another language. Exceptions can be thrown from one language to another.

Programmers do not have to learn a new language in order to use .NET. The same tools can work for all .NET languages. You can debug from one language into another.

SAFE EXECUTION ENVIRONMENT

With the CLR, a compiler generates MSIL instructions, not native code. It is this managed code that runs. Hence, the CLR can perform runtime validations on this code before it is translated into native code. Types are verified. Subscripts are verified to be in range. Unsafe casts and uninitialized variables are prevented.

The CLR performs memory management. Managed code cannot access memory directly. No pointers are allowed. This means that your code cannot inadvertently write over memory that does not belong to it, possibly causing a crash or other bad behavior.

The CLR can enforce strong security. One of the challenges of the software world of third-party components and downloadable code is that you open your system to damage from executing code from unknown sources. You might want to restrict Word macros from accessing anything other than the document that contains them. You want to stop potentially malicious Web scripts. You even want to shield your system from bugs of software from known vendors. To handle these situations, .NET security includes *Code Access Security* (CAS).

SIMPLER DEPLOYMENT AND ADMINISTRATION

With the CLR, the unit of deployment becomes an *assembly*, which is typically an EXE or a DLL. The assembly contains a *manifest*, which allows much more information to be stored.

An assembly is completely self-describing. No information needs to be stored in the registry. All the information is in one place, and the code cannot get out of sync with information stored elsewhere, such as in the registry, a type library, or a header file.

The assembly is the unit of versioning, so that multiple versions can be deployed side by side in different folders. These different versions can execute at the same time without interfering with each other.

Assemblies can be private or shared. For private assembly deployment, the assembly is copied to the same directory as the client program that references it. No registration is needed, and no fancy installation program is required. When the component is removed, no registry cleanup is needed, and no uninstall program is required. Just delete it from the hard drive.

In shared assembly deployment, an assembly is installed in the Global Assembly Cache (or GAC). The GAC contains shared assemblies that are globally accessible to all .NET applications on the machine. A download assembly cache is accessible to applications such as Internet Explorer that automatically download assemblies over the network.

PERFORMANCE

You may like the safety and ease-of-use features of managed code, but you may be concerned about performance. It is somewhat analogous to the concerns of early assembly language programmers when high-level languages came out.

The CLR is designed with high performance in mind. JIT compilation is designed into the CLR. The first time a method is encountered, the CLR performs verifications and then compiles the method into native code (which contains safety features, such as array bounds checking). The next time the method is encountered, the native code executes directly.

Memory management is designed for high performance. Allocation is almost instantaneous, just taking the next available storage from the managed heap. Deallocation is done by the garbage collector, which Microsoft has tweaked for efficiency.

Why Use a CLR?

Why did Microsoft create a CLR for .NET? Let's look at how well the goals just discussed could have been achieved without a CLR, focusing on the two main goals of safety and performance. Basically, there are two philosophies. The first is compile-time checking and fast native code at runtime. The second is runtime checking.

Without a CLR, we must rely on the compiler to achieve safety. This places a high burden on the compiler. Typically, there are many compilers for a system, including third-party compilers. It is not robust to trust that every compiler from every vendor will adequately perform all safety checking. Not every language has features supporting adequate safety checking. Compilation speed is slow with complex compilation. Compilers cannot conveniently optimize code based on enhanced instructions available on some platforms but not on others. What's more, many features (such as security) cannot be detected until runtime.

Design of Common Language Runtime

So we want a runtime. How do we design it? One extreme is to use an interpreter and not a compiler at all. All the work is done at runtime. We have safety and fast builds, but runtime performance is very slow. Modern systems divide the load between the front-end compiler and the back-end runtime.

INTERMEDIATE LANGUAGE

The front-end compiler does all the checking it can do and generates an intermediate language. Examples include

- P-code for Pascal
- Bytecode for Java

The runtime does further verification based on the actual runtime characteristics, including security checking.

With JIT compilation, native code can be generated when needed and subsequently reused. Runtime performance becomes much better. The native code generated by the runtime can be more efficient, because the runtime knows the precise characteristics of the target machine.

MICROSOFT INTERMEDIATE LANGUAGE

All managed code compilers for Microsoft .NET generate MSIL. MSIL is machine-independent and can be efficiently compiled into native code.

MSIL has a wide variety of instructions:

- Standard operations such as load, store, arithmetic and logic, branch, etc.
- Calling methods on objects
- Exceptions

Before executing on a CPU, MSIL must be translated by a JIT compiler. There is a JIT compiler for each machine architecture supported. The same MSIL will run on any supported machine.

METADATA

Besides generating MSIL, a managed code compiler emits metadata. Metadata contains very complete information about the code module, including the following:

- Version and locale information
- All the types
- Details about each type, including name, visibility, etc.
- Details about the members of each type, such as methods, the signatures of methods, etc.

Metadata is the "glue" that binds together the executing code, the CLR, and tools such as compilers, debuggers, and browsers. On Windows, MSIL and metadata are packaged together in a standard Windows PE file. Metadata enables "Intellisense" in Visual Studio. In .NET, you can call from one language to another, and metadata enables types to be converted transparently. Metadata is ubiquitous in the .NET environment.

Types

Types are at the heart of the programming model for the CLR. A type is analogous to a class in most object-oriented programming languages, providing an abstraction of data and behavior, grouped together. A type in the CLR contains the following:

- Fields (data members)
- Methods
- Properties
- Events

There are also built-in primitive types, such as integer and floating-point numeric types, strings, and so on. In the CLR, there are no functions outside of types, but all behavior is provided via methods or other members.

JIT COMPILATION

Before executing on the target machine, MSIL is translated by a JIT compiler to native code. Some code typically will never be executed during a program run. Hence, it may be more efficient to translate MSIL as needed during execution, storing the native code for reuse.

When a type is loaded, the loader attaches a stub to each method of the type. On the first call, the stub passes control to the JIT, which translates to native code and modifies the stub to save the address of the translated native code. On subsequent calls to the method, the native code is called directly.

As part of JIT compilation, code goes through a verification process. Type safety is verified, using both the MSIL and metadata. Security restrictions are checked.

COMMON TYPE SYSTEM

At the heart of the CLR is the CTS. The CTS provides a wide range of types and operations that are found in many programming languages. The CTS is shared by the CLR and by compilers and other tools.

The CTS provides a framework for cross-language integration and addresses a number of issues:

- Similar, but subtly different, types (for example, **Integer** is 16 bits in VB6, but **int** is 32 bits in C++; strings in VB6 are represented as BSTRs and in C++ as **char** pointers or a **string** class of some sort; and so on)
- Limited code reuse (for example, you can't define a new type in one language and import it into another language)
- Inconsistent object models

Not all CTS types are available in all languages. The CLS establishes rules that must be followed for cross-language integration, including which types *must* be supported by a CLS-compliant language. Built-in types can be accessed through the **System** class in the Base Class Library (BCL) and through reserved keywords in the .NET languages.

Managed Data and Garbage Collection

Managed code is only part of the story of the CLR. A significant simplification of the programming model is provided through *managed data.* When an application domain is initialized, the CLR reserves a contiguous block of storage known as the *managed heap.* Allocation from the managed heap is extremely fast. The next available space is simply returned, in contrast to the C runtime, which must search its heap for space that is large enough.

Deallocation is not performed by the user program but by the CLR, using a process known as *garbage collection.* The CLR tracks the use of memory allocated on the managed heap. When memory is low, or in response to an explicit call from a program, the CLR "garbage collects" (or frees up all unreferenced memory) and compacts the space that is now free into a large contiguous block.

Summary

PerlNET enables you to use Perl as your language while programming in the .NET environment. In this chapter, you received an orientation to the overall architecture and features of .NET.

Microsoft .NET is a new platform that sits on top of the operating system and provides many capabilities for building and deploying desktop and Web-based applications. .NET has many features that create a much more robust Windows operating system.

The .NET Framework includes the Common Language Runtime (CLR), the .NET Framework class library, the Common Type System (CTS), the .NET languages, and Visual Studio.NET.

The CLR manages the execution of code and provides useful services. The design goals of the CLR included simple application development, safety, simple deployment, support of multiple languages, and good performance.

.NET uses managed code that runs in a safe environment under the CLR. .NET compilers translate source code into Microsoft Intermediate Language (MSIL), which is translated at runtime into native code by a just-in-time (JIT) compiler.

An assembly is a grouping of types and resources that work together as a logical unit. Types and the CTS are the heart of the CLR. Garbage collection is used by the CLR to automatically reclaim unreferenced data.

In Chapter 2, we begin a tutorial on the Perl language, and in Part 2 we will learn about PerlNET.

Writing Simple Programs in Perl

*T*he goal of this chapter is to allow you to write simple Perl programs with a minimum of effort. Topics include preparing and executing Perl programs and a quick introduction to language elements, including data types, simple I/O, and control flow constructs.

Your First Perl Program

Several issues face a programmer who is about to write his or her first program in an unfamiliar programming language. How is the text for the program prepared? How do I translate this program into something that can be executed by the machine? How is it executed? These issues reside more or less outside of the programming language. Then there are other issues that are more directly related to the programming language itself. These include topics such as data types and control flow constructs. This chapter discusses both types of beginning issues.

Preparing Your Perl Program

For modest programs such as the ones that we demonstrate in this chapter, the first step is to prepare the source code for your program. In order to do this, you can use your favorite text editor. On your Windows machine, you might use Notepad or Edit. The choice of editor is yours. Just be certain that you do not use a word processor such as Microsoft Word. Word processors insert special codes into your files, whereas editors do not. These special codes interfere with the subsequent translation of your source code.

If you have Visual Studio and Visual Perl (see Appendix A), you can use this friendly integrated development environment (IDE). For the convenience of Visual Perl users, we provide solution (.sln) and project (.perlproj) files for each Perl program. We store each Perl program in its own folder within the chapter directory. Thus, the Perl programs in this chapter are in the **Chap02** folder.

The name of the file that you create—the name of your Perl program—is totally up to you. There are no real conventions in the Perl community about what to name Perl source files. However, we always use files whose names end with the extension **.pl**.

Viewing Your Source Code

Once you have typed your code into your editor and saved your file, you may wish from time to time to view your source file. In a DOS window, you can use the **type** command. Or, if the file contains more lines than you can fit on your display, you can use the **more** command. Often in this section of the book we will want to display a file so that you can compare the results of a program with the code that produced it. We use the **type** command to display the file. Also, we always use a mythical % as the system prompt.

Observations from a Small Perl Program

Code
Example

Let's say that you have entered a small Perl program into a file named **small.pl**. See the folder **Small**.

```
% type small.pl
#
#       small.pl
#
$name = "Michael";              # a string
$id = 1;                        # an integer
print "Name is\t$name\n";
print "Id is\t$id\n";
%
```

There are several things to notice in the program above. The **#** character is the comment character. The Perl translator ignores it and everything else up to and including the end of the line character. It is the place for the programmer to add explanations about the working of the code.

Each Perl statement must end in a semicolon. The semicolon is a statement separator, not a statement terminator. The last line of the program does not need to end with a semicolon, but it is a good idea to place one there anyway.

The program above is simple enough that before we explain it further, we wish to show you how to execute it.

Executing a Perl Program

Code
Example

Executing a Perl program is a simple matter. Give the name of the Perl command on the command line and follow it by the name of the file you wish to execute. See the folder **Demo**.

```
% perl demo.pl
Name is   Michael
Id is     1
%
```

Unlike compiled languages, such as C and C++, Perl does not produce any object files—that is, intermediate files that need to be linked to produce an executable. Rather, your program is translated and executed as the Perl interpreter reads it.

Perl Variables

A variable is a symbolic name for a location in memory. A programming language usually defines the types of variables it will allow. For example, in C some types include **int**, **char**, **float**, and **double**. Java allows similar types. In Perl the situation is a little different.

Perl distinguishes between three different data types. A scalar represents a single value. An array represents an ordered collection of these values indexed from 0. A hash represents an unordered collection of scalars whose values can be indexed by their key. Perl uses punctuation to distinguish between these three kinds of variables.

Perl also differs from many programming languages in that the programmer does not have to define a variable before using it.

Scalar Variables

A scalar represents a single value. The single value could be a whole number, a number with a decimal point, a character, a string, or the contents of a file. Of importance is that the data contained in a scalar is treated as one item.

The name of a scalar variable must begin with the $ character. Beyond the $, the name must start with a letter or underscore and may contain letters, underscores, and digits.

In Perl it is not unusual for a variable to contain an integer at one point in a program and a string at another point in the program. This might be syntactically sacrilegious to some programmers, but in practice it tends to simplify programs. In either case, the program above uses two scalars:

```
$name = "Michael";               # a string
$id = 1;                         # an integer
```

Strictly speaking, the pair of " characters are not needed except when you wish to enclose some special characters or white space characters.

```
$name = "Michael";              # quotes not needed
$name = Michael Saltzman;       # error
$name = "Michael Saltzman";     # quotes needed for space
$name = "Michael\nSaltzman";    # quotes needed for \n
```

The numbers in Perl are stored as signed integers if possible or as double-precision floating-point values in the machine's native format otherwise. The values with floating point are not infinitely precise. This is very important because comparisons like (15/6 == 1/6*15) can fail suddenly.

DISPLAYING VARIABLES AND TEXT

To display information in a Perl program, use the **print** function. Notice that the program above uses the **print** function on two occasions:

```
print "Name is\t$name\n";
print "Id is\t$id\n";
```

The double quotes above are used to enclose the text part of what is printed. Inside these double quotes, scalar variables are interpreted. The special sequence \t and \n represent the **tab** and **newline** characters, respectively.

The above **print** functions could have been combined into a single **print** function.

```
print "Name is\t$name\nId is\t$id\n";
```

Array Variables

The second kind of variable in Perl is the array variable. This data structure represents an ordered set of scalars, retrievable by an index starting at 0. Here are a few examples of arrays.

```
@days = (Sun, Mon, Tues, Wed, Thurs, Fri, Sat);
@holidays = ("Labor Day", Christmas, "New Years");
@powersOf2 = (1, 2, 4, 8, 16, 32, 64, 128, 256, 512);
```

Perl arrays are very special because their size is dynamic and thus it is a simple matter to grow or shrink them. This is a departure from many conventional languages where array sizes are fixed upon declaration.

Each of the arrays above is initialized with the set of elements within the parentheses. To compute the size of an array, simply assign the array to a scalar:

```
$size = @days;       # size = 7
$size = @powersOf2;  # size = 9
$size = @holidays;   # size = 3
```

To fetch a single scalar from an array of them, you must use the subscript operator, a set of square brackets enclosing an index:

```
$first = $days[0];                    # Sun
$xmas = $holidays[1];                 # Christmas
$twotothefifth = $powersOf2[5];       # 32
```

You can even use negative subscripts to fetch values from the end of the array:

```
$last = $days[-1];                    # Sat
$xmas = $holidays[-1];                # New Years
$twototheeight = $powersOf2[-2];      # 256
```

Note also that the elements of an array can come from various sources and can be of mixed types:

```
@combined = (@days, @powersOf2, @holidays)
$size = @combined                     # size = 20
@record = (Michael, 57, Columbia, MD);
```

You can also take the elements from an array and separate them into a list of elements:

```
($name, $age, $city, $state) = @record
# $name="michael", $age = 57, etc
```

When you do this, be sure that the number of elements in the array is at least as long as the number of elements in the list to which items are being assigned. Also be careful to understand the difference between the following two assignments:

```
$item = @record;                      # item = 4
($item) = @record;                    # item = Michael
```

The first assignment takes an array and assigns it to a scalar. This always produces the size of the array. The second assignment takes the array and assigns it to a list of one element. Only the first element of the array is assigned. It's also possible to assign one list to another. The line below swaps the extreme elements in **@record**.

```
($record[0], $record[-1]) = ($record[-1], $record[0]);
```

After the line above has been executed, the value of **@record** is

```
(MD, 57, Columbia, Michael);
```

The elements at the beginning of the array and the end of the array have been swapped.

PRINTING ARRAYS

Code Example

An array can be printed with the **print** function. In the simplest case, you may wish to print the entire array. By default the array elements are placed next to each other. By enclosing the entire array in a set of double quotes, a space is placed in between the array elements. This is a common way to print all of the elements. Here is an example of printing an array and some elements within it in various ways. See the folder **Array**.

```
% type arrays.pl
#
#    arrays.pl
#
@x = (1,2,3,4,5);
print @x;              # default
print "\n";
print "@x\n";          # one space between items
print '@x';            # no @ interpretation
print "\n";
print "$x[0]\n";       # print a single element
% perl arrays.pl
12345
1 2 3 4 5
@x
1
%
```

The first printing of the array prints the items without any spaces between them. The second printing of the array uses double quotes. In this case the data items are printed with a single space separating them. This is the preferred way of printing array elements. The third printing of the array uses single quotes. Anything printed within single quotes is printed literally. Finally, a single array element is printed.

Hash Variables

The third kind of variable in Perl is the hash array, a data structure that holds pairs of elements, where the first element of the pair is a key and the second element of the pair is a value that is retrieved by the key. Hashes are often called *associative arrays*. Hashes provide a fast way of performing table look-ups. Here is how you define a hash:

```
%roles =  { Susan => President,
            Michael => Technical,
            Erin => "Technical Services",
            Patti => Instructor,
            Tom => Marketing,
            Bob => Sales
       };
```

First, note that a hash is defined by using the % character. Otherwise, the initialization is like an array with the provision that there be an even number of elements so that they can be paired together. To find an element in the hash, you simply use the first part of a pair as an index:

```
$roles{Susan}        yields       President
$roles{Michael}      yields       Technical
```

The expression **$roles{Susan}** is a scalar resulting in the value represented by the key **Susan**—that is, the value **President**.

By the way, it is possible that the same Perl program include a scalar, an array, and a hash, all with the same name. Because of this, a hash is subscripted with curly braces, {}, whereas a plain old array is subscripted with square brackets, [].

Both hashes and arrays can contain arbitrarily complex data, but we have not yet seen how to do this.

PRINTING HASHES

Hashes represent unordered data. When you place a pair into a hash table, you are not concerned with ordering. This is different than an array, where you might be concerned, for example, with sorting. Because of this, there is less of a need, if any, to print an entire hash. Therefore, the % symbol has no meaning inside double quotes. Note the following way of attempting to print a hash. See the folder **Roles**.

Code Example

```
% type roles.pl
#
#    roles.pl
#
%roles = (
    Susan => President,
    Michael => Technical,
    Erin => "Technical Services",
    Patti => Instructor,
    Tom => Marketing,
    Bob => Sales
    );
```

```
print %roles;
print "\n";
print "%hash\n";
print '%hash\n';

% roles.pl
TomMarketingPattiInstructorSusanPresidentBobSalesMichaelTe
chnicalErinTechnical Services
%hash
%hash\n
%
```

The first print did display all of the items in the hash even though it is not in an easy form to read. The second and third attempts to print the hash use sets of double and single quotes respectively. In each of these cases, the % is not interpreted.

Simple Input and Output

In order to make programs more useful, there has to be a way for the program to receive input and to produce output. Some programs can be very useful simply by gathering input interactively from a user. Others may need to get their information from a disk file or two. Likewise, many programs need to produce output meant for a user's eyes, while still others may need to create a disk file or modify one. In this section we explore how Perl handles files.

Keyboard Input

When a Perl program begins, there are certain names that have already been associated with standard files. These names are called file handles. One such file handle, **STDIN**, is associated with the keyboard. Use this file handle when you wish to read from the keyboard.

In connection with file handles, there is also an input operator whose symbols are the angled brackets, **<>**. This operator directs Perl to read a line from the file handle specified within the angled brackets. The following line of Perl code reads a line from the standard input, the keyboard:

```
$line = <STDIN>;
```

Code
Example

You can use code such as the above to interactively obtain a line of information from the user. See the folder called **Input**.

```
%type input.pl
#
#    input.pl
#
print "Enter your name ";
$name = <STDIN>;
print "Enter your age ";
$age = <STDIN>;
print "Hi $name";
print "When did you turn $age";
% perl input.pl
Enter your name michael
Enter your age 57
Hi Michael
When did you turn 57
%
```

When you use this form of input, the data received by the program includes the newline character. If you wish to delete this character, use the **chomp** function. You can chomp any scalar, but it will delete the last character only if it is the newline character. There is also a **chop** function that indiscriminately removes the last character of a scalar.

```
$value = "thee\n";
chomp($value);           # value = thee
chomp($value);           # value = thee
chop($value);            # value = the
```

Input from Disk Files

Code
Example

When the input to your program comes from a user, you can rely on the **STDIN** file handle. However, programs also need to be able to handle input that comes from a disk file. In this case, the programmer needs to create a file handle and associate it with the disk file. This is accomplished by using the **open** function. Here is an example. The program is in the folder **ReadDisk**, which also contains a file called **input**.

```
% type readdisk.pl
#
#    readdisk.pl
#
open(INPUT, " input");
$line = <INPUT>;
print "line 1: $line";
$line = <INPUT>;
print "line 2: $line";
%
```

The **open** function takes a file handle, a name that you provide, and the name of the disk file, and creates the association between them. The file name can also be a relative or complete path name. In any case, from then on within that program, each line of the form

```
$line = <INPUT>;
```

reads a line from the file associated with the handle **INPUT**. In our case, the disk file is named **input**. File handles are conventionally coded using uppercase characters. Here is a sample input file and subsequent output from the running of the above program:

```
% type input
There once was a language named Perl
Which gave programmers quite a whirl
% perl readdisk.pl
line 1: There once was a language named Perl
line 2: Which gave programmers quite a whirl
%
```

The Standard Output

Code Example

The **print** function is more versatile than what we have seen thus far. It can take a list of arguments rather than a single argument. The elements of this list can be simple variables or expressions. Here is an example illustrating these concepts. See the folder **Compute**.

```
% type compute.pl
#
#       compute.pl
#
print "Enter an integer ";
chomp($f = <STDIN>);
print "Enter another integer ";
chomp($s = <STDIN>);
print "$f * $s = ", $f * $s, "\n";
% perl compute.pl
Enter an integer 10
Enter another integer 20
10 * 20 = 200
%
```

The last **print** function above has three arguments separated by commas. Each one is printed in turn.

```
"$f * $s = ",
$f * $s,
"\n";
```

Notice how the multiplication operator is treated literally inside of the double quote characters, whereas when exposed, it is treated as the multiplication operator. This is generally true for all operators; that is, when quoted, they lose their special meaning.

Output to Disk Files

In the few Perl programs that we have seen thus far, any output generated with **print** has been sent implicitly to the display. We could make this more explicit by using the file handle **STDOUT**, which is associated with the display. In other words, the following two lines are equivalent:

```
print "How are you? ";
print STDOUT "How are you? ";
```

However, the second line above opens up the possibility that another file handle could be used. If you wish to send data to a disk file, you must first use the **open** function to associate your newly created disk file with a file handle.

```
open(OUTPUT, "> output");
print  OUTPUT "This data is going to 'output'";
```

Code Example

When you open a file for output, the second argument to the **open** function requires the > punctuation. You could also have used the < punctuation to open a file for reading, but in the absence of punctuation, reading is the default mode. Here is a program that gets some input from a user and then sends this data to a disk file. See the folder **Io**.

```
% type io.pl
#
#       io.pl
#
print "Enter your name ";
$name = <STDIN>;
print "Enter your age ";
$age = <STDIN>;
open(OUTPUT, "> data");
print OUTPUT "Your name is $name";
print OUTPUT "Your age is $age";
% perl io.pl
Enter your name Michael
Enter your age 57
% type data
Your name is Michael
Your age is 57
%
```

printf Function

Code Example

The **printf** function in Perl is similar to the **print** function, but it takes format specifiers that aid in the placement of variables in the output stream. The easiest way to illustrate the **printf** function is to show some examples. See the folder **Printf**.

```
% type printf.pl
#
#    printf.pl
#
$a = 10;
$b = "Perl";
$c = 10/3;
printf "%10d %10s %10.2f\n", $a, $b, $c;
% perl printf.pl
10        Perl         3.33
%
```

Notice that the **printf** has a list of things to print: **$a**, **$b**, and **$c**, but that this list is preceded with a list of format items: **%10d**, **%10s**, and **%10.2f**. The formats are matched with the list of items to be printed. All items not prefixed with a % symbol are printed literally. **%10d** specifies that this item is to be printed as a decimal number in a width of at least 10 positions. **%10s** specifies that this item is to be printed as a string in a width of at least 10 positions. **%10.2f** specifies that this item is to be printed as a decimal number with 2 positions to the right of the decimal point and at least 10 positions in all. Any of the format items can have a minus sign in front of the number to indicate left adjustment.

Closing Files

Whenever you use the **open** function to create an association between a file handle and a disk file, you need to be careful when you are finished using the file. Each program in execution is given a limit on the number of files that can be opened concurrently. Each time the open function is successful, a slot in a system table is used. When you are finished using the file, you can free that slot by using the **close** function. In general, your code may look like this:

```
open(THEFILE, "myfile");
#
#    process file
#
close(THEFILE);
```

Of course, under certain conditions, the **open** function may fail. We discuss these possibilities later.

Control Flow Constructs

Like any modern programming language, Perl has a wide variety of control flow constructs. They are typically subdivided into looping constructs and decision-making constructs.

Decision-Making Constructs

Decision-making constructions in Perl center around various **if** constructs. There is also an **unless** construct whose main appeal is in error checking.

IF

Decisions in Perl are made with the keyword **if**. Depending upon the particular logic of the program, there may also be an **else** portion to go along with the **if**. In the simple example shown here, the opening and closing curly braces are necessary even in the case where there is only one statement in the body of either the **if** or the **else** portion. The tested expression is either true or false. If true, the body of the **if** is executed. If false, the body of the **else** is executed.

```perl
print "enter a value ";
chomp($value = <STDIN>);
if ( $value >= 0 )
{
    print "$value is non-negative\n"
}
else
{
    print "$value is negative\n";
}
```

In the above code, >= is the Perl "greater than or equal to" operator for numerical operands. We see all of these relational operators later in Chapter 3 of this book.

UNLESS

Perl also uses the **unless** keyword. Its logic is exactly the opposite of **if**. The above code could have been written as shown here, but its meaning is not as straightforward.

```perl
print "enter a value ";
chomp($value = <STDIN>);
unless ( $value >= 0 )
{
    print "$value is negative\n"
}
```

```
else
{
    print "$value is non-negative\n";
}
```

As you will see later, the keyword **unless** is used mostly in error checking.

ELSIF

A common programming problem is to determine which of a set of possibilities is true. Here is a snippet of Perl code that solves this problem:

```
print "Enter a grade ";
chomp($grade = <STDIN>);
if ( $grade >= 90 )
{
    print "$grade is an A\n";
}
elsif ( $grade >= 80 )
{
    print "$grade is a B\n";
}
elsif( $grade >= 70 )
{
    print "$grade is a C\n";
}
else
{
    print "$grade is a F\n";
}
```

In the code above, the optional **else** clause is executed when no other tests are true. In the event that one of the other tests is true, then the body for that test is executed followed by whatever follows the nested construction. Note that the "else if" portions of code are spelled **elsif**.

Looping Constructs

Looping constructs allow for program iteration. In many cases, the iteration is used to step through a data structure such as an array. In other cases, the looping construction may allow the user to repeatedly choose from a set of menu choices.

FOREACH

In many cases, the **foreach** loop is a perfect construction for iterating over a set of elements in an array. In this construction, there is a control variable, **$item** in the example below, that is bound in turn to each element of a list of values. The body of the loop is enclosed in curly braces. Here is an example that tests each element of the array to see if it is positive or negative.

```
@values = (10, 20, -30, -40, 0);
foreach $item (@values)
{
        if ( $item > 0 )
        {
                print "$item is positive\n";
        }
        elsif ( $item < 0 )
        {
                print "$item is negative\n";
        }
}
```

$item represents in turn each item in the **@values** array. What is not obvious in the above example is that **$item** is actually a synonym to each successive item in the array for each pass through the loop. This is more clearly seen in the next example, where **$item** is actually modified. This of course causes a change to the array element to which **$item** is currently referring.

```
@values = (10, 20, -30, -40, 0);
foreach $item (@values)
{
    $item = $item * 2;
}
```

In the above code, the **foreach** loop doubles each element in **@values**.

FOR

The **for** loop is similar to its equivalent in C, C++, and Java. The **for** statement itself has three parts that need to be separated from each other by semicolons: an initialization, a test, and a modification. The body of the **for** is enclosed in curly braces. As long as the test is true, the body is entered. See the folder **SumInts1**.

Code Example

```
% type sumints1.pl
#
#    sumints1.pl
#
print "Enter a number: ";
chomp($number = <STDIN>);
for ($i = 1; $i <= $number; $i = $i + 1)
{
        $sum = $sum + $i;
}
print "Sum of first $number integers is $sum\n";
```

```
% perl sumints1.pl
Enter a number: 10
Sum of first 10 integers is 55
%
```

WHILE

The **while** loop satisfies many looping problems that do not involve arrays. Here is an example that asks the user for a few numbers and then sums the integers between the two of them. See the folder **SumInts2**.

```
% type sumints2.pl
#
#    sumints2.pl
#
#print "Enter low integer ";
chomp($low = <STDIN>);
print "Enter high integer ";
chomp($high = <STDIN>);
$f = $low;
while($f <= $high)
{
        $sum = $sum + $f;
        $f = $f + 1;
}
print "Sum of integers between $low and $high is $sum\n";
%

% perl sumints2.pl
Enter low integer 10
Enter high integer 15
Sum of integers between 10 and 15 is 75
%
```

The **while** test always evaluates to true or false. Anything evaluating to zero is false. All else is true. When the tested value is true, the body of the loop is entered; otherwise, the code beneath the loop is executed.

A **while** loop can be very handy in stepping through the lines of a file. Here is a program that reads a file and displays the file with line numbers. The program reads the filename entered by the user. See the folder **Numbers**.

```
% type numbers.pl
#        numbers.pl
#
print "Enter file name ";
chomp($filename = <STDIN>);
open(INPUT, "$filename");
$num = 1;
while($line = <INPUT>)
```

```
{
        print "$num\t$line";
        $num = $num + 1;
}

% perl numbers.pl
Enter file name numbers.pl.
1    #
2    #           numbers.pl
3    #
4    print "enter file name ";
5    chomp($filename = <STDIN>);
6    open(INPUT, "$filename");
7    $num = 1;
8    while($line = <INPUT>)
9    {
10          print "$num\t$line";
11          $num = $num + 1;
12   }
%
```

Now, suppose you wanted to keep all the lines from the file in memory at the same time rather than processing them one at a time. One way to proceed is by using a **while** loop. Each line that you read can be stored in the next element of an array. Perl arrays are dynamic, so there is no need to know the size of the array ahead of time.

```
$i = 0;
while($line = <STDIN>)
{
        $lines[$i] = $line;
        $i = $i + 1;
}
```

The code above works fine, but in Perl there is a shorter way. When the Perl interpreter sees an array as the recipient of the <HANDLE> operators, it simply reads all lines from the file associated with HANDLE into the array as if you had written your own loop. Thus, the loop from above can be written as

```
@lines  = <STDIN>;
```

UNTIL

The **until** loop is similar to the **while**. With the **while** loop, you do something *while* a condition is true. With the **until** loop, you do something *until* the con-dition is true. Here is a simple example:

```
$x = 0;
until ($x == 10)
```

```
{
    print "$x\n";
    $x++;
}
```

The code above prints the integers 0 through 9, because when **$x** is 10, the loop test fails. Note the **==** operator to test for algebraic equality.

DO WHILE

Code Example

Finally, there is yet another looping construct in Perl—the **do while**. This construct is not as commonly used as the other looping constructs, but it does guarantee at least one pass through its body. Unlike the other looping constructs, the test for loop termination is at the end of the loop, so you are guaranteed at least one pass through the loop body. See the folder **DoWhile**.

```
% type dowhile.pl
#
#   dowhile.pl
#
%map = ( 1 => "Add", 2 => "Delete", 3 => "Exit" );
do
{
        print "Choose an item\n";
        print "1) Add\n2) Delete\n3) Exit\n";
        chomp($answer = <STDIN>);
        print "You chose $map{$answer}\n";
} while($answer != 3);
% perl dowhile.pl
Choose an item
1) Add
2) Delete
3) Exit
1
You chose Add
Choose an item
1) Add
2) Delete
3) Exit
3
You chose Exit
%
```

Notice that the keywords **do** and **while** are separated from each other by the loop body. The body is entered and executed, and then the test for loop completion is performed. If the test is true, the loop is repeated.

ENDLESS LOOPS

Code Example

In most programs, a loop should have a natural way of ending. However, programming being what it is, there are many cases where a loop goes on endlessly through some faulty programming. For example, in the following program, the user enters the name of a file and the line number. The program should print that line from the file. See the folder **Bug**.

```
% type bug.pl
#
#        bug.pl
#
print "enter filename ";
chomp($filename = <STDIN>);
open(INPUT, "$filename");
print "which line should I display ";
$num = <STDIN>;
$i = 0;
while($i < $num)
{
        $line = <INPUT>;
}
print $line;
%
```

Can you spot the bug in the program above? The programmer forgot to increment **$i** inside the loop. In this case, the program will loop forever even though eventually there will be no more lines in the input file. To terminate a runaway program such as this, simply press the Ctrl-C sequence.

Some programs intentionally have an endless loop. For these programs, the programmer must provide a graceful exit strategy. For example, suppose you wanted to write a Perl program that evaluated Perl expressions. You could start as follows:

```
while(1)
{
     print "Enter expression (or end to quit) ";
     chomp($exp = <STDIN>);
}
```

Here, the **while** test is always true. Anything other than zero could have been used, but conventionally the value **1** is used. Before any evaluation is performed, the programmer should allow the user a way out of the loop.

```
while(1)
{
     print "Enter expression (or end to quit) ";
     chomp($exp = <STDIN>);
```

```
            if ( $exp eq "end" )
            {
                    exit(0);
            }
    }
```

Code Example

The code uses the string comparison operator **eq** to determine if the user entered the sting **end**. In this case, the **exit** function is called to terminate the program. The argument sent to **exit** might be used in a batch file, for example. The final piece is to evaluate the expression entered by the user. For this we use the **eval** function. Here is the entire program and its execution. See the folder **Calc**.

```
% type calc.pl
#
#       calc.pl
#
while(1)
{
        print "Enter expression (or end to quit) ";
        chomp($exp = <STDIN>);
        if ( $exp eq "end" )
        {
                exit(0);
        }
        print eval($exp), "\n";
}
% perl calc.pl
Enter expression or end to quit 3 + 5 * 4
23
Enter expression or end to quit 2 ** 10 - 1
1023
Enter expression or end to quit end
%
```

Modifier Form of Control Flow Constructs

Perl forces you to use a set of curly braces even when an **if** or a **while** has one statement for its body.

```
while ($line = <STDIN>)
{
    print $line;
}

if ( $line eq "end")
{
    exit(0);
}
```

There is, however, a modifier form of these control structures. Using this form, place the one statement in front of the control structure. The two constructs from above would be written as

```
print $line while ($line = <STDIN>);

exit(0) if ( $line eq "end");
```

The **unless** and the **until** constructs can also be written with the modifier form.

Altering Control Flow

There are often programming situations where you need to perform a lookup within a data structure such as an array. You either find the item for which you conducted the search or you do not. Once you have found the item, you need to exit from the search loop. There are other situations where you also may need to alter control flow from within a loop.

last

Code
Example

The program below reads a list of hotels from a file. The user is then asked to enter the name of a hotel. The program loops through the list of hotels, trying to find the user's input among the hotels from the file. See the folder **Hotels**.

```
% type hotels.pl
#
# hotels.pl
#
open(HOTELS, "hotels");
@hotels = <HOTELS>;
while(1)
{
        print "enter hotel name ";
        $hotel = <STDIN>;
        $found = 0;
        foreach $item (@hotels)
        {
                if ($item eq $hotel)
                {
                        $found = 1;
                        last;
                }
        }
        print "found $hotel\n" if ($found)
}
%
```

In the inner loop above, if the hotel is found, the **last** statement sends control flow to the first statement beneath the loop in which **last** was executed.

next

On other occasions, you may wish to forego the rest of the statements in a particular loop in favor of the next iteration of the loop. This is a task for the **next** statement, which causes the next iteration of the loop to occur. Suppose we wanted to process only the positive numbers in an array. We could proceed as follows:

```
@numbers = (100, -30, 200, -40, 500);
foreach $number (@numbers)
{
        next if $number < 0;
        print "$number is positive\n";
}
```

redo

Code
Example

Perl also has a **redo** statement. This allows you to redo the current iteration of a loop. You might use this in sequences such as in the following example. See the folder **Grades**.

```
% type grades.pl
#
#    grades.pl
#
print "How many grades? ";
chomp($grades = <STDIN>);
for ($i = 1; $i <= $grades; $i = $i + 1)
{
        print "Enter grade # $i: ";
        chomp($grade = <STDIN>);
        if ( $grade < 0 || $grade > 100 )
        {
                print "$grade is illegal\n";
                redo;
        }
        $grades[$i - 1] = $grade;
}
print "Your $grades grades are: @grades\n";
% perl grades.pl
How many grades? 3
Enter grade # 1: 85
Enter grade # 2: 120
120 is illegal
Enter grade # 2: 90
```

```
Enter grade # 3: 95
Your 3 grades are: 85 90 95
%
```

Special Perl Variables

As you learn Perl, you will become familiar with many special Perl variables, each of which arms the Perl programmer with a more elegant way of writing some code. Probably the most common special variable is named $_. This variable plays a few important roles in the life of a Perl programmer.

The Default Input and Output Variable $_

Earlier, we presented a segment of code that read lines from the standard input and printed them.

```
while($line = <STDIN>)
{
    print $line;
}
```

Within a loop, if you do not name a variable to be the recipient of the input, Perl uses the variable $_ by default. Likewise, if you do not give any arguments to the **print** function, then $_ is printed by default. Thus, the above code could have been written as follows:

```
while(<STDIN>)
{
    print;
}
```

As you learn more about Perl, you will see other cases where $_ is used implicitly.

The Line Number Variable $.

If you wanted to add line numbers to the code from above, you could provide your own variable. Or, you could use the built-in $. variable. Each time you read a line from a file, Perl increases this variable. Thus, the following code produces line numbers:

```
while(<STDIN>)
{
    print "$.\t$_";
}
```

Or, you could write a program to count the lines in the input file, as shown here:

```
while(<STDIN>)
{
}
print "lines: $.\n";
```

The Default Array Element Separator $"

Code Example

We have seen that when you print an entire array, you need to place the array within double quotes, or else the array elements will be juxtaposed next to one another. Placing the array within double quotes causes a space to separate the array elements. The variable $" controls the character that separates the array elements when they are surrounded by double quotes in the **print** function. See the folder **Array**.

```
% type array.pl
#
#   array.pl
#
$" =",";
@data = (1,2,3);
print "@data\n";
$" =":";
print "@data\n";
$" =".";
print "@data\n";
% perl array.pl
1,2,3
1:2:3
1.2.3
%
```

The Error Message Variable $!

There will be occasions when you wish to terminate your program because of errors. One such occasion occurs when you try to open a file for reading and the file does not exist. The **open** function returns the value 1 when it succeeds. You can test for this condition and use the **die** function to terminate your program when **open** does not return this value. The **die** function takes a string, which typically contains your reason for terminating. Or, you could use the system's error message, which is contained in the **$!** variable.

```
$x = open(FILE, "myfile");
if ( $x == 1 )
{
        print "success: do something\n";
}
```

```
else
{
        print "SYSTEM ERROR IS -> $!\n";
        die "program terminated\n";
}
```

The Special Variable Controlling Buffering $|

The variable $| controls buffering. If set to nonzero, then any prints on the currently selected output file will immediately be flushed. However, this is not the default behavior, and thus if you want to turn off buffering, you have to write a line of Perl such as

```
$| = 1;      # turn off buffering
```

Summary

This chapter presented high-level features of the Perl programming language. We presented materials on the three types of variables: scalar, array, and hashes. Then we presented materials on file handles for performing file I/O. Next, we discussed the many control flow constructs, such as **if**, **while**, **do**, **until**, **for**, and **foreach**. We also talked about the ways in which you can alter loop control flow using **last**, **next**, and **redo**. Finally, we discussed some special Perl variables, such as $_, $", and $!.

Operators in Perl

A Perl expression is a syntactically correct combination of operators and operands. Perl has a plethora of operators. Many of them originated with C language, and some of them are particular to Perl. In this chapter, we explore all of the operators, including those used for bit manipulation, string manipulation, and regular expressions.

Perl Operators

Perl has an abundance of operators. Many of them come from the C programming language, some come from the UNIX shells, and others are strictly particular to Perl. Before we see the complete set of Perl operators, we must explain some preliminary concepts.

Precedence Versus Associativity

Operator precedence defines the order in which operators are to be executed. Operator associativity defines the order when there are ties in the precedence. For example, most languages define multiplication to be higher in precedence than addition, and thus the following evaluates to 17, and not 21.

```
$x = 2 + 5 * 3;
```

But what if an expression involves operators of the same precedence?

```
$x = 200 / 5 * 10;
```

The precedence does not tell us anything, because / and * are at the same level in the hierarchy. To evaluate this expression, we need to know the associativity of these operators. Is it left to right or right to left?

As it turns out, the associativity of these particular operators is left to right. Therefore, the above expression has the value 400. If you wanted to assure that the multiplication was executed first, then you could use a set of parentheses.

```
$x = 200 / (5 * 10);
```

The above expression now has a value of 4, because whatever is in parentheses is evaluated first. In the case of nested parentheses, the innermost set is evaluated first.

Table 3-1 lists the hierarchy of Perl operators. Operations on level 1 have the highest precedence, level 2 operators have the next highest precedence, and so on. The first column lists the level of precedence, the second column gives the names of the operators on this level, and the third column gives a brief description of the operators on this level.

Operators on levels 3, 4, and 18 associate right to left. Operators on levels 2, 9, 10, 11, and 16 do not have any associativity. All other levels associate left to right.

TABLE 3-1   *Table of Operators, Precedence, and Associativity*

Level	Operator	Description
1	( ), [ ], { }	function call, subscript, block
2	++, –	auto-increment, auto-decrement
3	!, not	logical NOT
	~	bitwise NOT
	-	unary minus
4	**	exponentiation
5	=~	pattern match
	!~	not a pattern match
6	*, /	multiplication, division
	%, x	modulus, repetition
7	+, -, .	addition, subtraction, concatenation
8	<<, >>	left shift, right shift
9	-d, -f, etc.	file test operators

TABLE 3–1	Table of Operators, Precedence, and Associativity (continued)

Level	Operator	Description
10	<	numeric less than
	<=	numeric less than or equal
	>	numeric greater than
	>=	numeric greater than or equal
	lt	string less than
	le	string less than or equal
	gt	string greater than
	ge	string greater than or equal
11	==	numeric equality
	!=	numeric inequality
	<=>	numeric signed comparison
	eq	string equality
	ne	string inequality
	cmp	string signed comparison
12	&	bitwise logical AND
13	|, ^	bitwise OR, exclusive OR
14	&&, and	logical AND
15	||, or	logical OR
16	..	range operator
17	?:	conditional expression
18	=, +=, etc.	assignment operators
19	,	comma operator

Operators Dictate Behavior

Knowing about operators in Perl is very important because often it is the operators that determine how a variable is treated. For example, in the following expression,

```
$x = "20abc" + "3xyz"
```

it appears as if we are attempting to add two strings. The + operator tells Perl to treat the strings as if they were numbers. Perl does the best that it can, since the strings are not really representations of numbers. The result in **$x** is 23. However, if we use the Perl concatenation operator, the dot, the expression below evaluates to the string **20abc3xyz**.

```
$x = "20abc"  .  "3xyz"
```

Operators Taken from C Language

This section presents the Perl operators that derive from the C language. Many of these allow for the writing of succinct code.

Assignment Operators

Most operators are binary in nature; that is, they have two operands. For example, the addition operator is binary. In the line of code below, **$y** and **$z** are the two operands.

```
$x = $y + $z;
```

Any binary operator can be written using the assignment operator rather than using the longer and more traditional approach. Here are some traditional assignment statements using some simple arithmetic operators.

```
$x = $x + 5;          # addition
$x = $x / 2;          # division
$x = $x * 2;          # multiplication
$x = $x ** 5;         # exponentiation
```

Perl has a set of operators that are collectively referred to as the assignment operators. These operators consist of any binary operator followed by the assignment symbol. Here are a few examples of the assignment operators. Each statement below is functionally equivalent to the respective statement above.

```
$x += 5;              # addition
$x /= 2;              # division
$x *= 2;              # multiplication
$x **= 5;             # exponentiation
```

These operators may save you some typing and therefore save you some errors. For example, compare the following two statements. Which is easier to type?

```
$table[$table_index] = $table[$table_index] + $increment;
$table[$table_index] += $increment;
```

Increment and Decrement Operators

Since incrementing and decrementing a variable are two very common operations, Perl allows you to use some special operators, the auto-increment and auto-decrement operators, to perform these operations. These operators can also save you from some typing errors. Each of the following statements adds 1 to the variable **$x**.

```
$x++;
++$x;
```

In the above code, each **++** causes **$x** to be increased by 1. However, there is a distinction between applying the **++** before the variable, a pre-increment, or after the variable, a post-increment. A pre-increment first increments the variable and then uses the incremented value. A post-increment uses the value of the variable before it is incremented. If either of these increments is part of a larger expression, you must be careful about whether you want the pre-increment or post-increment version of the operator. See the folder **PrePost**.

```
% type prepost.pl
#
#    prepost.pl
#
$x = 10;
$y = 20;
print $x++, "\n"; # prints $x, then increments $x
print ++$y, "\n"; # increments $y, then prints it
$c = $x++ + ++$y; # increment $y, do $x + $y, increment $x
print "$c\n";
% perl prepost.pl
10
21
33
%
```

In the last expression above, **$y** is incremented before it is used, and **$x** is incremented after it is used. The pre-decrement and post-decrement operators work similarly. Be careful not to put the **++** or the **--** operators inside quotes in expressions such as the following. They will be treated literally rather than as operators.

```
$x = 12;
print "$x++\n";              # prints 12++
```

Modulus (Remaindering) Operator

The modulus operator % gives you the remainder were you to divide one number by another. This can be used in a variety of problems. For example, to determine if a number is divisible by 10, you might code as shown below.

```
print "$num divisible by 10\n" if (( $num % 10 ) == 0);
```

Here, the remainder of dividing **$num** by 10 is compared against 0. Incidentally, the precedence of the % operator is higher than the precedence of the numerical equality operator **==**, and thus you might have coded the above as

```
print "$num divisible by 10\n" if ( $num % 10  == 0);
```

Finally, since we are using the modifier form of the **if**, the parentheses are also unnecessary.

```
print "$num divisible by 10\n" if  $num % 10  == 0;
```

Conditional Operator

Another notational convenience is the conditional expression. This operator can be used to express the same idea expressed in an **if** statement. This operator has three operands. The first operand is tested for true or false in the same way that the **if** condition is tested. The other two operands represent the value of this operation when the first operand evaluates to true or false respectively. Notice the following two cases:

```
1) $x = 10;
   $y = 20;
   if ( $x > $y )
   {
        $max = $x;
   }
   else
   {
        $max = $y;
   }

2) $max = $x > $y ? $x : $y;
```

In the second case, **$x > $y** is evaluated. If true, the expression between the **?** and **:** is assigned to **$max**. Otherwise, the expression to the right of the **:** is assigned to **$max**. Thus, the conditional expression is of the form

```
e1 ? e2 : e3
```

The value of this expression is either **e2** or **e3** depending upon whether **e1** is true or false respectively. Here are some other uses of this expression.

```
$ans = 120;
$ans = $x % 2  == 0 ? "even" : "odd";     # $ans = "even"
$ans = $x % 2 ? "odd" : "even";           # $ans = "even"
$ans = $x ? "not zero" : "zero";          # $ans = "not
zero"
```

The Comma Operator

Perl has a comma operator, the **,** symbol. There is little need for this operator, but we include it both for completeness and to assure that you understand a few Perl idioms.

In Perl, the semicolon is a statement separator. However, the same statement may have many comma-separated assignments. For example, the following sequence of statements,

```
$a = 10;
$b = 20;
$c = $a + $b;
```

may be written as

```
$a = 10, $b = 20, $c = $a + $b;
```

although there is no particular advantage of doing so. Since you may use this technique in any place where you might code a Perl statement, the following is also possible.

```
for ($i = low, $j = high; $i < $j; $i++, $j--)
{
# some code here
}
```

You may also use the comma operator in any conditional, but beware how this is evaluated.

```
while($a = <STDIN>, $a ne "quit\n")
{
        print $a;
}
```

In this context, the comma operator's value is strictly the value of the last expression in the series. Actually, the above expression is somewhat useful, since it allows you to iterate through a set of interactive responses until the user enters the **quit** string.

Later, we present information that allows you to extract an array slice—an array composed of selected array elements. To use this technique, you need to know about the comma operator. Here is a preview.

```
@list = (2,4,6,8,10);
$first = $list[0];        # retrieve the first element
$last =  $list[4];        # retrieve the last element
@both = @list[0,4];       # retrieve both elements
@both = $list[0,4];       # You probably didn't mean this.
```

The last two lines attempt to use an array slice to extract the zeroth and fourth elements of the array, but only one of them is correct. To obtain a slice, you must use the @ notation. Thus, only the first statement below is correct, and therefore the comma operator is evaluated in an array context yielding elements 0 and 4.

```
@both = @list[0,4];       # retrieve both elements
@both = $list[0,4];       # You probably didn't mean
this.
```

The latter statement above uses the **$** rather than the **@**. Thus, the comma operator is evaluated in a scalar context and evaluates to a 4, the last of the comma-separated items.

Bit Manipulation Operators

A programmer can spend many years writing software before running into a problem where the manipulation of bits is needed. On the other hand, if you are a systems programmer, then you have undoubtedly run into many situations where these techniques are needed.

```
Bitwise Logical not      ~
Bitwise Logical and      &
Bitwise Logical or       |
Bitwise Exclusive or     ^
shift right              >>
shift left               <<
```

Here are a few examples of rudimentary bit manipulation operations. You can represent octal and hexadecimal constants in Perl by using a leading **0** or leading **0x** respectively in front of a number. These constants are used in bit manipulation problems. Here are a few elementary bit operations.

```
$x = 0555;       #      ..000 101 101 101
$z = ~$x         #      ..111 010 101 010
$a = 045;        #      ..000 000 100 101
$b = 066;        #      ..000 000 110 110
$c = $a | $b     #      ..000 000 110 111
$d = $a & $b     #      ..000 000 100 100
$d = $d << 1     #      ..000 001 001 000
```

Code Example

The lines of code above are provided so that you can see the results of various bit manipulation operations. To see a real example, examine the following code, which counts the number of bits that are set in a variable. See the folder **Bits**.

```
% type bits.pl
#
#    bits.pl
#
$count = 0;
print "Enter a number ";
$val = <STDIN>;                    # read a number
$save = $val;
while( $val != 0 )                 # is it zero?
{                                  # no
    $count++ if ($val & 01);       # add 1 if right bit == 1
    $val >>= 1;                    # right shift 1 bit
}
print "($count) 1 bits in $save\n";
% perl bits.pl
Enter a number 31
(5) 1 bits in 31
%
```

As long as **$val** is non-zero, the bit on the extreme right is tested to see if it is a1. If it is, it is counted. In either case, **$val** is shifted one bit to the right, and the process is repeated.

Native Perl Operators

The operators in this section are Perl operators not found in the C language.

Range Operator

The range operator is a pair of dots (..). It has many uses in Perl. Perhaps the most useful is to create a sequence of elements to fill an array. The code below sums the numbers in the range 1 to 100.

```
@numbers = (1..100); # the numbers 1, 2, 3,...,100
foreach $item (@numbers)
{
    $sum += $item;
}
```

Rather than explicitly writing out the values in a particular sequence, the range operator generates them for you. This operator can be used with numbers or with characters. The code below prints the uppercase and lowercase characters.

```
foreach $item (a..z, A..Z);
{
    print "$item";
}
```

String Operators

Perl is very good at string manipulation. There are many string operators and functions that we must discuss. We look at the operators first. The concatenation operator is the dot (.). If you have some strings and you must combine them, it is a routine matter. The program below reads lines from the standard input, exchanges the newline character for the visible sequence **NL**, and joins all the lines together. See the folder **Glue**.

Code
Example

```
% type glue.pl
#
#   glue.pl
#
while($line = <STDIN>)
{
        chomp($line);
        $tot = $tot . $line . "NL";

}
print length($tot), "\n";
print "$tot\n";              # print the long string.
% perl glue.pl
line 1
line 2
line 3
^Z                          # control-z to end the input
24
line 1NLline 2NLline 3NL
%
```

Code
Example

There is also a replication operator, **x**, which is used to repeat a string a given number of times. Here is some code to demonstrate how this operator works. See the folder **Repeat**.

```
% type repeat.pl
#
#   repeat.pl
#
print "Enter a string ";
chomp($string = <STDIN>);
print "Enter a repeat factor ";
chomp($thismany = <STDIN>);
$result = $string x $thismany;
print "($string) repeated ($thismany) times is ($result)";
% perl repeat.pl
Enter a string hello
Enter a repeat factor 3
(hello) repeated (3) times is (hellohellohello)
%
```

Be careful when you use the repetition operator.

```
$number = 5;
$number = $number * 4          # number = 20
$number = $number x 4;         # number = 20202020
```

TABLE 3–2	Relational Operators	
Meaning	**Numeric**	**String**
Greater than	>	gt
Greater than or equal	>=	ge
Less than	<	lt
Less than or equal	<=	le
Equal	==	eq
Not equal	!=	ne
Signed equality	<=>	cmp

Relational Operators

We've already used some relational operators without giving any specific details. Relational operators have two different flavors: numeric and string. Table 3-2 summarizes which operators are used for string comparisons and which operators are used for numerical comparisons.

As you can see, the **==** operator is used for numerical equality, whereas **eq** is used for string equality. Be careful to use the correct operator here. The program below prints the square root and the square for input entered by the user. The user signals he or she is finished entering any input by entering the string **end**.

```
while(1)
{
        print "input a number ";
        chomp($val = <STDIN>);
        last if ( $val == end );
        print "$val ", $val * $val, " ", sqrt($val), "\n";
}
```

In the above code, it is important to use **eq** rather than **==** in checking for the ending string. If you erroneously use **==**, then an input of 0 will match favorably against **end**, which is not what you want.

cmp and <=> are similar in nature to the C language **strcmp** function in that they return **-1** if the left operand is lower than the right operand, **1** if the opposite condition is true, and **0** if the operands are equal.

Logical Operators

Logical operators are those that operate on compound conditions. In Perl, logical operators behave as short-circuit operators; that is, they stop evaluating when they have determined the value of the condition. The logical operators are

```
Logical not          !
Logical and          &&
Logical or           ||
```

You may also use the English words **not**, **and**, and **or** as respective synonyms for the above operators.

Short-circuit operators add efficiency to programs. For example, if **$x** has the value 0, then it would be inefficient to evaluate the second and third comparisons of the compound condition below.

```
if ( $x == 0 || $y == 0 || $z == 0)
{
# some code here
}
```

Sometimes this can make a difference in the flow of data through your program. For example, in the code below, a line is read only if **$x** does not have the value 0.

```
if ($x == 0 || ($y = <STDIN>) )
{
# some code here
}
```

In this particular example, the inner parentheses are necessary. To understand why this is the case, first notice that there are three operators in the evaluated condition. Without the inner parentheses, they will be evaluated in the order ==, ||, and =, as if the condition had been parenthesized as

```
if (((($a == 0) || $b ) = <STDIN> )
```

The evaluation of the || is either true or false, thus generating a 1 or a 0. In either case, this constant value cannot be the recipient of the line input with **<STDIN>**.

Here are a few examples of the use of the logical operators.

```
print "$a is between 0 and 9" if ( $a >= 0 && $a <= 9);
print "$a is between 0 and 9" if ( $a >= 0 and $a <= 9);

print  "$a is not a digit" if ( ! ($a >= 0 && $a <= 9));
print  "$a is not a digit" if ( not ($a >= 0 && $a <= 9));

print  "$a is zero or one" if ( $a == 0 || $a == 1);
print  "$a is zero or one" if ( $a == 0 or $a == 1);
```

Regular Expression Operators

A regular expression is a set of metacharacters that form patterns that are used to match strings. Every string either matches a particular regular expression or it doesn't. Regular expressions are enclosed within a pair of slashes. For example, if you wanted to determine whether the variable **$name** matched the pattern **tele**, you would code as follows.

```
print "$name matches tele\n" if ( $name =~ /tele/ );
```

All matches are case sensitive. If you wish to make the matches case insensitive, place an **i** in back of the pattern.

```
print "$name matches tele\n" if ( $name =~ /tele/i );
```

You can also use a set of **#**'s or a set of **!**'s to delimit the pattern. In these cases, the match operator **m** is required. Thus, the following three statements are different ways of encoding the same test.

```
print "$name matches tele\n" if ( $name =~ /tele/i );
print "$name matches tele\n" if ( $name =~ m!tele!i );
print "$name matches tele\n" if ( $name =~ m#tele#i );
```

If you want to match against the special variable **$_**, then you can omit the **=~** part of the test. Thus, you often see code such as

```
while(<STDIN>)           # read a line into $_
{
    print if /Susan/;    # print $_ if $_ contains Susan
}
```

In addition to simply finding matches, you can also make a replacement if a match is found. In this case, you must use the **s** operator. This operator requires a target regular expression and a replacement string. In each example below, if **$name** matches the string **Mike**, then it is replaced with **Michael**.

```
print $name if ( $name =~ s/Mike/Michael/i );
print $name id ( $name =~ s#Mike#Michael#i );
print $name id ( $name =~ s!Mike!Michael!i );
```

Remember that the **\t** sequence represents the tab character and the **\n** sequence represents the newline character. Thus, each of these sequences counts as a single character in the code above. If you wish to make the substitution in the string **$_**, you can code as follows.

```
print if ( s/Mike/Michael/i );
```

Regular Expression Metacharacters

In the above regular expression examples, simple matches were explained. Regular expression matching is usually more complicated than that and often involves characters with special meanings. For example, the ∧ and $ characters are used to find matches at the beginning and at the end of a string respectively.

```
print  if ( /sub/ );  # print $_ if it contains sub
print  if ( /^sub/ ); # print $_ if it contains sub at
                      # beginning of line
print  if ( /sub$/ ); # print $_ is it contains sub at
                      # end of line
print  if ( /^sub$/ );# print $_ if it contains only sub
                      # (i.e same sub at beginning and
end)
```

The ∧ and the $ are referred to as anchors because they anchor the match to a particular place, i.e., the beginning or the end of a string.

Other special characters are referred to as single character matches because they match a single character. The dot (.) character is one of these. For example, in the pattern **/th.s/**, the dot matches any character. Thus the pattern might be expressed as "any four-letter pattern whose first, second, and fourth characters are **t**, **h**, and **s** respectively and whose third character is any single character." Each of the following strings matches the pattern.

```
this, that, these, those, eleventh series
```

Note that in the example above, the dot was matched by the space character.

The brackets match any single character contained within the brackets. For example, the pattern **/th[iae]s/** is similar to the previous pattern, but the third character is limited to either an **i**, **a**, or **e**. Bracketed expressions have some shorthand notations as well. For example, **[0123456789]** can be encoded as **[0-9]**, and the lowercase alphabet can be encoded as **[a-z]**. Thus, the following expression matches a pattern whose first character is a capital **A** and whose next characters are any digit, a lowercase character, and a capital **Z**.

```
/A[0-9][a-z]Z/
```

Some characters are multicharacter matches. For example, the + character allows you to express the idea of "one or more" of something. In the example below, the pattern is one or more digits followed by one or more white space characters followed by one or more alphanumeric characters.

```
/[0-9]+[\t\n ]+[a-zA-Z0-9]+/
```

In addition Perl allows the following.

```
\w  Match a "word" character (alphanumeric plus "_")
\W  Match a non-word character
\s  Match a whitespace character
```

```
\S   Match a non-whitespace character
\d   Match a digit character
\D   Match a non-digit character
```

Another important metacharacter is the **?**. The question mark is used to signify an optional character: that is, zero or one of something. The regular expression below specifies the string must begin optionally (i.e., there can be zero or one) with a plus or a minus sign followed by any number of digits.

```
/^[+-]?\d+$/
```

The * character means zero or more of something. It is often used in connection with the **.** character to mean "a long string." For example, the following regular expression matches the longest string bounded by a digit on the left and a lowercase character on the right.

```
/[0-9].*[a-z]/
```

Remembered Patterns

Often, you will want to extract a portion of a match. For example, you may want to extract the area code if a string contains a telephone number. The following two patterns match a telephone number in the United States.

```
/\d\d\d-\d\d\d-\d\d\d\d\D/
/((\d\d\d)-\d\d\d-\d\d\d\d)\D/
```

In the second pattern, there are two sets of parentheses. The inner set surrounds the area code portion of the match, while the outer set surrounds the entire phone number. The parentheses do not count toward the match, but rather if there is a match, they tell Perl to remember that portion of the match. You can print the remembered patterns by using the special variables **$1**, **$2**, and so on. Thus, the following program prints area codes and phone numbers from any telephone numbers that are found. See the folder **Tele**.

```
% type tele.pl
#
#
#
while(<STDIN>)
{
        print "Area code for $1 is $2 \n"
        if /((\d\d\d)-\d\d\d-\d\d\d\d)\D/;
}
% perl tele.pl
My phone number is 301-555-1212
Area code for 301-555-1212 is 301
What is yours
Glad you asked.  Mine is 401-555-1213
Area code for 401-555-1213 is 401
%
```

String Functions

There is a close relationship between an operator and a function. For example, Perl uses ** for exponentiation, whereas some languages use the **pow** function to achieve the same result. Likewise, Perl uses the % symbol for the remaindering operation, while other languages use the **MOD** function to achieve the same result. Thus, in this section we present some simple but useful functions that you can use on scalars.

The length Function

The **length** function returns the length of a scalar.

```
$string="This\tstring\nconsists\nof a few\nlines\n";
$len = length($string);                    #    length = 36
```

Remember that the \t sequence represents the tab character and the \n sequence represents the newline character. Thus, each of these sequences counts as a single character in the code above.

The index and rindex Functions

The **index** function returns the first position (zero-based) within a string where a second string is found or **-1** if the second string is not found. The **index** function can also have a third argument: an integer specifying how much to skip in the first string before you start indexing.

```
$s = "if you don't succeed, try try again";
$pos1 = index($s,"try");                   # pos = 22
$pos2 = index($s, "Try");                  # pos = -1
$pos3 = index($s, "try", $pos1 + 1);       # pos = 26
```

The **rindex** function behaves like **index** but returns the index of the last occurrence of the second string.

```
$s = "He had had had where she had had had had";
$pos = rindex($s, "had");                  # pos = 37
```

The substr Function

The **substr** function returns a portion of a string starting at a specified position for a specified length. If the length is not given, the entire string from the specified beginning position is returned.

```
$var = "HOME=/users/home";
$where = index($var, "=");
$name = substr($var, 0, $where);
```

Code Example

```
$val = substr($var, $where + 1);          # HOME
print "$name\n$val\n";                     # /users/home
```

The **substr** function may also be used to alter a string. That is, it can be used on the left-hand side of an assignment. See the folder **Substr**.

```
% type substr.pl
#
#    substr.pl
#
$test = "Java is inferior";
substr($test, 8, 5) = "super";
print "$test\n";
substr($test, 0, 4) = "Perl";
print "$test\n";
substr($test, 0, 0) = "My My: ";
print "$test\n";
%
```

The first **substr** above changes **infer** to **super**. Next, **Java** is changed to **Perl**. And finally, My My: is prepended to the phrase.

```
% perl substr.pl
Java is superior
Perl is superior
My My: Perl is superior
%
```

Functions Dealing with Case

Code Example

The functions **lc** and **uc** return the lowercase and uppercase versions of the argument strings respectively. The functions **lcfirst** and **ucfirst** return the argument strings with only the first character changed to the appropriate case. See the folder **Cases**.

```
% type cases.pl
#
#    cases.pl
#
print "Enter a string: ";
$string = <STDIN>;
print "LOWER CASE: ", lc($string);
print "FIRST CHAR: ", lcfirst($string), "\n";
print "UPPER CASE: ", uc($string);
print "FIRST CHAR: ", ucfirst($string);
% perl cases.pl
Enter a string: a SIMPLE string
LOWER CASE: a simple string
FIRST CHAR: a simple string
```

```
UPPER CASE: A SIMPLE STRING
FIRST CHAR: A simple string
%
```

File Inquiry Operators

There may be many occasions where a programming task depends upon the type of one or more files. For example, you may need to know whether a name represents a file or whether a file is a directory. Perl has several operators that can help you toward these tasks. Table 3-3 shows some of these operators.

TABLE 3–3	Some File Inquiry Operators
Operator	**Meaning**
-e	File exists.
-z	File has zero size.
-s	File has nonzero size (returns size).
-f	File is a plain file.
-d	File is a directory.
-T	File is a text file.
-B	File is a binary file (opposite of -T).
-M	Age of file in days

Code Example

Here is a program that illustrates a few of these operators. See the folder **FileStat**.

```
% type filestat.pl
#
#    filestat.pl
#
print "Enter a filename ";
chomp($fn = <STDIN>);
if ( -e $fn )
{
        print "$fn exists\n";
        $days = (-M $fn) * 24 * 60 * 60;
        print "Modifed: $days seconds ago\n";
        $size = -s $fn;
        print "Size is: $size bytes\n";
}
else
```

```
{
        print "No such file as $fn\n";
}
% filestat.pl
Enter a filename filestat.pl
filestat.pl exists
Modifed: 92 seconds ago
Size is: 290 bytes
%
```

Most of the operators return a nonzero value if true. A few of them, such as the **-M** and the **-s** operators, return a numerical value. The **-M** operator returns the number of days since the file was last modified. In the example above, this number was multiplied by 24 * 60 * 60 so that the output reflected the number of seconds since the file was last modified.

Summary

This chapter has presented the plethora of Perl operators. We divided them into several classes, such as those taken from the C programming language and those that are native to the Perl language. We then looked at some string operators and string functions. Finally, we looked at some file inquiry operators.

Array and Hash Functionality

*I*t is difficult to write meaningful programs without using arrays. In this chapter we explore many of the functions used to manipulate arrays, including Perl's special array that stores key/value paired data.

In this section we use the words array and list quite often. The distinction between them in Perl is a narrow one. For our purposes, an array is a named list.

Array Manipulation

Unlike the arrays in many popular programming languages, Perl arrays are not of fixed length. This makes it simple to expand or contract an array in Perl. Many array functions are provided in Perl to operate on arrays in various ways. The first group of functions allows you to dynamically change the size of an array.

Functions that Alter the Size of an Array

Perhaps the most important functions used by Perl programmers are those that allow Perl arrays to grow or shrink. This section demonstrates many of these Perl functions.

SPLIT

The **split** function takes a scalar variable and returns an array. The array is composed of the fields of the scalar delimited by whatever characters you specify. In its simplest case, **split** splits $_ on whitespace characters—blanks, tabs, and newlines. **countwords.pl**, shown next, uses **split** to count words in the standard input. See the folder **CountWords**.

```
% type countwords.pl
#
#    countwords.pl
#
while(<STDIN>)
{
    @words = split;        # split the line into 'words'
    $words += @words;      # add to the number of words
}
print "Total words = $words\n";
%
```

The following line uses the array **@words** in a scalar context, which means that the number of elements in the array are added to **$words**.

```
$words += @words;
```

split can be used on any variable and with any delimiters. Regular expressions can be used as the criteria on which to split the scalar.

```
@fields = split("\t", $line);     # split line on tabs
@fields = split(",", $line);      # split line on commas
@fields = split(/\d+/, $line);    # split line on digits
```

Additionally, a nice use of **split** is to provide a third argument specifying the total number of fields that **split** will return.

```
@fields = split("\t", $line, 2);
```

PUSH, UNSHIFT

The **push** function adds one or more elements to the end of an array.

```
@array = (5,10);              # array = 5, 10
push(@array, 20);             # array = 5, 10, 20
push(@array, 15,25);          # array = 5, 10, 20, 15, 25
```

The following example reads lines and creates an array consisting of those words that are numbers. A regular expression is used to determine if a word is a number. Only then is the number pushed onto the array. See the folder **Numbers**.

```
% type numbers.pl
#
#    numbers.pl
#
while(<STDIN>)
{
        @words = split;
        foreach $item (@words)
```

```
            {
                    push(@numbers, $item) if $item =~ /^\d+$/;
            }
}
print "@numbers\n";
%
```

unshift is similar to **push** except that the elements are added to the beginning of the array rather than to the end of it.

POP, SHIFT

The **pop** function is used to remove the last element of an array. Here is an example that reads a line that presumably consists of a series of numerical values. The entire line is split into a series of numbers, then each number is popped off the array and processed. The processing here is simple: We just compute the square of the number. See the folder **Pop.**

```
% type pop.pl
#
#        pop.pl
#
print "enter some numbers ";
chomp($_ = <STDIN>);
@numbers = split;
while(@numbers)
{
        $x = pop(@numbers);
        print "$x\t", $x * $x, "\n";
}
%
```

The **while** test treats the array in a scalar content, returning its size. As each element of the array is popped, the size of the array changes. Eventually, the array will be empty.

shift is similar to **pop** except that the elements are removed from the beginning of the array rather than from the end of it.

SPLICE

splice can be used to insert elements into an array, displacing those where the insertion occurred. For example, the following invocation inserts the names Susan, Erin, and Patti, while removing Mike and Dave.

```
@emps = (Maria, Mike, Dave, Bob);
@removed = splice(@emps, 1, 2, Susan, Erin, Patti);
```

The first argument specifies the array to be affected. The next two arguments specify a starting position and a length. Remaining arguments are the values to be inserted. The starting position is zero based. If the length is zero, then the values are inserted.

Code Example

Here is a program that generates some random numbers and inserts them into an array so that the array elements are always in order. This may not be the most efficient way to sort an array, but it does demonstrate how to insert using **splice**. See the folder **Splice**.

```
% type splice.pl
#
#   splice.pl
#
print "How many random numbers? ";
$items = <STDIN>;
for ($i = 0; $i < $items; $i++)
{
        $random = int( rand() * 100 );
        print "number is $random\n";
        $found = 0;
        $amt = @vector;
        for ($k = 0; $k < $amt; $k++)
        {
                if ( $random < $vector[$k])
                {
                        splice(@vector,$k,0,$random);
                        $found = 1;
                        last;
                }
        }
        push (@vector, $random) if ($found == 0);
}
print "Sorted array is: @vector\n";
%
```

The **rand** function generates a random number between zero and almost one. To get these numbers into the range zero to almost 100, multiply by 100. To remove any fractional values, use the **int** function. Once the random number is generated, we need to see where it should be placed in the array so that the array is always ordered. The line

```
splice(@vector,$k,0,$random);
```

places the new random number in the array in its proper place. Here is a sample run of the program.

```
% perl splice.pl
How many random numbers? 4
number is 34
number is 77
```

```
number is 36
number is 83
Sorted array is: 34 36 77 83
%
```

Functions that Operate on Entire Arrays

The functions in this section receive arrays and manipulate them in some specified way.

REVERSE

The **reverse** function takes an array and returns a new array consisting of the original elements, but reversed.

```
@result  = reverse(@names);
```

The original array is unchanged. If you want to change it, you'll have to code, as shown next.

```
@names  = reverse(@names);
```

SORT

sort takes an array and returns a new array containing the original elements, but in dictionary-sorted order. The original array is unaltered.

```
@result  = sort(@names);
```

Code
Example

Here is a small program summarizing the **reverse** and the **sort** functions. See the folder **RevSort**.

```
% type revsort.pl
#
#       revsort.pl
#
@names = (Mike, Susan, Erin, Patti, Dave, Maria);
print "Original: @names\n";
@reversed = reverse(@names);
print "Reversed: @reversed\n";
@sorted = sort(@names);
print "Sorted:   @sorted\n";
@revsort = reverse(sort(@names));
print "Rev Sort: @revsort\n";
% perl revsort.pl
Original: Mike Susan Erin Patti Dave Maria
Reversed: Maria Dave Patti Erin Susan Mike
Sorted:   Dave Erin Maria Mike Patti Susan
Rev Sort: Susan Patti Mike Maria Erin Dave
%
```

Be careful if you wish to sort numbers. In order to do this, you need to know about subroutines, a topic that we visit in Chapter 5.

GREP

The **grep** function takes a criterion and a list, and returns an array of those elements in the list that match the criterion. The criteria can be a regular expression, a file operator, or even a subroutine. Later we see how to use a subroutine in this context. For now, we show a few examples using a regular expression and a file inquiry operator. See the folder **Grep1**.

```
% type grep1.pl
#
#    grep1.pl
#
#print "Enter some numbers ";
$line  = <STDIN>;
@elements = split(' ', $line);
@numbers = grep(/^\d+$/, @elements);
print "The numbers are @numbers\n";
% perl grep1.pl
Enter some numbers 10 20 hi there 30 40
The numbers are 10 20 30 40
%
```

In the above code, the line is split into fields and then **grep** is used to filter out the non-numbers. You can also give the **grep** function a file inquiry operator. See the folder **Grep2**.

```
% type grep2.pl
#
#       grep2.pl
#
print "Enter some names ";
$line  = <STDIN>;
@elements = split(' ', $line);
@files = grep(-f, @elements);
print "Files are @files\n";
% perl grep2.pl
Enter some names . .. grep1.pl grep2.pl this that
Files are grep1.pl grep2.pl
%
```

In this case, the criterion is the file inquiry operator **-f**. The code represents an idiom to select file names from a group of names.

JOIN

The **join** function takes an array and a scalar, and produces a string consisting of each element in the array separated from one another by the scalar. Here is a popular idiom using this function. Suppose we have a list of names and we want to print them in sorted order. This is not a difficult problem, but suppose we try to be terse and hand the result of the sort to the print function.

```
@names = (mike, dave, tom);
print sort(@names);
```

The output for the above code segment is

```
davemiketom
```

The output is hard to read because there are no spaces between the array items. If you recall that putting quotes around the array causes a space between each of the output items, then you might be tempted to code as follows.

```
@names = (mike, dave, tom);
print "sort(@names)";
```

However, the output reveals that function names are not recognized within double quotes. Here is the output.

```
sort(mike dave tom)
```

This is where the **join** function comes to the rescue. You can code as follows and **join** will place whichever scalar you specify as the first argument as the separator between the array elements.

```
@names = (mike, dave, tom);
print join(" ", sort(@names)), "\n";
```

Now the output is

```
dave mike tom
```

Hashes (Associative Arrays)

This section deals with a special kind of array in Perl called a hash. Hashes, sometime called associative arrays, contain paired data. Each pair in the hash contains a key that acts as an index to a value that is associated with it. Hashes represent a simple yet powerful idea whose use makes programs more efficient and maintainable.

Hash Functionality

In this section we explore the functionality built into Perl for manipulating hashes. We start with an example hash that maps rock groups to their lead singers. See the folder **Groups**.

```
% type groups.pl
#
#   groups.pl
#
%groups = (  U2 => Bono,
             Stones => "Mick Jagger",
             Aerosmith => "Steve Tyler",
             Heartbreakers => "Tom Petty",
             Journey => "Steve Perry",
             Queen => "Freddie Mercury",
         );
while(1)
{
    print "Enter a Rock Super Group ('quit' to quit) ";
    chomp($group = <STDIN>);
    last if ($group =~ /^quit/i);
    print "Lead singer for $group is $groups{$group}\n";
}
% perl groups.pl
Enter a Rock Super Group ('quit' to quit ) U2
Lead singer for U2 is Bono
Enter a Rock Super Group ('quit' to quit ) Queen
Lead singer for Queen is Freddie Mercury
Enter a Rock Super Group ('quit' to quit ) Beatles
Lead singer for Beatles is
Enter a Rock Super Group ('quit' to quit ) quit
%
```

The big advantage of a hash is that the programmer does not have to perform a lookup. The expression **$groups{$group}** uses the variable **$group** as the index to the value associated with it. If you happen to evaluate this expression for a pair that is not present, then the output is simply empty. You can see that occurring above when the user asks for the Beatles. Note also that the {}'s are used to index a hash, whereas the []'s are used to index an array. This is because in Perl the same program could have an array and a hash with the same name.

Incidentally, the **%groups** hash could also have been formed using the array initialization syntax. In this case, for each pair of elements within parentheses, the first item is the key and the second item is the value.

```
%groups=(  U2, Bono, Stones, "Mick Jagger", Aerosmith,
           "Steve Tyler", Heartbreakers, "Tom Petty",
           Journey, "Steve Perry", Queen,"Freddie Mercury"
           );
```

It is also possible to take an existing array and assign it to a hash, as shown below. When you do this, be sure that the pairs are arranged correctly.

```
@groups= (U2, Bono, Stones, "Mick Jagger", Aerosmith,
           "Steve Tyler", Heartbreakers, "Tom Petty",
```

```
          Journey, "Steve Perry", Queen,
          "Freddie Mercury"
          );
%groups = @groups;
```

EXISTS

Before you actually form an expression such as **$groups{$groups}**, you are advised to check whether that entry exists. You can use the function **exists** for this purpose. Rather than indiscriminately printing the value of **$groups{$group}**, you should first determine if there is an entry for this key. Thus, the code above should have been written as

```
if ( exists ($groups{$group}) )
{
    print "Lead singer for $group is $groups{$group}\n";
}
else
{
    print "No information on $group\n";
}
```

ADDING AND DELETING VALUES

Although most problems involving hashes call for the direct lookup of an entry in the hash table, problems involving hashes are dynamic. This means that when the program is executing, there are often requests for adding and deleting entries. To delete an entry, simply code as follows, using the **delete** function.

```
if ( exists( $group{$group} ) )
{
    delete $groups{$group}
}
```

Adding an element is as simple as the following.

```
$groups{Eagles} = "Don Henley";
$groups{Wings} = "Paul McCartney";
```

KEYS AND VALUES

There are many occasions when you must know the entire set of keys. You can use the **keys** function for this. The code below can be used to retrieve the keys.

```
foreach $key (keys(%groups))
{
    print ++$i, "\t", $key, "\n";
}
```

```
1    Heartbreakers
2    Journey
3    Aerosmith
4    Stones
5    Queen
6    U2
```

You may have noticed that the keys are displayed in no special order. If you want to impose an order on them, you can sort the keys first.

```
foreach $key (sort (keys(%groups)))
{
    print ++$i, "\t", $key, "\n";
}
```

```
1    Aerosmith
2    Heartbreakers
3    Journey
4    Queen
5    Stones
6    U2
```

You can also retrieve all the values whenever you wish by using the **values** function.

```
foreach $value (values(%groups))
{
    print ++$i, "\t", $value, "\n";
}
```

```
1    Tom Petty
2    Steve Perry
3    Steve Tyler
4    Mick Jagger
5    Freddie Mercury
6    Bono
```

EACH

Another function that may prove useful for manipulating hashes is the **each** function. This function delivers each pair in some unspecified order until there are no more pairs. The following idiom can be used to iterate over all the pairs.

```
while(($key, $value) = each(%groups))
{
    print "$key -> $value\n";
}
```

```
Heartbreakers -> Tom Petty
Journey -> Steve Perry
Aerosmith -> Steve Tyler
```

```
Stones -> Mick Jagger
Queen -> Freddie Mercury
U2 -> Bono
```

Useful Hash Examples

If you have not seen hashes before, you might be amazed at the places where they can be used. The following examples show some application areas where this data type is useful. Notice in these examples that the hashes are built dynamically in response to the requirements of the program. This is different from the **%groups** hash above, where that hash was initialized before accepting user input.

Counting Words in a File

Code
Example

This example demonstrates how to use a hash to count the frequency of words in a file. The strategy is to read lines from a file and split each line into its words. Then each word can be used as an index into a hash where the associated value can be the count for each word. Here is the code. See the folder **Freq**.

```
% type freq.pl
#
#        freq.pl
#
while(<STDIN>)
{       @words = split;
        foreach $word (@words)
        {
                $words{$word}++;
        }
}
foreach $word (sort(keys(%words)))
{
        print "$word occurred $words{$word}\n";
}
%
```

The important piece of code above is

```
$words{$word}++;
```

which is of course a shortcut for

```
$words{$word} = $words{$word} + 1
```

and which simply adds 1 to the count for the word indexed by **$word**.

Finding Unique Words

In the next example, we wish to record the unique words in a document. We do this by examining each word found in the input to determine whether it has been seen already. If it has not been seen, we simply add it to the hash and associate some value with it, a 1 in this case. The next time this word is encountered, it will already have been marked as seen. In the end, we just print out the keys. See the folder **Uniq**.

```
% type uniq.pl
#
#       uniq.pl
#
while(<STDIN>)
{
   @words = split;
   foreach $word (@words)
   {
        $seen{$word} = 1 if (!exists($seen{$word}));
   }
}
print join("\n", sort(keys(%seen)));
%
```

Built-in Arrays and Hashes

We have introduced a few special Perl variables, such as **$.** and **$_**. Perl also has a few built-in arrays.

@ARGV

One special array in Perl is the **@ARGV** array. This array is the collection of strings passed in on the command line. For example, if you execute your Perl program as

```
% perl program.pl these are a few pieces of data
```

then the array **@ARGV** contains the strings

```
these are a few pieces of data
```

Here is a program that will familiarize you with some common uses of the **@ARGV** array. The program raises the first argument to the second argument power. The first part of the program is error checking. See the folder **Power**.

```
% type power.pl
#
#        power.pl
#
die "usage: perl power.pl base power\n" unless $#ARGV ==
1;
die "first argument must be a number\n" unless $ARGV[0] =~
/^\d+$/;
die "second argument must be a number\n" unless $ARGV[1]
=~ /^\d+$/;
print $ARGV[0] ** $ARGV[1], "\n";
% perl power.pl
usage: perl power.pl base power
% perl power.pl 2a 4
first argument must be a number
% perl power.pl 2 4a
second argument must be a number
% perl power.pl 2 4
16
%
```

Since **@ARGV** is an array, **$ARGV[0]** is the first element and **$ARGV[1]** is the next element. Likewise, **$#ARGV** is the subscript of the last element. Thus, if there are two arguments, then **$#ARGV** will have the value 1. With this is mind, you will see that the following line assures that there are two arguments passed to this script.

```
die "usage: perl power.pl base power\n" unless $#ARGV ==
1;
```

The **die** function prints whatever error message you supply and then terminates your program. If you do not supply your own message, then a default message will be supplied for you. When you do supply your own message, be sure to supply the newline character as well. This will suppress the default message.

The <ARGV> File Handle

Code
Example

Although arguments on the command line can be arbitrary strings, they are often the names of files. Suppose you wanted to write a Perl program that displayed each file whose name appeared on the command line, along with their line numbers. You could proceed as follows. See the folder **ReadFiles**.

```
% type readfiles.pl
#
#        readfiles.pl
#
foreach $file (@ARGV)
{
```

```
        next unless -f $file;
        open(FILE, "$file");
        print ++$i, "\t", $_ while(<FILE>);
        close(FILE);
}
%
```

This would work fine, but Perl has an easier strategy. The file handle **ARGV** is such that when reading from it you are actually reading from each file on the command line. Thus, the following program is equivalent to the previous one.

```
print "$.\t$_" while(<ARGV>);
```

When you use the file handle **ARGV**, you might want to be able to detect the end of each file. Here is a program that does the detection and uses the special scalar **$ARGV** to print the name of the file from which you are reading. When you execute the **close** function on the handle **ARGV**, the line counter **$.** is reset. See the folder **Eof**.

```
% type eof.pl
#
#         eof.pl
#
while (<ARGV>)
{
        print "$ARGV\t$.\t$_";
        close (ARGV) if ( eof );
}
%
```

The Special %ENV Array

On your system, if you open up a DOS window and execute the **set** command, you will see many lines of the form VAR=VALUE. These are the so-called environment variables. These variables can be accessed from a Perl program by using the built-in hash named **%ENV**. This hash contains environmental variables and their values. Here are a few examples of how this array can be used. See the folder **Env**.

```
% type env.pl
#
#         env.pl
#
print "My Prompt is $ENV{PROMPT}\n";
print "My User Name is $ENV{USERNAME}\n";
print "My System Root is $ENV{SYSTEMROOT}\n";
% perl evn.pl
My Prompt is $P$G
My User Name is michael
```

```
My User System Root is C:\WINNT
%
```

Summary

This chapter presented information about Perl arrays and hashes. We studied many kinds of array functions, including those that create arrays, such as **split** and **splice**, and those that return them, such as **sort** and **reverse**. We also studied the purposes of hashes and some useful hash functions, such as **keys** and **values**. Finally, we gave some examples of applications areas where a hash provides the best solution to a problem.

Subprograms

*A*ll programming languages give developers the ability to create their own subroutines, blocks of code that allow generality and reuse. This chapter examines the principles of subroutines in Perl.

All high-level languages offer ways in which a large program may be partitioned into manageable pieces. This divide-and-conquer strategy leads to easier debugging, maintenance, and readability. Different programming languages use different names for these partitions of reusable code. Some of these names are methods, subprograms, procedures, functions, and subroutines. Perl tends to use the latter two names more than the other names.

Organization of Subroutines

A solid programming strategy is to write programs in small, manageable, reusable pieces. This division of labor in Perl is accomplished through the use of programmer-written subroutines, operating system calls, built-in subroutines, and library functions. To the Perl programmer, they all look the same. Part 1 of this book concentrates on programmer-written subroutines.

Although programmer-written subroutines may be defined anywhere within a Perl script, in practice they are usually defined in separate files and then imported into any program that needs them. However, for simplicity, the first few subroutines that we demonstrate will be defined at the top of the file that needs them. The general form of a subroutine is as follows:

```
sub subName
{
    body of subroutine;
}
```

Once a subroutine is defined ahead of its first use, it can be invoked in any of the following ways; the last line is preferred.

```
&subName()
&subName
subName;
subName()
```

Code Example

Here is an example of a subroutine. Each time it is called, it prints the company name, city, and state. See the folder **Org**.

```
% type org.pl
#
#        org.pl
#
sub header
{
        print "=============\n";
        print "/training/etc\n";
        print "Columbia, ";
        print "MD.\n";
        print "=============\n";
}
print "print the header\n";
header();                        # call the subroutine
print "header is printed\n";
% perl org.pl
print the header
=============
/training/etc
Columbia, MD.
=============
header is printed
%
```

When Perl executes your code, it skips over any subroutines and executes them only when they are invoked, as shown above. The subroutine named **header** works perfectly well as it is written, but it lacks generality. Users of this subroutine should be able to pass as arguments to the subroutine, for example, the company name, the city, and the state.

Passing Arguments to Subroutines

In Perl, when a subroutine is invoked, the arguments to the subroutine are collected in a special array named @_. This array comes into existence only when a subroutine is invoked. Inside the subroutine, if you need to fetch the individual elements of @_, you can reference them as **$_[0]**, **$_[1],** and so on. Here is a version of the **header** subroutine, which allows arguments to be passed to it. See the folder **Org2**.

```
% type org2.pl
#
#   org2.pl
#
sub header
{
        print "==============\n";
        print "$_[0]\n";
        print "$_[1], ";
        print "$_[2].\n";
        print "==============\n";
}
header("/training/etc", "Columbia", "MD");
header("Toy Factory", "Miami", "FL");
% perl org2.pl
==============
/training/etc
Columbia, MD.
==============
==============
Toy Factory
Miami, FL.
==============
%
```

local Versus my

Variables that you might use inside a subroutine are global variables. If you modify such a variable, it has a residual effect when you leave the subroutine. Notice the following code. See the folder **Global**.

```
% type global.pl
#
#        global.pl
#
sub header
{
        print "inside sub: before change: $message\n";
        $message = "A new message";
        print "inside sub: after change :  $message\n";
}
$message = "The original message";
print "message: Before sub: $message\n";
header();
print "message: After sub: $message\n";
% perl global.pl
```

```
message: Before sub: The original message
inside sub: before change: The original message
inside sub: after change :  A new message
message: After sub: A new message
%
```

You can see that once **$message** was changed inside the subroutine, it had a lasting change throughout the program. To avoid problems like this, Perl provides a way to limit the scope of a variable to a specific subroutine and all those subroutines called from it. This is known as *dynamic scoping*. The **local** function allows you to create variables that behave in this way. See the folder **LocalTest**.

Code
Example

```
% type localtest.pl
#
#   localtest.pl
#
$x = 10;
$y = 20;
sub first
{
        print "Inside first: $x $y\n";
        print 'Create local vars: $x and $y', "\n";
        local($x, $y) = (100,200);
        print "After creating local vars: $x, $y\n";
        print "Call second\n";
        second();
        print "Return from second: $x, $y\n";
}
sub second
{
        print "Inside second: $x $y\n";
        print "Adding 1 inside second\n";
        $x++;
        $y++;
}
print "Before function calls: $x $y\n";
first();
print "After function calls: $x $y\n";
% perl localtest.pl
Before function calls: 10 20
Inside first: 10 20
Create local vars: $x and $y
After creating local vars: 100, 200
Call second
Inside second: 100 200
Adding 1 inside second
Return from second: 101, 201
After function calls: 10 20
%
```

In the above program, the two variables $x and $y are used before any functions are called. If we never localized these variables, there would be only one set of them. Localizing them within the **first** function creates a second set of these variables whose lifetimes are not only for this subroutine but also for any subroutine that **first** may call. When **second** is called, it modifies these variables. You can see these modified values near the bottom of **first**. Finally, when we return from these subroutines, the original set of variables have maintained their original values.

On the other hand, the **my** function gives you a way to limit the scope of a variable to a specific subroutine, excluding those called from within it. This is called *lexical scoping*. **my** is always preferred to **local**. Here is a subroutine that uses a **my** variable to sum the elements of an array passed to it. See the folder **Totals**.

Code
Example

```
% type totals.pl
#
#       totals.pl
#
sub totals
{
        my($sum) = 0;
        foreach $item (@_)
        {
                $sum += $item;
        }
        $sum;
}
print "Enter a list of values ";
$_ = <STDIN>;
@data = split;
print "sum of @data is ", totals(@data), "\n";
% perl totals.pl
%
Enter a list of values 10 20 30 40
sum of 10 20 30 40 is 100
%
```

Note also that the calls below represent legitimate calls to the **totals** subroutine. In each case, the various argument lists are flattened out into one long list.

```
@data = (10,20,30,40);                        # 100
@items = (100,200,300);                       # 600
$result = totals(@data, @items);              # 700
$result = totals(10,20,30, @data, 40,50 60);  # 310
```

Named Parameters

Code Example

In most cases, the order in which parameters are sent to subroutines is very important. For example, suppose you write a subroutine that computes the value of a base raised to a power. If you wanted to compute the result of raising 2 to the fifth power, then the first call below would be correct and the second call would be incorrect. See the folder **Raise1**.

```
%type raise1.pl
#
#    raise1.pl
#
sub raise
{
    my($base, $power) = @_;
    my $result = 1;
    for ( $i = 0; $i < $power; $i++)
    {
            $result *= $base;
    }
    $result;
}
$result = raise(2,5);          # correct - base first
print "$result\n";             # 32
$result = raise(5,2);          # incorrect - base second
print "$result\n";             # 25: 5 squared
%
```

If you name the parameters, then their order is irrelevant. You can name parameters by passing the arguments, as shown here.

```
$result = raise(base => 2, power => 5);
$result = raise(power => 5, base => 2);
```

Incidentally, this technique is used when you write graphical user interfaces using the **Tk** module (see the book *Modern Perl Programming* by Michael Saltzman).

When you use named parameters, the subroutine needs to be written carefully. The name/value pairs must be copied to an associative array and then fetched from it. This is how we would rewrite the **raise** subroutine. See the folder **Raise2**.

Code Example

```
% type raise2.pl
#
#    raise2.pl
#
sub raise
{
    my(%params) = @_;
    my($base) = $params{base};
```

```
        my($power) = $params{power};
        my $result = 1;
        for ( $i = 0; $i < $power; $i++)
        {
                $result *=   $base;
        }
        $result;
}
$result = raise(base => 2,power => 5);
print "$result\n";
$result = raise(power => 5, base => 2);
print "$result\n";
%
```

Using this technique, you can also supply default parameters. In this case, the default values are copied directly into the associative array and then replaced with the actual arguments supplied by the user of the subroutine. See the folder **Raise3**.

Code Example

```
% type raise3.pl
#
#   raise3.pl
#
sub raise
{
        my(%params) = ( base => 2,
                        power => 5,
                        @_
                      );
        my($base) = $params{base};
        my($power) = $params{power};
        my $result = 1;
        for ( $i = 0; $i < $power; $i++)
        {
                $result *=   $base;
        }
        $result;
}
$result = raise();                        # 2 to the 5th
print "$result\n";
$result = raise(base => 3);               # 3 to the 5th
print "$result\n";
$result = raise(power => 10);             # 2 to the 10th
print "$result\n";
$result = raise(base => 3, power => 4); # 3 to the 4th
print "$result\n";
%
```

Returning a Value from a Subroutine

In the previous section, we concentrated on parameter issues. However, you can think of a function as a black box with inputs and outputs. The inputs are the parameters and the outputs are the value or values returned from the subroutine. In this section we concentrate on the values returned from a subroutine.

All Functions Return Something

In languages such as C, C++, and Java, a specific function either returns a value or it does not. In these languages, you need to explicitly specify a return type for those functions returning a value, and you also need to explicitly specify the type **void** for those functions that do not return a value.

In Perl, we would like to achieve the same behavior. However, as you will soon see, every Perl function returns a value. Thus, to use a function as if it does not return a value, you simply ignore the returned value. In this case, you would invoke the function as we did before.

```
header();
```

If a function does return a value, then you need to invoke the function in a specific context. Any of the following invocations of a mythical **compute** function would use the value returned from the function.

```
$x = compute();            # store returned value in $x

print compute();           # print returned value

while(compute() > 0)       # compare returned value to 0
{
}

if ( compute() < 0 )       # compare returned value to 0
{
}
```

Code Example

Functions Returning a Scalar

Subroutines can return any type of value. The subroutine below returns a scalar, the largest value from a list of values. See the folder **Largest**.

```
% type largest.pl
#
#   largest.pl
#
sub largest
{
```

```
        my($large) = shift @_;
        foreach $item (@_)
        {
                $large = $item if $item > $large;
        }
        return $large
}
print "enter a list of values ";
$_ = <STDIN>;
@data = split;
print "largest item among @data is ", largest(@data),
"\n";
% perl largest.pl
Enter two numbers 5 10 15 40 30 20 10
largest item among 5 10 15 40 30 20 10 is 40
%
```

The **return** statement is responsible for returning a value from a function. In this case, the returned value is simply printed. As it turns out, the **return** statement is not necessary, because Perl will always return the last expression evaluated inside a function. Thus, the function could have been written as follows.

```
sub largest
{
        my($large) = shift @_;
        foreach $item (@_)
        {
                $large = $item if $item > $large;
        }
        $large;
}
```

Even an innocuous function such as the following would return a value.

```
sub hello
{
    print "hello there\n";
}
```

You might wonder about the value returned from **hello**. As usual, it is the value of the last expression evaluated. In this case, it would be the value from the **print** function. Although nobody ever uses it, **print** actually does return a value, typically the number of characters printed. So even though **hello** does return a value, it is usually ignored. You would invoke **hello** as

```
hello();
```

and not as

```
$x = hello();
```

Functions Returning an Array

Code Example

You can also write subroutines that return arrays. To return an array, just make sure the last expression evaluated in the function is an array. Here's an example of a subroutine that receives a list of items and returns an array consisting of those items in the list that are numbers. See the folder **Numbers**.

```
% type numbers.pl
#
#       numbers.pl
#
sub numbers
{
        my(@numbers);
        foreach $item (@_)
        {
            push (@numbers, $item) if $item =~ /^[-+]?\d+$/
;
        }
        @numbers;
}
print "Enter a list of values ";
$_ = <STDIN>;
@data = split;
print "Numbers from are @data are ",
join(" ", numbers(@data)), "\n";
% perl numbers.pl
Enter a list of values 10 20 mike 30 40 sue
Numbers from (10 20 mike 30 40 sue) are 10 20 30 40
%
```

Returning Other Types

Perl subroutines are not limited to returning a scalar or an array. They can return associative arrays or references as well.

There is another possibility. Suppose you wanted to write a subroutine that returned the number of elements in an array that are even numbers. This is a simple function to write.

```
sub types
{
    my($count);
    foreach $item (@_)
    {
            $count++ if ( $item % 2 == 0 );
    }
    $count;
}
```

Now suppose you want the same function to return the count of even numbers or the count of both even and odd numbers, depending upon the context. Such a subroutine might be called in either of the following ways.

```
$evens = types();              # return count of even numbers
($evens, $odds) = types();     # return count of even and odd
                               # numbers
```

Code Example

To write such a function, where the return type is contextual, Perl uses the **wantarray** function. This function returns a nonzero value when the context is an array and a zero value otherwise. See the folder **WantArray**.

```
% type wantarray.pl
#
#        wantarray.pl
#
sub odd_or_even
{
        my($odds, $evens) = (0,0);
        foreach $item (@_)
        {
                $evens++ if ($item % 2) == 0;
                $odds++ if $item % 2 == 1;
        }
        return wantarray() ? ($evens, $odds) : $evens;
}
@data = (1,2,3, 4, 4, 4, 5, 6);
print "Test in scalar context\n";
$evens = odd_or_even(@data);
print "$evens even numbers in @data\n";
print "Test in array context\n";
($evens, $odds ) = odd_or_even(@data);
print "$evens even numbers in @data\n";
print "$odds odd numbers in @data\n";
% perl wantarray.pl
Test in scalar context
5 even numbers in 1 2 3 4 4 4 5 6
Test in array context
5 even numbers in 1 2 3 4 4 4 5 6
3 odd numbers in 1 2 3 4 4 4 5 6
%
```

Perl Libraries

All of the subroutines above have been written in the file where they are invoked. To make these and other programmer-written subroutines reusable, you must place them in a file and instruct Perl to include them in any program that needs them. The file where you place these subroutines are essentially Perl library files. There are a few ways of accomplishing this task.

The require Function

One way of importing a file into your program is to use the Perl **require** function. To illustrate how this function works, let's take a few of the functions we have seen thus far and place them in a file by themselves. Although the name of this file is not significant, we will call it **library.pl**. Keep in mind that this file will not be executed on its own, but will be imported into other applications that need one or more of its functions.

```
% type library.pl
#
#    library.pl
#
sub numbers
{
        my(@numbers);
        foreach $item (@_)
        {
          push (@numbers, $item) if $item =~ /^[-+]?\d+$/;
        }
        @numbers
}
sub largest
{
        my($large) = shift @_;
        foreach $item (@_)
        {
          $large = $item if $item > $large;
        }
        $large
}
1;       # see next paragraph
```

In order to use any of the functionality in the library file that we just constructed, we need to load this file into any application that requires any of these functions. The loading is accomplished by the **require** function. Like other functions, **require** evaluates the last expression that it reads. If the last expression evaluates to nonzero, then **require** succeeds. Otherwise, it fails. All Perl libraries must have their last expression evaluate to true (i.e., nonzero). By con-

Code Example

vention, Perl programmers use the value 1, as we saw in **library.pl**. Here is a program that uses this library. See the Folder **MyApp**.

```
% type myapp.pl
#
#   myapp.pl
#
require "library.pl";
print "Enter some values ";
$_ = <STDIN>;
@data = split;
print "Nums in @data: ", join(" ", numbers(@data)), "\n";
print "Largest in @data: ",  largest(@data), "\n";
% myapp.pl
Enter some values 10 20 mike jane 30 40
Nums in 10 20 mike jane 30 40: 10 20 30 40
Largest in 10 20 mike jane 30 40: 40
%
```

The @INC Array

There is another issue with libraries. The library file above needs to be placed in a directory in the file system where Perl can find it. This is where Perl uses the built-in array **@INC**. This array contains a colon-separated set of directories where Perl looks to find required files. You can place a library file in any directory as long as you add this directory to the **@INC** array. When you install Perl, the **@INC** array will already have some directories in it. One is the current directory and another is called **site**. This is a good place for your libraries.

One way of adding a directory to the **@INC** array is to either **push** or **unshift** it there. Of course, you would have to do this in every program that needed to use this library.

```
push(@INC, "c:/perl/site");
```

Another way to do this is to use the **-I** flag on the command line each time you wish to execute a Perl program requiring a certain library.

```
% perl -I/perl/site myapp.pl
```

Perhaps the best way is to use the **PERL5LIB** environment variable. This variable should contain the set of directories where your libraries exist. If this variable exists, Perl will check it to determine where to look for libraries. How you set the environment variable depends on which version of Windows you are using. One way is to place a line like the following in your startup file.

```
C:> set PERL5LIB=C:\perl\site
```

One final note about the **@INC** array: It is not absolutely required. Instead, you could use long path names. However, the more you type, the more errors you will make. Here is how your code will look if you use long path names.

```
require "c:/perl/site/mylib.pl";
```

The Standard Perl Library

As we have seen, programmers can always build their own libraries. There is, however, a Standard Perl Library that is delivered with the Perl distribution and located in the **lib** subdirectory of your Perl installation. This library contains many useful functions for Perl programs. We illustrate the use of this library with the **ctime** function that delivers the date and time as a string. You do not need **@INC** here because the standard library directory is automatically searched. See the folder **Time**.

```
% type time.pl
#
#    time.pl
#
require "ctime.pl";
$time = time;                  # builtin time function
print "$time";                 # as an integer
$x=&ctime($time);              # standard library function
print $x;                      # date format
% perl time.pl
1015454406
Wed Mar 6 17:40:06 2002
%
```

The **time** function is built into Perl. It returns the number of seconds that have elapsed since Jan 1, 1970. This is a form of data compression, since using this technique, it takes only 4 bytes to store a date. If you give this value to the **ctime** function, it returns a date and time string.

If you wish to obtain pieces of the time, such as the day of the week or the month of the year, you should use the **localtime** function. This function returns an array consisting of various time parts. Be careful when using this function. The year is reported as a number since 1900. The month is reported in the range 0 through 11 (0 == January). The weekday is reported as a number in the range 0 through 6 (0 == Sunday). See the folder **LocalTime**.

```
% type localtime.pl
#
#       localtime.pl
#
($sec,$min,$hour,$mday,$mon,$year,$wday,$yday,$isdst) =
localtime();
print "DAY OF THE YEAR: $yday\n";
```

```
print "DST: ", $isdst == 1 ? "on" : "off", "\n";
print "TIME OF DAY: $hour:$min:$sec\n";
print "DATE: ", $mon+1, "/", $mday, "/", $year+1900, "\n";
% perl locatime.pl
DAY OF THE YEAR: 138
DST: on
TIME OF DAY: 7:29:14
DATE: 5/19/2002
%
```

Observing the above program, you will see that the **localtime** function returns an array of nine elements. We used almost all of them above. We had to add 1900 to the year and 1 to the month to coincide with how most of us expect to see these values.

Packages

The scope of a variable refers to that section of the program where a variable can be accessed. In a Perl program without any subroutines, all variables are global to the program. We've seen how a scope can be limited to a subroutine either dynamically, with **local**, or lexically through the use of **my** variables. Now we will look at the Perl **package** capability that allows for a further division of scope.

By default, a program has one package—the **main** package. You can create other packages by using the **package** statement. Packages provide a separate namespace so that you can avoid naming collisions. These collisions may happen if you are using libraries from two different sources and each source happens to choose the same name for a function or a variable. Below is a simple package contained in a file named **Hotel.pl**. See the folder **HotelApp**.

```
% type hotel.pl
#
#    Hotel.pl
#
package Hotel;
$name="The Perl Hotel";
sub reservation
{
        print "reservation at $name\n";
}
sub cancellation
{
        print "cancellation at $name\n";
}
1;
%
```

In Perl, there is the notion of a default package. When a Perl program begins, the default package is the main package. In order to use symbols from another package, you must use the :: operator to make qualified references. First, however, you must use **require** to load the new package. In one sense, packages are nothing more than named libraries. Here is an application that uses the **Hotel.pl** library. See the folder **HotelApp**.

```
% type hotelApp.pl
#
#    hotelApp.pl
#
require "Hotel.pl";
print $Hotel::name, "\n";
Hotel::reservation();
Hotel::cancellation();
%
```

When the program begins, all references are assumed to be references to the default package, **main**. If you wish to make references to another package, you must qualify the reference with the :: operator.

```
print $Hotel::name, "\n";
Hotel::reservation();
Hotel::cancellation();
```

You can always change the default package name with a **package** statement so that references can be made more easily.

```
print $Hotel::name, "\n";
Hotel::reservation();
Hotel::cancellation();
package Hotel;              # Hotel is now the default package
print $name, "\n";
reservation();
cancellation();
```

In the latter part of the above code, **Hotel** becomes the default package. Of course, this means that any names in the **main** package will now have to be qualified.

```
$message = "A simple message";
print "$message\n";            # main in the default package
print $Hotel::name, "\n";
Hotel::reservation();
Hotel::cancellation();
package Hotel;                 # Hotel is the default package
print $name, "\n";
reservation();
cancellation();
```

```
print "$main::message\n";
package main;              # main is the default again
print "$message\n";
```

Perl built-in variables such as **$.** and **$_** always belong to the **main** package and thus never have to be referred to using the **::** convention. **my** variables, on the other hand, are never part of a package, thus they can never be referenced using the **::** notation.

Modules and Use

If a file contains a package, the package is usually fully contained in that file, but this is not a requirement. A file could consist of more than one package. Likewise, a package could be spread out over more than one file. However, neither arrangement is a common occurrence. The name of the file in which a package is defined is irrelevant in Perl 4. Most files that define packages in Perl 4 were conventionally named **something.pl**.

Beyond Perl 4, a more systematic approach is used. There is now a tight coupling between the file name and the package name. For example, if a package is named **Math**, then the file must be named **Math.pm**. In this approach only one package must be defined per file. Files that follow this approach are called Perl modules. Modules are imported into your program with the **use** statement.

The **use** statement loads only files whose names end in **.pm**—a Perl module, as described above. When you use **use**, you need to omit the **.pm** portion of the file you are loading.

```
use Math;
use English;
use Cwd;
```

There is also a technical difference between **use** and **require**. The former is executed during the first pass of the Perl interpreter, whereas the latter is executed during execution of the Perl program. Thus, the following will not work properly.

```
$name = "Math";
use $name;
```

Additionally, when **use** is used, the functions within the module are imported into the main package. Many Perl modules (.pm files) now ship with the Perl distribution. We will take a closer look at these modules later in Chapter 8. For now, we show how to use a few simple modules.

The module **Cwd** contains the function **getcwd()**, which returns the name of the current directory. In the program below, the system call **chdir()** is used a few times to change to a different directory. Each time there is a directory change, its name is printed by a call to **getcwd()**. See the folder **Pwd**.

```
% type pwd.pl
#
#    pwd.pl
#
use Cwd;
$cur = getcwd();               # get current directory name
print "Current directory is ($cur)\n";
print "changing to $ARGV[0]\n";
chdir ($ARGV[0]);              # change to directory $ARGV[0]
$pwd = getcwd();
print "Current directory is now ($pwd)\n";
print "Changing to $cur\n";
chdir ($cur);
print "Current directory is ($cur)\n";
% perl pwd.pl ..
Current directory is (C:/OI/NetPerl/Chap05/Pwd)
changing to ..
Current directory is now (C:/OI/NetPerl/Chap05)
Changing to C:/OI/NetPerl/Chap05/Pwd
Current directory is (C:/OI/NetPerl/Chap05/Pwd)
%
```

Another handy module is the **Benchmark** module that is used to determine how long it takes to execute some code. For example, if you have two different algorithms to compute a factorial, you may want to know which one is faster. In the program below, one algorithm computes the factorial recursively and the other computes the factorial using iteration. See the folder **Fact**.

```
% type fact.pl
#
#    fact.pl
#
use Benchmark;
sub recur
{       my($item) = @_;
        return $item if ( $item == 1 );
        return $item * recur($item - 1);
}
sub iter
{       my ($item) = @_;
        my ($prod) = 1;
        while($item > 1)
        {
                $prod *= $item;
                $item--;
        }
        $prod;
```

```
}
timethese(500000, {     'iter'  => 'iter(10);',
                        'recur' => 'recur(10);'
                  }
);
```

The **timethese** function from the **Benchmark** module runs each function as many times as you specify (500,000 in the example above) and then produces the time it takes to run them.

```
% perl fact.pl
Benchmark: timing 500000 iterations of iter, recur...
iter: 10 wallclock secs ( 8.66 usr + 0.00 sys =  8.66 CPU)
recur: 23 wallclock secs (22.60 usr + 0.00 sys = 22.60
CPU)
%
```

Writing Special Sort Functions

Some Perl functions require that you write your own function to alter the default behavior of the Perl function. The best example of this is the **sort** function. Whenever data is sorted, there are two phases to the algorithm: the comparison phase, to see if elements are out of order, and the exchange phase, to put them in order. The default comparison for the **sort** is to compare items lexicographically. This is why the following program produces the output that is displayed. See the folder **DefSort**.

```
% type defsort.pl
#
#      defsort.pl
#
@numbers = (1, 15, 100, 250, 2, 200, 15, 25);
print join("\n", sort(@numbers));
% perl defsort.pl
1
100
15
15
2
200
25
250
%
```

If you want to sort these values numerically, you need to provide your own comparison algorithm. Then, when the sort function compares two

Code Example

items, it will call your comparison routine. The restrictions on your algorithm are twofold.

- You must use the two special variables **$a** and **$b** in your subroutine.
- The value returned from your subroutine must be either greater than zero, zero, or less than zero, depending upon how the two values compare.

Here is the correct way to sort numerically. See the folder **NumSort**.

```
% type numsort.pl
#
#        numsort.pl
#
sub numcompare
{
        if ( $a > $b )
        {
                1;
        }
        elsif ( $a < $b)
        {
                -1;
        }
        else
        {
                0;
        }
}
@numbers = (1, 15, 100, 250, 2, 200, 15, 25);
print join("\n", sort numcompare (@numbers));
%
```

The subroutine can be written more tersely by using the signed comparison operator **<=>**.

```
sub numcompare
{
        $a <=>$b;
}
```

There may be various ways in which you want to sort your data. The following example may be a stretch, yet it does illustrate the principle. Suppose you wish to sort lines of a file based on their length. Here is a program that does just that. The program reads the file named **para**.

```
% type para
This example will
demonstrate how
you can write custom sorts.
```

Code Example

```
For example, to sort by
line lengths.
%
```

See the folder ByLength.

```
% type bylength.pl
#
#       bylength.pl
#
sub bylength
{
        length($a) <=> length($b);
}
die "Need an argument\n" unless $#ARGV == 0;
die "Argument must be a file\n" unless -f $ARGV[0];
open(INPUT, "$ARGV[0]");
@lines = <INPUT>;
@result = sort bylength(@lines);
print @result;
% perl bylength.pl para
line lengths.
demonstrate how
This example will
For example, to sort by
you can write custom sorts.
%
```

In the program above, the lines themselves are sent to the **bylength** sub-routine, but it is their lengths that are compared.

We can complicate the problem a bit by trying to print the original line numbers along with the lines. This is a nice problem because it ties together many of the things we have seen in Perl thus far. It requires not only a custom sort but also that we keep a hash that maps line numbers to lines. That's not all: It also requires that we sort on the values of a hash and not on the keys. See the folder **LineNums**.

```
% type linenums.pl
#
#       linenums.pl
#
sub bylength
{
        length( $lines{$a} ) <=> length( $lines{$b} );
}
die "Need an argument\n" unless $#ARGV == 0;
die "Argument must be a file\n" unless -f $ARGV[0];

open(INPUT, "$ARGV[0]");
```

```
while(<INPUT>)
{
        $lines{$.} = $_;
}
@keys = sort bylength(keys(%lines));
foreach $key (@keys)
{
        print "$key\t$lines{$key}";
}
% perl linenums.pl para
5  line lengths.
2  demonstrate how
1  This example will
4  For example, to sort by
3  you can write custom sorts.
%
```

The program begins by doing some error checking on the command-line argument. Then each line from the input file is read into a hash keyed by its line number. The **sort** sends a pair of keys to the special **sort** function, but the comparison is *not* on the length of the keys but rather on the length of the values associated with the keys.

```
length( $lines{$a} ) <=> length( $lines{$b} );
```

Summary

This chapter presented the details of writing your own functions in Perl. We discussed the topics of passing arguments to subroutines and returning values from subroutines. Then we discussed Perl libraries, which are files of Perl subroutines. One of these libraries, the Standard Perl Library, ships with all Perl distributions. We also discussed various issues regarding where variables can be accessed within a program. This discussion included topics such as **local**, **my**, and the **package** statement. Finally, we discussed the occasional need to write your own function to alter the behavior of a standard function.

Perl References

*R*eferences provide the cornerstone for all advanced work using Perl, including object-oriented programming, graphical user interface (GUI) programming, .NET programming with Perl, and database programming. This chapter explores all of the details of using Perl references.

References to Various Perl Datatypes

References are pointers. A reference variable stores an address. In this way you can store a pointer to a huge chunk of data and later dereference the pointer to get at the data.

What Is a Reference?

You can think of a Perl reference as a scalar whose value is the address in memory of where a piece of data is stored. The piece of data may be a simple value, such as a string, or it might be more complex, such as a record consisting of a name, an occupation, and a series of elements relating to the occupation. In Perl, a reference is a scalar variable that contains the address of some arbitrarily complex piece of data.

Scalar References

One way to create a reference is by using the \ symbol. You can think of this symbol as the "address of" symbol, because that is what it returns. Here's an example of creating a reference.

```
$data = 20;                    # scalar: integer value of 20
$rdata = \$data;               # reference: address of $data
```

The scalar **$rdata** is a reference to **$data**, which is itself a scalar. Once a reference to a variable is created, you may use it to access the variable that is being referenced. In order to access a variable through a reference, you must use $, the scalar dereferencing operator. Assembly language programmers will recognize this as indirect addressing. All of the ideas having to do with a reference to a scalar are collected into the following example. See the folder **Scalar**.

```
% type scalar.pl
#
#    scalar.pl
#
$data = 20;
$rdata = \$data;               # create the reference
print "$data\n";               # print the data directly
print "$rdata\n";              # print the reference
print "$$rdata\n";             # print the data indirectly
$$rdata = 50;                  # change the data indirectly
print "$data\n";               # prove it
% perl scalar.pl
20
SCALAR(0x1ab2cb8)
20
50
%
```

If you print a reference, you'll get an address. Normally, this is not what you want, so don't forget to put the extra $ in front of the reference to get the value to which it refers.

Array References

References can be created to any of Perl's data types. To create a reference to an array, proceed as follows.

```
@values = ( 10, 20, 30 );      # create array
$rvalues = \@values;           # create reference to it
```

As before, if you print **$rvalues**, you get the following.

```
ARRAY (0xbe742c)
```

To get the actual array through the reference, you need to use the array dereferencing operator @.

```
print "@$rvalues";             # prints 10 20 30
```

Or, if you want any element of the array—for example, one of the scalars inside the array—then you would use the scalar dereferencing operator **$**.

```
print "$$rvalues[0]";        # prints  10
print "$$rvalues[1]";        # prints  20
print "$$rvalues[2]";        # prints  30
print "$$rvalues[-1]";       # prints  30
```

Here's a program that summarizes the ideas behind a reference to an array. See the folder **Array**.

```
% type array.pl
#
#    array.pl
#
@values = ( 10, 20, 30);
$rvalues = \@values;          # create the reference
for ( $i = 0; $i < @$rvalues; $i++)
{
     print "$$rvalues[$i]\n"; # access element via reference
}
@$rvalues = (120,130,140);    # change array through reference
print "@values\n";
% perl array.pl
10
20
30
120 130 140
%
```

References to arrays have great utility in Perl. Recall that when arguments are sent to a Perl function, they are all collected into the special array @_. If you need to distinguish between two or more arrays sent to a function, this collection strategy becomes a hindrance. However, if you passed references instead of actual arrays, then you could simply dereference them inside the subroutine.

Here is an example of a subroutine that returns the sum of the elements in each array passed to the subroutine. Keep in mind that in this example, the arrays are not passed to the subroutine, but rather a reference to each array is passed. Thus, @_ is filled with references to the real arrays and not with the data in the real arrays. To get to the real arrays, the references must first be dereferenced. See the folder **Sums**.

```
% type sums.pl
#
#       sums.pl
#
sub sums
{
        my($sum);
        my(@ans);
        foreach $array (@_)
        {
                $sum = 0;
```

```
                    foreach $item (@$array)
                    {
                            $sum += $item;
                    }
                    push(@ans, $sum);
            }
            @ans;
}

@a = (10,20,30);
@b = (100,200,300,600);
@c = (5000, 2000, 3000, 4000);
@totals = sums(\@a, \@b, \@c);
print "@totals\n";
% perl sums.pl
60 1200 14000
%
```

The subroutine has nested loops. The outer loop iterates over each reference in the @_ array.

```
foreach $array (@_)
{

}
```

The inner loop dereferences each of the references.

```
foreach $item (@$array)
{
    $sum += $item;
}
```

Prototypes

The program above works fine, but there is a slight burden to the user of the **sums** function. The user must remember to pass references rather than the arrays themselves. It would be nice if the user could pass the actual array and have the subroutine behave as if references were passed. This is where a Perl prototype is useful.

A prototype is a set of symbols that informs the Perl subroutine about the type of the incoming parameter. These symbols are placed within a set of parentheses following the name of the function at its definition. Some of the symbols that may be used are

$ Force scalar context on incoming arguments.

\@   Force array reference context.

;   Rest of arguments are optional.

In our example, we would like to have at least one argument and, let's say, as many as four arguments to be treated as array references. Thus, we would code

```
sub sums(\@;\@\@\@)
{
    # as before;
}
```

The line that invokes the **sums** function would now be

```
@totals = sums(@a, @b, @c);
print "@totals\n";
```

The only restriction is that the caller must not use the **&** symbol to invoke the subroutine.

Hash References

Code
Example

You may also create a reference to a hash. As usual, the reference operator is \, but this time **%** is the dereferencing operator. See the folder **Hash**.

```
% type hash.pl
#
#   hash.pl
#
%convert = (  1 => one, 2 => two, 3 => three );
$ref = \%convert;
#
#   print all the keys - a likely event
#
print join("\n", keys(%$ref)), "\n";
#
#   print a value from a key - the most likely event
#
print $$ref{1}, "\n";
%
```

In the above code, notice that **%$ref** is the entire associative array and that **$$ref{1}** is the scalar resulting from the **1** key.

```
% perl hash.pl
1
2
3
one
%
```

SYNTACTIC SUGAR

To make the encoding of certain dereferences more meaningful, Perl allows a friendlier notation than what we have seen thus far. Suppose we have the following.

```
@data = (10,20,30,40);
$rdata = \@data;
```

We have seen above that to retrieve an element of the array **@data** through the reference **$rdata**, you can code

```
$$rdata[0];
```

However, there is another notation that is more user friendly and inherently more meaningful.

```
$rdata->[0]
```

There is also an alternative notation for hash references so that if you have a hash such as

```
%states = ( MD => Annapolis,
            CA => Sacramento,
            NY => "New York City"
          );
```

and a reference to a hash such as

```
$rhash = \%states;
```

you can retrieve values from the hash by using either of the following notations.

```
print "$$rhash{NY}\n";          # New York City
print "$rhash->{NY}\n";         # New York City
```

References to Subroutines

Any Perl data type can have a reference. Thus far, we've seen references to arrays, hashes, and scalars. We now examine references to subroutines. The code below shows how to create a reference to a subroutine and how to invoke the subroutine through the subroutine dereference operator **&**.

```
sub square
{
    $_[0] * $_[0];
}
$sref = \&square;               # create reference
$ans = &$sref(10);              # dereference
print "$ans";                   # prints 100
```

Now that we know the mechanics of referencing subroutines, we can show an example of sending both an array and a subroutine as arguments to a subroutine. See the folder **Compute**.

```
% type compute.pl
#
#    compute.pl
#
sub square
{
    $_[0] * $_[0];
}
sub cube
{
    $_[0] * $_[0] * $_[0];
}

sub compute
{
    my($array,$function) = @_;
    foreach $item (@$array)
    {
        $item = &$function($item);
    }
}
@values = (10,20,30);
compute(\@values,\&square);
print "@values\n";
@data = (5,6,7);
compute(\@data,\&cube);
print "@data\n";
% perl compute.pl
100 400 900
125 216 343
%
```

In the above code there are two calls to the **compute** function.

```
compute(\@values,\&square);
compute(\@data,\&cube);
```

In each case, the arguments are an array reference and a subroutine reference. Therefore, inside the subroutine, we can access each of the arguments through **my** variables defined in the following statement:

```
my($array,$function) = @_;
```

$array is a reference to an array, and **$function** is a reference to a function. The **foreach** loop calls the function on each element of the array and changes that element. It will be changed to either its square or its cube, depending upon which function is sent during the call to **compute**.

```
foreach $item (@$array)
{
    $item = &$function($item);
}
```

Remember that within a **foreach** loop, the iterating variable is a synonym for the actual array element to which it is bound. Thus, the following statement actually changes an array element, the one referred to by **$array**.

```
$item = &$function($item);
```

Anonymous References

The references that we have seen thus far have been to variables that have already had storage allocated for them.

```
@data = (10,20,30,40);          # allocate the array
$rdata = \@data;                # create a reference to it
%states = (                     # allocate a hash
            MD => Annapolis,
            CA => Sacramento,
            NY => "New York City"
          );
$rhash = \%states;              # create a reference to it
```

In some cases you will want to take another approach; that is, you will want to create a reference to anonymous storage.

Anonymous Arrays

The syntax for an anonymous array uses the [ ] operator. When Perl sees this operator in the following context, the address of the data within the [ ] is created. In the code below, **$refa** is simply a reference to an array. It can be used as before. The only difference between **$refa** and any array references that we have seen prior to this section is that **$refa** is a reference to an anonymous array.

```
$refa = [10, 20, 30];          # $refa is address of 10,20,30
print "The entire array -> @$refa\n";   # 10 20 30
print "A single element -> $$refa[0]\n";        # 10
print "Alternative notation", $refa->[0];       # 10
```

It would be a logical error to code as

```
@refa = [10, 20, 30];
```

This would simply create an array of one element whose value was the address of wherever the data 10, 20, and 30 was stored. The important notion here is that the expression

```
[10, 20, 30]
```

is a reference in the same sense that **$ref** is a reference in the second line below.

```
@data = (200, 300, 400);
$ref = \@data;
```

Anonymous Hashes

You may also have a reference to an anonymous hash. Recall that anonymous arrays use the [ ] notation. Likewise, anonymous hashes use the { } notation. In the code below

```
$states = {  MD => Annapolis,
             CA => Sacramento,
             NY => "New York City"
          };
print "$$states{NY}\n";
print $states->{NY}, "\n";
```

$states is an anonymous hash; that is, it points to a hash that has no name. Notice that curly braces are used here as opposed to a set of parentheses that usually encloses a set of hash initializers. You can use **$states** in the same way that you can use **$s** below.

```
%morestates =    ( RI => Providence,
                   CT => Hartford,
                   MA => Boston
                 );
$s = \%morestates;
print "$$s{NY}\n";
print "$s->{NY}\n";
```

Anonymous Scalars

It is also possible to define a reference to an anonymous single value, a scalar. In this way, you can define constants in Perl.

```
$PI = \3.14159;
$$PI++;                   # illegal, it's a constant
print $$PI;               # legal - prints 3.14159
```

Complex Data Structures

We now want to use references to build some higher level data structures.

Two-Dimensional Arrays

Suppose you want to build an array with two dimensions. Conceptually, you might think of this as rows and columns, but Perl thinks of this as an array of arrays. A first attempt may result in something like

```
@a1 = (10,20,30);
@a2 = (100,200,300);
@matrix = (@a1, @a2);
```

but this simply creates one flat array with six elements.

```
print "@matrix"; # prints 10,20,30,100,200,300
```

Code Example

Instead, you could populate an array with references to anonymous arrays. See the folder **TwoDim**.

```
% type twodim.pl
#
#   twodim.pl
#
@twodim = (          [10, 20, 30],
                     [40, 50, 60],
                     [70, 80, 90]
             );
print "@twodim\n";
print "$twodim[0]\n";
print "$twodim[1]\n";
print "$twodim[2]\n";
%
```

Each item of the form

```
[10, 20, 30]
```

is a reference, and thus **@twodim** is an array of references to anonymous arrays. If you execute the program above, you will see the following output.

```
% perl twodim.pl
ARRAY(0x176f09c) ARRAY(0x17650f4) ARRAY(0x176516c)
ARRAY(0x176f09c)
ARRAY(0x17650f4)
ARRAY(0x176516c)
%
```

The first print above prints all the elements of the array, which of course are simply references to anonymous arrays. From this, it follows that the last three prints print single references. To get at the actual data in these anonymous arrays, you must dereference each anonymous array.

How you actually perform the dereferencing depends upon which chunk of data you wish to access. If you want to print each row, you can simply dereference each anonymous array reference.

```
foreach $row (@twodim)
{
    print "@$row\n";
}
```

Perl also allows some shortcuts here. The simplest way to get at a particular element is to use two subscripts.

```
print $twodim[0][0]          # prints the 10
print $twodim[0][1]          # prints the 20
print $twodim[1][0]          # prints the 40
```

Two-dimensional arrays may also be built on the fly. For example, if the first access to an array in your program is

```
$data[5][6] = 0;
```

then you have created an array of 42 elements (not 30, because array subscripts start at 0, not 1).

Code
Example

Finally, you may have a jagged array, one in which there are a different number of elements in each row. See the folder **Disparate**.

```
% type disparate.pl
#
#   disparate.pl
#
@values = (  [1, 2, 3, 4, 5 ],
             [Mike, Judy, Joel],
             [Prov, Boston]
           );
for ( $i = 0; $i < @values; $i++)
{
    for ($j = 0; $j < @{$values[$i]}; $j++)
    {
        print $values[$i][$j], " ";
    }
    print "\n";
}
% perl disparate.pl
1 2 3 4 5
Mike Judy Joel
Prov Boston
%
```

The outer loop performs three iterations, one for each reference in the array. In a scalar context, **@values** yields 3, the number of elements in the **@values** array. Since the array is not rectangular, the number of inner loop iterations depends upon how many elements are contained within each referenced array.

The following expression used in a scalar context yields the correct number of elements in each row.

```
@{$values[$i]}
```

There is yet another approach we can take. We can have a reference to a bunch of references. If you are a C programmer, you may know this idiom as a pointer to a bunch of pointers—similar to **argv**.

```
$t =     [    [1, 2, 3, 4, 5 ],
              [Mike, Judy, Joel],
              [Prov, Boston]
         ];
```

$t is a reference to three anonymous references. To get at any of the elements, there needs to be an additional indirection with respect to previous array examples.

```
print "$t \n";               # ARRAY ref
print "$$t[0]\n";            # ARRAY ref
print "$$t[1]\n";            # ARRAY ref
print "$$t[0][0]\n";        # 1
print "$$t[1][0]\n";        # Mike
print "@{$$t[2]}\n";        # Prov Boston
```

Complex Hashes

All of the hashes thus far have consisted of pairs, where each pair consisted of a key and a simple value. The value can be arbitrarily complex—it could be a scalar, an array, another hash, a subroutine, or any other complex data that you need. For example, in the following hash, each name is mapped to an anonymous array.

```
%courses = (    Mike  =>     [CPP, Java, Perl],
                Patti =>     [HTML, C],
                Dave  =>     [JSP, XML]
           );
```

If we wanted to display the courses that **Mike** teaches, we could simply dereference the expression **$courses{Mike}**. The code would be

```
print @{$courses{Mike}};
```

If we wanted a particular course, we could just supply the appropriate subscript on the previous expression. For example, the following expression would display Java.

```
print @{$courses{Mike}}[1];
```

Thus, we could use the following to print all of the courses.

```
foreach $key (keys(%courses))
{
    print @{$courses{$key}}, "\n";
}
```

Each **$courses{$key}** reference above returns a reference to an array, which then must be dereferenced with @. If we wanted to build an array of all of the courses, we could code

```
foreach $key (keys(%courses))
{
    foreach $course (@{$courses{$key}})
    {
        push(@courses, $course);
    }
}
```

Rather than having an actual hash, we could have a reference to one. This would change the notation a bit.

```
$fac = {    Mike   =>    [CPP, Java, Perl],
            Patti =>    [HTML, C],
            Dave   =>    [JSP, XML]
        };
print @{$$fac{Mike}}, "\n";
foreach $key (keys(%$fac))
{
    print @{$$fac{$key}}, "\n";
}
```

Note that a reference to an anonymous array uses the [ ] notation

```
$anonarray = [ 10, 20, 30 ];
```

whereas a reference to an anonymous hash uses the { } notation.

```
$hash = {   a => b, c=> d };
```

Collections of Records

A record is a set of related data fields. For example, the name, address, and phone number are a set of fields that, when taken together, form a payroll record. Keep in mind that Perl does not have any formal treatment of records, and thus the programmer must be creative. Most programmers keep track of records by using anonymous hashes. If you are a C programmer, you can appreciate the similarity between record creation in C and Perl. The C approach might be

```
struct record {
    char name[100];
    int age;
};
typedef struct record RECORD;
RECORD create(char *name, int age)
{
    RECORD r;
    strcpy(r.name, name);
    r.age = age;
    return r;
}
main()
{   struct record a,b;
    a = create("Mike",54);
    printf("%s %d\n", a.name, a.age);
}
```

In Perl, the record would be constructed as

```
sub create
{
    my($name,$age) = @_;
    my $rec =        {     name => $name,
                           age => $age
                     };
    $rec;
}
$a = create("Mike",54);
print $a -> {name}, "\n";
print $a -> {age}, "\n";
```

create is a function that inserts its input into a hash keyed by meaningful field names: **name** and **age**. The important issue is that the hash is anonymous, and thus the result is stored in a reference. When the subroutine returns this reference, the "record" is created.

Collections of these records can be built and references to them can be stored in lists. Then they can be manipulated using Perl's powerful list manipulation functions, such as **push**, **pop**, **shift**, and **unshift**.

The next program reads a file of records and builds a list of references. We will assume that the file contains lines of space-separated triplets, such as "name, age, city." See the folder **GetRecs** and the input file **RECDATA**.

```
% display recdata
```

```
Mike 57 Columbia
Susan 40 Columbia
Bob 57 Plantation
Erin 28 Annapolis
Patti 36 Columbia
Tom 36 Columbia
Maria 40 Pikesville
Dave 36 Odenton
% type getrecs.pl
#
#   getrecs.pl
#
sub create
{   my($name, $age, $city) = @_;
    my $emp   = {   name => $name,
                    age => $age,
                    city => $city
                };
    return $emp;
}
open(INPUT, "RECDATA") || die "can't find RECDATA\n";
while(<INPUT>)
{       @info = split;
        $record = create(@info);
        push(@list, $record);
}
while(@list)
{       $x =   pop(@list);
        print "RECORD #: ", ++$ct, "\n";
        print "NAME: $x->{name}\n";
        print "AGE:  $x->{age}\n";
        print "CITY: $x->{city}\n";
        print "-------------\n";
}
%
```

The main part of the program reads lines from the input file and splits them on white space. These values are sent to the **create** method, where a hash reference is created and filled with this data. Each reference is added to the **@list** array. The rest of the program is simply a loop, which pops off one reference at a time from the **@list** array until it is empty. Each record is then printed a field at a time. Later we will see how hashes are used in object-oriented programming. Here is the execution of the program.

```
% perl getrecs.pl
RECORD #: 1
NAME: Dave
AGE:  36
CITY: Odenton
-------------
```

```
RECORD #: 2
NAME: Maria
AGE:  40
CITY: Pikesville
--------------
RECORD #: 3
NAME: Tom
AGE:  36
CITY: Columbia
--------------
RECORD #: 4
NAME: Patti
AGE:  36
CITY: Columbia
--------------
RECORD #: 5
NAME: Erin
AGE:  28
CITY: Annapolis
--------------
RECORD #: 6
NAME: Bob
AGE:  57
CITY: Plantation
--------------
RECORD #: 7
NAME: Susan
AGE:  40
CITY: Columbia
--------------
RECORD #: 8
NAME: Mike
AGE:  57
CITY: Columbia
--------------
%
```

Sorting Based on a Key Field

Now suppose we want to sort this record based on a particular field. We know from previous experience with sorting that we will have to write some custom subroutines.

```
@keys = sort custom_sub (@list);
```

Code Example

In the above line, the sort routine will repeatedly pass two references to its comparison algorithm. The trick is to have the reference point to the field that we want sorted. Based on how these fields compare, the references are placed in an order that reflects that comparison. Here's the program that sorts on the name field. See the folder **NameSort**.

```
% type namesort.pl
#
#    namesort.pl
#
sub create
{
    my($name, $age, $city) = @_;
    my $emp =        {        name => $name,
                              age => $age,
                              city => $city
                     };
    return $emp;
}
open(INPUT, "RECDATA") || die "can't open RECDATA\n";
while(<INPUT>)
{
    @info = split;
    $record = create(@info);
    push(@list, $record);
}
sub byname
{
    $a->{name} cmp $b->{name};
}
@sorted = sort byname(@list);
print "SORTED BY NAME\n";
foreach $item (@sorted)
{
    print "$$item{name} $$item{age} $$item{city}\n";
}

% perl namesort.pl
SORTED BY NAME
Bob 57 Plantation
Dave 36 Odenton
Erin 28 Annapolis
Maria 40 Pikesville
Mike 57 Columbia
Patti 36 Columbia
Susan 40 Columbia
Tom 36 Columbia
%
```

If we want to sort by age, we simply change the special comparison function to

```
sub byage
{
    $a->{age}   <=> $b->{age};
}
```

```
@sorted = sort byage(@list);

% perl agesort.pl
SORTED BY AGE
Erin 28 Annapolis
Tom 36 Columbia
Dave 36 Odenton
Patti 36 Columbia
Susan 40 Columbia
Maria 40 Pikesville
Mike 57 Columbia
Bob 57 Plantation
%
```

References to References

Data structures can be arbitrarily complex. In most of the previous examples, the references that we used were pointing to data. However, there is no reason why they cannot point to other references that point to data. The next example involves teams and their players. Each team has a name, a nickname, and a set of players. Each player has a name and a position. A player can be built with a reference to an anonymous hash.

First, we create a few players.

```
sub makeplayer
{
    my($name, $position) = @_;
    my $pass = { name => $name,
                 position => $position,
               };
    $pass;
}
$p1 = makeplayer(Dixon, "Shooting guard");
$p2 = makeplayer(Blake, "Point guard");
$p3 = makeplayer(Baxter, "Center");
$p4 = makeplayer(Mouton, "Small forward");
$p5 = makeplayer(Wilcox, "Power forward");
```

Each item above is a reference to a player. Now we can build a team that contains these players. Each team will contain a name, a nickname, and a set of players

```
sub maketeam
{
    my($name, $nickname, @players) = @_;
    my $team = { name => $name,
                 nickname => $nickname,
                 players => [@players]
               };
```

```
        $team;
}
@players = ($p1, $p2, $p3, $p4, $p5);
$team = maketeam("U of Maryland", Terps, @players);
```

Now we create a function called **roster**. This function receives a reference to a team and prints information about the players on that team.

```
sub roster
{
    my ($f) = @_;
    my ($log) = $f->{players};
    print $f->{name}, " ($f->{nickname})", "\n";
    foreach $p (@$log)
    {
            print $p->{name}, "\t";
            print $p->{position},  "\n";
    }
}
```

When **roster** is invoked, it stores the team reference and then obtains a reference to the players:

```
my($log) = $f->{players};
```

After the name and nickname are printed, the function loops through the **players** array.

```
foreach $p (@$log)
{
    print $p->{name}, "\t";
    print $p->{position},  "\n";
}
```

Code
Example

Here is the entire code minus the **roster** subroutine. See the folder **Teams**.

```
#   teams.pl
#
sub makeplayer
{
    my($name, $position) = @_;
    my $pass = { name => $name,
                 position => $position,
               };
    $pass;
}
sub maketeam
{
    my ($name, $nickname, @players) = @_;
    my $team = {         name => $name,
                         nickname => $nickname,
```

```
                                players => [@players]
                                };
        $team;
}
$p1 = makeplayer(Dixon, "Shooting guard");
$p2 = makeplayer(Blake, "Point guard");
$p3 = makeplayer(Baxter, "Center");
$p4 = makeplayer(Mouton, "Small forward");
$p5 = makeplayer(Wilcox, "Power forward");
@players = ($p1, $p2, $p3, $p4, $p5);
$team = maketeam("U of Maryland", Terps, @players);
roster($team);
% perl teams.pl
U of Maryland (Terps)
Dixon        Shooting guard
Blake        Point guard
Baxter       Center
Mouton       Small forward
Wilcox       Power forward
%
```

Code Example

We could create a further level of complexity by creating a few more teams and then creating an array of teams. Finally, we could pass a pattern and the **teams** array to a function that prints those players matching the pattern. The program below uses this function to print the guards on all the teams. See the folder **Players**.

```
% type players.pl
#
#   players.pl
#
sub printplayers
{
    my ($pat, @teams) = @_;
    foreach $team (@teams)
    {
        my ($log) = $team->{players};
        print $team->{name}, "($team->{nickname})", "\n";
        foreach $p (@$log)
        {
            if ( $p->{position} =~ /$pat/ )
            {
                print "\t", $p->{name}, "\t";
                print $p->{position},  "\n";
            }
        }
    }
}
$p1 = makeplayer(Dixon, "Shooting guard");
```

```
$p2 = makeplayer(Blake, "Point guard");
$p3 = makeplayer(Baxter, "Center");
$p4 = makeplayer(Mouton, "Small forward");
$p5 = makeplayer(Wilcox, "Power forward");
@players1 = ($p1, $p2, $p3, $p4, $p5);
$team1 = maketeam("U of Maryland", Terps, @players1);

$p6 = makeplayer(Williams, "Shooting guard");
$p7 = makeplayer(Duhon, "Point guard");
$p8 = makeplayer(Boozer, "Center");
$p9 = makeplayer(Dunleavy, "Small forward");
$p10 = makeplayer(Jones, "Power forward");
@players2 = ($p6, $p7, $p8, $p9, $p10);
$team2 = maketeam("Duke U", "Blue Devils", @players2);

@teams = ($team1, $team2);
printplayers(guard, @teams);
% perl players.pl
U of Maryland (Terps)
    Dixon Shooting guard
    Blake Point guard
Duke U (Blue Devils)
    Williams     Shooting guard
    Duhon        Point guard
%
```

Summary

This chapter discussed the topic of Perl references. A reference is a pointer—the address of a piece of data of arbitrary size. Perl references are the cornerstone of advanced Perl constructions, including lists of lists, higher dimensional arrays, and arbitrarily complex data structures, all of which we have seen in this chapter. We also were exposed to anonymous data structures of various types.

Object-Oriented Programming

With the success of graphical user interfaces (GUIs), the software world has gone object crazy. Object-oriented software offers the developer rich rewards in productivity because it makes programs easier to maintain and understand. This chapter gives the details of object-oriented programming in Perl.

The Vocabulary of Object Orientation

Before we learn how to write object-oriented programs in Perl, we must develop an object-oriented vocabulary. Then we can describe how objects are created and manipulated.

Objects

In the real world, we commonly think of anything physical as an object. In software, we extend this notion to things that are conceptual. Thus, you can think of anything that is physical or conceptual as an object.

Some examples of objects are a **Bank Account**, a **File**, a **Person**, a **Linked List**, and a **Circle**. Typically, a particular application is built to solve problems in a domain-specific area. Any such application would likely have many objects in it. For example, banking software would have many **Account** objects in it. An operating system would have many **File** and **Job** objects in it.

Characteristics of an Object

Every object has a set of attributes collectively referred to as the *state* of the object. For example, a **Mortgage** object would have, among other things, a name, a loan amount, a payment amount, and so on. Thus, the state of a **Mortgage** object is the collection of its data items, such as **name**, **loanAmount**, and **payment**. Note that attributes tend to be nouns. As you will discover later in this book, .NET distinguishes between two different kinds of attributes.

Each object will function in various ways. The collection of these functions can be thought of as the *behavior* for the object. For example, a **Mortgage** object has behavior such as **create**, **makePayment**, **getBalance**, and so on. Behaviors tend to be verbs. Thus, every object has state and behavior.

Behavior refers to the collection of actions that the object can perform. Behavior is sometimes referred to as actions, functions, operations, procedures, or methods. The term *method* is the most often used term. To ensure that these points are clearly understood, a few simple examples follow.

Suppose we have a **Car** object—call it **MyCar**. Instance data for **MyCar** would include length, height, color, model, and so on. The collection of this data is called the **state** of the object.

Methods for **MyCar** would include such actions as **start**, **stop**, **drive**, and **turn_left**. The collection of these functions is called the behavior of the object.

Object Versus Class

Every object contains data and behaves in a particular way based on the **class** to which it belongs. A class is like a blueprint or a template out of which objects are created. An object is composed from many pieces of data. The level of complexity of an object is completely determined by the class from which it was instantiated.

Each behavior for an object is implemented by a Perl method that is defined in the file where the class definition is kept. The class definition is always kept in a **.pm** file, the contents of which are organized in a particular way. We will describe this organization as we move through this chapter. As a preview, a **Mortgage** class would be defined in a file named **Mortgage.pm**. Each method that can be executed on a particular Mortgage would be defined in this file.

Unlike traditional object-oriented languages, such as C++ and Java, in Perl there is no keyword named **class**. Rather, a class is just a Perl module, a **.pm** file, with certain other prerequisites.

Defining and Using Objects

A class usually provides a method for creating an object as well as methods for defining the behavior of an object. Although you may name the creation method whatever you wish in most Perl dialects, in .NET it must be named **new** in honor of both C++ and Java, where it is likewise mandatory.

Code Example

The data contained in an object is composed of many pieces. A **Student** object, for example, might contain a **NAME**, a **MAJOR**, and a set of **COURSES**. One way to model this in Perl is to create an anonymous hash and then retrieve items from it. See the folder **Object**.

```
% type object.pl
#
#    object.pl
#
$student = {
    NAME => Mike,
    MAJOR => Math,
    COURSES => [Calc, Trig, DiffE ]
};
print $student->{NAME},"\n";              # the name
print $student->{MAJOR},"\n";             # the major
print "@{$student->{COURSES}}", "\n";     # the courses
print "@{$student->{COURSES}}[0]", "\n";  # 0th course
% perl object.pl
Mike
Math
Calc Trig DiffE
Calc
%
```

Constructing Objects

The above code demonstrates a way to create a set of related data. But an object should be constructed more formally and in such a way that it knows to which class it belongs. In particular, there should be a way to create as many new **Student** objects as an application requires. What is needed is correct packaging. In order to do this, we create a file whose first line is

```
package Student;
```

This is the start of what ultimately will be the creation of a new data type named **Student** that will have an entire set of methods describing the behavior of a **Student** object. In this file, we place a method for the creation of a **Student** object. The code in this method will look similar to the code above. An application could use this method as many times as it wished in order to create as many **Student** objects as it needed. Methods to implement Student behaviors are required as well. We will see them shortly. Here's a version of **Student.pm**. See the folder **UseStudent**.

```
% type Student.pm
#
#   Student.pm
#
package Student;
sub new
{
    my($pkg, $name, $major, @courses) = @_;
    my $s = {   NAME => $name,
                MAJOR => $major,
                COURSES => [ @courses ]
            };
    bless $s, $pkg;              # see later for details
    return $s;
}
1;
%
```

The first method that we illustrate is called **new**. Its purpose is to construct a new **Student** object. This method must be named **new** in .NET. Further, this method is typically referred to as the constructor for the **Student** class because it is used to construct new **Student** objects. The intent is to invoke the constructor and pass to it the arguments it needs to build a **Student** object. The Perl syntax for invoking the constructor is shown below. For reasons that will become clear shortly, we also pass the package name as the first argument.

```
@courses = (Calc, Trig, DiffE);
$s1 = Student::new(Student, Mike, Math, @courses);
```

Although the notation above can be used, there is an alternative and equivalent way in which to invoke the **Student::new** method.

```
$s1 = new Student(Mike, Math, @courses);
```

The alternative method is closer to the C++ and Java syntax. When you use this form, Perl translates it to the original form. The following two statements are thus equivalent.

```
$s1 = new Student(Mike, Math, @courses);
$s1 = Student::new(Student, Mike, Math, @courses);
```

There is also a third notation that is equivalent to the first two.

```
$s1 = Student->new(Mike, Math, @courses);
```

The **new** method creates a reference to an anonymous hash and then fills the hash with the parameters. Before this method returns the reference, it adds to the reference an additional property—the package name—in this case, **Student**. This is accomplished with the **bless** function. Now the reference is a blessed hash reference and not simply a hash reference.

```
bless $s, $pkg;
```

Code Example

This additional property will be necessary when we call methods on the hash and when we discuss inheritance. An application using a **Student** object might look like this. See the folder **UseStudent**.

```
% type useStudent.pl
#
#    useStudent.pl
#
use Student;
@courses = qw(Calc Trig DiffE);
$s1 = new Student(Mike, Math, @courses);
print $$s1{NAME}, "\n";
print $s1->{MAJOR}, "\n";
print "@{$$s1{COURSES}}", "\n";
print @{$s1->{COURSES}}[0], "\n";
% perl student1.pl
Mike
Math
Calc Trig DiffE
Trig
%
```

Information Hiding

Although the above code works fine, the retrievals leave a few things to be desired. First, many of the retrievals use a cumbersome syntax. We would like to avoid this. Second, the retrievals above place a burden on the writer of the code. The writer must be familiar with the field names. For example, see if you can determine why the code below would produce incorrect results.

```
use Student;
@courses = (Calc, Trig, DiffE);
$s1 = new Student(Mike, Math, @courses);
print $$s1{name}, "\n";
print $s1->{name}, "\n";
print "@{$$s1{COURCES}}", "\n";
print @{$s1->{COURCES}}[0], "\n";
```

The reason is that the developer has misspelled the last two indices. It should be *COURSES*, not COURCES. Users of the **Student.pm** file, that is, users of the **Student** class, should not have to worry about any information inside the **Student.pm** file, let alone the spelling of any of the keys.

These problems may be overcome by writing methods that deliver object data rather than allowing direct access to the data. The disallowance of direct access to object data is called *information hiding*. Most object-oriented languages generate a compiler error when direct access to hidden data is attempted. Perl just expects you to "play by the rules," as it has no such feature as hidden data.

Accessor and Mutator Methods

A good class is expected to provide methods to retrieve data from an object. These methods are called accessor methods. Likewise, a good class is expected to provide methods to alter the state of an object. These methods are called mutator methods. Other methods might simulate other behavior. For example, in the **Student** class, there could be a method that determines how many courses a student is taking.

The Student class should have methods that allow the setting and getting of object data. Functionality like **setname** and **getname** should be supported.

```
use Student;
$s1 = new Student(Mike, Math, Trig, Calc);
$s1 -> setname(Michael);
$name1 = $s1->getname();
```

When a method is called on a blessed reference, such as in the last two lines above, Perl knows to look in the appropriate **.pm** file to find the correct method. In reality, Perl turns the last two calls above into

```
Student::setname($s1, Michael);
Student::getname($s1);
```

so that the reference is always passed as the first argument to the method in question. Here is the revised **Student.pm** file. This file contains the methods **getname()** and **setname()**.

```
package Student;
sub new
{   my($pkg, $name, $major, @courses) = @_;
    my $s = {        NAME => $name,
                     MAJOR => $major,
                     COURSES => [ @courses ]
              };
    bless $s, $pkg;
    return $s;
}
sub getname
{   my ($ref) = shift;                # store reference
    $ref->{NAME};                     # return the name
```

```
}
sub setname
{    my ($ref, $name) = @_;            # store ref and new name
     $ref->{NAME} = $name;            # assign new name
}
1;
```

Other Instance Methods

A real class would have some other methods as well. Here are some possibilities.

```
@courses = $s1 -> getcourses();
$s1 -> addcourses(Geometry, Algebra);
$numcourses = $s1 -> numcourses();
$course = $s1 -> getcourse(1);
```

Here is how you might write these additional methods.

```
sub getcourses
{
    my($ref) = @_;                     # ref to student
    @{$ref->{COURSES}};                # all the courses
}
sub addcourses
{
    my($ref, @courses) = @_;           # ref + new courses
    push( @{$ref->{COURSES}}, @courses);# push onto list
}
sub numcourses
{
    my($ref) = @_;                     # ref to student
    scalar(@{$ref->{COURSES}});        # number of courses
}
sub getcourse
{
    my($ref, $num) = @_;               # ref + index
    @{$ref->{COURSES}}[$num];          # return a course
}
```

In each method, a reference to a student is automatically passed in as the first argument. In each case,

```
$ref->{COURSES}
```

is a reference to a reference to the courses, and thus,

```
@{$ref->{COURSES}}
```

is the array of courses. The benefit of each method is that the difficult Perl constructions are encapsulated within the methods. Users of these methods are freed from details of the encapsulated code.

Writing an Accessor and a Mutator as One Method

Remember that an accessor method retrieves the value of some object data.

```
$s1 = new Student(Susan, Dynamics, Statics, Art);
$name1 = $s1->getname();
```

Also, recall that a mutator method sets the value for some object data.

```
$s1 = new Student(Susan, Dynamics, Statics, Art);
$s1->setname("Soozie");
```

Some Perl programmers use the same function to both get and set object data. In order to do this, the programmer takes advantage of the fact that in setting object data, there is one real argument passed to the method, while in getting the object data, there are zero real arguments sent to the method. Let's suppose we call this method **name**. The code for invoking both getting and setting the name would be

```
$s1 = new Student(Susan, Dynamics, Statics, Art);
$s1->name("Soozie");              # set the name
$thename = $s1->name();           # get the name
```

You can see that in setting the name, there is no need to capture the returned value from this method, although if you wanted, you could write the function so that it returned the old value of the name. Here's the code for the dual-purpose **name** method.

```
sub name
{
    my $ref = shift;
    if ( @_ )               # if another argument
    {                       # then must be setting the name
        my($oldname) = $ref->{NAME};
        $ref->{NAME} = shift;
        $oldname;
    }
    else                    # if no other args
    {                       # then must be getting the name
        $ref->{NAME};
    }
}
```

As usual, the first argument is the reference and it is shifted into **$ref**. Then **@_** is tested to see if any arguments remain. If there is one, the old name is tucked away in **$oldname**, the new name is shifted into the hash, and **$old-name** is returned. If there are no remaining arguments, the current name is returned.

If **name** is invoked with an argument, it could be used in two ways.

```
#    simply set name and ignore the returned value.
#
$s1->name("Michael");
#
#    set the name but remember the previous name
#
$oldname = $s1->name("Michael");
```

Destructors

Some classes may use resources when objects are constructed. For example, a class that encapsulates the details for a **File** object might create a file handle when a **File** object is constructed. It is essential that this resource be given back to the system when the object that used it is no longer in use. Toward this end, Perl executes the special subroutine **DESTROY** if you provide it in your class. Object-oriented languages refer to this method as the destructor. It must be named **DESTROY**, and it will be called automatically whenever the space for an object is reclaimed.

In the previous Student example, a **DESTROY** method is not needed because no resources are used. If we provided one, it would still be executed each time a blessed reference was no longer in use. Here's an example of the **DESTROY** method. Keep in mind that most of the work in this particular **DESTROY** method is for illustrative purposes. Strictly speaking, it is not necessary for this class. See the folder **Destroy**.

```
sub DESTROY
{
    my ($ref) = shift;
    print "destroying ";
    print $ref -> {NAME}, "\n";
}
% type destroy.pl
#
#    destroy.pl
#
use Student;
sub dosomething
{
    my($s2) = new Student(Jane, Math, Trig);
}
$s1 = new Student(Mike, Math, Trig, Calc);
dosomething();
$s3 = new Student(Peter, Math, Trig, Calc);
```

```
% destroy.pl
destroying Jane
From destructor: 1 objects
destroying Mike
From destructor: 1 objects
destroying Peter
From destructor: 0 objects
%
```

Notice that the objects are destroyed when zero references point to them or when the program terminates. The object defined within the subroutine is removed from memory when the subroutine terminates. Thus, it is the first object for which the **DESTROY** method is called. Objects created within the same block of code are destroyed in the opposite order of creation.

Class Data and Class Methods

Each object has its own set of data. However, some programs may require that there be data of a *class* rather than of an *object*. This kind of data exists on a per-class basis rather than on a per-object basis. In .NET, such data may also be referred to as *static* data (C#) or *shared* data (VB.NET). If your application contains 10 student objects, there would be only be one instance of any class data.

Class data can be realized by using **my** variables at file scope. For example, suppose we wish to track the number of objects currently allocated at any given time in a program. We would make the following additions to the **Student.pm** file.

1. Add a **my** variable.

```
my $count = 0;
```

2. Add the following line to the constructor.

```
$count++;
```

3. Add the following line to the destructor.

```
$count--;
```

At this point we might also want to add a method that can return the number of objects that have been created. Such a method is shown below.

```
sub howmany
{
    return $count;
}
```

The interesting thing about the **howmany** method is that it does not operate on objects but on the class. Here is a program that uses the **howmany**

Code Example

method. Notice how it is invoked compared to how the other methods are invoked. See the folder **Count**.

```
Student::howmany()          # called upon the class
print $s3->getname();        # called upon an object

% type count.pl
#
#    count.pl
#
use Student;
sub dosomething
{
    my $s2 = new Student(Jane, Math, Trig);
    print Student::howmany(), " objects\n";
}
$s1 = new Student(Mike, Math, Trig, Calc);
print Student::howmany(), " objects\n";
dosomething();
$s3 = new Student(Peter, Math, Trig, Calc);
print Student::howmany(), " objects\n";
% perl count.pl
1 objects
2 objects
destroying Jane
From destructor: 1 objects
2 objects
destroying Mike
From destructor: 1 objects
destroying Peter
From destructor: 0 objects
%
```

Inheritance

The **bless** function gives more information to a reference. It makes the reference be of a type: **Student** in this case. This has several uses in Perl, as we shall see. Using public methods to access private data is not the only benefit of the object-oriented approach. Another important principle, **inheritance**, is the cornerstone of object orientation.

Inheritance is one of the principal ways of implementing code reuse. The following are examples of inheritance relationships.

- A **Directory** is a type of **File**.
- A **Manager** is a type of **Employee**.
- A **Car** is a type of **MovingVehicle**.
- A **Circle** is a type of **Shape**.

Sometimes inheritance is characterized as the **is-a** relationship. In the **File–Directory** relationship, we say that a **Directory** *is-a* **File**. Likewise, a **Circle** *is-a* **Shape**. Other common terminology is that **File** is the superclass of **Directory**. Also, **Shape** is the superclass of **Circle**. Likewise, **Circle** is a subclass of **Shape** and **Directory** is a subclass of **File**.

If we already have a **File** class, we should not have to build the **Directory** class from the beginning. Since a **Directory** is a **File**, any **Directory** object should be able to reuse (without rewriting) all of the **File** methods.

To illustrate inheritance, suppose that we have a special kind of student— a **GradStudent**. For simplicity, let's say a **GradStudent** is a **Student** with a salary. The **GradStudent** class needs to specify that it is a derived class of **Student**. This is done by using the special **@ISA** array, as you will see below. All methods defined in the **Student** package can be reused by any **GradStudent** object.

GradStudent must implement a constructor and possibly a destructor, as well as any incremental behavior that specializes a **GradStudent**, such as **getsalary** and **setsalary**.

Using SUPER in Inheritance

The constructor for the subclass typically needs to call the constructor in its superclass. This is accomplished by using the keyword **SUPER**. Here is the constructor for a **GradStudent**. Notice how **SUPER** is used in the **new** method in the file **GradStudent.pm**. See the folder **GradStudent**.

```
% type GradStudent.pm
#
#    GradStudent.pm
#
package GradStudent;
use Student;
#
#    The next line tells Perl that
#    GradStudent is derived from Student
#
@ISA=qw(Student);
#
#    GradStudent's new
#
sub new
{
    my $pkg = shift;
    my ($name, $major, $salary, @subjs) = @_;
#
#    Call new in the SUPER (Student) class
#    In the call, $pkg == GradStudent
#
    my $obj=$pkg->SUPER::new($name, $major, @subjs);
```

```
    $obj ->{'SALARY'} = $salary;
    $obj;
}
sub salary
{
    my($pkg) = shift;
    @_ ? $pkg ->{SALARY} = shift : $pkg ->{SALARY};
}
1;
```

When a **GradStudent** object is created, the data for it is passed to the constructor **new** in the same way that the **Student new** constructor was called when a **Student** was constructed. Then there is a call to the **Student** constructor. It is necessary for the **GradStudent** constructor to call the **Student** constructor in order to construct the **Student** portion of a **GradStudent**.

```
my $obj=$pkg->SUPER::new($name, $major, @subjs);
```

The line above calls the **new** method in the **Student** class in such a way that the first argument in the call is **GradStudent**. This is because **GradStudent** is the value of **$pkg**. When **Student::new** returns, the returned reference has been blessed as a **GradStudent**, not as a **Student**. Finally, the **salary** field is added to the reference and the reference is returned.

The line

```
@ISA=qw(Student);
```

Code
Example

tells Perl that the **GradStudent** class is a subclass of **Student** and thus any **GradStudent** object can freely reuse all **Student** methods. Here is a program that demonstrates the use of the **GradStudent** class. See the folder **UseGradStudent**.

```
% type UseGradStudent.pl
#
#   useGradStudent.pl
#
use Student;
use GradStudent;
$stu1 = new Student(Mike, Math, Alg, Calc, Trig);
print $stu1->getname(), "\n";
print $stu1->getmajor(), "\n";
$gs=new GradStudent(Dave, Math, 25000, Calc, Trig);
#
#   reuse Student functionality
#
print $gs->getname(), "\n";
print $gs->getmajor(), "\n";
#
#   a new method
#
print $gs->salary(), "\n";
```

The methods **getname()** and **getmajor()** are implemented in the **Student.pm** file. Since a **GradStudent** is a **Student** (because of the **@ISA** array), these methods may be used on **Student** and **GradStudent** objects. Code reuse is a major benefit of inheritance. The **salary()** method is implemented only for a **GradStudent**.

Polymorphism

Consider a set of classes related through inheritance. The classic example is a set of classes derived from a geometric **Shape** class. Each class, say **Circle**, **Square**, and **Triangle**, would have its own **area** and **perimeter** methods. Each of these methods would have a class-specific implementation. The skeleton code for an application for such a scenario would be:

```
$circle1 = new Circle(5);          # create a Circle
$square1 = new Square(10);         # create a Square
print $square->area(),"\n";        # area of Square
print $circle1->perimeter(),"\n"; # perimeter of Circle
```

The capability of a language to differentiate among several methods, all of which have the same name in the same inheritance hierarchy, is called *polymorphism*. Polymorphism is implemented in Perl through the **bless** function. When an object is blessed, it is bound to a class. When a method is called upon this object, the chosen method comes from the class bound to the object.

Here is an example to illustrate polymorphism with respect to the **Shapes** hierarchy.

Although we will never have a **Shape** object, we need to create a **Shape** class in order to factor out some common methods and data that apply to all subclasses.

```
% type Shape.pm
#
#    Shape.pm
#
package Shape;
sub new
{
    my ($pkg, $val) = @_;
    my ($shref) = { value => $val };
    print "Creating a $pkg of size $val\n";
    bless $shref, $pkg;
    return $shref;
}
sub getvalue
{
    my ($pkg) = @_;
    return $pkg -> {value};
```

```
}
1;
%
```

The **new** method of the **Shape** class will never be called directly. It will, however, be called by the **new** method of any **Shape** subclasses, such as **Circle** and **Square**. The **getvalue()** method will be used by all derived classes to retrieve parameter information, such as the radius for a circle or the side for a square.

Next, we show the **Circle** and **Square** classes.

```
% type Circle.pm
#
#    Circle.pm
#
package Circle;
@ISA = ('Shape');
sub new
{
    my ($pkg, $rad) = @_;
    $pkg ->SUPER::new($rad);
}
sub perimeter
{
    my ( $pkg) = @_;
    return 2 * 3.14159 * $pkg -> {value};
}

sub area
{
    my ( $pkg) = @_;
    return 3.14159 * $pkg -> {value} ** 2;
}
sub type()
{
    "Circle";
}
1;
% type Square.pm
#
#    Square.pm
#
package Square;
@ISA = ('Shape');
sub new
{
    my ($pkg, $rad) = @_;
    $pkg ->SUPER::new($rad);
}
sub perimeter
```

```
{
    my ( $pkg) = @_;
    return   4 * $pkg -> {value};
}
sub area
{
    my ( $pkg) = @_;
    return  $pkg -> {value} ** 2;
}
sub type
{
    "Square";
}
1;
%
```

Code
Example

The **Circle** and **Square** classes implement their own versions of **area** and **perimeter** but rely on the **Shape** class for a common version of **getvalue()**. Finally, here is a program that uses these classes. See the folder **UseShapes**.

```
% type useShapes.pl
#
#        useShapes.pl
#
use Shape;
use Circle;
use Square;
$sq1 = new Square(10);
$sq2 = new Square(20);
$c1  = new Circle(5);
$c2 =  new Circle(10);
push(@array, $c1, $c2, $sq1, $sq2);
foreach $s (@array)
{
    print "TYPE IS:\t",    $s->type(), "\n";
    print "PARAM IS:\t",   $s->getvalue(), "\n";
    print "AREA IS:\t",    $s->area(), "\n";
    print "CIRCUM IS:\t", $s->perimeter(), "\n";
    print "_____\n";
}
% perl useShapes.pl
Creating a Square of size 10
Creating a Square of size 20
Creating a Circle of size 5
Creating a Circle of size 10
TYPE IS:  Circle
PARAM IS: 5
AREA IS:  78.53975
CIRCUM IS:31.4159
```

```
TYPE IS:   Circle
PARAM IS: 10
AREA IS:   314.159
CIRCUM IS:62.8318
```

```
TYPE IS:   Square
PARAM IS: 10
AREA IS:   100
CIRCUM IS:40
```

```
TYPE IS:   Square
PARAM IS: 20
AREA IS:   400
CIRCUM IS:80
```

```
%
```

@array contains references to either **Circle** or **Shape** objects. When a method is invoked on these objects, Perl checks to see if the class to which this object is blessed contains this method. If it does, it is invoked. If it does not, then the superclass is checked. The superclass is known through the use of the **@ISA** array.

Methods whose behavior is invariant over specialization should belong to the **Shape** class and be used as a default implementation for subclasses. **getvalue** is one of these methods. Methods whose behavior varies on a class-specific basis should belong to the specific class. **area()**, **perimeter()**, and **type()** are a few of these methods.

Summary

This chapter presented the concepts of object-oriented programming. An object is an entity that contains data and is able to perform certain actions. Both of these characteristics are contained within a class definition, which is stored within a **.pm** file that implies a particular package. We showed how to construct objects and use them. We discussed inheritance, the ability to reuse methods defined in one class on objects from another class. We also discussed polymorphism, the ability to detect the type of an object while the program is running.

The Comprehensive Perl Archive Network

We have seen that Perl comes with many built-in functions. This set of functions has been extended by those provided with the Standard Perl Library that is shipped with any standard download of the Perl system. We have seen how to extend this wealth of functionality with our own home-grown functions.

Beyond this functionality, there is a repository of Perl modules and documentation that you can download form the Comprehensive Perl Archive Network, more commonly referred to as CPAN. This section deals with the format and the information contained in these archives.

Format of Perl Modules

Recall that a Perl module is a **.pm** file that contains a package statement together with some other items, including documentation. Perl documentation is typically called POD (Plain Old Documentation). Before we present the categories of modules found on CPAN, we discuss what you can expect to find in any of the CPAN modules that you might download.

Building a Module

To illustrate the different pieces of information that you may find in any module, we will build one of our own. The first step is to create a **.pm** file. All **.pm** files need to have the package specifier as the first line of the file. The name of the file and the name of the package need to be the same (except for the suffix **.pm**).

Suppose we wish to build a package that handles complex numbers. We would create a file named **Complex.pm** whose first line has a package statement.

```
% type Complex.pm
package Complex;
1;
%
```

Remember that this module will be used by other applications, so the last line evaluated when this modules is imported must be nonzero.

Adding Functions to a Module

A module contains a set of related functions. In the case of the **Complex** module, we start with a function to create a complex number and a function to print one.

```
% type Complex.pm
package Complex;
sub create
{
        my ($r, $i) = @_;
        my ($complex) = {
                          real => $r,
                          imag => $i
                          };
        $complex;
}
sub display
{
        my($ref) = @_;
        print $ref->{real}, "+", $ref->{imag}, "i";

}
1;
```

Any application needing the functionality of the **Complex** module would proceed as follows.

```
use Complex;
$x = Complex::create(2,3);
Complex::display($x);                    #  prints 2+3i
```

If there are many references to the functions in the **Complex** module, it may be both tiresome and error prone to continuously have to use the **Complex** prefix. There is a way around this dilemma.

Exporting Symbols

Any module that allows its functions or other symbols to be exported must inherit from the **Exporter** module. The following code would typically be placed immediately after the package statement.

```
use Exporter;
@ISA = (Exporter);
@EXPORT = (create, display);
```

Recall that the **@ISA** array is used to create an inheritance relationship. In this case, **Complex** inherits from **Exporter**. The **Exporter** module has an **import** function that is called automatically whenever Perl processes a **use** statement for a module.

The **@EXPORT** array holds the name of the symbols that can be used without the package specifier. In other words, given the three lines above, the application using the **Complex** module can be coded as

```
use Complex;
$x = create(2,3);
display($x);                        #  prints 2+3i
```

Even though this strategy works fine, the more names that are entered into a namespace, the less efficiently your program will run. Thus, there is an alternative way to import symbols.

If the module writer uses the **@EXPORT_OK** array instead of the **@EXPORT** array, the symbols contained in **@EXPORT_OK** become candidates for exporting. The user of the **Complex** module must then explicitly arrange to import them.

```
#   Complex.pm
package Complex;
use Exporter;
@ISA = (Exporter);
@EXPORT_OK = (create, display);

#   Complex.pl
use Complex (create, display);
$x = create(2,3);
display($x);                        #  prints 2+3i
```

Our **Complex** module is for illustrative purposes. Were it real, we would have methods to perform the normal calculations on complex numbers, such as adding, subtracting, multiplying, and dividing them. Here is an example of the multiplication of two complex numbers.

```
sub mult
{
    my ($r1, $r2) = @_;
```

```
my ($rr, $ir);
$rr=$r1->{real}*$r2->{real} - $r1->{imag}*$r2->{imag};
$ir=$r1->{real}*$r2->{imag} + $r2->{real}*$r1->{imag};
my ($hash) = { real => $rr,
               imag => $ir
             };
$hash;
}
```

The **mult** method would be invoked as in the following program. See the folder **Complex**.

```
% type Complex.pl
#
#   Complex.pl
#
use Complex (create, display, mult);
$x = create(2,3);
$y = create(3,4);
display($x);                    #   prints 2+3i
print "\n";
display($y);                    #   prints 3+4i
print "\n";
$z = mult($x, $y);
display($z);                    #   prints -6+17i
% perl Complex.pl
2+3i
3+4i
-6+17i
%
```

Note that the Perl distribution comes with a **Complex** module.

A Real Module: Roman.pm

This section presents the details on an actual module, **Roman.pm**, that you can download. See later in this chapter for the details on how to download this module.

To demonstrate the similarities between the **Complex** module and an actual module such as **Roman.pm**, we first demonstrate the use of this module.

Using Roman.pm

Roman.pm has methods to convert from roman numerals to arabic and from arabic to roman numerals. We present a small program that asks the user for a

Code Example

roman numeral. After verifying it, it is converted to arabic. Next, the arabic is doubled and then converted to roman numerals. We doubt that you will be using this module often, but it is worth studying because its simplicity makes it easier to understand the principles of writing and using modules. See the folder **Roman**.

```
% type roman.pl
#
#    roman.pl
#
use Roman;
print "Enter number in roman numerals ";
chomp($roman = <STDIN>);
if (isroman($roman))
{
    $arabic = arabic($roman);
    print "arabic for $roman is $arabic\n";
    $arabic = $arabic * 2;
    $roman = roman($arabic);
    print "$roman is twice the original roman numeral\n";
}
else
{
    print "$roman is not roman numerals\n";
}
% perl roman.pl
Enter number in roman numerals xiv
arabic for xiv is 14
xxviii is twice the original roman numeral
%
```

Looking Inside Roman.pm

Now that we have seen how to use **Roman.pm**, let's take a peak inside the module. One of the things you will notice is that there is a striking similarity between the format of **Complex.pm** and **Roman.pm**. To reinforce this, we use bold print to highlight the common points.

```
% type Roman.pm
package Roman;

=head1 NAME

Roman - Perl module for conversion between Roman and
Arabic numerals.

=head1 SYNOPSIS

    use Roman;
```

```
        $arabic = arabic($roman) if isroman($roman);
        $roman = Roman($arabic);
        $roman = roman($arabic);

=head1 DESCRIPTION

This package provides some functions which help conversion
of numeric notation between Roman and Arabic.

=head1 BUGS

Domain of valid Roman numerals is limited to less than
4000, since proper Roman digits for the rest are not
available in ASCII.

=head1 CHANGES

1997/09/03 Author's address is now <ozawa@aisoft.co.jp>

=head1 AUTHOR

OZAWA Sakuro <ozawa@aisoft.co.jp>

=head1 COPYRIGHT

Copyright (c) 1995 OZAWA Sakuro.  All rights reserved.
This program is free software; you can redistribute it
and/or modify it under the same terms as Perl itself.

=cut

$RCS = '$Id: Roman.pm,v 1.2 1997/09/03 01:35:23 ozawa Exp
$';

require Exporter;
@ISA = qw(Exporter);
@EXPORT = qw(isroman arabic Roman roman);
sub isroman
{   # details not shown here
}
sub arabic
{   # details not shown here
}
sub roman
{   # details not shown here
}
1;
```

The pieces that are common to all modules are

- package name
- inheriting from the **Exporter** module
- last expression evaluated is 1
- exporting symbol names

Of course, you also have noticed many lines that do not look like Perl code and in general begin with the assignment (=) symbol. These lines are the documentation of the module and are the subject of the next section.

Plain Old Documentation

In the last several years, there has been a trend in software development that espouses the coupling of code and documentation in the same file. Prior to this trend, documentation was usually tasked separately, increasing the chances for inconsistencies between code and documentation.

Perl modules typically contain documentation along with code. The documentation is accomplished through a mini-markup language called Plain Old Documentation, or POD. The documentation is intended as markup for tools that come with the Perl distribution. The result of using the tools on a particular module will be HTML, text, or something else, depending upon the tool.

Using POD

When a POD translator reads a module, it looks for tags such as those shown below and uses the tags to format its output. Permissible tags are

- =head1 heading
- =head2 heading
- =item text
- =over N
- =back
- =cut
- =pod
- =for X
- =begin X
- =end X

When the Perl translator reads a module, it compiles and executes Perl code, but it leaves alone the lines between and including the POD tags.

Using the pod2html Tool

One executable that is delivered with the Perl distribution is the **pod2html** tool. Figure 8-1 is a screenshot of the HTML that results from applying this tool to the **Roman.pm** file. The rendering has been shortened so it can fit on the page. If you are familiar with HTML, it might be informative to match the POD documentation with the resulting rendering.

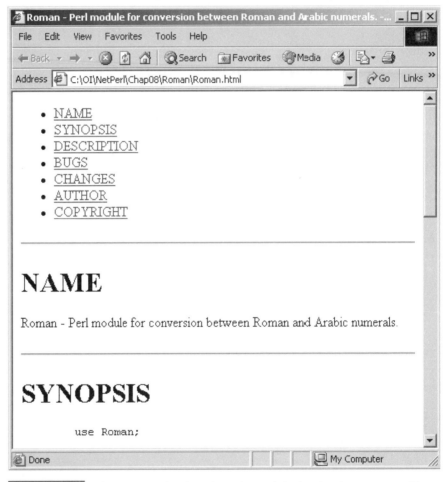

FIGURE 8-1   *The HTML results of applying the pod2html tool to the Roman.pm file.*

Downloading Perl Modules with ppm

The Perl community has been a closely knit community over the years. It includes the many software developers who have freely donated software written to the informal Perl module specification that we have been discussing. Much of this software resides on either the CPAN or the ActiveState repositories. See *www.cpan.org* or *www.activestate.com*.

The Perl Package Manager

In the previous sections, we discussed a module named **Roman.pm**. We used this module to reinforce the principles that are common to all modules. We downloaded this module using the Perl Package Manager, **ppm3.bat**, utility that is delivered with the ActiveState version of Perl. This utility allows you to search a vast repository of Perl modules. We demonstrate the use of this utility in this section.

ppm3.bat allows you to manage modules. This management includes the installation, removal, listing, and updating of modules. **ppm3.bat** is run either from the command line or by executing the **ppm3.bat** batch file that brings up a shell window. In either case, you should be connected to the Internet before you start it up.

Once **ppm3.bat** is started, you can enter the **help** command to see a list of **ppm3.bat** commands. User responses are in boldface.

```
% ppm3.bat
PPM-Programmer's Package Manager version 3.0 beta 3.
Copyright (c) 2001 ActiveState SRL. All Rights Reserved.

Entering interactive shell. Using Term::ReadLine::Stub as
readline library.

Profile tracking is not enabled. If you save and restore
profiles manually, your profile may be out of sync with
your computer. See 'help profile' for more information.

Type 'help' to get started.

ppm> help
Type 'help command' for more detailed help on a command.
Commands:
describe -describes packages in detail
exit -leaves the program
help -prints this screen, or help on 'command'
install -installs packages
profiles -manage PPM profiles
properties -describes installed packages in detail
query -queries installed packages
```

The output for the help command has been edited slightly so that we can concentrate on the most commonly used commands. Use the install command to download and install a module. Use the name of the module without the **.pm** suffix.

```
ppm> install Roman
Install package 'Roman?'  (y/N): y
Installing package 'Roman' ...
Installing \Perl561\html\site\lib\Roman.html
Installing \Perl561\site\lib\Roman.pm
Installing \Perl561\site\lib\auto\.packlist
ppm>
```

ppm3.bat announces the names of the files that it is loading on your machine. **Roman.html** is the supporting HTML documentation for **Roman.pm**. **.packlist** is a manifest specifying which files were downloaded. At some point, if you wish to remove the module, simply execute the remove command. In the following scenario, we started to remove **Roman.pm** but responded no to the **ppm3.bat** interaction. Finally, as shown below, we exited.

```
ppm> remove Roman
Remove package 'Roman'  (y/N): n
ppm> exit
%
```

The Comprehensive Perl Archive Network

The largest repository of Perl modules resides on the CPAN and mirror sites. Figure 8-2 is a screenshot of the CPAN home page at *www.cpan.org*.

This page is divided into three sections: frequently asked questions (FAQs), browsing, and searching. You may want to use the Searching link to search for a Perl module by name, author name, or other search criteria.

If you select the Browsing link, you can look for modules alphabetically and then download the one you want. First, select **Browsing**, then **modules**, then **all modules**. You will be greeted with an exceedingly long alphabetized list of modules. Just select the one you want to begin the download process.

Another way to proceed is to select **Browsing**, **Modules**, and **The Module List**. This gives you a list of modules by category. Here is a partial list of those categories.

1. Module Listing Format
2. Perl Core Mods, Language Extensions, and Doc Tools
3. Development Support
4. Operating System Interfaces, Hardware Drivers
5. Networking, Device Control (modems), and IPC

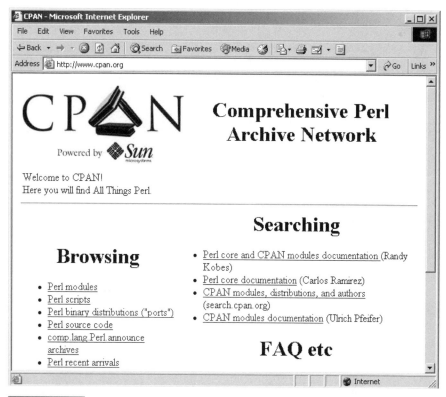

FIGURE 8–2 CPAN offers the largest repository of Perl modules.

6. Data Types and Data Type Utilities
7. Database Interfaces
8. User Interfaces
9. Interfaces to or Emulations of Other Prog Languages
10. File Names, File Systems, and File Locking
11. String Processing, Language Text Processing
12. Internationalization and Locale
13. Authentication, Security, and Encryption
14. World Wide Web, HTML, HTTP, CGI, MIME
15. Server and Daemon Utilities
16. Archiving, Compression, and Conversion
17. Images, Pixmap, and Bitmap Manipulation

If you wanted to download the **Net::FTP** module, you would select item 5 and then search until you found the **Net::FTP** module.

By the way, sometimes package names can have the appearance of being nested. For example, there is a file named **Path.pm** that is delivered with the standard Perl distribution. The first line of this file is

```
package File::Path;
```

For package names containing a **::**, the double colon is treated as a directory separator. Therefore, you can expect a directory named **File** to contain the file **Path.pm**. **FTP.pm** would be installed in the directory **Net**. Of course, both **File** and **Net** would be located in an **@INC** directory.

Summary

This chapter presented the format of a Perl module. We discussed the **Exporter** module, the **@ISA** array, and the ability of a module to export symbols. After building the rudiments of a **Complex** module, we compared our work with a real module, **Roman.pm**. Then we showed how to download any module using the Perl Package Manager. Finally, we discussed the CPAN repositories of Perl modules and how you can use CPAN to download any of the modules located there.

PROGRAMMING WITH PERLNET

PROGRAMMING WITH PERLNET

Part 2 covers in detail the use of PerlNET to bring together the worlds of .NET and Perl. We show you how to use .NET classes in Perl programs. We discuss how to create .NET components using Perl. We cover different types of PerlNET components and demonstrate them with a rich set of sample programs. Important .NET classes are surveyed, and there is coverage of using .NET in specific areas, including graphical user interfaces, database programming, and using ADO.NET, ASP.NET, and Web services.

First Steps in PerlNET

*T*his chapter opens the gate into the exciting world of programming Perl within the .NET environment. We start our journey with simple program examples. You will learn how to compile and run PerlNET programs. The new statements that make Perl to the .NET Framework interaction easy to use are introduced. After discussing PerlNET program structure and the use of namespaces, we demonstrate how to incorporate the input and output .NET classes into our programs. Finally, we present the full example program, which involves user interaction and shows how to bring into use Perl-specific constructions inside the .NET environment.

Your First PerlNET Program

As a first step in PerlNET programming, we write a simple program to introduce you to the basics of the new language. Our program outputs a single line of text. Here is the code for the first sample.

```
#
# Hello.pl
#
use namespace "System";
use PerlNET qw(AUTOCALL);

Console->WriteLine("Hello from Perl!");
```

Code
Example

The above code is saved in the **Hello** folder for this chapter. Optionally, you can just type the program in your favorite editor. If you are using Visual Perl (see Appendix A), you can open the solution **Hello.sln**. If you are not using Visual Perl, just ignore the solution and project files.

It is commonly known that Perl is a script language and as such is processed by Perl interpreter. So, the first reaction ("Perl instinct") is to type the following line:

```
perl Hello.pl
```

and to get a "Hello from Perl!" line as an output. If you decided to try it, you got the following probably familiar but unpleasant response:

```
can't locate namespace.pm in @INC (@INC contains: . . .)
at Hello.pl line 4
BEGIN failed - compilation aborted at Hello.pl line 4.
```

Well, this is the moment to remind ourselves that from now on we will use Perl language (or more precisely, its extended version, PerlNET) to target our programs to the .NET environment. Therefore, we should be able to map any Perl program into MSIL (Microsoft Intermediate Language) assembly, which in turn can be executed by the .NET CLR (Common Language Runtime).

The work of compiling and building an assembly is done by **plc.exe** (PerlNET compiler), which comes with the PerlNET distribution. Simply run the following command from your command prompt in the **Hello** directory:

```
plc Hello.pl
```

As a result, **Hello.exe** will be created. Now, you can test your first PerlNET program by executing **Hello.exe**. You should get the following output:

```
Hello from Perl!
```

Congratulations! You've just written, built, and executed your first fully functional PerlNET program. Reward yourself with a cup of coffee, and let's move on to the program discussion.

Sample Overview

The first two lines after the starter comment in our sample are **pragmas**. These are instructions that tell the Perl interpreter how to treat the code that follows the pragma. Usually, you define pragmas at the beginning (header) of your Perl program, and then you write the code. Let us look at the first pragma.

```
use namespace "System";
```

This pragma tells Perl to look up types in the **System** namespace.[1] As a result, we can use the unqualified type **Console** throughout our program. This means

---

1. All classes in .NET are divided into namespaces. Namespaces are discussed later in this chapter.

that we can write **Console** whenever referring to the **System.Console** class. This class encapsulates a rich functionality of the input/output operations.

Now let us look more closely at the second pragma.

```
use PerlNET qw(AUTOCALL);
```

In short, this line allows us to use the standard Perl call-method syntax when invoking **static** methods (**class** methods) of .NET classes. If we do not import **AUTOCALL**, then we must use the **call** function of the PerlNET module (we discuss this module shortly), as follows:

```
PerlNET::call("System.Console.WriteLine",
              "Hello from Perl!");
```

The first argument to the **call** function is the **static** method name to call. Starting from the second argument, you should specify the arguments list that you pass to the **static** method. If you specified the **System** namespace with the **use namespace** pragma, then you may omit it and write just **Console.WriteLine** when specifying the **static** method to the **call** function:

```
PerlNET::call("Console.WriteLine","Hello from Perl!");
```

Combining the two pragmas described above allows us to easily access .NET classes.

```
Console->WriteLine("Hello from Perl!");
```

This statement calls the **static** method **WriteLine** of the **Console** class, which is located in the **System** namespace. The **WriteLine** method is passed a string to output as argument.

PerlNET Module

In the previous section, we introduced the PerlNET module. Throughout this book, we will make wide usage of this module by importing useful functions that help the Perl language tap into the .NET environment.

Whenever you decide to use one of the functions provided by the PerlNET module, you may choose from two forms of syntax:

```
PerlNET::call("System.Console.WriteLine", "Hello");
```

or you may import the function from PerlNET and write as follows:

```
use PerlNET qw(call);
. . .
call("System.Console.WriteLine", "Hello");
```

In most cases, we prefer to use the second form of syntax in this book—importing all the function from the PerlNET module at the header of our Perl file. If you should use several PerlNET module functions, then you may enumerate them in the single **use** statement instead of importing each separately:

```
use PerlNET qw(AUTOCALL call enum);
```

PLC Limitations

As we saw in the previous sections, **plc.exe**, the PerlNET compiler, is used to build our programs and create assemblies. During compilation, **plc** checks a Perl file for syntactic accuracy. However, this check does not verify the correct spelling of .NET type names or the correct number of arguments passed to .NET methods. This means that you may misspell some .NET class or type name, but the PerlNET compiler will not let you know about this and will create an assembly. As a result, you will be informed about the error only at runtime.

Consider the following code (**HelloErr**), where we intentionally misspelled **Console** and wrote **Consol**:

```
#
# HelloErr.pl
#
use strict;
use namespace "System";
use PerlNET qw(AUTOCALL);

Consol->WriteLine("Hello, World.\n");
```

If we compile this program, we get no errors and **HelloErr.exe** is created. However, if we run **HelloErr.exe**, then the following error is displayed:

```
System.ApplicationException: Can't locate type Consol
. . .
```

The PerlNET compiler creates the .NET assembly, but internally our code is still being interpreted by the Perl Runtime Interpreter component, which passes our commands to .NET. It serves as a mediator between PerlNET programs and the .NET environment. Therefore, if we write two statements, the first correct and the second with error, then the Perl interpreter will execute the first statement, and on the second, we will get an error message:

```
Console->WriteLine("Hello from Perl");
Consol->WriteLine("Hello, World.\n");
```

The output will be

```
Hello from Perl
System.ApplicationException: Can't locate type Consol
. . .
```

PerlNET programs, like any Core Perl scripts, should pass through extensive runtime testing before being released.

Main Function

Let's look at a simple program written in C# that performs the same action as our first sample: It displays the single line "Hello from C#." (If you don't know C#, you can refer to Appendix B, "C# Survival Guide for PerlNET Programmers.") We saved the program in the **HelloCs** folder.

```csharp
// Hello.cs
using System;

class Hello
{
   public static void Main(string[] args)
   {
      Console.WriteLine("Hello from C#");
   }
}
```

As you can see, we defined a class with a single static method **Main**, and this is the minimum requirement of each .NET program.

Unlike C# or other .NET-compliant languages, in PerlNET you are not required explicitly to define the **Main** function and wrap your program by the class, which means that our PerlNET programs may be written just as a sequence of statements (like script) and saved in a **.pl** file. In Chapter 12, we will see that, after compiling, our programs are implicitly wrapped by the class that has the static **Main** method. This method is an entry point to our program, and it encapsulates all the statements that we wrote in the **.pl** file in the script-like manner. However, you may want to define the **Main** method explicitly. We will see that it is useful when we learn how to create a graphical user interface in Chapter 14.

Here is how we may rewrite our first sample with the **Main** function definition.

```perl
#
# HelloMain.pl
#
use namespace "System";
use PerlNET qw(AUTOCALL);

=for interface
   public static void Main(str[] args);
=cut
```

```
sub Main
{
   Console->WriteLine("Hello from Main function");
}
```

**Code
Example**

The code for the program resides in **HelloMain**. This program introduces additional syntactic structures that are not present in Core Perl. The first thing you may notice is the following POD **=for interface** block:

```
=for interface
   public static void Main(str[] args);
=cut
```

We will make wide use of these blocks when learning about creating .NET components later in the book. Perl is a dynamic type language and recognizes neither method modifiers (**public**, **static**) nor types. As we want to preserve Perl features and still tap into the .NET environment, we are required to find a compromise that is acceptable to both sides. The solution is to use a special **=for interface** block, where all .NET-specific definitions go on. As you can see, our sample defines the **Main** method with the same modifiers, return type, and signature as the C# program.

Namespaces

Earlier in this chapter, we introduced the term **namespace**. In general, all classes in .NET are divided into namespaces to prevent name conflicts. Thus, classes with the same name may reside under the different namespaces. For example, **Samples.Car** and **Examples.Car** are different classes with the same name. We may distinguish them by their namespace.

When writing a program, you may refer to classes or types with a fully qualified name, a name in which the namespace precedes the class name. You can specify the fully qualified name either by delimiting the namespace and class name with two colons or by placing the whole name (both namespace and class) in double quotes and delimiting with a dot.

```
System::Console->WriteLine("Hello");     # Correct
System.Console->WriteLine("Hello");      # Error
"System.Console"->WriteLine("Hello");    # Correct
q(System.Console)->WriteLine("Hello");   # Correct
```

Throughout the book we specify which namespaces to use in the header of our PerlNET programs with the **use namespace** pragma.

Expressions

Internally, PerlNET uses Perl interpreter. This allows us to incorporate all the standard Perl features and expressions in our PerlNET programs. This means that all samples that we introduced in Part 1 may be compiled and executed in the .NET environment without any changes. Let us demonstrate this by a simple Core Perl program, the standard Perl script **freq.pl** for counting word occurrences, which we presented in Chapter 4. Here is the code for the script.

```
#
# freq.pl
#
while(<STDIN>)
{
    @words = split;
    foreach $word (@words)
    {
        $words{$word}++;
    }
}
foreach $word (sort(keys(%words)))
{
    print "$word occurred $words{$word}\n";
}
```

Now, we may run the script either using Perl interpreter,

```
perl freq.pl
```

or by compiling into a .NET assembly and running the assembly:

```
plc freq.pl
freq.exe < text.txt
```

In any case, we get the same result: All word occurrences in text from standard input are calculated and printed. Here is the output for both cases when the input was originated from the following file:

```
Almost everybody can learn Perl programming
Not everybody likes to learn
```

Output:

```
Almost occurred 1
Not occurred 1
Perl occurred 1
can occurred 1
everybody occurred 2
learn occurred 2
likes occurred 1
programming occurred 1
to occurred 1
```

Marshalling Types

Until this chapter, we wrote Core Perl programs without worrying about typing, as Perl has a dynamic typing system. .NET is a strong-typed environment: There is one-to-one correspondence between variables and types. In other words, every variable has one and only one type associated with it.

We do not have to change our attitude with respect to types if our PerlNET program contains Core Perl statements only. However, the problem may occur when working with .NET components and classes.[2] As we saw in our first sample program, working with .NET classes involves calling methods.[3] Many of the methods expect arguments, and we have to supply arguments of the correct type. Consider the following code example from the **Marshalling\Types** folder.

```
#
# Types.pl
#
use strict;
use namespace "System";
use PerlNET qw(AUTOCALL);

my $x = "0";
print Math->Cos($x);
```

This program introduces the static method **Cos** of the **Math** class located in the **System** namespace. This class provides constants and static methods for trigonometric, logarithmic, and other common mathematical functions.

We expect our program to print the numeral **1**, because we rely on Perl for converting the **$x** variable from string scalar into floating-point number scalar, as we use **$x** in the numeric context. Unfortunately, building and running the program ruins our expectations, and instead of printing **1** in output, the program exits with the following error message:

```
System.ApplicationException: Can't locate public static
method Cos(System.String) for System.Math.
```

The error means that we supplied an argument with an incorrect type to the **Cos** function, which expects a floating-point number. Perl context-based conversion did not work here because PerlNET runtime modules that serve as a bridge between Perl and .NET environments convert scalars into specific .NET

---

2. We discuss working with .NET components in detail in Chapter 10. We mention it here for problem-illustrating purposes.

3. In this chapter we work with static .NET methods only, but the discussion of marshalling types is relevant for all .NET methods.

types. PerlNET defines different rules than Core Perl defines for type conversions when we call .NET methods and pass to them Perl scalars.

Internally, Perl caches multiple representations of a value for each variable:

- String
- Integer
- Numeric (float)

In other words, Perl "remembers" the last representation of a value and sometimes it interprets the type not in the way we want it to.

Back to our example. We assigned 0 to our **$x** variable. The type of value is **String**, and this is how it is remembered by **$x**. To fix it, we should clear the part of **$x**'s memory that remembers the type as **String**. There are several ways to do it. We may perform mathematical operations on **$x** that will not change it (e.g., add zero or multiply by 1) and store the result back to **$x** (the first way in the example below) or pass the mathematical expression to the method without assigning to the variable (the second way shown). Optionally, we may use the **Convert** class from the **System** namespace. Its **ToDouble** function will return a numeric value (the third way). Here are some possible ways to rewrite the **Cos** statement in our **Types.pl** program.

```
$x = $x + 0;
print Math->Cos($x);                        # 1-st way
. . .
print Math->Cos($x*1);                       # 2-nd way
. . .
print Math->Cos(Convert->ToDouble($x)); # 3-rd way
```

After you pick up the way you like it, rebuild and run the program. You should get a clean execution. We saved the correct version of the program in **Marshalling\TypesFix**.

Code
Example

However, such solutions will work only for float (double) numbers. To avoid any ambiguity in interpreting your Perl scalar variables, PerlNET offers a set of special casting functions for value types. We explain these functions and marshalling types in Chapter 10 when we discuss calling methods.

Input/Output

As we stated in the previous section, all Core Perl constructions may be brought into use in PerlNET. Input/output issues are not an exception.

Performing Output

Instead of using a long call to the **WriteLine** method of the **Console** class, we can write

```
print "Hello from Perl!\n";
```

and we will get the same result as if had written

```
Console->WriteLine("Hello from Perl!");
```

The reason we use the **Console** class rather then Core Perl **print** is to demonstrate the .NET concepts on simple examples and to show the .NET way to do things. You may combine Core Perl and .NET statements to perform output. However, you may run into buffering problems when running the program in some environments, so that your program output would not be in the original order that you meant when designing the program. This may occur when you test your Managed Exe Perl project in Visual Studio running it with Ctrl-F5 (we present the Visual Studio description in Appendix A). The reason for this is that the .NET methods and Core Perl functions use different buffers for output and you do not control the order in which these buffers are flushed. To prevent this, you should add the following statement, which instructs Perl not to buffer the output, at the beginning of your program:

```
$| = 1;
```

Examine the **IO\ Buffering** sample.

```
#
# Buffering.pl
#
use strict;
use namespace "System";
use PerlNET qw(AUTOCALL);

$| = 1;
Console->WriteLine("1");
print "2\n";
Console->WriteLine("3");
```

If you comment the **$| = 1** statement, then the output in the Visual Studio Run window will look like what follows.

```
1
3
2
```

This is definitely not the order of printing we meant. If you uncomment the assignment, this will restore the original output order.

Getting Input

Most applications involve user interaction. Core Perl offers a simple way to treat user input:

```
<STDIN>;
```

As you probably guessed, the .NET SDK introduces several methods to treat user input. We will show how to take benefit of these methods.

You may implement a simple text-based user interface with the **ReadLine** method of the **Console** class. This method does not take any parameters and returns the string that it reads from the standard input device.

Before we present a sample program, we should explain another feature of the **WriteLine** method: placeholders. When performing output, often you need to include variables or expressions whose values are known only at run-time. The **WriteLine** method reserves a place for the expression in the output string. For each expression, there are placeholders {0}, {1}, and so on. The expressions should be placed after closing quotes and should be delimited by commas. Here is the simple example.

```
my $x = 3;
Console->WriteLine("x={0};x+1={1};x^2={2}",$x,$x+1,$x**2);
```

The output is

```
x=3;x+1=4;x^2=9
```

The following sample takes as input float number **x** and calculates its exponent. We use the static method **Exp** of the **Math** class. Our program demonstrates two ways of calculating the exponent.

```
#
# Exp.pl
#
use namespace "System";
use PerlNET qw(AUTOCALL);

Console->WriteLine("Please enter a number:");

# Get input from user
my $x = Console->ReadLine();

Console->WriteLine("1)exp({0}) = {1}", $x, Math->Exp($x));
Console->WriteLine("2)exp({0}) = {1}", $x, Math->E ** $x);
```

You may find the above program in the **IO\Exp** folder. To compile the program type

```
plc Exp.pl
```

Code Example

If you did not make any syntax mistakes, the compilation should accomplish successfully. Now run **Exp.exe**. Enter some number when the program asks you to, and examine the response. You should get an error message:

```
System.ApplicationException: Can't locate public static
method Exp(System.String) for System.Math.
```

The problem is caused by the **Math->Exp($x)** statement. If we comment the whole line, compile, and run again, there should not be any error messages. The output may look as shown below.

```
Please enter a number:
1
2)exp(1) = 2.71828182845905
```

By now, you should know how to fix the first **WriteLine** statement to get a clean execution. The **ReadLine** method of the **Console** class returns **System.String** that PerlNET runtime module delivers to our program as a Perl string scalar. The solution is to clear the string representation. We do it by passing the **$x+0** value to the **Exp** method.

```
Console->WriteLine("1)exp({0}) = {1}", $x, Math->Exp($x+0));
```

We saved the correct version of the program in **IO\ExpFix**. Now, after rebuilding and running the exponent program again, you should get no error messages.

```
Please enter a number:
2.5
1)exp(2.5) = 12.1824939607035
2)exp(2.5) = 12.1824939607035
```

Main Sample

In this section, we combine the knowledge that we provided throughout this chapter. We present the full example program, which you should easily understand. We use the **Console** class, since we want you to feel comfortable when combining .NET types with Core Perl statements and expressions.

Our sample performs calculations of binary operations (+, −, *, /). It gets as an input an expression (**x op y**) where **x** and **y** are integer positive numbers and **op** is one of the four operators mentioned above. Our .NET program validates the input using Perl regular expressions (!) and then evaluates the expression. To test the following code, refer to the **MainSample\BinOper** folder.

```
#
# BinOper.pl
```

```
#
use namespace "System";
use PerlNET qw(AUTOCALL);
use strict;

# Full qualified type reference
q(System.Console)->WriteLine("Please enter expression to
                            evaluate:");

# Get an expression from the user - Another way to refer to
# Console class
my $expr = System::Console->ReadLine();

#remove whitespaces from $expr
$expr =~ s/\s*//g;

# Check for valid format
if ($expr =~ /(^\d+)([\+,\-,\*,\/]{1})(\d+$)/)
{
    # Evaluate user expression
    my $result = eval $expr;

    # Check if the result is OK
    if (!defined $result)
    {
        die "Illegal operation: $expr";
    }

    # Output - Refer to Console without namespace
    # specification
    Console->WriteLine("Result: {0}\n", $result);
}

# Handle wrong input
else
{
    die "Incorrect expression format";
}
```

As you can see, we take advantage of the powerful Perl constructions to validate input. **eval** simply evaluates an expression if it was supplied in correct form. The **die** statement is used to handle errors. Examples of running the program may look like this:

```
Please enter expression to evaluate:
64 + 36
Result: 100
------------
Please enter expression to evaluate:
d-5
```

```
Incorrect expression format at binoper.pl line 38.
------------
Please enter expression to evaluate:
10 / 0
Illegal operation: 10/0 at binoper.pl line 27.
```

Take some time to play with the program. Supply different inputs and examine the response. Enjoy!

Summary

In this chapter. we touched on the basics of Perl programming within the .NET environment. The combination of Perl and the .NET extensions is called PerlNET. Pragmas were introduced to simplify program code. All classes in .NET are divided into namespaces. **System** namespace exposes **Console** class (among many others), which provides static methods for performing input/output operations and can be used in any PerlNET programs. These methods may be replaced by Core Perl statements (**print** and **<STDIN>**). All other standard Perl constructions and features are supported in PerlNET as well.

There are several ways to write an application. You may choose a script-like form or an object-oriented approach by supplying interface definitions and explicitly defining the **Main** function.

.NET has a wide range of classes that may be incorporated into our programs. We saw how to use classes, which provide static methods: **Console**, **Math**, and **Convert**. In the next chapter, we will learn in detail about the .NET components and review the most popular and useful classes.

Using .NET Components in PerlNET Programs

*I*n Chapter 9, we placed the first bricks of the PerlNET programming foundation by introducing the simple examples of using .NET classes. In this chapter, we take this topic further and discuss .NET components in detail. First, we give general information about .NET types exposed by Framework components. **System.Object**, the base class type from which all types in .NET inherit, is discussed. Then we concentrate on incorporating components into our programs and discuss practical issues, such as how to construct an object of a class type exposed by a component, how to work with properties and fields of objects, how to call methods, and more. You should pay special attention to how parameters with value types are marshaled by PerlNET when passed to methods of .NET classes. Afterwards, we take a tour to review commonly used types included in the standard .NET components: enumerations, strings, arrays, collections, and more. This chapter does not cover creating components, as the two next chapters deal with it. Upon completing this chapter, you should be able to build powerful applications based on the .NET technology, and it will be an additional step towards understanding how Perl language is integrated within the .NET environment.

Components Overview

Component Object Model (COM) technology preceded .NET. It defined the standards for developing robust, scalable applications based on components from independent parties. You could create a COM object and then use it in a client program through interfaces that are exposed by the object. Interfaces are immutable, so if a new version of the component was released, you would not have to recompile the client program. You could just continue working with it.

.NET and COM share much of the philosophy, but .NET takes the component development issue much further by introducing a more flexible platform for component reuse and interoperation.

Prior to learning how to create our own components, we will learn how to benefit from existing ones in our PerlNET programs. Generally, components are independent program units that expose namespaces; namespaces contain classes, and classes in turn provide different functionalities that we will utilize in our applications.

.NET Classes

Microsoft .NET Framework offers to software developers a rich set of classes with a wide range of functionality. The **Console**, **Math**, and **Convert** classes that we met in the previous chapter are just three of more than 2,500 .NET classes that may be used in our .NET applications. Here is a partial list of main programming fields where you may find the .NET class library very helpful:

- Base class library (basic functionality such as strings, arrays, and formatting)
- Networking
- Security
- Remoting
- Diagnostics
- I/O
- Database
- XML
- Web services that allow us to expose component interfaces over the Internet
- Web programming
- Windows user interface

.NET Types and PerlNET

The .NET types that we use in PerlNET may be divided into two major groups: value types and reference types. Value type variables store the value itself, while reference type variables store a reference (an address in memory where the data is located). References are useful for compound types, and usually we use them to work with instances of .NET class types—objects.

Whenever a .NET method returns an object, PerlNET stores a reference to it unless this object represents one of the value types: **System.Int32**, **System.Double**, **System.Decimal**, and so on. Here are the .NET value types of our interest (they all reside in the **System** namespace):

- Boolean
- Char
- SByte
- Int16
- Int32
- Int64
- Byte
- UInt16
- UInt32
- UInt64
- Single
- Double
- Decimal

PerlNET stores value types as boxed objects, maintaining their .NET type information, instead of converting them into regular Perl scalars. Such boxed objects may be a result of either storing the return value of some .NET method (in case the method returns one of the above mentioned value types) or constructing a value type object using special cast functions defined in the PerlNET module.

When we call .NET methods and pass Perl scalars, the latter are converted into corresponding .NET objects by PerlNET runtime modules and are passed to .NET. Some scalars must be cast to the correct value type as expected by the .NET method.[1]

We explain the process of casting, marshaling, and working with value types later in this chapter when we discuss calling methods. We will demonstrate this with concrete examples.

System.Object

.NET is a strong-typed object-oriented environment. Every .NET type has a class associated with it. This includes even value types: for example, the **System.Int32** class represents **int** type and the **System.Double** represents the **double** type. Every class in .NET directly or indirectly inherits from the same root class: **System.Object** (inheritance in .NET and its implementation in PerlNET is discussed in Chapter 12). This class defines several methods, such as

---

1. Perl strings are scalars and PerlNET automatically converts them into the **System.String** class objects. We do not need to perform any casting operation before passing string scalars to .NET methods.

ToString and **Equals**. Every .NET class overrides or inherits as is the **System.Object** methods.

Class Usage in General

Usually, to benefit from the functionality provided by a class (or encapsulated in a class), we construct an object of that class. Then, we get a reference to the newly created object (instance of the class) and work with this object by invoking its methods or accessing its properties or fields. Finally, when we finish working with the object, we dispose it; that is, we free the memory that we allocated when constructing it. We examine an object's life cycle in a .NET application in the next section.

There are cases when we do not need to create an object in order to use certain classes. These classes define so-called static methods that provide general functionality and are not bound to the specific properties. You access static methods through the name of a class. We already encountered static methods when we used the **WriteLine** method of the **Console** class without instantiating an object.

An Object's Life Cycle

Every object in a .NET application passes through three major stages during its life cycle:

- Constructing
- Working with object
- Disposing

To make our samples real rather than theoretical, we illustrate the above stages on the **StringBuilder** class objects. **StringBuilder** is located in the **System.Text** namespace. It provides some methods for an easy string building, as follows from its name.

Constructing

You can construct an object of a class by calling the **new** class method—the same method-calling syntax as in Core Perl:

```
my $obj = StringBuilder->new();
```

As a result, our program allocates memory for storing an object, and the invoked constructor performs some initialization. If there were no errors, then the **new** method returns a reference to a new instance. We assign this reference to **$obj**. Through **$obj** we access the methods and the properties. In other words, we work with the object (second stage of the object's lifecycle).

Optionally, you may pass parameters to the **new** method.

```
my $obj = StringBuilder->new("Hello");
```

The constructor accepts parameters and may perform some initializations based on values of these parameters.

Another way to instantiate an object is to use the **ctor** helper function of the PerlNET module to invoke the constructor:

```
my $obj = PerlNET::ctor("StringBuilder", "Hello");
```

In this statement, the first argument to **ctor** is the class/type name to construct. Starting from the second argument, you should specify the arguments list that you pass to the constructor. If you intend to invoke the default constructor, then your arguments list should be empty:

```
my $obj = PerlNET::ctor("StringBuilder");
```

Note that not all the classes have the default constructor.

Working with Objects

After we obtain a reference to an object, we may fully exploit its functionality provided through the class interface. Normally, when working with the object, you would perform the following actions:

- Call methods on object
- Get or set object's properties and fields

We discuss calling methods on an object and working with its properties and fields later in this chapter.

Disposing

Fortunately, we do not have to worry about disposing an object explicitly. The .NET environment introduces a *garbage collection* mechanism (similar to Java) that frees memory occupied by the unreferenced objects. The object becomes unreferenced when we exit the scope of the reference definition in our application.

Calling Methods

We can access .NET methods through the standard Perl method-calling syntax. We pass arguments to methods the same way as we do it in Core Perl:

```
$foo->Method(@args);
```

Look at the following fragment:

```
my $obj = StringBuilder->new("How");
$obj->Append(" Are You?");
print $obj;
```

After constructing an object and storing a reference to it in **$obj**, we call the **Append** method, passing to it " Are you?" string as an argument. The method will append this string to the "How" string and the last statement will print

```
How Are You?
```

Every .NET class inherits the **ToString** method from **System.Object**. The class either overrides this method or uses the base class version of the method. If we call **ToString** on the **StringBuilder** object, then it will return the encapsulated string. PerlNET automatically invokes the **ToString** method on any object reference that is used in string context. Hence, the last statement in the above fragment works correctly and we do not have to perform any conversions on **$obj**.

Static Methods

If you plan to work with static methods in your PerlNET application, you have two options to invoke them:

- Using PerlNET::call
- Arrow syntax with AUTOCALL

PERLNET::CALL

When working with the **call** helper function, as its first argument you pass a method to invoke as a string (you have to prefix the method with name of the class that exposes this static method). The second argument of **call** is an argument list that you pass to your static method. You may enumerate all the arguments, delimiting them with commas. For example, here is how we may obtain the maximum of two numbers, 3 and 5. Though the answer is obvious for us, we would like to check if the same is true for the **Max** method of the **Math** class.

```
use namespace "System";

my $bigger = PerlNET::call("Math.Max", 3, 5);
print $bigger;
```

Another way to pass arguments to the static method when using **call** is to build a Perl array (list) of them.

```
use namespace "System";

my @args = (3, 5);
my $bigger = PerlNET::call("Math.Max", @args);
print $bigger;
```

When your static method takes no parameters, like **Console.ReadLine**, then you should supply an empty arguments list in one of the forms of your choice.

```
use namespace "System";
. . .
PerlNET::call("Console.ReadLine", ());   # Right
PerlNET::call("Console.ReadLine", );     # Right
PerlNET::call("Console.ReadLine");       # Right
PerlNET::call("Console.ReadLine", "");   # Wrong!
```

AUTOCALL

The second alternative that PerlNET offers is using standard Perl method-calling syntax (arrow syntax) on a .NET class name. For example,

```
Math->Max(3, 5);
```

To use the above form, you should import **AUTOCALL** from the PerlNET module:

```
use PerlNET qw(AUTOCALL);
```

This instructs Perl to retry all the calls as .NET calls, for which no Perl method was found. Supplying parameters in such calls is the same as in all .NET calls. You may either delimit your parameters with comma or pass a list. In case of methods such as **ReadLine**, just leave the brackets empty or pass an empty list:

```
use PerlNET qw(AUTOCALL);
Console->ReadLine();
```

STATIC METHODS SUMMARY

Summarizing our discussion about the static methods, we recommend the second alternative, using **AUTOCALL**, which will result in more readable code, and the inefficiency of retrying the calls is insignificant. Besides, it makes programming in PerlNET an even more pleasant experience.

Marshalling Types

Whenever you invoke a method—either static or non-static—and supply some arguments, you have to make sure that these arguments are of the correct type. This means that if some class defines a method that expects a **double** value, you cannot pass a string to it, unlike in the case of Core Perl subroutines.

```
my $a = Math->Exp("1.5");    # Wrong! .NET call
my $b = Math->Exp(1.5);      # Correct - .NET call
my $c = exp(1.5);            # Correct - Core Perl
my $d = exp("1.5");          # Correct - Core Perl
```

To assure that we supply arguments with the correct type to a .NET method, you should use special *cast* functions imported from the PerlNET module. They translate Perl scalars into all the basic .NET value types. As a result, the translated value represents a corresponding .NET value type object. Table 10-1 shows the possible casting operations between Perl and .NET.

TABLE 10–1	*Value Types Conversion in PerlNET*
System	**PerlNET**
Boolean	bool
Char	char
SByte	sbyte
Int16	short
Int32	int
Int64	long
Byte	byte
UInt16	ushort
UInt32	uint
UInt64	ulong
Single	float
Double	double
Decimal	decimal

For example, **PerlNET::decimal** produces a **System.Decimal** value. Note that the PerlNET cast functions' names are the same as corresponding C# data types.

PerlNET automatically converts all value types into strings as needed and also implements autoincrement and autodecrement operators for them, covering the whole valid value range. The wraparound behavior is the same as of the underlying .NET types.

```
my $byte = PerlNET::byte(255);
++$byte;
```

yields the same result as

```
my $byte = PerlNET::byte(0);
```

Normal arithmetic operations, however, will convert the .NET value types into Perl integers or floating-point numbers. That means that the result is no longer a .NET value type, and that values exceeding 32-bit integers (for **long**, **ulong**, and **decimal** types) may not be converted correctly. Numeric comparisons for these three types will also not work.

```
use PerlNET qw(uint);
...
my $word = uint(42);
$word += 7;

# need to convert back to System.UInt32 as $word is now
# just a Perl int
$obj->Method( uint($word) );
```

Note that you will override the built-in **int()** function if you import **PerlNET::int()** into your program.

```
use PerlNET qw(int);
...
# use CORE::int() to call builtin Perl int() function
# my $int = CORE::int($val*1.68);
```

With the help of these cast functions, we may pass to .NET methods even variables or constants that store Perl strings.

```
my $s = "1.5";
my $res = Math->Exp(PerlNET::double($s));      # Correct!
my $res2 = Math->Exp(PerlNET::double("1.5")); # Correct!
```

Properties and Fields

When working with .NET objects, we may alter them not only by using methods, but also by accessing properties and fields that the object has. In most cases, properties and fields share the same syntax for their access. However, there are some significant differences in their implementation in .NET.

Properties

The encapsulation principles suggest that we store the data inside our instances in private *fields* (private members[2]) and we access this data through special accessor and mutator methods. .NET implements these principles by introducing the notion of *properties*. We access properties through the hash-reference syntax. We assign values to properties or read their values, but actually, .NET calls for us special getter and setter methods. Consider the following code:

```
use namespace "System.Text";
use PerlNET qw(AUTOCALL);
. . .
my $obj = StringBuilder->new("How Are You");
my $len = $obj->{Length};                        # $len = 11
```

First, we construct the **StringBuilder** object and initialize it with the string `"How Are You"`. The **Length** property holds the length of the string encapsulated inside the **StringBuilder** object. We assign to **$len** the value of the **Length** property. **Length** is a read/write property, which means that we can get and set its value. The following fragment demonstrates setting the **Length** property:

```
my $obj = StringBuilder->new("How Are You");
print $obj, "\n";
$obj->{Length} = 3;
print $obj,"\n";
```

We set the **Length** property to 3. Therefore, the last characters are cut off the encapsulated string. The actual string value is stored in the private field. The output of the above fragment is

```
How Are You
How
```

As we have just demonstrated, properties implement a higher level of abstraction than do member variables. When we change an object's property, some actions might have to be taken besides storing its value. The same thing is true when reading the object's property. The property might be calculated based on some private fields' values. Examine the following piece of code:

```
my $obj = StringBuilder->new("Central")
print $obj, "\n";
$obj->{Length} = 4;
print $obj, "\n";
```

---

2. We may draw a parallel between .NET fields and C++ member variables.

The output is

```
Central
Cent
```

As you can see, we follow the standard procedure of constructing the **StringBuilder** object, initializing it with the `"Central"` string. Then we output the value of the encapsulated string. With the third statement, we alter the **Length** property, setting it to 4. Pay attention to the fact that we did not explicitly touch the string value inside our **StringBuilder** object. However, when we output it again with the last statement, we obtain another value. This means that the third statement with the simple assignment altered the string:

```
$obj->{Length} = 4;
```

In fact, when we set a property, a special function called setter (mentioned earlier) is invoked. Optionally, you may call the setter method through the object reference. You pass to it the value you assign to the property, and it executes some code according to this value. The name of the setter method is **set_XXX**, where **XXX** is the property name. For the **Length** property, the setter name is **set_Length**, and it cuts off the last characters of encapsulated string or expands it by adding spaces, so that the length of the resulting string will be equal to the value you supply. Let us demonstrate the direct setter invocation.

```
$obj->set_Length(4); # Same as: $obj->{Length} = 4;
```

In the same manner, the getter method of the form **get_XXX** is defined for properties. It is invoked when we read the value of the property. In the case of the **Length** property, the two following lines are identical:

```
my $len = $obj->{Length};
my $len = $obj->get_Length();
```

get_Length calculates the length of the **StringBuilder** instance.

Read-only properties have only getter methods. Write-only properties have only setter methods. Finally, read-write properties have both: getter and setter methods.

Some properties may optionally take parameters. In this case, we cannot use the convenient hash-reference syntax. Instead, we have to invoke getter and setter methods explicitly supplying the expected parameters in the arguments list.

Fields

Fields are member variables of the class, and when getting or setting field values, we directly access its memory location. In contrast to properties, no methods are invoked to perform field getting or setting. Fields never accept parameters.

Most of the .NET classes do not expose any fields as part of their interface, and we access their values through the properties. However, the programmer of some class may decide to make fields visible to class users. In this case, we use hash-reference syntax to access fields (the same syntax we use when working with properties). For instance, if the hypothetical class **House** stores the number of floors in the **NumOfFloors** field, then here is how the code of getting and setting this field may look.

```
$h = "House"->new(@args);    # Construct House object
                             # and initialize with some args
$h->{NumOfFloors} = 5;       # Assignment
print $h->{NumOfFloors};     # prints 5 (get field value)
```

Static Properties and Fields

Some .NET class may give you access to its static properties or fields. They are common to all the instances of that class. PerlNET defines a special syntax for working with such class members. We would like to introduce **get** and **set** helper functions that are part of the PerlNET module, and with their help, we will gather access to static properties and fields.

Suppose the class **MyClass** exposes the static property **StaticProperty** and static field **StaticField**. The following lines demonstrate the use of **get** and **set**.

```
use PerlNET qw(get set);
. . .
# Assign $p to StaticProperty of MyClass
set("MyClass.StaticProperty", $p);
# Retrieve the value of StaticProperty
my $prop = get("MyClass.StaticProperty");

# Assign $f to StaticField of MyClass
set("MyClass.StaticField", $f);
# Retrieve the value of StaticField
my $fld = get("MyClass.StaticFields");
```

More About Types

Recall our explanations about marshalling types to .NET methods. We stated that a developer should take care of correct typing of arguments by using special cast functions. Since methods may have several versions (method overloading), PerlNET cannot know what argument types should be used until the specific overloaded signature is chosen. After all, we choose the signature according to the types and/or number of parameters, and not otherwise. Hence, the exact types are essential when working with objects.

The good news is that when working with properties or fields, we have more freedom with typing. Since the type of property or field is known, PerlNET has enough information to try to coerce the type of assigned value to the type of chosen property or field. This is true only when you use hash-reference syntax for property or field assignment. Hence, it is legal to write the following:

```
my $obj = StringBuilder->new("Central")
print $obj, "\n";       # prints "Central"

# PerlNET will convert Perl string into integer
$obj->{Length} = "4";
print $obj, "\n";       # prints "Cent"
```

Indexers

.NET enlarges the set of properties by introducing another kind: indexed properties (we refer to them as indexers). Many types define the concept of default indexer. This concept is taken from arrays (we discuss arrays later in this chapter); that is, we supply an index (which, by the way, does not have to be an integer) and get a value with accordance to this index. Usually, an indexer is defined when an object has elements of the same type in a specific order.

In the case of the **StringBuilder** class, the string encapsulated within it is built up from characters that are standing in the specific order. Therefore, **StringBuilder** exposes an indexer. When you access this property, you are required to supply an integer index as an argument. This index is passed to the getter method, which returns a character standing on the index-th place.

For properties that expect an integer index, PerlNET offers array-style syntactic sugar: access to the property supplying the index in square brackets.

```
my $obj = StringBuilder->new("Yevgeny");
my $c = $obj->[0];           # $c = "Y"
my $d = $obj->[3];           # $d = "g"
```

We assign to **$c** and **$d** the first and the fourth characters respectively of the "Yevgeny" string. And, you can always call the getter method explicitly. Usually, the name of an indexer property is **Item**, but there are exceptions, and **StringBuilder** uses the **Chars** name. Here is how to invoke the getter.

```
my $obj = StringBuilder->new("Jeka");
my $c = $obj->get_Chars(2);        # $c = "k"
```

When the property is indexed by a noninteger value (e.g., string), the square bracket syntax cannot be used in your PerlNET programs. You should access such a property through its **get_XXX** method.

Setting indexed properties is similar to setting regular properties, with one distinction—in addition to a new value, you should supply an index. This is how we can simply turn "Life" into "Wife":

```
my $obj = StringBuilder->new("Life");
$obj->[0] = 'W';
```

Note that in the last statement, we did not use the casting **char** function. The reason for this is that PerlNET automatically translates one-character strings into a **char** value type as part of general type coercing that we explained earlier.

Stock Management: Step 1

Let us summarize using .NET classes with a sample program, which manages the stock of a small store. The program supports three commands:

- add: adds new item to stock
- quit: exit program
- help: show help

If a user chooses to add an item, he or she is asked to enter a name for a new item. Our program generates a new **id**, and we build a string in the following format:

```
<id> <item_name>
```

Afterwards, we capitalize all first letters of words in the item name and store the information. To make our program more ambitious, the stock information is stored in the text file **Stock.txt**. To perform the file output operations, we introduce another .NET class: **StreamWriter**. We construct the **StreamWriter** object and pass to its constructor a file name and appending mode. The file name will be always **Stock.txt**. The appending mode is a **boolean** parameter: If it is set to **true**, then all the information we write will be appended to the end of the file; otherwise, the file will be overwritten. In both cases, if the **Stock.txt** file does not exist, we create a new empty file upon the construction.

```
my $sw = StreamWriter->new("Stock.txt", true);
```

To marshal boolean parameters correctly, the PerlNET module defines **true** and **false** symbols that we import from it.

```
use PerlNET qw(AUTOCALL true false);
```

We perform writing to the file with the **WriteLine** method of **StreamWriter**, which gets a string to write as an argument.

```
$sw->WriteLine("new item");
```

When we finish working with the file, we close it by invoking the **Close** method.

```
$sw->Close();
```

Each time we run our program, we rewrite the **Stock.txt** file. Here is the program code.

```
#
# Stock.pl
#
use strict;
use namespace "System";
use namespace "System.IO";
use namespace "System.Text";
use PerlNET qw(AUTOCALL true false);

# Create file or overwrite existing
my $sw = StreamWriter->new("Stock.txt", false);
$sw->Close();
my $id = 0;
Console->WriteLine("Welcome to Stock Management System");
Console->WriteLine("For the list of commands type help\n");
Console->Write(">>");

my $command = Console->ReadLine();
while ($command ne 'quit')
{
   if ($command eq 'add')
   {
      $id++;
      my $str = StringBuilder->new();
      $str->Append(Convert->ToString($id));
      Console->WriteLine("Please enter item name:");
      my $name = Console->ReadLine();
      # Convert multiple white chars to space
      $name =~ s/\s+/ /g;
      # Remove leading space
      $name =~ s/^\s//g;
      $str->Append(" ");
      $str->Append($name);
      # Make first letter of each word capital
      for(my $i=1; $i<$str->{Length}; $i++)
      {
         if ($str->[$i-1] eq " ")
         {
            $str->[$i] = uc($str->get_Chars(int($i)));
```

```
            }
        }
        # Open "Stock.txt" for appending and add new item
        my $sw = StreamWriter->new("Stock.txt", true);
        $sw->WriteLine($str->ToString());
        $sw->Close();
        Console->WriteLine("Item added. ID = {0}", $id);
    }
    elsif ($command eq 'help')
    {
        Console->WriteLine("List Of Commands:\n");
        Console->WriteLine("add\t- add new item to stock");
        Console->WriteLine("quit\t- exit program");
        Console->WriteLine("help\t- print this list\n");
    }
    else
    {
        Console->WriteLine("Unrecognized command\n");
    }
    Console->Write(">>");
    $command = Console->ReadLine();
}
Console->WriteLine("\nGoodbye.");
```

Code Example

This code resides in the **Stock\Step1** folder under the chapter samples directory. Here is the sample run and contents of the **stock.txt** file:

```
C:\OI\Chap10\Stock\Step1>stock.exe
Welcome to Stock Management System
For the list of commands type help

>>help
List of Commands:

add    - add new item to stock
quit   - exit program
help   - print this list

>>add
Please enter item name:
mobile phone
Item added. ID = 1
>>add
Please enter item name:
excellent  Notebook
Item added. ID = 2
>>quit

Goodbye.
```

```
C:\OI\Chap10\Stock\Step1>type stock.txt
1 Mobile Phone
2 Excellent Notebook
```

Throughout this chapter, we will alter this sample by adding new commands and changing the implementation of the existing ones.

Useful Types

After learning how to work with .NET classes in your PerlNET programs, it is a good idea to introduce the most useful types and classes.

Enumerations

Enumeration types are used to define a set of named constants with common ground, such as days of week, file attributes. Constants that are defined in an enumeration are also called **enumeration members**. Namespaces inside components may expose enumerations. In PerlNET, we can access these constants (enumeration members) using the **enum** helper function, which we import from the PerlNET module. We should supply this function with one argument, fully qualified constant name, in the following format:

```
"namespace.enumeration.constant"
```

If you specified namespace by the **use namespace** pragma, then you can omit it when referring to the enumeration member. Here is how we can access the file attributes enumeration constants that the **System.IO** namespace exposes:

```
my $ar = PerlNET::enum("System.IO.FileAttributes.Archive");
```

Depending on the context in which you use enumeration objects, they return either numeric or string values. Consider the following fragment:

```
use namespace "System.IO";
use PerlNET qw(enum);

my $ar = enum("FileAttributes.Archive");
print $ar;
print $ar+0;
```

The output will be

```
Archive
32
```

In addition, we may use combinations of enumeration members. For example, suppose a file has both the attributes **Archive** and **ReadOnly**. Here is how we combine them.

```
my $attr =
PerlNET::enum("FileAttributes.Archive,ReadOnly");
```

Enumerations whose members can be combined are called **flag** enumerations. If we present their integer value in the binary form, then it will have exactly one bit set to 1. By combining the flags, we set specific bits in the resulting value; that is, we perform a bitwise **or**.

Strings

System.String is another .NET class type, which encapsulates a wide range of operations on strings. However, you cannot create the **System.String** object in your PerlNET programs, because the PerlNET runtime module automatically converts all **System.String** objects to the Perl scalar strings before you get them in your program. Whenever you supply a Perl string to a .NET method, PerlNET constructs the **System.String** object from your string, and the .NET method gets the data in the correct format. All the conversions are highly optimized, so you do not have to worry about efficiency when you work with strings.

As in many other fields, Core Perl provides strong background for sophisticated text handling. It is enough to mention Perl regular expressions. So, the fact that we cannot access **System.String** methods does not derogate from our PerlNET programs.

Notwithstanding the unavailability of this class for PerlNET, there are cases when we will refer **System.String**. We will learn in Chapter 12 that there are situations when we cannot use Core Perl arrays, so the best way to overcome this difficulty is to resort to the help of .NET arrays, which we discuss in detail in the next section. Suppose we need to create an array of strings. When constructing a .NET array, we should supply the .NET type of elements that we want to be stored in the array. As you probably guessed, in the case of strings, we use the **System.String** class type. We show how it is done in the next section when we enhance our Stock Management system.

Arrays

All .NET arrays inherit from the **System.Array** class type, which provides rich functionality when working with array objects. .NET array elements have to be of the same type, which you should specify when constructing a .NET array object. All arrays that are constructed in any PerlNET program will be of fixed length, which is determined upon construction. In this section, we first discuss one-dimensional arrays, and then we review multidimensional and jagged arrays. Compared to Core Perl arrays, the functionality of the .NET arrays seems limited. Whenever possible, we prefer to use Core Perl arrays in our PerlNET programs. However, there are cases when we cannot take advantage of them and our options are limited to the .NET arrays (we learn about such situations in Chapter 12), so we should dedicate some time to learn and practice with the .NET arrays.

ONE-DIMENSIONAL ARRAYS

We can construct a one-dimensional .NET array by specifying the .NET type and array size in square brackets and calling **new** method with no arguments.

```
my $arr = "StringBuilder[10]"->new();
```

Optionally, we can create an array from already existing objects by passing references to them to the constructor. In this case, we leave the square brackets empty.

```
my $str1 = StringBuilder->new("Yevgeny");
my $str2 = StringBuilder->new("Avi");
my $str3 = StringBuilder->new("Katrin");

my $arr  = "StringBuilder[]"->new($str1, $str2, $str3);
```

After we create the array, we cannot change its size. This is one of the disadvantages of the .NET arrays, which we may eliminate by using **Collections**. We discuss **Collections** later in this chapter.

To iterate through arrays, you may use the standard **for** loop. As in Core Perl, the .NET arrays are zero-based. **System.Array** exposes the **Length** property, which holds length of an array and may be used for stopping conditions when iterating. To access elements of an array, we use the array-reference syntax, because we access array members through an indexer:

```
for (my $i = 0; $i < $arr->{Length}; $i++)
{
   print $arr->[$i], "\n";
}
```

System.Array implements the **IEnumerable** interface. Interfaces are discussed in Chapter 12. For now, it is enough to understand that by implementing some interface, a class acquires an additional ability. In our case, PerlNET offers an easy way of iteration through all classes that implement the **IEnumerable** interface. For such classes, we can use a **foreach** loop in conjunction with the **PerlNET::in** helper function. This is how we can rewrite the previous code fragment:

```
use PerlNET qw(in);
. . .
foreach $str(in $arr)
```

```
{
   print $str, "\n";
}
```

In both cases, the output would look as follows:

```
Yevgeny
Avi
Katrin
```

The disadvantage of using **foreach** iteration is that we lose the index information.

STOCK MANAGEMENT: STEP 2

After we learn how to use the .NET arrays in PerlNET programs, we may rewrite our code for stock management and replace file operations by in-memory arrays operations. In addition, we add the new command **show**, which asks the user for the item ID and displays the information for the corresponding item. To show the whole list of the items, a user should type –1 instead of the ID. We list the code for the **add** and **show** commands as well as for creating arrays. The complete code resides in the **Stock\Step2** directory. The lines of the code that deal with arrays are bolded. In this example, we limit the stock to 100 items, as we create an array at the beginning of the program and its size is immutable. We may resolve such limitation by creating a new, bigger array each time the current is full and copying all the elements to the new array, but this solution is too expensive, and we will see how collections solve this in a more elegant way.

Code Example

```perl
#
# StockArr.pl
#
use strict;
use namespace "System";
use namespace "System.Text";
use PerlNET qw(AUTOCALL in);

my $id = -1;
# Create Strings array for 100 items
my $items = "String[100]"->new();
 . . .
   if ($command eq 'add')
   {
      $id++;
      my $str = StringBuilder->new();
      $str->Append(Convert->ToString($id));
      Console->WriteLine("Please enter item name:");
      my $name = Console->ReadLine();
      # Convert multiple white chars to space
```

```
        $name =~ s/\s+/ /g;
        # Remove leading space
        $name =~ s/^\s//g;
        $str->Append(" ");
        $str->Append($name);
        # Make first letter of each word capital
        for(my $i=1; $i<$str->{Length}; $i++)
        {
            if ($str->[$i-1] eq " ")
            {
                $str->[$i] = uc($str->get_Chars(int($i)));
            }
        }
        $items->[$id] = $str->ToString();
        Console->WriteLine("Item added. ID = {0}", $id);
    }
    elsif ($command eq 'show')
    {
        Console->WriteLine("Please enter id or -1 for all");
        my $itemid = Console->ReadLine();
        if ($itemid > $id || $itemid < -1)
        {
            Console->WriteLine("No such item");
        }
        else
        {
            if ($itemid >= 0)
            {
                Console->WriteLine("{0}",
                                $items->[int($itemid)]);
            }
            else
            {
                for(my $i = 0; $i <= $id; $i++)
                {
                    Console->WriteLine($items->[$i]);
                }
            }
        }
    }
. . .
Console->WriteLine("\nGoodbye.");
```

Here is the sample run.

```
Welcome to Stock Management System
For the list of commands type help

>>add
Please enter item name:
gamepad
```

```
Item added. ID = 0
>>add
Please enter item name:
computer dictionary
Item added. ID = 1
>>show
Please enter id or -1 for all
1
1 Computer Dictionary
>>show
Please enter id or -1 for all
-1
0 Gamepad
1 Computer Dictionary
>>quit

Goodbye.
```

MULTIDIMENSIONAL ARRAYS

We use multidimensional arrays to treat multidimensional data. They are limited to three dimensions. If you define a two-dimensional array, it will be rectangular: All rows will have the same number of elements. Similarly, the three-dimensional array will be cubic. Two-dimensional arrays are the most popular among multidimensional arrays. They are used to represent tables, matrices, and any other tabular data. We provide here samples for the two-dimensional arrays. The transition to three dimensions is intuitive. When creating a multidimensional array, you may either specify its dimensions in square brackets, delimiting with a comma:

```
my $table1 = "System.Int32[5,5]"->new();
```

or leave the last dimension empty and specify initial values as arguments to the constructor:

```
my $table2 = "System.Int32[5,]"->new(1..15);
```

In the first case, an empty 5x5 array is created (by default, initialized with zeros). In the second case, we create a 5x3 array initialized with values from 1 to 15.

When supplying initial values, take care that the number of elements you provide is enough to fill all the rows. If you write

```
my $table2 = "System.Int32[5,]"->new(1..14);  # Wrong!
```

you will get a runtime error from the PerlNET module:

```
Incomplete args at /PerlApp/PerlNET.pm line 86.
```

This happened because the last row is filled with only four elements, not five. The rule is to supply such a number of elements that can be divided on the first dimension size without a remainder.[3] In the case of **$table2**, the number of elements should be divisible by 5.

For multidimensional arrays, the **Length** property holds the number of the elements in the whole array.

```
my $table1 = "System.Int32[5,5]"->new();
my $table2 = "System.Int32[5,]"->new(1..15);

print $table1->{Length};          # Prints 25
print $table2->{Length};          # Prints 15
```

To obtain size of a dimension, you can use the **GetLength** function, specifying the dimension index as a parameter: 0 for the first, 1 for the second, and so on.

```
my $x = $table2->GetLength(0);
my $y = $table2->GetLength(1);
print $x, "x", $y, "\n";          # prints "5x3"
```

We can access the two-dimensional array elements by specifying two indices for special getter or setter functions, as there is no syntactic sugar for the multidimensional arrays.

```
$table1->SetValue(8, 0, 1); # Element from first row
                            # and second column is set to 8
print $table1->GetValue(0, 1);# Will print 8
```

Following is the full example program, which will print a multiplication table using a two-dimensional array. The code for this program may be found in the **Arrays\MultTable** directory.

Code
Example

```
#
# MultTable.pl
#
use strict;
use namespace "System";
use PerlNET qw(AUTOCALL);

# Create two-dimensional array
my $mult = "System.Int32[10,10]"->new();
# Fill in the multiplication table
for(my $i = 0; $i < 10; $i++)
{
    for(my $j = 0; $j < 10; $j++)
    {
        $mult->SetValue(int($i*$j), int($i), int($j));
```

---

3. As for three-dimensional arrays, the number of elements in the list should be divisible by a product of the first two dimensions. For example, if the first two dimensions are 3 and 4 respectively, the number of elements may be 12, 24, and so on.

```
        }
    }

    # Print multiplication table
    for(my $i = 0; $i < $mult->GetLength(0); $i++)
    {
        for(my $j = 0; $j < $mult->GetLength(1); $j++)
        {
            print $mult->GetValue(int($i), int($j)), "\t";
        }
        print "\n";
    }
```

Here is the output:

```
0    0    0    0    0    0    0    0    0    0
0    1    2    3    4    5    6    7    8    9
0    2    4    6    8    10   12   14   16   18
0    3    6    9    12   15   18   21   24   27
0    4    8    12   16   20   24   28   32   36
0    5    10   15   20   25   30   35   40   45
0    6    12   18   24   30   36   42   48   54
0    7    14   21   28   35   42   49   56   63
0    8    16   24   32   40   48   56   64   72
0    9    18   27   36   45   54   63   72   81
```

Creating arrays with three dimensions is similar.

```
my $cube1 = "System.Int32[3,3,3]"->new();      # Empty array
my $cube2 = "System.Int32[3,3,]"->new(1..27);  # initialized
print $cube1->GetValue(0, 0, 0);    # Prints 0
print $cube2->GetValue(1, 1, 1);    # Prints 14
$cube1->SetValue(10, 0, 0, 0);      # Sets element value
print $cube1->GetValue(0, 0, 0);    # Prints 10
```

JAGGED ARRAYS

Jagged array is another name for an array of arrays. Jagged arrays may represent multidimensional data without limiting the number of dimensions, and they do not have to be rectangular (for two-dimensional), or cubic (for three-dimensional), and so on. The best way to create a jagged array is to construct an array of **System.Array** objects (outer array) and then create an array for each element (inner arrays). As all objects (outer and inner arrays) are .NET arrays, they implement the **IEnumerable** interface, and we can iterate easily through them with the **foreach** statement. Here is a simple program (from the **Arrays\JaggedArray** folder), which creates an array of arrays with different lengths and then outputs their contents.

Code
Example

```
#
# JaggedArray.pl
```

```perl
#
use strict;
use namespace "System";
use PerlNET qw(AUTOCALL in);

# Construct array of 10 arrays
my $jag = "System.Array[10]"->new();
for(my $i = 0; $i < 10; $i++)
{
    # Create new array element
    $jag->[$i] = "System.Int32[]"->new(1..$i);
}

# Iterate through rows of jagged array
foreach my $row(in $jag)
{
    # Iterate through columns (through array element)
    foreach my $col(in $row)
    {
        print $col, " ";
    }
    print "\n";
}
```

Here is the output of the sample program.

```
1
1 2
1 2 3
1 2 3 4
1 2 3 4 5
1 2 3 4 5 6
1 2 3 4 5 6 7
1 2 3 4 5 6 7 8
1 2 3 4 5 6 7 8 9
```

As all arrays (outer and inner) are one-dimensional, we can use the syntactic sugar of square brackets to access the array elements. We may also access the inner arrays' properties, such as **Length**. Here is how we can rewrite the loop of printing the contents of our jagged array.

```perl
for(my $i = 0; $i < $jag->{Length}; $i++)
{
    for(my $j = 0; $j < $jag->[$i]->{Length}; $j++)
    {
        print $jag->[$i][$j], " ";
    }
    print "\n";
}
```

The output will be the same.

As we stated before, jagged arrays do not have limitations on a number of the dimensions. We demonstrate here how to create a three-dimensional array, and you can make the transition to higher dimensions by induction (the sample resides in **Arrays\Jagged3Dim**).

```perl
#
# Jagged_3dim.pl
#
use strict;
use namespace "System";

# Create Outer array
my $jag = "Array[3]"->new();

# Create Inner arrays for each dimension
for(my $i = 0; $i < 3; $i++)
{
    $jag->[$i] = "Array[3]"->new();
}
for(my $i = 0; $i < 3; $i++)
{
    for(my $j = 0; $j < 3; $j++)
    {
        $jag->[$i][$j] = "Int32[]"->new(1..$j+1);
    }
}

# Output contents of 3-dim jagged arrays
for(my $i = 0; $i < 3; $i++)
{
    for(my $j = 0; $j < 3; $j++)
    {
        for(my $k = 0; $k < $$jag[$i][$j]->{Length}; $k++)
        {
            print $jag->[$i][$j][$k], " ";
        }
        print "\n";
    }
}
```

Here is the output.

```
1
1 2
1 2 3
1
1 2
1 2 3
1
1 2
1 2 3
```

To summarize the jagged arrays topic, we recommend using them when the multidimensional data that you want to treat does not have to be rectangular or cubic. By doing this, you save the memory. Besides, accessing elements of jagged arrays is simpler, and they do not have any limitations, except the size of your computer memory, on the number of the dimensions.

Collections

Collections are another set of .NET class types. The **System.Collections** namespace exposes them. Collections provide a flexible data structure for storing (collecting) objects. As all .NET types inherit from **System.Object**, we can store different types in a single collection. Collections are automatically expanded when we add elements and collapsed when we remove them. The functionality is very close to arrays. However, there are many actions we do not need to perform, such as resizing or shifting the elements, if we remove some element from the middle.

One of the most useful collection types the .NET class library offers is **ArrayList**. This class provides all the functionality of an array, and its length is not fixed. As do all collections, **ArrayList** has **Add** and **Remove** methods through which we can easily manipulate our data. The **Remove** method gets an object as a parameter, looks inside the collection for the object that is equal to the parameter object, and removes the found object. The **Count** property returns the number of objects inside collection.

```
use strict;
use namespace "System.Collections";

my $col = ArrayList->new(); # Construct collection
$col->Add("Yevgeny");         # Add 3 elements
$col->Add("Avi");
$col->Add(5);
print $col->{Count};          # prints 3
$col->Remove(5);              # Remove 3-rd element
print $col->{Count};          # prints 2
```

You can access elements of a collection (get and set) exactly as you do elements of an array—through an indexer.

```
use namespace "System.Collections";

my $col = ArrayList->new();
$col->Add("Eugene");
$col->Add("Avi");
$col->Add(5);
$col->[2] = 25;          # Set an existing element
for(my $i = 0; $i < $col->{Count}; $i++)
```

```
{
   print $col->[$i], " ";      # Get element
}
```

And here is the output.

```
Eugene
Avi
25
```

STOCK MANAGEMENT: STEP 3

After we learned a new class for storing lists of objects, we may rewrite our stock management program and use **ArrayList** to store our data. This way, we are not bound by a fixed array. In addition, we enhance our program by the new command **rmv**, which asks for ID and removes the specified element. Following is the code for creating the collection and the **add** and **rmv** commands. The complete program is stored in the **Stock\Step3** directory.

```
#
# StockCol.pl
#
use strict;
use namespace "System";
use namespace "System.Text";
use namespace "System.Collections";
use PerlNET qw(AUTOCALL in);

$| = 1;
# Create file or overwrite existing
my $id = -1;
my $items = "ArrayList"->new();
. . .
   if ($command eq 'add')
   {
      . . .
      $items->Add($str->ToString());
      printf("Item added. ID = %d\n", $id);
   }
   elsif ($command eq 'show')
   {
      . . .
   }
   elsif ($command eq 'rmv')
   {
      printf("Please enter id or -1 for all\n");
      my $itemid = Console->ReadLine();
      if ($itemid == -1)
      {
         printf("All items will be deleted!\n");
         printf("Confirm? (y/n)\n");
```

```
        my $response = Console->ReadLine();
        if (uc(substr($response, 0, 1)) eq "Y")
        {
            $items->Clear();
        }
    }
    else
    {
        # Remove specific item
        foreach my $item(in $items)
        {
            my @a = split(' ', $item);
            if (int($a[0]) == int($itemid))
            {
                $items->Remove($item);
            }
        }
    }
    if ($items->{Count} == 0) { $id = -1; }
}
. . .
Console->WriteLine("\nGoodbye.");
```

Here is the output of the sample run.

```
. . .
>>add
Please enter item name:
blue mousepad
Item added. ID = 0
>>add
Please enter item name:
blanc cd
Item added. ID = 1
>>add
Please enter item name:
CDRW
Item added. ID = 2
>>show
Please enter id or -1 for all
-1
---------------------
0 Blue Mousepad
1 Blanc Cd
2 CDRW
---------------------
>>rmv
Please enter id or -1 for all
1
>>show
Please enter id or -1 for all
```

```
-1
--------------------
0 Blue Mousepad
2 CDRW
--------------------
>>rmv
Please enter id or -1 for all
-1
All items will be deleted!
Confirm? (y/n)
y
>>show
Please enter id or -1 for all
-1
--------------------
--------------------
>>quit
Goodbye.
```

Summary

In this chapter, we reviewed classes and types that standard .NET Framework components expose to us. All the .NET types inherit from **System.Object**. We should use the **new** method to construct .NET objects in our PerlNET programs. We use hash-reference syntax to access properties or fields and standard Perl calling-method syntax for invoking methods of the constructed objects. Classes may expose indexed properties (indexers). We may treat such classes as arrays. .NET strings cannot be used directly in PerlNET. We may use a variety of .NET arrays in our programs: one-dimensional, multidimensional (limited to three dimensions), and jagged arrays. Finally, we presented collections and demonstrated their use on the **ArrayList** class. Collections provide more flexibility in treating lists of data than do .NET arrays. In the next chapter, we learn how to create our own .NET components that we may reuse in PerlNET or other .NET-compliant languages as regular .NET objects.

Creating .NET Components: Pure Perl Types

We have used PerlNET to create monolithic applications that use standard .NET classes and types. In this chapter, we create our own components so that different applications written in any .NET-compliant language may reuse them. We learn component development from the simple class created in C#, then referenced and used in our PerlNET program exactly as any other standard .NET class. Then, we explain how to implement class functionality in PerlNET, using most of the knowledge acquired in Chapter 7. We explain how to define methods and properties for Perl packages so that every .NET program may access them. Finally, we show how to make existing Perl modules (e.g., from CPAN) available to .NET programs.

Component Development

As we developed our PerlNET applications in previous chapters, we put all the functionality in a single file. Such applications are referred to as *monolithic*. The technique of monolithic development is useful when we have to perform simple and focused tasks. We aim at writing short, effective, and readable code as much as possible. Obviously, when the requirements from our software grow, writing monolithic applications results in numerous lines of code, which leads to inefficient and unreadable programs. Besides, if our application resides on a network (probably inside some intranet) and it serves a large number of users, then we may reach an unpleasant situation of service denial. Thus, our goal is to develop scalable, robust applications that respond to growing demands of users, can serve large numbers of requests (in the case of implementing some kind of server), and perform a wide range of tasks according to predefined specifications.

The solution is to break our application into small, effectively working and integrable components. This way, we divide functionality between these components that will be used as bricks for constructing whole applications. We may use the same component as many times as we want (not beyond the memory limit) and compose our software from different components. In addition, we do not have to keep in memory all the components throughout the application life cycle—we can instantiate objects from the classes exposed by components, and the garbage collector will dispose these objects when we no longer need them. This is exactly the same scheme as with standard classes of .NET Framework that we discussed in Chapter 10.

The technique of dividing functionality into components is a part of object-oriented design (OOD), through which our applications will pass.

Components Definition

We define each component by a package (Perl Module), exactly as the classes are defined in Chapter 7, and in most of the cases each module contains one package. However, sometimes it is convenient to put several packages inside a single file to create a library of components.

For each component, prior to its definition, we have to decide what PerlNET type it shall represent, and according to our decision, we will follow the rules of implementation for the chosen PerlNET type.

PerlNET Types

As we stated in Chapter 1, a type in .NET is analogous to a class. *PerlNET types* (the class packages that we will develop in PerlNET) may be divided into Pure Perl types, .NET types, and Mixed types. Do not let the name *Pure Perl types* confuse you, as they are fully functional in the .NET environment and enjoy all the Core Perl benefits, but some .NET design possibilities are unreachable for them. The second (.NET types) will have more flexibility in using .NET features while being limited on the Core Perl side. Finally, the third (Mixed types), as their name suggests, mix the functionality of both Pure Perl and .NET types, but mostly they behave as .NET types.

We dedicated this chapter to programming and designing of Pure Perl types. Chapter 12 concentrates on .NET and Mixed types in PerlNET.

With component development, we achieve scalability and robustness for our applications. We also take advantage of other benefits:

- Simpler and shorter code

- Easier debugging[1]
- Code reusability
- Efficiency

Therefore, after convincing you in favor of the component development (hopefully, our explanation was persuasive), we demonstrate this technique with a simple example.

Component Sample

We will write our first component in C# and not in PerlNET, as you would expect. This choice is not casual, as the C# language was written especially for .NET, while considering all the tiniest details of this environment, and that is why the structure of programs written in C# is much closer to the structure of .NET assemblies. Therefore, it is rather natural to start advanced programming learning of any .NET-compliant language with C#, as we gain an additional insight into the .NET Framework. We will continue this approach of using C# to delve more deeply into .NET in Chapter 13.

C# Sample

Code
Example

Our example provides simple functionality of a stock item. The code resides in **Stock\Cs**. Our class defines a constructor, two properties, and one method. The code is quite simple and intuitive. First, just read the code and try to understand it. Then, read our explanations following the listing. These explanations are brief, as C# is out of the scope of this book, but this is enough to understand the concept. You may refer to Appendix B for a more detailed discussion of C# and its syntax. Here is the code in C# for our sample.

```
//
// StockItem.cs
using System;

// Define namespace for class
namespace OI.Samples
{
    public class StockItem
    {
        // Member variables (fields) for storing
        // properties
        private int m_id;          // Item ID
        private string m_name;     // Item Name
```

---

1. Currently, you cannot debug your PerlNET programs. However, ActiveState is working on adding this feature to Visual Perl.

```
// Constructor
public StockItem(int id, string name)
{
   this.m_id = id;          // Initialize ID
   this.m_name = name;      // Initialize Name
}
// Definition of read-only ID property
public int ID
{
   // Only "get" function
   get
   {
      return m_id;
   }
}
// Definition of read-write Name property
public string Name
{
   // "get" and "set" functions
   get
   {
      return m_name;
   }
   set
   {
      m_name = value;
   }
}
// Output Item Information
public void OutputItem(bool lines)
{
   if (lines)
      Console.WriteLine("--------------------");

   Console.WriteLine("{0}\t{1}",this.m_id,
                              this.m_name);

   if (lines)
      Console.WriteLine("--------------------");
   }
  }
}
```

The **StockItem.cs** file defines the **StockItem** class in the **OI.Samples** namespace. We declared two private member variables for the class: **m_id** and **m_name**. The **private** modifier makes these variables inaccessible from outside, which means that they are visible only for the methods of the **StockItem** class. Every class must have a constructor.[2] In C#, a constructor must have the same name as the class. In our case, the constructor has the following proto-type:

```
StockItem(int id, string name);
```

As you can see, the constructor expects two parameters, **id** and **name**, whose values are assigned to **m_id** and **m_name** respectively.

Next, we have the read-only **ID** property defined. In programs that use the **StockItem** class, we would not be able to set this property. In addition, we defined the **Name** property, which is read-write. This means that we would be able to get and set it using all known ways to do it.

Finally, we defined the public method for performing output of stock item details:

```
public OutputItem(bool lines);
```

This method expects one boolean parameter, **lines**. If **lines** is true, then lines are printed before and after the stock item details; otherwise, only stock item details are displayed.

As you probably noticed, the above class does not have **Main** function that we mention in Chapter 9 when we describe .NET program structure. It is not a mistake, as we will build the **StockItem** class as a library and not as an executable. This means that we cannot use **StockItem** as a standalone pro-gram, because we intend it to be referenced and used in other .NET programs.

First, let us build the **StockItem** library. This can be easily done with the C# command line compiler **csc.exe**:[3]

```
csc /target:library StockItem.cs
```

As a result of running the above command, **StockItem.dll** will be created. Other .NET programs can use this library now in order to work with the **StockItem** class.

PerlNET Client Program

To make our demonstration complete, we present a program in which we ref-erence the **StockItem** class and illustrate its usage. Such a program may be referred to as a client program, as it makes use of the **StockItem** component-

---

2. If you do not define a constructor, then the C# compiler will generate the *default* constructor that accepts no arguments and has an empty body. As we will see later, this is true for PerlNET as well.

3. Optionally, you may double-click the solution file in the sample directory and open it in Visual Studio.NET, where you can build your applications or components with F7. In Appendix A, we explain how to use Visual Perl. In case of C# projects, the keyboard shortcuts are the same as in Visual Perl.

provided functionality. All the principles of using .NET components in the PerlNET programs we learned in the previous chapter remain in force when we work with custom components (ones that are not part of .NET Framework). Therefore, the code we write in PerlNET for our client program of the **StockItem** component will look familiar and comprehensible to you.

We wrote the PerlNET client program, which reflects the common way of custom .NET components usage. You may find it in the **Stock\StockItemCli** directory under the chapter samples directory. Here is the code for this program.

```perl
#
# StockItemCli.pl
#
use strict;
use namespace "System.Collections";
use namespace "OI.Samples";
use PerlNET qw(AUTOCALL in);

$| = 1;
my $items = ArrayList->new();

# Create 5 items and add them to collection
for(my $i = 0; $i < 5; $i++)
{
   my $item = StockItem->new(int($i), "item " . $i);
   $items->Add($item);
}

# Output second item
$items->[1]->OutputItem(PerlNET::true);

# Output all 5 items
print "------------------------\n";
foreach my $item(in $items)
{
   $item->OutputItem(PerlNET::false);
}
print "------------------------\n";

# Access read-only property
print "ID of Second Item: ";
print $items->[1]->{ID}, "\n";

# Access read-write property
print "Name of Second Item: ";
print $items->[1]->{Name}, "\n";
```

```
# Alter read-write property
$items->[1]->{Name} = "Pencil";
print "New Name of Second Item: ";
print $items->[1]->{Name}, "\n";
```

Before running and examining the output of this program, we should clarify several important points. Recall the C# code for the **StockItem** component where we defined the **OI.Samples** namespace. This namespace exposes the **StockItem** class. Hence, in order to be able to use the unqualified name **StockItem**, we write

```
use namespace "OI.Samples";
```

We construct the **StockItem** class objects by calling the **new** method, as for every other .NET class.

```
my $item = StockItem->new(int($i), "item " . $i);
```

Now, after the code is ready, let us try to compile it with the usual **plc** command that we learned to use in Chapter 10.

```
plc StockItemCli.pl
```

Run this command in the sample directory and examine the output. Despite that we did not make any syntax errors, the compilation was not successful. The error message will be similar to this:

```
D:\DOCUME~1\ADMINI~1\LOCALS~1\Temp\432.cs(7,7): error
CS0246: The type or namespace name 'OI' could not be found
(are you missing a using directive or an assembly
reference?)
Stopped with exit code 1
```

So, what did we do wrong? Well, we forgot to tell the compiler where to look for the **OI.Samples** namespace, which exposes the **StockItem** class. As you remember, prior to writing our client program, we built a library for the **StockItem** component, **StockItem.dll**, and now we should reference it by modifying our command line as follows:

```
plc StockItemCli.pl -reference=StockItem.dll
```

Referenced Components

The referenced component should reside in the same directory as the client program. Otherwise, we have to write the path to the DLL (dynamic-link library) when referencing it. In any case, when running the client exe-program, our DLL should be in the same directory as our executable. In order to assure the correct functioning of the sample programs, please compile the component first and then copy the resulting DLL to the client program folder. Refer to the **readme.txt** file in the chapter's samples directory for more details.

Now, as **StockItemCli.exe** was built successfully, we may run it and get the following output:

```
------------------------
1      item 1
------------------------
------------------------
0      item 0
1      item 1
2      item 2
3      item 3
4      item 4
------------------------
ID of Second Item: 1
Name of Second Item: item 1
New Name of Second Item: Pencil
```

Your Own PerlNET Component

Most of the components that we will create throughout this book will expose one class. However, there is no limitation on the number of classes that reside inside one component (library). Hence, when discussing classes' definition, we assume that they reside in different components unless we specify otherwise.

Class Interface

Whenever designing a new class, we first think about the way it should be used and we try to make our class users' lives as easy and comfortable as possible. In other words, we think about a convenient interface[4] through which the users will access our class. Interface is a compound notion, and here we will try to divide it into simpler parts and explain each separately. We hope that in this case, a "divide and conquer" technique will turn out to be a fruitful one.

Class interface usually is composed of the following elements:

- Properties
- Fields[5]
- Methods
- Constructors
- Attributes

---

4. In this chapter we are using the term interface in its general sense of an external specification. In Chapters 12 and 13 we will see that .NET has a special notion of interface.

5. Fields are not applicable to Pure Perl types that we describe in this chapter. Hence, we omit the discussion of fields.

Properties and methods may belong to two major parts of class interface: visible (public) and invisible (private). In general, a visible part contains properties and methods that may be accessed by class users. An invisible part consists of properties, fields, and methods that are private to our class; that is, access to them is permitted only to other class members. Modifiers, which we will discuss later in this chapter, control the visibility.

As we have stated, .NET is a strongly typed environment. Therefore, when we define methods, we should explicitly specify argument types as well as return types of our methods and types of properties and fields that belong to the class interface.

Typing

There are several often used .NET value and class types for which aliases were created in PerlNET. We can use these aliases in **for interface** POD (Plain Old Documentation) blocks for defining types of properties, fields, return values of methods, and arguments types. Table 11-1 shows the .NET types and the corresponding aliases in PerlNET.

TABLE 11-1	*PerlNET Aliases for .NET Types*
.NET Type	**PerlNET Alias**
Boolean	bool
Char	char
Sbyte	sbyte
Int16	short
Int32	int
Int64	long
Byte	byte
UInt16	ushort
UInt32	uint
UInt64	ulong
Single	float
Double	double or num
Decimal	decimal
Object	any
String	str

As you can see, this table is almost identical to the cast table (Table 10-1) in Chapter 10. However, there are some amendments: The **System.Double** class has two aliases, and there are two new entries for **System.Object** and **System.String**. The value types are the same as in C#.

If you want to use a type that is not listed in the table above, you can always write its fully qualified name. However, if the **use namespace** pragma was turned on for the namespace where the type of your interest resides, then the unqualified name may be used. For example, if we want to define that our method returns an integer value, we can do it in three different ways:

```
=for interface
   # using alias
   int SomeMethod();
   # using full-qualified name
   System.Int32 AnotherMethod();
=cut
. . .
# Using unqualified name
use namespace "System";
=for interface
   Int32 YetAnotherMethod();
= cut
. . .
```

We use the same aliases and types in specifying the type of arguments.

```
int SomeMethod(str s, System.UInt32 i);
```

We will see more detailed examples of typing when we discuss methods and properties definitions later in this chapter.

To specify that a return value of an argument is an array, we use the square brackets:

```
str[] Words(str sentence);
```

The **Words** method returns an array of strings.

You may encounter a situation in which your method returns a Perl list and not a .NET array to the .NET client application. In this case, it is useful to convert the Perl list into a .NET array of a correct type, as not all our client applications are able to work with Perl-specific structures. To force the conversion into a .NET array before returning a value, we use **wantarray!** method modifier.

```
=for interface
   static wantarray! str[] Words();
=cut
. . .
sub Words
{
   return qw(Car Bicycle Ship);
}
```

The **Words** method returns the .NET string array. We will see the use of the **wantarray!** method modifier when we discuss wrapping existing Perl modules.

Attributes

The first attribute we are going to use is

```
[interface: pure]
```

With help of this attribute, we specify that our PerlNET component will be written in the Core Perl manner (Pure Perl type). This chapter is dedicated to Pure Perl components only.

We present additional attributes when we discuss inheritance issues in the next chapter. We use attributes to define interfaces and/or methods with special features. Attributes are placed in square brackets inside **for interface** POD blocks. When the attribute is relevant to an interface as whole, it is preferable to put such attribute in the first line of the first **for interface** block for better readability. Attributes that affect a specific method should be placed above that method definition. We will see method attributes usage when we will learn about graphical user interfaces and Windows Forms in Chapter 14.

Constructors

Every .NET class should expose at least one version of a constructor—a special method for initializing class instances (methods are discussed later in this chapter). Inside the **for interface** blocks, the constructor name should be identical to the name of the class. The **new** subroutine defines the code for the constructors. We can define more than one constructor. Constructors should differ by their signatures—types and/or quantity of parameters they expect. This technique is called constructor overloading and is widely used in object-oriented languages, such as C++ and Java. Even if we defined several constructors in POD blocks, there remains only one **new** subroutine. You should examine the parameters inside the body of **new** and determine which version of constructor was called. In addition, a **static** modifier should be specified for every constructor, since these are class methods that we call before the new class instance exists. Constructors of Pure Perl classes return class objects, but we may omit the return type for them.

Following are examples of constructors' definitions. First, we show the **Car** class with a single constructor. The sample is stored in the **Car\Step1\SingleConstructor** directory.

Code Example

```
#
# Car.pm
#
package OI::Samples::Car;
=for interface
    [interface: pure]
    # Return type specified
    static Car Car(str Model);
=cut
```

```
sub new
{
    # Constructor body
    my ($self, $Model) = @_;
    my $s = bless {}, $self;

    print "Car1: Model = ", $Model, "\n";
    # Do something with $Model and $s
    return $s;
}
```

Additionally, we demonstrate constructor overloading with the **Car2** class. The code is in the **Car\Step1\TwoConstructors** directory.

Code
Example

```
#
# Car2.pm
#
package OI::Samples::Car2;
=for interface
    [interface: pure]
    # Return types omitted
    static Car2(str Model);
    static Car2(str Model, int Year);
=cut
sub new
{
    # We determine which version of constructor was
    # called
    my ($self, $Model, $Year) = @_;
    my $s = bless {}, $self;

    if (!defined $Year)
    {
        # First version was called
        print "Car2: Model only was passed\n";
    }
    else
    {
        # Second version was called
        print "Car2: Model and Year were passed\n";
    }
    return $s;
}
```

Our two classes (**Car** and **Car2**) are "dummy" for now, as they do not provide any functionality. However, as we build on these classes, they will grow and may become even "Rolls Royce" classes. We wrote a small client program to illustrate the use of these classes and to show their constructors in action. However, before we can work with our classes, we should compile them and build the components. **plc.exe** will do the job for us. The command line will differ from those we used to compile into executables, as now our targets are libraries (DLLs) where our classes will reside. In order to compile the **Car** package, run the command shown below in the command prompt when you are in the same directory where **Car.pm** is located.

```
plc Car.pm -target="library"
```

In the same manner, compile the **Car2.pm** package.

```
plc Car2.pm -target="library"
```

As a result, you built two DLLs, which we will reference in the client program.

You may find the code for our client in the **CarCli\Step1** directory.

Code
Example

```
#
# CarCli.pl
#
use namespace "OI.Samples";

# Car class has single constructor
# We pass it Car Model as string
my $c = Car->new("SuperCar");

# Car2 class has two constructors
# We create two objects using two constructors
my $diesel = Car2->new("Diesel");
my $turbo  = Car2->new("Turbo", int(2001));
```

This simple client program should reference two components (**car.dll** and **car2.dll**). Therefore, after we copy these two DLLs into the same directory where our program resides, the command line for building an executable should look as follows:

```
plc CarCli.pl -reference="car.dll" -reference="car2.dll"
```

Running **CarCli.exe** will display the following information:

```
Car1: Model = SuperCar
Car2: Model only was passed
Car2: Model and Year were passed
```

OVERLOADING BY TYPE

You should pay special attention to the cases when you wish to overload the constructor only by type of parameters and not by their quantity, as the **defined** function will not be helpful. To distinguish the types, the PerlNET module offers a **typeof** function that you may import. This function returns a reference to the **Type** class object, which is initialized with the type that we passed as a parameter to the function. The **Type** class resides in the **System** namespace of .NET Framework and represents the declarations of classes. We may use it to query a class for information about our objects at runtime. To check whether a certain object is an instance of a class, we use the **IsInstanceOfType** method of the **Type** class and pass it the reference to the object. For demonstration purposes, let us take the above **Car** class and change it so it has two constructors, as follows:

```
static Car(int Model);
static Car(str Model);
```

We may now construct our **Car** objects, passing to them the **Model** parameter as an integer or as a string. We should handle the different versions of the constructor accordingly.

```
use PerlNET qw(typeof);
use namespace "System";
. . .
sub new
{
   my ($self, $Model) = @_;
   my $s = bless {}, $self;

   # We have to find out the type of $Model
   if (typeof("Int32")->IsInstanceOfType($Model))
   {
      print "Integer version\n";
   }
   elsif (typeof("String")->IsInstanceOfType($Model))
   {
      print "String version\n";
   }
   return $s;
}
```

We would like to emphasize that for **typeof**, you cannot use PerlNET aliases of .NET types and you have to supply the exact fully qualified name of the .NET type (or omit namespace if you used the **use namespace** pragma, as we did in our sample above).

Defining Properties

Properties for .NET classes play the same role as properties for Core Perl classes. Using properties, we may define different states for our class objects. The general syntax for property definition is shown next.

```
=for interface
   # Optionally other methods/properties
   . . .
   [Access Modifier] <Property Type> PropertyName;
=cut
. . .
# Code for getting/setting property
sub PropertyName
{
```

```
   # Handle getting or setting
}
. . .
```

The access modifier of a property defines its visibility. By default, properties are accessible by all class users. We will explain about different kinds of access modifiers later in this chapter. For now, no access modifier will be applied in our samples. A property type should be one of the .NET-supported types or the PerlNET alias to such a type from Table 11-1. The property name is the name the class user should use to access our property. In addition, a subroutine with the property name should be defined. This subroutine will handle getting and setting operations on our property, as we will explain later.

In the .NET environment, properties are divided into three kinds:

- Read-only
- Write-only
- Read-write

Read-only properties, as their name suggests, may be read and may not be mutated. Write-only may be mutated only. Finally, read-write properties may be read and mutated. Unfortunately, PerlNET has no special syntax for defining the kind of property. However, we can handle this by other means.

When a class interface exposes some property, there has to be a defined subroutine with the same name as property in the body of the Perl module (exactly as in Core Perl modules). After the module is built into a component (DLL), our interface exposes two methods for each defined property, **get_XXX** and **set_XXX**, where XXX is the property name. Whenever the property is accessed or mutated, the PerlNET runtime module readdresses the call to the same subroutine with the name of the property in our Perl module. If we read the property, then no arguments besides the package are passed. If we set the property, the new value is passed as an argument in addition to the package. Hence, we can determine by the arguments list whether our property is being read or mutated and act accordingly. In addition, read-only or write-only behavior may be simulated.

Let us enrich the **Car** class with some properties:

```
=for interface
   str Model;
   int Year;
   int Age;
=cut
```

As you can see, our **Car** class exposes three properties. **Model** and **Year** are read-write and **Age**, which calculates car age (based on **Year** property), is read-only. Until now, there is no difference in definition of read-write and read-only properties. This difference will be reflected in the corresponding subroutines code. **Model** and **Year** are much alike; therefore, we present only the **Year** subroutine:

```perl
sub Year
{
   my($self, $value) = @_;
   # decide if Year is being read or mutated
   if (defined $value)
   {
      # Property is being mutated
      $self->{Year} = $value;
   }
   else
   {
      # Property is being read
      return $self->{Year};
   }
}
```

The code for the **Age** property is slightly different, as we want to simulate the read-only behavior:

```perl
sub Age
{
   my($self, $value) = @_;
   # decide if Age is being read or mutated
   if (defined $value)
   {
      # Property is being mutated
      # Do nothing as Age is Read-only
      return;
   }
   else
   {
      # Property is being read
      # Calculate number of years from
      # Year (of production) to current year.
      my @cur_time = localtime(time);
      my $cur_year = $cur_time(5) + 1900;

      return $cur_year - $self->{Year};
   }
}
```

As you notice, when there is an attempt to set the **Age** property, the call to **set_Age** is readdressed to **sub Age** with an additional value parameter, and the subroutine immediately returns and no error is reported at runtime. Therefore, you may add your own error message to indicate to the developer that he or she cannot set the read-only property. The code below will not mutate the **Car** object.

```perl
my $c = "Car"->new("Turbo", 1999);
$c->{Age} = 5; # No effect - we simulate read-only behavior
```

In the same manner, we may imitate write-only behavior, which is rarely used when defining properties.

Initialization of properties is most likely to happen during the stage of construction. Here is the code for the altered version of the **Car** class constructors. All the calls to constructors are readdressed to the same subroutine, **new**.

```perl
sub new
{
    # We determine which version of constructor was
    # called
    my ($self, $Model, $Year) = @_;
    my $s = bless {}, $self;

    if (!defined $Year)
    {
        # First version was called
        # Call subroutine Model to set the property
        $s->Model($Model);
    }
    else
    {
        # Second version was called
        # Set both properties
        $s->Model($Model);
        $s->Year($Year);
    }
    return $s;
}
```

The **Age** property is not initialized, as we calculate it based on the **Year** property.

Defining Methods

The ability to define states for class objects by setting certain properties is not enough, since very often our classes should provide some functionality and actually do something. For this purpose, we use methods—special member functions—that implement class functionality based on current values of properties and/or parameters.

Generally, you should use the following syntax to define a method properly:

```perl
=for interface
    # Optionally other methods/properties
    . . .
```

```
   # Method definition
   [modifiers] <return type> MethodName([args]);
=cut
 . . .
# Code for the method
sub MethodName
{
   # Do something useful
}
 . . .
```

We may optionally start our method's definition with modifiers, which tell the compiler and/or .NET environment about special characteristics, such as visibility (access modifiers). If a method is independent of the properties' values, then it is preferable to declare such method as a static or class method (it is done by putting a **static** modifier in the method definition). Hence, it may be invoked without instantiating a class object. If the method has some dependency on the properties, then it will be nonstatic (without a **static** modifier). In addition, a static method does not get a package as its first argument, unless it is a constructor. We will meet more modifiers when we discuss the inheritance in .NET in the next chapter.

A return type follows modifiers or starts the line of the definition if no modifiers are applied. It is mandatory to write the return type for each method we define.[6] If the method does not return a value, its return type should be **void**. After the return type, we write the method name. In brackets we define for each parameter of the method a pair—**<arg type>, <arg name>**—delimited with commas. Optionally, the method can get no arguments. If this is the case, we leave the brackets empty. The code for the method is defined inside the subroutine with the same name as our method. There may be several versions of the method (method overloading). These versions must differ by their signature.

We handle overloaded versions of methods exactly the same way as we do for constructors, using **defined** or **typeof** functions inside the corresponding method subroutine.

For better understanding, we illustrate defining methods on our **Car** class. We define two nonstatic methods: **OutputCarInfo** prints formatted information about the car. **CalculateCarAge** returns the age of the car. This method has two versions: without parameters and with one integer **Year** parameter. The former version returns the current age of the car—the **Age** property. The latter version returns the age of the car in the year specified as parameter **Year**. Calls to these two methods are readdressed to the same **CalculateCarAge** subroutine; inside that we should decide which version was called by examining

---

6. The only exceptions for this rule are class constructors. We may omit the return type in their definitions.

the arguments list and act accordingly. In addition, there is one static method, **ClassInfo**, which outputs help information about the **Car** class interface.

```
# Interface definition
=for interface
   void OutputCarInfo();
   int CalculateCarAge();
   int CalculateCarAge(int Year);
   static void ClassInfo(str delim);
=cut
# Output information about the car
sub OutputCarInfo
{
   my $self = shift;
   print "Car model: ", $self->Model(),"\n";
   print "Year of production: ";
   print $self->Year(),"\n";
   print "End of report\n";
}
# Calculate car age - two version in one subroutine
sub CalculateCarAge
{
   my ($self, $year) = @_;
   if (defined $year)
   {
      return $year-$self->Year();
   }
   else
   {
      return $self->Age();
   }
}
# static method - no package as first parameter
sub ClassInfo
{
   my $delim = shift;
   print "Read-Write Properties: ";
   print "Model", $delim, "Year\n";
   print "Read-Only Properties: Age\n";
   print "Non-static Methods: ";
   print "OutputCarInfo", $delim, "CalculateCarAge\n";
   print "Static Methods: ";
   print "ClassInfo\n";
   print "End of Report\n";
}
```

Access Modifiers

The object-oriented paradigm offers a concept of information hiding. This means that the information, which is used inside a class only, should not be accessible by the class users. In Core Perl we assumed that class users "play by the rules" and do not access private object parts (through hash reference). In PerlNET this concept is fully implemented, and other .NET programs that are clients of our .NET component will not be able to gather access to the private parts of our class. This became possible by introducing **access modifiers** for methods definitions:

- public
- private
- protected

If no access modifier is applied for a method or a property, the corresponding class member is assumed to be **public**—in other words, accessible for everybody.

When we want to hide the class members, we use either **private** or **protected** modifiers. If the **private** modifier appears in a method or a property definition, then the corresponding member is accessible by other class members **only**. The **protected** modifier hides the class members, but allows access to the methods in the inherited classes from the base class where the protected method or property was defined. We will see a sample of using **protected** in Chapter 12 when we discuss inheritance.

We decided to hide the **Age** property from the users, as it is already accessible indirectly when passing no parameters to the **CalculateCarAge** method. Therefore, we apply the **private** modifier to the **Age** property inside the interface definition. Other code remains intact.

```
=for interface
    private int Age;
=cut
```

Code Example

The full version of the **Car** class that we developed throughout the chapter is located in **Car\Step2** under the chapter samples directory.

Car Client Program

Code Example

The client program, which exploits the functionality of the **Car** class, resides in **CarCli\Step2**. Here is the client code for your convenience.

```
#
# CarCli.pl
#
use strict;
use namespace "OI.Samples";
use PerlNET qw(AUTOCALL);

# Use static method and output Car class info
# Delimiter string is passed as parameter
"Car"->ClassInfo(", ");
```

```perl
# Construct Car object BMW
my $bmw = "Car"->new("BMW 327i", 1997);

# Output BMW car information
print "------------------------------\n";
print "Car Info\n";
print "--------\n";
$bmw->OutputCarInfo();

my ($age_2000, $cur_age);
$age_2000 = $bmw->CalculateCarAge(2000);
$cur_age  = $bmw->CalculateCarAge();
print "Car age in 2000 was: ", $age_2000, "\n";
print "Car age now is: ", $cur_age, "\n";

# Upgrade car to the newer of the same model
print "Upgrading to 2002...\n";
$bmw->{Year} = 2002;
$cur_age  = $bmw->CalculateCarAge();
print "Age of new car is: ", $cur_age, "\n";

# Change model of BMW
print "Replacing by 518...\n";
$bmw->{Model} = "BMW 518";

# Print upgraded car information
print "------------------------------\n";
print "New Car Info\n";
print "------------\n";
$bmw->OutputCarInfo();

print "------------------------------\n";
```

Here is the output:

```
Read-Write Properties: Model, Year
Read-Only Properties: Age
Non-static Methods: OutputCarInfo, CalculateCarAge
Static Methods: ClassInfo
End of Report
-------------------------------
Car Info
--------
Car model: BMW 327i
Year of production: 1997
End of report
Car age in 2000 was: 3
Car age now is: 5
Upgrading to 2002...
Age of new car is: 0
```

```
Replacing by 518...
-------------------------------
New Car Info
------------
Car model: BMW 518
Year of production: 2002
End of report
-------------------------------
```

StockItem Example

For the sake of variety, we offer in this section another sample of a PerlNET component with full code. This sample is the translation of the C# sample that we presented at the beginning of this chapter. The PerlNET component has the same interface as its C# analogue, so its usage is identical to the C# component.

EXAMPLE CODE

Here we present the code, which is followed by short explanations. After reading and understanding the previous sections of this chapter, you should find this code very easy to deal with. The code is located in the **Stock\PerlNET\StockItem.pm** file under the chapter samples directory.

```perl
#
# StockItem.pm
#
package OI::Samples::StockItem;

use strict;
use PerlNET qw(bool);

# Constructor
=for interface
    [interface: pure]
    static StockItem(int id, str name);
=cut

# Properties
=for interface
    int ID;
    str Name;
=cut

# Method
=for interface
    void OutputItem(bool lines);
=cut

# Constructor definition
```

```perl
sub new
{
   my $self = shift;
   my ($id, $name) = @_;
   my $s = {ID => $id,
            Name => $name};
   bless $s, $self;
   return $s;
}

# ID read-only Property
sub ID
{
   my($self, $value) = @_;
   if (defined $value)
   {
      # We want make ID read-only, so we just return
      return;
   }
   else
   {
      $self->{ID};
   }
}

# Name read-write Property
sub Name
{
   my($self, $value) = @_;
   if (defined $value)
   {
      $self->{Name} = $value;
      return;
   }
   else
   {
      $self->{Name};
   }
}

# OutputItem method
sub OutputItem
{
   my($self, $lines) = @_;
   if (bool($lines))
   {
      print "--------------------------\n";
   }
   print $self->{ID}, " ", $self->{Name}, "\n";
   if (bool($lines))
```

```
    {
        print "--------------------------\n";
    }
}
```

To compile this PerlNET component, run **plc** in the following form:

```
plc StockItem.pm -target="library"
```

StockItem.dll will be created, and we may reference it when compiling the **StockItemCli** program, which was created to test the C# component at the beginning of this chapter. The output will be identical:

```
------------------------
1       item 1
------------------------
------------------------
0       item 0
1       item 1
2       item 2
3       item 3
4       item 4
------------------------
ID of Second Item: 1
Name of Second Item: item 1
New Name of Second Item: Pencil
```

EXAMPLE DISCUSSION

The code we have just presented for the PerlNET **StockItem** component may be used by Core Perl programs as easily as any other Perl module. There are several blocks in the code that are necessary for integrating into the .NET environment or that have another meaning when used in .NET. Here we present their .NET interpretation.

```
package OI::Samples::StockItem;
```

This line defines **StockItem** inside the **OI.Samples** namespace. This means that the fully qualified name for our class will be **OI.Samples.StockItem**.

You should additionally notice several **=for interface** POD blocks. To remind you, they are used to expose methods and properties definitions to the .NET environment (class interface definition), and they have no effect when the package is used with Core Perl. These blocks do not have to be divided into several parts—you can write all the definitions in one POD block. We did it for the sake of accuracy and readability of our code.

```
# Constructor
=for interface
    [interface: pure]
    static StockItem(int id, str name);
=cut
```

The constructor for the class should have the same name as the class. In the same manner, we defined properties and methods.

```
# Properties
=for interface
   int ID;
   str Name;
=cut

# Method
=for interface
   void OutputItem(bool lines);
=cut
```

We define the code for methods and properties getters and setters with the **sub** keyword, exactly as with Core Perl subroutines.

Using PerlNET Components in C#

We stated before that our PerlNET components can be easily integrated in other .NET programs. These programs may be written in any .NET-compliant language. In this section, we back this statement with a C# client program that works with the **Car** class, which we developed throughout the chapter. The C# code is simple and quite intuitive.

```csharp
//
// CarCli.cs
//

// Standard System namespace
using System;
// Our Car class namespace
using OI.Samples;

class CarCli
{
   public static void Main(string[] args)
   {
      // Use static method and output Car class info
      // Delimiter string is passed as parameter
      Car.ClassInfo(", ");

      // Construct Car object BMW
      Car BMW = new Car("BMW 327i", 1997);

      // Output BMW car information
      Console.WriteLine("--------------------------");
      Console.WriteLine("Car Info");
```

```
        Console.WriteLine("--------");
        BMW.OutputCarInfo();
        int age_2000, cur_age;
        age_2000 = BMW.CalculateCarAge(2000);
        cur_age  = BMW.CalculateCarAge();
        Console.Write("Car age in 2000 was: {0}\n",
                                       age_2000);
        Console.WriteLine("Car age now is: {0}\n",
                                       cur_age);

        // Upgrade car to the newer of the same model
        Console.WriteLine("Upgrading to 2002...");
        BMW.Year = 2002;
        cur_age  = BMW.CalculateCarAge();
        Console.Write("Age of new car is: {0}\n",
                                       cur_age);
        // Change model of BMW
        Console.WriteLine("Replacing by 518...");
        BMW.Model = "BMW 518";

        // Print upgraded car information
        Console.WriteLine("New Car Info");
        Console.WriteLine("------------");
        BMW.OutputCarInfo();

        Console.WriteLine("-------------------------");
    }
}
```

To compile this program, use the C# compiler and run the following commands (first to build **car.dll** and then to build **CarCli.exe**):

```
plc Car.pm -target="library"
csc /reference:car.dll CarCli.cs
```

The output for the C# **Car** class client is

```
Read-Write Properties: Model, Year
Read-Only Properties: Age
Non-static Methods: OutputCarInfo, CalculateCarAge
Static Methods: ClassInfo
End of Report
------------------------------
Car Info
--------
Car model: BMW 327i
Year of production: 1997
End of report
Car age in 2000 was: 3
Car age now is: 5
```

```
Upgrading to 2002...
Age of new car is: 0
Replacing by 518...
New Car Info
------------
Car model: BMW 518
Year of production: 2002
End of report
-------------------------------
```

The code for the C# sample is located in the **CarCli\Cs** folder under the chapter samples directory.

Wrapping Existing Perl Modules

One of the most powerful features of PerlNET is the ability to make the existing Perl packages available to the .NET environment. This feature may be applied to Perl modules that were downloaded from CPAN or to any others. Whenever you decide to provide Perl module functionality to .NET, you should create a .NET component using PerlNET that will expose its class interface. This interface should define all the functionality that you wish to be available to .NET applications. Actually, this way we create a wrapper class for the Perl module. The role of this class is to readdress .NET calls to the corresponding module subroutines.

There are two major types of modules:

- Library of subroutines
- Classes

By *library of subroutines,* we mean modules that offer subroutines unified under the same topic, but do not represent any class module—that is, should not be instantiated with the **new** method prior to usage. We saw the sample **Roman.pm** for such a module type in Chapter 8. When programming for .NET, we must define a class. Therefore, for this type of module, we create a class with all **static** methods and without a constructor, as we should not instantiate objects for such class.[7]

If we are going to wrap a **class module**, then we define nonstatic methods and properties in our PerlNET class interface. In both cases, the **[interface: pure]** attribute has to present inside the interface definition as we deal with the Core Perl modules.

In this section, we will show one sample of the wrapping for each module type. The **Roman** module will serve as the example of **Library of subrou-**

---

7. PerlNET will create the default constructor for the class, which will do nothing.

tines. We will take the **Whitespace** module from CPAN, which cleans up bogus spaces, as our **class module** example.

Library of Subroutines Sample

We present the sample for wrapping the **Roman** module, which was described in Chapter 8. One of the rules of wrapping is to give the same package name and namespace as of the original module to our PerlNET package for a .NET component. Therefore, the **Roman** method, which translates the arabic numbers into roman numbers with the uppercase letters, should have a different name. Otherwise, it will be considered as the constructor for the **Roman** class, and this is not what we want. Hence, in the interface definition, we declare the **romanUC** method. The subroutine for this method readdresses the call to the original **Roman** function. You must require the **Roman** module after the interface definition. Here is the code with the renamed **Roman** method (we placed the sample in the **Wrapping\Roman** folder).

Code
Example

```
#
# Roman.pm
#
package Roman;

use strict;

=for interface
   [interface: pure]
   static str roman(int ar);
   static str romanUC(int ar);
   static bool isroman(str rom);
   static int arabic(str rom);
=cut

require Roman;

sub romanUC
{
    return Roman::Roman(shift);
}
```

Class Sample

Here is how wrapping is done for the **Whitespace** class module from CPAN (you may find the code in **Wrapping\WhiteSpace**).

```
#
# Whitespace.pm
#
```

```perl
package Whitespace;

use strict;

=for interface
   [interface: pure]
   static Whitespace(str infile);
   static Whitespace(str infile, str outfile);
   int detect();
   int cleanup();
   wantarray! str[] Status();
   str error();
   int leadclean();
   int trailclean();
   int indentclean();
   int spacetabclean();
   int eolclean();
=cut

require Whitespace;

sub Status
{
   my $self = shift;
   my @arr = %{$self->status()};
   return @arr;
}
```

When wrapping a Perl module, we have the freedom to decide which methods to expose to .NET and which not to. This is why we did not include all the methods enumerated in the **Whitespace** class module. When wrapping the **Whitespace** class module, we had to perform some workaround on the **status** method. This method returns a hash with counters for all whitespaces that were detected. The .NET environment does not "know" how to handle Perl hashes, so we cannot use the returned hash. However, we can convert any hash into a list (array) of strings. We implant our function **Status** into class interface (the function should have a different name from module function— changing case of the first letter is enough). In the body of the **Status** function, we call the original **status** and assign the return value to an array, which is returned to the .NET environment. Since **Status** returns an array, we have to add the **wantarray!** method modifier in the function definition.

```perl
wantarray! str[] Status();
```

The **Whitespace** class can be initialized with one or two filename parameters; hence, we overload the constructor. Before the definition of the constructors, we write the **[interface: pure]** attribute.

Using Wrapped Components in C#

Here we present a short C# client program that uses the **Whitespace** wrapped module to perform the clean-up operations on the **input.txt** file.

```csharp
//
// WhitespaceCli.cs
using System;

public class WhitespaceCli
{
    public static void Main(string[] args)
    {
        // construct object
        Whitespace ws = new Whitespace("input.txt",
                                        "output.txt");

        // Detect bogus whitespaces
        int det = ws.detect();
        string err = ws.error();

        // Check if there was an error
        if (err != null)
        {
            Console.WriteLine(err);
            return;
        }
        Console.Write("{0} bogus whitespaces found\n",
                                                det);

        if (det > 0)
        {
            // Output information
            // about detected whitespaces
            string[] stat = ws.Status();
            foreach (string s in stat)
            {
                Console.WriteLine(s);
            }

            // Perform input file clean-up
            ws.cleanup();
        }
    }
}
```

The code for this program is located in the **Wrapping\WhitespaceCli** folder under the chapter samples directory. In addition, see the **Wrapping\Roman-Cli** folder, which contains the client program for the **Roman** module.

Summary

In this chapter, we laid the foundation for understanding component development and discussed the advantages of this approach. We covered the topic of the interface definition in PerlNET in detail: defining constructors, properties, and methods, and using attributes. We presented the full example of a PerlNET component that may be easily integrated in any .NET application. In addition, we described wrapping of the existing Perl modules and showed the use samples of the resulting .NET components in the .NET programs.

Until now, we wrote Pure Perl components. In the next chapter, we will present .NET and Mixed types. Moreover, we will see how we can create complex components using advanced object-oriented techniques.

Component Development: In-Depth Discussion

*T*his chapter, as its name suggests, is dedicated to a closer and more detailed discussion of component development. In this chapter, we present two new types of PerlNET components: .NET types and Mixed types. While these two types have much in common, there are some differences in their capabilities and usage that we explain in this chapter. Next, we look inside assemblies with the help of the **ILDASM** tool to better understand the underlying principles of component development. Then, we cover .NET inheritance issues. Interfaces are an important part of the .NET environment, and we dedicate a section of this chapter to examining them. Finally, the secrets of exceptions and error-handling mechanisms are revealed. The chapter presents a rich set of examples to help you get on track with component development issues.

PerlNET Component Types

In Chapter 11 we learned about some good and powerful techniques of component programming in PerlNET. We focused on one type of component: Pure Perl. This choice was not casual, as developing such components is almost identical to developing Core Perl module packages. Moreover, the Core Perl scripts can transparently use these components, unless we used .NET classes when developing Pure Perl components. However, because of being so close to Core Perl, Pure Perl components are limited inside the .NET environment. Hence, we need another type of components to resolve these limitations. PerlNET offers us .NET types and Mixed types. We therefore must learn how to work with three different PerlNET types:

- Pure Perl
- .NET
- Mixed

We concentrate first on the main characteristics of each type and then give general advice on their use.

Pure Perl Components

First, let us summarize the rules for building a Pure Perl component. We may repeat the facts you already know in order to strengthen understanding of the material.

Component definition starts with declaring a package. Optionally, we may define namespace for the class in the following manner:

```
package Namespace::ClassName;
```

Pure Perl components must have an interface definition with the declaration of methods and properties that we are willing to expose to the .NET world. As a part of this interface, there should present the **[interface: pure]** attribute, which actually gives the instruction to treat the component as pure.

There may be several versions of class constructors (constructor overloading). All the constructors must have the same name, which is the name of the class exposed by the component. If a constructor overloading occurs, then each constructor must have a different signature. No matter how many constructors were defined for the class, the PerlNET runtime module will readdress the calls when constructing an object of our class to the same method, **new**. This method should be defined in the package and distinguish different versions of constructors according to the arguments list. The **new** method has to return a reference to a hash that was blessed to our package (class).

For each declared method, there should be defined a subroutine with the same name as the method. If we overload a method, then different versions must have different signatures (the same as constructor overloading). The call to the overloaded method will be readdressed to the same subroutine with the method's name, and the version of the method will be determined after examining the arguments.

For each property that we define, we should supply a subroutine with the same name as the property. This subroutine handles getting and setting operations on our properties. When setting the property, a new value is passed through the arguments list to the subroutine.

Whenever we call a nonstatic method, get or set a nonstatic property, the first argument that is passed to the corresponding subroutine is the reference to the hash that was returned by the **new** method when constructing new instance of the class (exactly as in case of Core Perl class modules). Therefore, the first line of each nonstatic method or property subroutine should get the hash so that we can call methods and access properties of the current instance of the class.

```
sub NonStaticMethodOrProperty
{
    my $self = shift;

    # Access $self hash
    . . .
}
```

or

```
sub NonStaticMethodOrProperty
{
    my ($self, @args) = @_;

    # Examine @args and Access $self hash
    . . .
}
```

Static methods work in a slightly different manner. As we explained earlier, static methods are invoked without instantiating of the class object. They provide general functionality rather than being bound to the specific properties. Therefore, the subroutines that correspond to the static methods do not get a reference to the hash, and the first entry in their arguments list is the first argument that was passed by a method caller.

```
sub StaticMethodOrProperty
{
    my @args = @_;
    # Examine args if were passed and do something
    . . .
}
```

We mentioned that there are some limitations to using Pure Perl components. This chapter tells us about advanced component development, including such operations as implementing .NET interfaces, deriving components from other .NET classes, inheriting from PerlNET components, and handling exceptions. Merely the latter is available to Pure Perl components. All the other operations may be employed for .NET and Mixed types.

.NET and Mixed Types

PerlNET provides you with tools to develop fully .NET-compliant components that may implement interfaces, inherit from other classes, serve as base classes, and so on. The classes that define these components are also referred to as .NET types. Of course, being so close to the .NET environment will limit the

.NET types in the use of Core Perl structures such as arrays or hashes. However, as we saw in Chapter 10, the .NET Framework offers alternate classes for these structures. In addition, Mixed types may be a good solution for combining Perl and .NET structures. Mixed types allow you to store the Perl references in a blessed hash.

We first describe the .NET types. Then it will be easy for you to understand the essence of their close relatives—Mixed types.

.NET TYPES

We would like to describe the milestones that we pass through when developing .NET type components. Developing .NET type components is similar to developing Pure Perl type components.

Type definition should start with declaring a package, exactly as in the case of Pure Perl types (with an optional namespace declaration for our class).

```
package Namespace::MyClass;
```

When we define a .NET type, the code should contain **=for interface** POD blocks with interface definition. The **[interface: pure]** attribute should *not* appear in any of these blocks. Constructors and methods definition syntax is the same as in Pure Perl types. However, for constructors there should be a defined subroutine with the same name as our class, and not **new**.

.NET types that we develop with PerlNET work in a different manner from Pure Perl, and PerlNET runtime modules handle them differently. One of the significant distinctions is that we work with reference to our object and not with reference to a hash. As a result, all the subroutines that implement constructors, methods, and properties handling get the reference to the .NET object, and we should work with this reference in our subroutines as with any other .NET object reference. For example, the subroutine for the constructor serves more as an initializer than as a constructor, as it gets as its first argument a reference to an already constructed object. All that remains to do is initialize our object state. Additionally, properties will be implemented slightly differently, as we cannot save their values in a hash anymore. The solution will be to use fields (another type of class members that we can declare when defining our interface).

When extracting an object reference from an arguments list, we use the **$this** name for the variable to store this reference. This is true for nonstatic methods. Static methods, as previously explained, do not get any reference as a first argument. Constructors are declared as static, but they are an exception, and their first argument is the reference to an already instantiated (by PerlNET runtime) object. This is how the first lines of our subroutines inside a package for .NET type may look:

```
sub NonStaticMethod
{
    # $this gets object reference
```

```
    # Same is true for constructor
    # subroutine
    my ($this, @args) = @_;

    # Work with $this and @args
    .  .  .
}

sub StaticMethod
{
    # No reference to this object
    # NOT true for the constructors
    my @args = @_;

    # Work with @args
    .  .  .
}

# Constructor for the class MyClass
sub MyClass
{
    # Get reference to this object
    # Despite the fact MyClass should be
    # declared as static
    my ($this, @args) = @_;

    # Perform Initializations
    .  .  .
}
```

We access our object's internal parts through an arrow reference syntax on the **$this** variable. You have to remember that **$this** is an object reference.

.NET TYPE SAMPLE

We translated the sample of the **StockItem** class from the previous chapter so that it answers the definition of a .NET type class. The changes are minor, but they are principal. We bolded the important lines of the code. After the listing there is a discussion dedicated to the changes we have made. You can find the code for the new version of the **StockItem** class saved under the chapter samples directory in the **StockItem\Step1** folder.

Code
Example

```
#
# StockItem.pm
#
package OI::Samples::StockItem;

use strict;
use PerlNET qw(bool);
```

```perl
# Constructor
=for interface
   # No [interface: pure] attribute
   static StockItem(int id, str name);
=cut

# Fields
=for interface
   private field int f_ID;
   private field str f_Name;
=cut

# Properties
=for interface
   int ID;
   str Name;
=cut

# Methods
=for interface
   void OutputItem(bool lines);
   static void ClassInfo(str delim);
=cut

# Constructor definition
sub StockItem
{
   # Get REFERENCE to the object
   my $this = shift;
   my ($id, $name) = @_;
   $this->{f_ID} = $id;
   $this->{f_Name} = $name;
}

# ID read-only Property
sub ID
{
   my($this, $value) = @_;
   if (defined $value)
   {
      # We want make ID read-only, so we just return
      return;
   }
   else
   {
      # Return field that stores property value
      $this->{f_ID};
   }
}
```

```
# Name - read-write Property
sub Name
{
   my($this, $value) = @_;
   if (defined $value)
   {
      # Set field that stores property value
      $this->{f_Name} = $value;
      return;
   }
   else
   {
      # Return field that stores property value
      $this->{f_Name};
   }
}

# OutputItem method
sub OutputItem
{
   my($this, $lines) = @_;
   if (bool($lines))
   {
      print "--------------------------\n";
   }
   print $this->{f_ID}, " ", $this->{f_Name}, "\n";
   if (bool($lines))
   {
      print "--------------------------\n";
   }
}

# static method - outputs name and version of the class
sub ClassInfo
{
   # No reference to object is passed
   # as this is static method
   my $delim = shift;
   print "Class Name: StockItem", $delim;
   print "Class Version: 1.0 .NET type\n";
}
```

There is no **[interface: pure]** attribute anymore, as this is a .NET type class. The constructor definition inside the **[for interface]** POD block stays intact. However, there is no **new** subroutine. It is replaced by a subroutine with the class name, **StockItem**. As in the case of Pure Perl, the constructor should be **static**.

You should notice a new **[for interface]** block with definitions of fields. Fields are member variables of a class. They are accessed directly through the memory location, using hash-reference syntax. No **get_XXX** and **set_XXX** methods are generated for fields, and we do not need to define any subroutine for handling get or set operations on fields. The most popular use of fields is to store private data of the object or current values of properties. We do not have a hash reference to our class anymore, and we cannot store and retrieve values of properties to and from a hash, as with Pure Perl types, but we do have a reference to our object, through which we may access the methods, the properties, and the fields that were defined in the class interface. In the **StockItem** sample, we applied the **private** modifier to both fields so that they will be invisible to class users. When this modifier follows the **field** keyword, it informs the compiler that we defined a field. This keyword should be present in every field definition before the type of the field.

Two properties definitions stayed intact from the Pure Perl version. We still have to define two subroutines to handle get and set operations. Theoretically, we could manage with fields only, but using properties, we may execute some code, perform some calculations before getting or setting a value, and limit access to the private data members.

Every subroutine for a nonstatic method or property gets a reference to an object, which we store in the **$this** variable. Through this reference, we have access to our object data and methods. The only static methods that get a reference to the object as a first argument are constructors (see constructor subroutine **sub StockItem**). Other subroutines for the static methods do not get this reference (see **sub ClassInfo**, the subroutine for the static method).

MIXED TYPES

Using .NET types does not allow us to store Perl-specific structures (arrays or hashes) as an instance data of our classes (packages). If you want to utilize the advanced features of .NET types and still store some instance data inside Core Perl arrays or hashes, then implementing a Mixed type is the right choice for you.

We will add the following attribute to specify that we intend to create a Mixed type component:

```
=for interface
    [interface: Mixed]
=cut
```

"Mixing" mainly occurs inside the arguments lists of every subroutine. PerlNET will implicitly provide the subroutines of a Mixed type with two parameters: **$this** (a reference to the object itself) and **$self** (a reference to a blessed hash for storing Perl references). The former references the object itself. With help of the latter, you may store or retrieve values from a blessed hash. You may store in the hash even references to subroutines. However, providing private methods results in more readable code.

Here is how you may retrieve both pointers and parameters in your sub-routine code:

```
sub SomeMethod
{
    my ($this, $self, @args) = @_;
    . . .
}
```

It is always better to see one full sample than to read a hundred explanations, so let's see a Mixed type in action.

MIXED TYPE SAMPLE

To demonstrate a Mixed type, we will create a component for simulating simplified casino roulette. We will write a Perl package that will treat the following scenario. Each participating gambler will choose a number between 0 and 36 and make a stake. Upon receiving all the stakes, a random number will be generated, and the results of the round will be printed. In case of the correct guess the gambler will win 36 times his or her stake; otherwise the prize will be zero.

There are many possibilities for implementation, but for pedagogical reasons, we will choose a Mixed type for our component. We will use a two-dimensional Perl array for storing gambling data, so that for each gambler, we will create a new row with two entries: the chosen number and the stake. The code is stored in the **Roulette** folder.

```
#
# Roulette.pm
#

package OI::Samples::Roulette;
use strict;

# Define Mixed type
=for interface
    [interface: mixed]
=cut

# Methods
=for interface
    # Add new stake
    void AddStake(int guess, num stake);
    # Roll the roulette - generate the result
    int Roll();
    # Output the results for all gamblers
    private void OutputResults(int number);
=cut

# Private Data Member: Last Gambler ID
```

```
=for interface
   private field int f_LastGambler;
=cut

sub Roulette
{
   my ($this, $self) = @_;
   $this->{f_LastGambler} = 0;
   $self->{Stakes} = [];
}

sub AddStake
{
   my ($this, $self, $guess, $stake) = @_;
   my $i = $this->{f_LastGambler};
   $self->{Stakes}->[$i][0] = $guess;
   $self->{Stakes}->[$i][1] = $stake;
   $this->{f_LastGambler}++;
}

sub Roll
{
   # We do not retrieve $self since we do not need it
   my $this = shift;

   my $result = int(rand(37));
   $this->OutputResults($result);

   return $result;
}

sub OutputResults
{
   my ($this, $self, $result) = @_;

   print "*************************\n";
   print "The winning number is: ", $result, "!\n";
   print "*************************\n";
   print "-------------------------\n";
   my ($guess, $stake, $prize);
   for (my $i = 0; $i < $this->{f_LastGambler}; $i++)
   {
      $guess = $self->{Stakes}->[$i][0];
      $stake = $self->{Stakes}->[$i][1];
      $prize = ($result == $guess ? 36*$stake : 0);
      printf("Gambler %d:\n", $i+1);
      printf("Your prize is: %.2f\n", $prize);
      print "-------------------------\n";
   }
}
```

Code
Example

The bolded lines of code treat the access to a blessed hash. Notice that there are no interface entries for the **Stakes** Perl array reference inside the **=for interface** blocks. All the class members that appear in the interface definition are accessed through the **$this** object reference, as in regular .NET types. The **$self** part of our class is not visible from outside to the class users, and they will have to "play" **Roulette** through the interface we provided.

To test our Mixed type, we wrote **RouletteGame**, a small client program. It makes three stakes and rolls the roulette. The output of the results is performed by the **OutputResults** private method of the **Roulette** class.

```
#
# RouletteGame.pl
#

use strict;
use namespace "OI.Samples";

# Instantiate Roulette
my $roulette = Roulette->new();

# Make three stakes
$roulette->AddStake(15, 2);
$roulette->AddStake(36, 1.5);
$roulette->AddStake(0, 3.5);

# Roll it
$roulette->Roll();
```

You shouldn't observe any differences between the use of the Mixed type and other .NET components. After running the program many times, we finally won a modest prize:

```
*************************
The winning number is: 36!
*************************

-------------------------
Gambler 1:
Your prize is: 0.00
-------------------------
Gambler 2:
Your prize is: 54.00
-------------------------
Gambler 3:
Your prize is: 0.00
-------------------------
```

We hope that you will be even luckier. Make your stakes, but don't forget to keep on reading the book.

Choosing a Type for the Component

As we saw, Pure Perl types are similar in usage and implementation to Core Perl class modules. They allow us to use the standard Perl structures, which are more efficient than the .NET equivalents. As a result, based on the original Perl technology, we may write powerful components that will easily integrate with other .NET applications. On the other hand, Pure Perl classes are limited inside the .NET environment, as they are *sealed*, which means that no other .NET class can inherit from them. Moreover, these classes cannot inherit from the other .NET classes and cannot implement .NET interfaces.

The best way to utilize a Pure Perl type is to wrap existing Perl modules by providing interface definitions for them, as shown in the previous chapter. Also, you may consider using Pure Perl types when you want your class to serve as both a .NET component and a Core Perl module. Of course, no .NET calls may be done.

.NET and Mixed types allow PerlNET to tap into the .NET environment. Here are some benefits that we gather by implementing these types:

- Implementing .NET interfaces
- Extending .NET classes
- Serving as base classes for other .NET types

.NET types and Mixed types are identical in all the aspects except for ability of the latter to store Perl references inside a blessed hash. Hence, we may treat them both as .NET types. Upon deciding to implement your component as .NET type, you should ask yourself about your preferences to store the data. If native Perl structures seem relevant to you, then make it a Mixed type. Otherwise, stay with a regular .NET type.

> **Note**
>
> The features of .NET types described in the rest of this chapter are applicable to both .NET and Mixed types unless we distinguish between them.

Summarizing this section, we emphasize that all PerlNET types you implement will be built as .NET components, and as such, they have many things in common. You will see this throughout the rest of this chapter, which is partly dedicated to the detailed explanations of how to work with .NET types in PerlNET. In addition, advanced topics that are applicable to both Pure Perl and .NET component types, such as exception handling, are covered.

Inheritance

An important feature of the object-oriented paradigm is the ability to specify a common functionality for different classes and implement it inside one class. All classes (descendants) that should share this functionality will inherit from that class (base class). We may also say that descendant classes extend a base class, increasing our code reusability and reducing the possibility of errors (useful for debugging).

PerlNET provides a convenient and easy-to-use way to inherit from .NET classes. In this section, you will find all the required information for implementing inheritance.

System.Object

In the previous section, we stated that only .NET types in PerlNET may extend other .NET classes. The **System.Object** class is kind of an exception to this rule. Every .NET class *must* inherit from **System.Object**, and Pure Perl classes must therefore inherit from **System.Object** as well. Moreover, even an executable PerlNET program is wrapped by a .NET class, which inherits from **System.Object**. We demonstrate with the following sample:

```
#
# Simplest.pl
#
print "The Simplest Program\n";
```

We may compile this Perl program with the **plc** program and convert it into .NET assembly. However, there is not even the tiniest hint of extending some class in this one line of code.

Code Example

To illustrate what we get upon compiling our program, we use **ILDASM** tool that is provided with the .NET Framework SDK. It takes us inside our assemblies, revealing their structure. First, compile **Simplest.pl** and then run the tool from the command line—type **ildasm**. You should see an empty window with a menu bar. Choose **File | Open** and then browse to **Simplest.exe** in the **Simplest** folder under this chapter's samples directory. You should see the window illustrated in Figure 12-1.

The square with three lines denotes a class inside our assembly. We clearly see that our assembly exposes two classes, although we did not define either of them in our simple program.

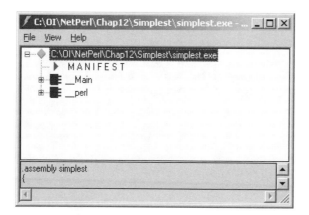

| FIGURE 12-1 | **ILDASM** *shows an assembly created by PerlNET.* |

The __**perl** class is generated by the Perl compiler and is added to every assembly that originates from PerlNET code. This class helps to interpret the code of our program or component by communicating with the PerlNET run-time modules.

The __**Main** class was automatically generated for our program by **plc**. We may expand its branch and look inside, as illustrated in Figure 12-2.

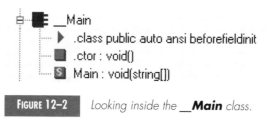

| FIGURE 12-2 | *Looking inside the* __***Main*** *class.* |

The first item in the __**Main** class, with the triangle from the left, is the class manifest. We can double-click this item to get more information about the class. If we do so, then a new window pops up with the following text:

```
.class public auto ansi beforefieldinit __Main
        extends [mscorlib] System.Object
{
} // end of class __Main
```

The second line of the class manifest states that our __**Main** class extends **System.Object**. Recall that we did not declare a class and there was no word about inheritance or extending in our simple program. Thus, the Perl compiler does this automatically. The same thing (inheriting from **System.Object**) occurs with every PerlNET component we compile with **plc**.

Besides the manifest, we see two other entries under the __Main branch. The first is a constructor that is called internally by the CLR. The second is the **Main** method. As previously stated, every .NET executable assembly contains a class with the **Main** method. Either we may define this method explicitly or **plc** will do it for us in addition to wrapping our simple program by a .NET class. The **Main** method is an entry point to our program. The CLR looks inside the executable assembly for the class with this method and calls it. If no such method is found, an error occurs. That is why the PerlNET compiler generates for us a class with the public **Main** method.

Deriving from .NET Classes

We just saw the demonstration of implicit inheritance from **System.Object**. Now, we will learn how to inherit from any non-sealed .NET class using PerlNET.

EXTENDS ATTRIBUTE

We would like to extend functionality of **StockItem** and write a new class named **BookItem**, which will represent any book in our stock. To inherit from **StockItem**, we have to use the **[extends: ...]** attribute in our class interface definition for the **BookItem** class.

```
package OI::Samples::BookItem;

# Using extends attribute
=for interface
    [extends: StockItem]
=cut
# Other interface definitions and subroutines
. . .
```

The .NET environment does not support multiple inheritance, which means that we can extend one class only. Therefore, the **[extends: ...]** attribute should appear at most once in our PerlNET class interface definition.

CREATING INHERITED COMPONENTS

Inheriting from other .NET classes gives us an option to use all the functions that were defined in the base class. However, we should perform some additional work. One of our tasks is to define a constructor for our new class, and there are no innovations in this—we do it the same way as we did for all our classes. Our package—from the **BookItem\Step1** folder—looks like this:

```
package OI::Samples::BookItem;

=for interface
    [extends: StockItem]
```

Code
Example

```
      static BookItem(int id, str name);
=cut

# Constructor subroutine
sub BookItem
{
   my($this, $id, $name) = @_;

   $this->{f_ID} = $id;
   $this->{f_Name} = $name;
}
```

This package does not give any extended functionality, but we will study it for a while and enrich its interface step by step. For now, we just copy the functionality of **StockItem**. When building the package with **plc**, we have to reference the DLL where the base class resides.

```
plc BookItem.pm -target="library"
-reference="stockitem.dll"
```

Running the above command results in the following error:

```
error CS1501: No overload for method 'StockItem' takes '0'
 arguments
```

This actually means that our **StockItem** class interface was not properly defined to serve as a base class for other PerlNET classes. Other .NET-compliant languages will inherit successfully from **StockItem**, but PerlNET requires that any base class defines a default constructor—a constructor with no parameters. Otherwise, we cannot extend the class in PerlNET. As a result, we have to perform modifications to **StockItem** and overload the constructor.

```
# Constructor
=for interface
   # Default constructor
   static StockItem();
   static StockItem(int id, str name);
=cut
```

Additionally, the implementations of the **StockItem** subroutine should be corrected.

```
sub StockItem
{
   # Get REFERENCE to the object
   my $this = shift;
   my ($id, $name) = @_;
   if (defined $id)
   {
      $this->{f_ID} = $id;
      $this->{f_Name} = $name;
```

```
   }
   else
   {
      # No arguments supplied - Default Constructor
      $this->{f_ID} = -1;
      $this->{f_Name} = "No Name";
   }
}
```

Code Example

After these modifications to **StockItem** and rebuilding of **StockItem.dll**, we can successfully build **BookItem.dll**. However, as we mentioned before, some errors appear only at runtime. We wrote a small client program (**BookItemCli**) for the **BookItem** class.

```
#
# BookItemCli.pl
#
use strict;
use namespace "OI.Samples";
use PerlNET qw(AUTOCALL);

my $book = BookItem->new(1, "PerlNET book");
$book->OutputItem(PerlNET::true);
```

BookItemCli.exe is built successfully, but when running it, we get an error:

```
System.ApplicationException: Can't locate any property or
field called 'f_ID' for OI.Samples.BookItem ...
```

What did we do wrong this time? As you can see, we accessed the **f_ID** and **f_Name** fields without defining them in the **BookItem** class.

```
sub BookItem
{
   my($this, $id, $name) = @_;

   $this->{f_ID} = $id;
   $this->{f_Name} = $name;
}
```

The inheritance principles tell us that we should be able to work with a base class interface. Our mistake was accessing two fields that are **private** to **StockItem** and hence not visible outside of this class. To keep these fields invisible to the **StockItem** class users on the one hand and to allow descendant classes to work with these fields on the other hand, we should apply the **protected** modifier to our fields in the interface definition of the base class.

```
package OI::Samples::StockItem;
. . . . . . . . . . .
# Fields
```

```
=for interface
      protected field int f_ID;
      protected field str f_Name;
=cut
```

This is enough to rebuild **StockItem.dll** and rerun **BookItemCli.exe**. Finally, we get clean execution with the following output:

```
---------------------------
1 PerlNET book
---------------------------
```

We placed the fixed version of the **StockItem** class in the **StockItem\Step2** directory.

OVERRIDING BASE CLASS METHODS

Many times when inheriting from some class, we would like to provide our own implementation for some base class methods or **override** methods. PerlNET has an appropriate method modifier we should apply inside interface definition of the descendant class. We should specify the method prototype we are going to override and apply the **override** modifier to the method.

```
=for interface
    override BaseClassMethodPrototype;
=cut
```

However, we cannot override every base class method, as such methods should have one of the following modifiers in the base class:

- abstract
- virtual
- override

Applying the **abstract** modifier is analogous to defining pure virtual function in C++. We do not implement this function, and all descendants must override it. With the **virtual** modifier, we instruct PerlNET that this function may be overridden in the inherited classes. Finally, the presence of the **override** modifier in the base class means that our base class provides its definition of the method from its base class. The **override** modifier has the same effect as **virtual**.

We may decide that the **BookItem** class should have its own **OutputItem** method implementation. Therefore, first we change the **StockItem** class by applying **virtual** modifier to the **OutputItem** method (**StockItem\Step3**). Then, we can make the following addition to the **BookItem** class package in the interface definition (**BookItem\Step2**):

```
=for interface
    override void OutputItem(bool lines);
=cut
```

The following subroutine implements the new version of **OutputItem**:

```
sub OutputItem
{
    my($this, $lines) = @_;
    if (bool($lines))
    {
        print "---------------------------\n";
    }
    print "Item type: Book\n";
    print $this->{f_ID}, " ", $this->{f_Name}, "\n";
    if (bool($lines))
    {
        print "---------------------------\n";
    }
}
```

This way, whenever a class user invokes the **OutputItem** method on the **BookItem** object, the new version presented above will be called.

INITIALIZATION OF EXTENDED CLASS

You can see that despite inheriting all the base class functionality, we had to initialize our fields in the **BookItem** class. This is not critical if we do just simple and not numerous initializations. However, it will be time and code consuming to rewrite the initialization code in each inherited class. Therefore, we need a way to eliminate these inconveniences as much as possible.

There two types of object initialization:

- Default
- Parametric

For each of these types, we suggest our solution to handle the problems mentioned above.

DEFAULT INITIALIZATION

Default initialization is used when all instances of a class get the same initial properties—the same state. We may assign property and field values in a default constructor that takes no parameters. This constructor works for descendant classes too, as the PerlNET runtime module automatically invokes the default constructor whenever we create the inherited class object. To demonstrate default initialization, we wrote two classes:

- **Circle** is the base class.
- **RandCircle** extends **Circle**.

The **Circle** class has one read-write **Radius** property and one method, **CalculateArea**. We have defined one default constructor. It initially sets the value of **Radius** to **5**. After the instance is created, we may get or set **Radius** of

Code Example

a circle and calculate its area with the **CalculateArea** method. Here is the class code, which is located in the **Circle** folder.

```perl
#
# Circle.pm
#
package OI::Samples::Circle;
use PerlNET qw(AUTOCALL);
use strict;

# Default constructor
=for interface
   static Circle();
=cut

# Calculate Area Method
=for interface
   num CalculateArea();
=cut

# Radius Property
=for interface
   int Radius;
=cut

# Field to store property value
=for interface
   protected field int f_Radius;
=cut

# Default constructor implementation
sub Circle
{
   my $this = shift;

   # Initialize field that stores property value
   $this->{f_Radius} = int(5);
}

# CalculateArea implementation
sub CalculateArea
{
   my $this = shift;
   return("System.Math"->PI*($this->{f_Radius}**2));
}

# Radius Property implementation
sub Radius
{
   my ($this, $value) = @_;
```

```
   if (defined $value)
   {
      # Set radius
      $this->{f_Radius} = $value;
   }
   else
   {
      return $this->{f_Radius};
   }
}
```

Now, we would like to implement the descendant **RandCircle** class, which will extend the **Circle** class functionality with one method, **RandRadius**. This method will generate a new circle radius value randomly and will assign it to the **Radius** property.

Note that we do not need to initialize the **Radius** property in the descendant class, as the default constructor of the base class will do this job for us. Here is the code for **RandCircle**.

```
#
# RandCircle.pm
#
package OI::Samples::RandCircle;

use namespace "OI::Samples";
use strict;

=for interface
   [extends: Circle]
   # We do no have to specify the default
   # constructor - PerlNET will generate one
=cut

# Random radius generating
=for interface
   void RandRadius();
=cut

# No need to implement the default constructor
# The Radius property is initialized in the base class

# Random Radius implementation
sub RandRadius
{
    my $this = shift;
    $this->{f_Radius} = int(rand(20) + 1);
}
```

To test **RandCircle**, we wrote a simple client program that resides in the **RandCircleCli** directory. Here is the code and the output of this program.

```
#
# RandCircleCli.pl
#
use strict;
use namespace "OI.Samples";

$| = 1;
my $circle = RandCircle->new();
print "Radius: ", $circle->{Radius}, "\n";
print "Area: ", $circle->CalculateArea(), "\n";
print "--------------------------\n";
$circle->RandRadius();
print "New Radius: ", $circle->{Radius}, "\n";
print "New Area: ", $circle->CalculateArea(), "\n";
```

Output:

```
Radius: 5
Area: 78.5398163397448
--------------------------
New Radius: 9
New Area: 254.469004940773
```

As you can see, the default constructor of the base class initialized the **Radius** property of the descendant class automatically. The PerlNET runtime module always invokes the base class constructor before the descendant class constructor.

PARAMETRIC INITIALIZATION

Programmers commonly use parametric initialization. It allows other developers to pass some parameters to a class constructor, and in this way to set the initial state of a new object. Initialization occurs inside the constructor subroutine. When we create an object of the inherited class, then we pass some parameters that should be assigned to properties of the base class and others for inherited class properties. The best way to handle this is to call the base class constructor and supply it with appropriate parameters. Unfortunately, there is no special syntax in PerlNET to call the base class constructor.

However, we suggest a solution to this problem. Recall that in the **BookItem** class we defined previously in this chapter, we had to manually initialize two fields, **f_ID** and **f_Name**. We were not able to call the second version of the base class constructor that gets **id** and **name** parameters, because PerlNET does not allow this. That is why we suggest defining in the base class an additional method. We will call it **_init**. This method will replicate the functionality of a constructor. It gets the same parameters as the constructor and performs the corresponding assignments. This way, we avoid unnecessary initialization code in inherited classes, as they can call the **_init** method from their constructor and supply this method with initialization parameters for the base class. There may be several overloaded versions of **_init** methods as there are a number of nondefault constructors. The base class constructors may call the **_init** method too for the sake of code accuracy. It is reasonable to use such a solution whenever we have more then one property or field to initialize.

Going back to our items classes, we should slightly change an implementation of the **StockItem** class to reflect the proposed specification from the previous paragraph. We present here only the changed code fragments. The full code version may be found in the **StockItem\Step4** directory.

```
#
# StockItem.pm
#
package OI::Samples::StockItem;

use strict;
use PerlNET qw(bool);

# Constructor
=for interface
   # No [interface: pure] attribute
   static StockItem();
   static StockItem(int id, str name);
=cut

# Initializer method same params as second constructor
=for interface
   protected void _init(int id, str name);
=cut

   . . .

# Constructor definition
sub StockItem
{
   # Get REFERENCE to the object
   my $this = shift;
   my ($id, $name) = @_;
   if (defined $id)
   {
      $this->_init(int($id), $name);
   }
   else
   {
      $this->_init(int(-1), "No Name");
   }
}

# Initializer implementation
sub _init
{
```

```
   my ($this, $id, $name) = @_;
   $this->{f_ID} = $id;
   $this->{f_Name} = $name;
}
```

The **BookItem** class constructor implementation will change accordingly and will become more accurate. Here is the new code (located in **BookItem\Step3**).

```
#
# BookItem.pm
#
package OI::Samples::BookItem;
use namespace "OI.Samples";
use strict;

# Constructor
=for interface
   [extends: StockItem]
   static BookItem(int id, str name);
=cut

# Constructor implementation
sub BookItem
{
   my($this, $id, $name) = @_;

   $this->_init($id, $name);
}
```

INHERITANCE SUMMARY

As we have just shown, we must think ahead when we develop a set of classes that implement inheritance principles. Let's review the main points that you should consider when designing base and descendant classes.

Any class that you are going to use as a base class for other PerlNET classes must have the *default constructor.* Any property, field, or method that you want to hide from class users but allow access for descendant classes should have the *protected* modifier inside an interface definition. It is preferable that *common initialization* code for all class instances reside inside the default constructor. If our class provides nondefault constructors and this class should serve as a base class, then the best way to avoid unnecessary initialization code in descendant classes is to define the *protected* **_init** method. This method would get some parameters to assign as initial values to properties (fields). This way, we can call this method from inherited classes and work around the inability to call nondefault constructors of the base class. If you are going to use your class as a base for C# classes, then you do not have to define the **_init** method, as C# has a special syntax for calling nondefault constructors of the base class. Consult Appendix B for more details.

Interfaces

When designing an object-oriented system, there often arises a need to define some functionality or some pattern for class behavior without providing any implementation. Interfaces provide us this feature in a .NET environment. Generally, an interface is a set of methods. Implementing an interface by a class means providing implementations for *all* methods of that interface. This is very similar to inheritance from an abstract class, but unlike in the case of inheritance, you may implement multiple interfaces in your classes. Unfortunately, PerlNET does not allow us to define our own .NET interfaces, but we can easily implement existing ones. You can create your own interfaces in other .NET languages, such as C#. You can see how that is done later in this chapter and in Appendix B.

Implementing .NET Interfaces

To better understand implementing .NET interfaces, let us take the existing .NET interface, **IComparable** (code convention is that interface names should start with I). This interface is exposed by the **System** namespace and consists of only one method, **CompareTo**, with the following prototype:

```
int CompareTo(Object o);
```

This method takes an object (other object) as an argument and compares it to the object on behalf of which the method was called (this object). If this object is greater than the other object, then the method should return a positive value. If this object is less than the other object, then the return value should be negative. In case of equality of this object and the other object, we should return zero. If some class implements the **IComparable** interface (i.e., provides implementation of **CompareTo** method), then we can easily sort our objects of this class inside **ArrayList** by applying the **Sort** method to the **ArrayList** object. Internally, the **Sort** method will call the **CompareTo** method on the objects inside the list and, according to comparison results, will sort the objects.

Generally, to implement some .NET interface, we should use the **[implements: ...]** attribute inside our PerlNET class **=for interface** POD blocks. Additionally, we should enumerate *all* the methods of the interface inside POD blocks, even if we provide an empty implementation for some methods.

```
package MyPackage;

=for interface
   [implements: SomeInterface]
   SomeInterfaceMethod_1;
   SomeInterfaceMethod_2;
   . . .
   SomeInterfaceMethod_N;
=cut

# Other definitions
. . .
```

SomeInterfaceMethod_X is the prototype of method number X defined by the interface. We may implement several interfaces. In this case we can list them in the single **implements** attribute:

```
[implements: IComparable, IEnumerable, ICollection]
```

Example and Discussion

Code
Example

If we want our **StockItem** class to implement the **IComparable** interface, then we should alter the **StockItem** module in the following manner (**StockItem\Step5**):

```
#
# StockItem.pm
#
package OI::Samples::StockItem;
use namespace "System";

=for interface
   [implements: IComparable]
   int CompareTo(Object o);
=cut

# IComparable implementation
sub CompareTo
{
   my($this, $other) = @_;

   # Return comparison result
   return($this->{f_ID} - $other->{ID});
}
# The rest of the module
. . .
```

To provide implementation for the methods of the interface, we should define subroutines with the methods' names inside the Perl module, as we did

Code Example

in the above fragment for the **CompareTo** method—we compare IDs of two items and return the result of the comparison.

The following PerlNET program (**SortItems**) demonstrates the easy way to sort the **StockItem** class objects after we implement the **IComparable** interface.

```
#
# SortItems.pl
#
use namespace "System.Collections";
use namespace "OI.Samples";
use PerlNET qw(in false);

my $items = ArrayList->new();
$items->Add(StockItem->new(int(2), "Item 2"));
$items->Add(StockItem->new(int(1), "Item 1"));
$items->Add(StockItem->new(int(3), "Item 3"));

print "Before Sort:\n";
foreach my $item (in $items)
{
    $item->OutputItem(false);
}
print "\n";

# Sort Array
$items->Sort();

print "After Sort:\n";
foreach my $item (in $items)
{
    $item->OutputItem(false);
}
```

The output of the **SortItems** program will look like this:

```
Before Sort:
2 Item 2
1 Item 1
3 Item 3

After Sort:
1 Item 1
2 Item 2
3 Item 3
```

All the descendant classes automatically implement all the interfaces of the base class with no need of additional definition inside the descendant or the base classes. Therefore, the **BookItem** class implements the **IComparable** interface as the descendant of **StockItem**.

Defining Interfaces

If we have to define our own interface, we do so in C# or in any other .NET-compliant language that supports creating .NET interfaces. The implementation technique is the same as for all .NET interfaces.

ROULETTE SAMPLE

We stated that Mixed types enjoy the same benefits as .NET types. We decided to combine the demonstration of defining our own interface with implementing it in the Mixed type **Roulette**, which we presented previously in this chapter.

We want to define a new interface, **IResettable**. It will have one method, **Reset**. Calling this method on an implementing class will cause the object to reset its state. In the example of the **Roulette** class, we will erase all the stakes that were previously made.

We have written the following interface definition in C#:

```
//
// IResettable.cs
//
namespace OI.Samples
{
    interface IResettable
    {
        void Reset();
    }
}
```

Code Example

Refer to the **IResettable** folder for the code and Visual C# project. We compile this file into a DLL **(IResettable.dll)** using the **csc.exe** C# compiler:

```
csc /target:library IResettable.cs
```

When rewriting and rebuilding the **Roulette** class, we will reference this library.

Our next step is to alter the **Roulette** code to provide the implementation of the **IResettable** interface. Remember that we deal with Mixed type, and all its nonstatic methods are automatically provided with two arguments that are not listed in the interface definition: **$this** and **$self**. The **Reset** method is not an exception.

We made the following additions to the code to implement the **IResettable** interface (the full code of the new **Roulette** class resides in the **ResettableRoulette** folder):

```
#
# Roulette.pm
#
```

Code Example

```
package OI::Samples::Roulette;
use namespace "OI.Samples";
. . .
# Implements IResettable interface
=for interface
    [implements: IResettable]
    void Reset();
=cut
. . .
# IResettable implementation
sub Reset
{
    my ($this, $self) = @_;
    $this->{f_LastGambler} = 0;
    $self->{Stakes} = [];
}
```

To build the newly written **Roulette** class, run PerlNET compiler (don't forget to build **IResettable.dll** and copy it to the **ResettableRoulette** folder).

```
plc Roulette.pm -target="library"
                -reference="IResettable.dll"
```

After the above modifications, we may clear all the stakes after each round in our roulette game (**ResettableRouletteGame**).

```
#
# RouletteGame.pl
#

use strict;
use namespace "OI.Samples";

# Instantiate Roulette
my $roulette = Roulette->new();

# Make two stakes
$roulette->AddStake(20, 3);
$roulette->AddStake(5, 2.5);

# Roll it
$roulette->Roll();

# Clear the stakes
$roulette->Reset();

# Make new stake
$roulette->AddStake(10, 4);

# Roll again
$roulette->Roll();
```

The output, depending on the number generated, may look like the following:

```
**************************
The winning number is: 25!
**************************
--------------------------
Gambler 1:
Your prize is: 0.00
--------------------------
Gambler 2:
Your prize is: 0.00
--------------------------
**************************
The winning number is: 10!
**************************
--------------------------
Gambler 1:
Your prize is: 144.00
--------------------------
```

Exceptions

.NET provides an *exception-handling mechanism*. As its name implies, this mechanism helps to take care of exceptional situations in our program. Generally, if an error occurs, then the code throws an exception that can be caught by the caller code, even if this is another module or component; that is, exceptions bubble up in the call stack. Fortunately, PerlNET provides a very easy way to work with exceptions. We use **die** functions and **eval** blocks to generate and to catch exceptions respectively.

Generating and Catching Exceptions

To generate an exception in the module or any other PerlNET program, we use the **die** function, passing to it a string with an error description. For example, we may set a rule for our **StockItem** class that class users may not pass negative ID to the constructor. If we encounter negative value for ID, we throw an exception with the appropriate message string. This is how we should change the **StockItem** constructor code to reflect this rule (**StockItem\Step6**):

```perl
# Constructor definition
sub StockItem
{
    # Get REFERENCE to the object
    my $this = shift;
    my ($id, $name) = @_;
    if (defined $id)
```

```
   {
      if ($id < 0)
      {
         die "Item ID should be positive";
      }
      $this->_init(int($id), $name);
   }
   else
   {
      $this->_init(int(-1), "No Name");
   }
}
```

To catch an exception, we should enclose the code, where an exception may occur, inside the **eval** block. If we do not do so, then the .NET Framework will catch the exception and will terminate our program execution, displaying an unpleasant message to the user. If a negative value is passed to **StockItem**, the output will be

```
PerlRuntime.PerlException: Item ID should be positive at
unknown in C:\...\StockItem.pm : line 65.
```

After printing the above message, the program exits. Obviously, this is not what we want. It is better to inform the user of an error and to continue execution if possible. Consider the following code:

```
use namespace "OI::Samples";

$item1 = StockItem->new(-1, "Item 1");
$item2 = StockItem->new(2, "Item 2");
```

Here, if we do not provide any additional code, the execution would stop when trying to create Item 1. However, we would like to let the user know that we did not create this item and move on to constructing Item 2. This can be done by using the **eval** blocks, as follows (you may refer to the **StockClient** folder to work with the sample).

```
#
# StockClient.pl
#
use strict;
use namespace "OI.Samples";

$| = 1;
my($item1, $item2);
my $res = eval {
$item1 = StockItem->new(-1, "Item 1");
};
if (!defined $res)
{
   print $@, "\n";
```

```
}
else
{
   print "Item was created successfully!\n";
}
my $res = eval {
$item2 = StockItem->new(2, "Item 2");
};
if (!defined $res)
{
   print $@;
}
else
{
   print "Item was created successfully!\n";
}
```

The above program produces the following output:

```
PerlRuntime.PerlException: Item ID should be positive at
unknown in C:\Dev\PerlDev\StockItemNET\StockItemExc.pm:line
74
Item was created successfully!
```

This program illustrates how we can proceed with the program execution despite that an exception occurred while creating the first stock item.

C# SAMPLE

Code Example

We can easily trap exceptions that PerlNET programs generate in other .NET languages. C# uses the **try** and **catch** blocks for this purpose. Here is a simple console application written in C# (**PerlNET2CS**), where we handle PerlNET exceptions.

```
//
// PerlNET2CS.cs
//
using System;
using OI.Samples;
class PerlNET2CS
{
   static void Main(string[] args)
   {
      Console.WriteLine("Enter Item ID:");
      string strID = Console.ReadLine();
      int id = Convert.ToInt32(strID);
      Console.WriteLine("Enter Item Name:");
      string strName = Console.ReadLine();
```

```
try
{
    Console.WriteLine("Constructing...");
    StockItem si = new StockItem(id, strName);
    Console.WriteLine("Item was created");
}
catch (Exception e)
{
    Console.WriteLine("Exception occurred:");
    Console.WriteLine(e.Message);
}
    }
}
```

If PerlNET code generates an exception using the **die** function, the .NET environment instantiates an **Exception** object. This object is passed to the **catch** block, which follows the **try** block, enclosing the fragment that generated the exception. We can refer to the **Exception** class's various methods and properties to find out what caused it. We chose to display the **Message** property, which holds the string that PerlNET module passed to the **die** function.

The above program expects two input values: an integer for the item's ID and a string for the item's name. If the ID is negative, then we should catch an exception. Otherwise, the **StockItem** object is successfully constructed. Here are two sample runs:

```
Enter Item ID:
1
Enter Item Name:
Item 1
Constructing...
Item was created
. . . . . . . . .
Enter Item ID:
-1
Enter Item Name:
item 1
Constructing...
Exception occurred:
Item ID should be positive
```

Summary

In this chapter, we discussed the advanced topic of component development in PerlNET. Every program or component we write in PerlNET represents a .NET class. The executable assemblies are implicitly provided with the **Main** function as their entry point.

To implement classes that are fully compliant with .NET, we use either .NET types or Mixed types. In both cases, the resulting classes will be non-sealed. We are able to inherit from existing .NET classes and implement .NET interfaces. In addition, Mixed types may store Perl references as private instance data in a blessed hash.

An exception-handling mechanism is available for all PerlNET components, including these implementing Pure Perl types. We use the **die** function to throw an exception and the **eval** block to catch exceptions.

.NET Framework Classes

We have seen how easy it is both to call .NET classes from Perl and to create .NET classes using PerlNET. In this chapter we study a few of the many .NET classes that are available to the PerlNET programmer. These classes should be viewed only as an appetizer to a very rich feast, as the .NET Framework class library has over 2,500 useful classes, which are now available to you as a Perl programmer, thanks to PerlNET. In later chapters we'll look at classes to help you create user interfaces, access databases, and create Web applications. In addition to learning about some useful classes, we will gain further insight into the structure of the .NET Framework and explore some new concepts, such as delegates.

We begin with an examination of the root class **Object**. This class itself does not provide a lot of functionality, but it defines some virtual methods that are sometimes important for you to override in your own classes. We continue the chapter with a discussion of the important concept of memory management, and we will see some important interactions between the Perl runtime environment and the .NET Common Language Runtime. The CLR provides a powerful *garbage collection* mechanism, which simplifies memory management in .NET programs.

We then study .NET classes for programming with directories and files. Next, we examine programming with multiple threads. The .NET Framework provides a clean threading model based on delegates, which we will see again in Chapter 14 when we deal with events in user interface applications.

System.Object

As mentioned in Chapter 10, every class in .NET is ultimately derived from the root class **Object**, which is in the **System** namespace. The class **ValueType** inherits directly from **Object**. **ValueType** is the root for all value types, such as structures and simple types like **Integer** and **Decimal**.

Public Instance Methods of Object

There are four public instance methods of **Object**, three of which are virtual and frequently overridden by classes.

EQUALS

```
public virtual bool Equals(Object obj);
```

This method compares an object with the object passed as a parameter and returns **true** if they are equal. **Object** implements this method to test for reference equality. **ValueType** overrides the method to test for content equality. Many classes override the method to make equality behave appropriately for the particular class.

TOSTRING

```
public virtual String ToString();
```

This method returns a human-readable string representation of the object. The default implementation returns the type name. Derived classes frequently override this method to return a meaningful string representation of the particular object.

GETHASHCODE

```
public virtual int GetHashCode();
```

This method returns a hash value for an object, suitable for use in hashing algorithms and hashtables. You should override this method if instances of your class will have hashes computed by .NET—for example, by being a key in a .NET hashtable class. (The C# compiler will give you a warning message if you override **ToString** and not **GetHashCode**.)

GETTYPE

```
public Type GetType();
```

This method returns type information for the object. This type information can be used to get the associated metadata through *reflection*. Although beyond the scope of this book, reflection is an extremely important concept in .NET, allowing extensive runtime information to be obtained about .NET data types. Reflection allows very dynamic programming and is used extensively by the PerlNET interpreter.

Protected Instance Methods

There are two protected instance methods, which can be used only within derived classes.

MEMBERWISECLONE

```
protected object MemberwiseClone();
```

This method creates a shallow copy of the object. To perform a deep copy, you should implement the **ICloneable** interface. We will discuss shallow and deep copy later in this chapter.

FINALIZE

```
protected virtual void Finalize();
```

This method allows an object to free resources and perform other cleanup operations before it is reclaimed by garbage collection. Finalization is non-deterministic, dependent upon the garbage collector. We discuss finalization later in this chapter.

Generic Interfaces and Standard Behavior

If you are used to a language like Smalltalk, the set of behaviors specified in **Object** may seem quite limited. Smalltalk, which introduced the concept of a class hierarchy rooted in a common base class, has a very rich set of methods defined in its **Object** class. I counted 38 methods.[1] These additional methods support features such as comparing objects and copying objects. The .NET Framework class library has similar methods, and many more. But rather than putting them all in a common root class, .NET defines a number of standard *interfaces*, which classes can optionally support. This kind of organization, which is also present in Microsoft's Component Object Model (COM) and in Java, is very flexible. We introduced the concept of generic .NET interfaces in Chapter 12, where we illustrated how your class can participate in .NET sorting routines if it implements the interface **IComparable**. In this section we focus on the simple methods of **Object**.

Using Object Methods in the StockItem Class

As a simple illustration of **Object** methods, let's look at our **StockItem** class before and after overriding the **Equals** and **ToString** methods.

---

1. The methods of Smalltalk's **Object** class are described in Chapters 6 and 14 of *Smalltalk-80: The Language and Its Implementation*, by Adele Goldberg and David Robson (Addison-Wesley, 1983).

Code Example

DEFAULT METHODS OF OBJECT

If our class does not provide any overrides of the virtual instance methods of **Object**, our class will inherit the standard behavior. This behavior is demonstrated in the implementation of **StockItem** in the folder **StockObj\Step1**. The solution contains two projects. The **StockItem** project creates a class library **StockItem.dll**, and the **StockObj** project provides an interactive test program to exercise the class library. This program is somewhat of a hybrid of Step 3 of the Stock Management example of Chapter 10 (which stored the list of stock items as an **ArrayList** of strings) and the **StockItem** example of Chapter 11 (which introduced a PerlNET component to represent a stock item). Our version also uses pure .NET input/output, with aid of the **InputWrapper** class described in Appendix A.

Here is Step 1 of the implementation of the **StockItem** class.

```
#
# StockItem.pm
#
package OI::Samples::StockItem;

use strict;
use namespace "System";
use PerlNET qw(AUTOCALL);

# Constructor
=for interface
    [interface: pure]
    static StockItem(int id, str name);
=cut

# Properties
=for interface
    int ID;
    str Name;
=cut

# Method
=for interface
    void OutputItem();
=cut

# Constructor definition
sub new
{
   my $self = shift;
   my ($id, $name) = @_;
   Console->WriteLine(
      "in constructor, id = {0}, Name = {1}", $id, $name);
   my $s = bless {}, $self;
```

```
      $s->ID(int($id));
      $s->Name($name);
      return $s;
}

sub ID
{
   my($self, $value) = @_;
   if (defined $value)
   {
      $self->{ID} = $value;
      return;
   }
   else
   {
      $self->{ID};
   }
}

# Name read-write Property
sub Name
{
   my($self, $value) = @_;
   if (defined $value)
   {
      $self->{Name} = $value;
      return;
   }
   else
   {
      $self->{Name};
   }
}

# OutputItem method
sub OutputItem
{
   my $self = shift;
   Console->WriteLine(
      "{0} {1}", $self->{ID}, $self->{Name});
}
```

Here is the exerciser program **StockObj.pl**.

```
#
# StockObj.pl
#
use strict;
use namespace "System";
use namespace "System.IO";
use namespace "System.Text";
```

```perl
use namespace "System.Collections";
use namespace "OI.Samples";
use PerlNET qw(AUTOCALL in);
require "InputWrapper.pl";

$| = 1;
my $items = ArrayList->new();
my $id = -1;
Console->WriteLine("Welcome to Stock Management System");
Console->WriteLine("For the list of commands type help");

my $command = GetString(">>");
while ($command ne 'quit')
{
    if ($command eq 'add')
    {
        $id++;
        my $name = GetString("item name: ");
        my $item = StockItem->new(int($id), $name);
        $items->Add($item);
        Console->WriteLine("Item added. ID = {0}", $id);
    }
    elsif ($command eq 'show')
    {
        Console->WriteLine("---------------------");
        foreach my $item(in $items)
        {
            $item->OutputItem();
        }
        Console->WriteLine("---------------------");
    }
    elsif ($command eq 'dump')
    {
        Console->WriteLine("---------------------");
        foreach my $item(in $items)
        {
            Console->WriteLine("{0} {1} {2}",
                $item->{ID}, $item->ToString(),
                $item->GetType());
        }
        Console->WriteLine("---------------------");
    }
    elsif ($command eq 'rmv')
    {
        my $itemid = GetString("id: ");
        my $item = StockItem->new(int($itemid), "");
        $items->Remove($item);
        if ($items->{Count} == 0) { $id = -1; }
    }
    elsif ($command eq 'help')
```

```
    {
        Console->WriteLine("List Of Commands:\n");
        Console->WriteLine("add\t- add new item to stock");
        Console->WriteLine("show\t- show items in stock");
        Console->WriteLine("dump\t- dump info about items");
        Console->WriteLine(
            "rmv\t- remove item/s from stock");
        Console->WriteLine("quit\t- exit program");
        Console->WriteLine("help\t- print this list");
    }
    else
    {
        Console->WriteLine("Unrecognized command");
    }
    $command = GetString(">>");
}
Console->WriteLine("\nGoodbye.");
```

The program creates an array list to hold stock items and then enters a command loop. The **add** command prompts for an item name, generates an item ID, instantiates a **StockItem** object, and adds this item to the array list. The **show** command iterates through the array list and displays each item using the **OutputItem** method. The **dump** command displays the ID of the item, its string representation using **ToString**, and the type (class) name using **GetType**. We discuss the **rmv** command in the next section.

Here is a sample run of the program.

```
Welcome to Stock Management System
For the list of commands type help
>>add
item name: notebook
in constructor, id = 0, Name = notebook
Item added. ID = 0
>>add
item name: monitor
in constructor, id = 1, Name = monitor
Item added. ID = 1
>>show
--------------------
0 notebook
1 monitor
--------------------
>>dump
--------------------
0 OI.Samples.StockItem OI.Samples.StockItem
1 OI.Samples.StockItem OI.Samples.StockItem
--------------------
>>rmv
id: 0
in constructor, id = 0, Name =
```

```
>>show
----------------------
0 notebook
1 monitor
----------------------
>>quit

Goodbye.
```

For the most part, the output is reasonable, but there are some anomalies. In the **dump** command, the string representation obtained by calling **ToString** just returns the name of the class and no information about the particular object instance. And the **rmv** command is not working properly, as can be seen by the notebook with ID of 0 not being removed.

Code
Example

OVERRIDING TOSTRING AND EQUALS

We fix these defects by overriding the **ToString** and **Equals** methods, as illustrated in the folder **StockObj\Step2**.

```perl
#
# StockItem.pm
#
...

# Method
=for interface
   void OutputItem();
   override bool Equals(Object obj);
   override str ToString();
=cut

...

# Equals method
sub Equals
{
   my($self, $obj) = @_;
   if ($self->{ID} eq $obj->{ID})
   {
      return PerlNET::true;
   }
   else
   {
      return PerlNET::false;
   }
}

# ToString method
sub ToString
```

```
{
   my $self = shift;
   return $self->{ID} . " " . $self->{Name};
}
```

Two object instances are defined to be equal if they have the same ID, and the string representation is given as the ID concatenated with the Name. Now let us examine the code for the **rmv** command in the exerciser program **StockObj.pl** (which is unchanged from Step 1).

```
...
elsif ($command eq 'rmv')
   {
      my $itemid = GetString("id: ");
      my $item = StockItem->new(int($itemid), "");
      $items->Remove($item);
      if ($items->{Count} == 0) { $id = -1; }
   }
   ...
```

The meat of the code is the two lines shown in bold. We construct an object with the same ID as the object to be removed, and then we call the **Remove** method of the **ArrayList** class. The .NET Framework implementation of the **ArrayList** class will iterate through the collection, searching for an object that **Equals** the object passed as an argument in the call to **Remove**. If such an object is found, it will remove it.

Running the Step 2 version of the program with the same commands now produces a clean result.

```
Welcome to Stock Management System
For the list of commands type help
>>add
item name: notebook
in constructor, id = 0, Name = notebook
Item added. ID = 0
>>add
item name: monitor
in constructor, id = 1, Name = monitor
Item added. ID = 1
>>dump
---------------------
0 0 notebook OI.Samples.StockItem
1 1 monitor OI.Samples.StockItem
---------------------
>>rmv
id: 0
in constructor, id = 0, Name =
>>show
---------------------
```

```
1 monitor
---------------------
>>quit

Goodbye.
```

Garbage Collection and Finalization

Memory management is a critical aspect of programming and can be the source of many errors. Whenever a resource is created, memory must be provided for it. And when the resource is no longer needed, the memory should be reclaimed. If the memory is not reclaimed, the amount of memory available for other resources is reduced. If such "memory leaks" recur often enough (which can happen in long-running server programs), the program can crash. Another potential bug is to reclaim memory while it is still required by another part of the program.

.NET greatly simplifies the programming of memory management through an automatic *garbage collection* facility. The CLR tracks the use of memory that is allocated on the managed heap, and any memory that is no longer referenced is marked as "garbage." When memory is low, the CLR traverses its data structure of tracked memory and reclaims all the memory marked as garbage. Thus the programmer is relieved of this responsibility.

Although a good foundation for resource management, garbage collection by itself does not address all issues. Memory allocated from the managed heap is not the only kind of resource needed in programs. Other resources, such as file handles and database connections, are not automatically deallocated, and the programmer may need to write explicit code to perform cleanup. The .NET Framework provides a **Finalize** method in the **Object** base class for this purpose. The CLR calls **Finalize** when the memory allocated for an object is reclaimed.

PerlNET is a hybrid of the .NET and Perl platforms, and as such, also has to take into account the memory management protocols of Perl. In particular, we will see that PerlNET invoke a class's **DESTROY** method (introduced in Chapter 7) when an object is deallocated.

In this section, we study the issues of memory management in .NET and Perl, including a discussion of **Finalize**, the **IDispose** interface, the Perl **DESTROY** method, and garbage collection in the CLR.

Finalize

System.Object has a protected method **Finalize**, which is automatically called by the CLR after an object becomes inaccessible. (Finalization for an object may be suppressed by a call to the method **SuppressFinalize** of the **System.GC** class.) Since **Finalize** is protected, it can only be called through the class or a derived class. The default implementation of **Finalize** does nothing. For any cleanup to be performed, a class must override **Finalize**. Also, a class's **Finalize** implementation should call the **Finalize** of its base class.

FINALIZE IN THE STOCKITEM CLASS

Code
Example

After our success in overriding **ToString** and **Equals**, it would be natural to next override **Finalize**. See the folder **StockObj\Step3bug**. The result is very different. Instead of smooth sailing, we get an error message in our face.

```
error CS0111: Class 'OI.Samples.StockItem' already defines
a member called 'Finalize' with the same parameter types
```

We can get a clue to the reason our program with **Finalize** failed by examining the assembly **StockItem.dll** from our previous good builds (Steps 1 and 2). Use the **ILDASM** tool, as described in Chapter 12. For Step 1 we see the definition of the **StockItem** class, as shown in Figure 13-1.

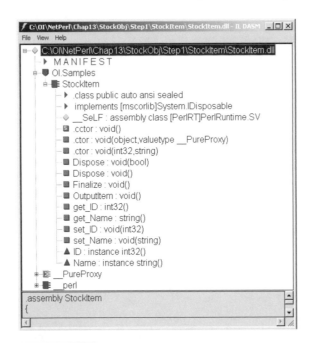

FIGURE 13-1   *Viewing the **StockItem.dll** assembly (Step 1) using ILDASM.*

Notice the properties **ID** and **Name** that we implemented along with the method **OutputItem**. Also note the absence of **ToString** and **Equals**, which we have not yet implemented in Step 1. But we have not implemented **Finalize** either, and that is shown as being present. Where did that **Finalize** come from?

The answer is that PerlNET implemented **Finalize** for us, and so when we try to implement it ourselves, we run into a conflict and the compiler gives us an error message.

DESTROY IN THE STOCKITEM CLASS

What do you suppose PerlNET does in its implementation of **Finalize**? Why, it calls **DESTROY**, of course. As we saw in Chapter 7, every class in Perl may implement a method **DESTROY**, which will be called when the last reference to an object goes away.

As an illustration, the implementation of **StockItem** in **StockObj\Step3** provides a **DESTROY** method that simply provides a debugging output statement, analogous to the code in the constructor.

```
sub DESTROY
{
   my $self = shift;
   Console->WriteLine($self->{ID} . " " . $self->{Name} . "
      destroyed");
}
```

The exercise program is unchanged. Here is a sample run, illustrating the same scenario from before of adding a notebook and a monitor and removing the notebook.

```
Welcome to Stock Management System
For the list of commands type help
>>add
item name: notebook
in constructor, id = 0, Name = notebook
Item added. ID = 0
>>add
item name: monitor
in constructor, id = 1, Name = monitor
Item added. ID = 1
>>show
---------------------
0 notebook
1 monitor
---------------------
>>rmv
id: 0
in constructor, id = 0, Name =
>>show
---------------------
```

```
1 monitor
---------------------
>>quit

Goodbye.
0 notebook destroyed
0   destroyed
1 monitor destroyed
```

There are several interesting features to this output. First, note that **DESTROY** is not called until the very end, even after "Goodbye." The notebook is *not* destroyed at the time it is removed from the list. The notebook becomes garbage at this point, but **Finalize** and hence **DESTROY** is not called until the garbage collector kicks in, which in this example is not until the program exits. In a larger, long-running application, memory may sometimes become low, and then the garbage collector will be called by the CLR to clean up all the garbage, resulting in **Finalize** being called for all these objects. We say that there is "non-deterministic finalization," which is very different from the memory management scheme in other environments, such as C++, where there are precise rules for when deallocation occurs (for example, when a stack-based object goes out of scope or a heap-based object is explicitly freed by a statement such as **delete** or **free**).

Dispose

For the most part, the automatic memory management scheme implemented by the CLR works very well, and the programmer need not be concerned about just when memory is cleaned up. But there are cases when the programmer needs better control. For example, suppose a class allocates some scarce resource such as a file handle or a database connection. If the file or database were closed in **DESTROY**, we could run into a problem if the resource encapsulated by the class becomes low, but there is still plenty of memory. The garbage collector may not kick in, and so **DESTROY** never winds up being called. But the program fails, because the resource runs out.

To deal with this not uncommon situation, the .NET Framework defines an interface **IDisposable** with a method **Dispose**, which a client of the class can call when it is through with a particular object.

If you examine Figure 13–1 again, you will see that PerlNET implements the **IDisposable** interface, which brings an implementation of the **Dispose** method.[2]

---

2. There are actually two **Dispose** methods, one with and one without a **bool** parameter. The method without the parameter is the one required by the **IDisposable** interface. The other method is used as part of a standard design pattern in which you can program carefully to avoid calling **Dispose** twice, keeping track of whether **Dispose** has been called by a boolean flag. This design pattern is discussed in the MSDN documentation that comes with the .NET Framework.

Code Example

DISPOSE AND THE STOCKITEM CLASS

We illustrate the use of **Dispose** with **StockObj\Step4**. When we remove an item, we call **Dispose** on it. (Actually, we call dispose on the item of the same ID but blank name, which we created for the purpose of calling **Remove**. Thus our example is rather artificial, but it was anyway, since there is no non-memory resource encapsulated by **StockItem**. The example should demonstrate the basic mechanism of **Dispose**.)

```
#
# StockObj.pl
#
...
   elsif ($command eq 'rmv')
   {
      my $itemid = GetString("id: ");
      my $item = StockItem->new(int($itemid), "");
      $items->Remove($item);
      $item->Dispose();
      if ($items->{Count} == 0) { $id = -1; }
   }
...
```

Here is a sample run of the program. Again, we add a notebook and a monitor, and remove the notebook.

```
Welcome to Stock Management System
For the list of commands type help
>>add
item name: notebook
in constructor, id = 0, Name = notebook
Item added. ID = 0
>>add
item name: monitor
in constructor, id = 1, Name = monitor
Item added. ID = 1
>>show
---------------------
0 notebook
1 monitor
---------------------
>>rmv
id: 0
in constructor, id = 0, Name =
0  destroyed
>>quit

Goodbye.
0 notebook destroyed
1 monitor destroyed
```

The object on which we called **Dispose** was destroyed as soon as **Dispose** was called.

Working with the CLR Garbage Collector

The .NET Framework provides the class **System.GC**, which you can use to work directly with the garbage collector. As a tiny illustration, consider **StockObj\Step5**, which adds a **gc** command. This command causes the **GC::Collect** method to be invoked, resulting in an immediate call to the garbage collector.

```
#
# StockObj.pl
#
use strict;
use namespace "System";
use namespace "System.IO";
use namespace "System.Text";
use namespace "System.Collections";
use namespace "System.Threading";
...
   elsif ($command eq 'gc')
   {
      GC->Collect();
      Thread->Sleep(100);
   }
...
```

After the call to **GC::Collect** we cause the current thread to sleep for 100 milliseconds to make sure that the garbage collection has actually taken place before we go on with the rest of the program. (We discuss multithreading in .NET later in the chapter.)

Here is the output, when yet again we add a notebook and a monitor and remove the notebook. Now the real notebook is destroyed as soon as we call **GC::Collect**. Only the monitor hangs around until the program exits.

```
Welcome to Stock Management System
For the list of commands type help
>>add
item name: notebook
in constructor, id = 0, Name = notebook
Item added. ID = 0
>>add
item name: monitor
in constructor, id = 1, Name = monitor
Item added. ID = 1
>>show
---------------------
0 notebook
```

```
1 monitor
---------------------
>>rmv
id: 0
in constructor, id = 0, Name =
0  destroyed
>>gc
0 notebook destroyed
>>quit

Goodbye.
1 monitor destroyed
```

Directories and Files

Our next topic, directories and files, is not particularly advanced but is quite fundamental. In this section we will first examine the **System.IO.Directory** class in the .NET Framework that allows us to work with directories. We will then look at file input and output, which makes use of an intermediary called a *stream*.

Directories

The classes supporting input and output are in the namespace **System.IO**. The classes **Directory** and **DirectoryInfo** contain routines for working with directories. All the methods of **Directory** are static, and so you can call them without having a directory instance. The **DirectoryInfo** class contains instance methods. In many cases, you can accomplish the same objective using methods of either class. The methods of **Directory** always perform a security check. If you are going to reuse a method several times, it may be better to obtain an instance of **DirectoryInfo** and use its instance methods, because a security check may not always be necessary. (We do not discuss security in this book. For a discussion of security in .NET, you may wish to refer to the book *Application Development Using C# and .NET,* another book in The Integrated .NET Series from Object Innovations and Prentice Hall PTR.)

Code
Example

We illustrate both classes with a simple program, **DirectoryDemo**, which contains DOS-like commands to show the contents of the current directory (**dir**) and to change the current directory (**cd**). A directory can contain both files and other directories. The method **GetFiles** returns an array of **FileInfo** objects, and the method **GetDirectories** returns an array of **DirectoryInfo** objects.[3] In this program, we use only the **Name** property of **FileInfo**. In the following section, we will see how to read and write files using streams.

---

3. The two lines shown in bold in the following code are particularly interesting. Each returns an array, of directories and files respectively. We simply use the standard Perl notation for arrays.

```perl
#
# DirectoryDemo.pl
#
use strict;
use namespace "System";
use namespace "System.IO";
use PerlNET qw(AUTOCALL in);
require "InputWrapper.pl";

sub ShowPath()
{
   my $curpath = Directory->GetCurrentDirectory();
   Console->WriteLine("path = " . $curpath);
}


$| = 1;
my $path = Directory->GetCurrentDirectory();
my $dir = DirectoryInfo->new($path);
Console->WriteLine("Welcome to Directory Demo");
Console->WriteLine("For the list of commands type help");
ShowPath();

my $command = GetString(">>");
while ($command ne 'quit')
{
   my $res = eval {
   if ($command eq 'cd')
   {
      $path = GetString("path: ");
      $dir = DirectoryInfo->new($path);
      Directory->SetCurrentDirectory($path);
      ShowPath();
   }
   elsif ($command eq 'dir')
   {
      my @files = $dir->GetFiles();
      Console->WriteLine("Files:");
      foreach my $f (in @files)
      {
         Console->WriteLine("   {0}", $f->{Name});
      }
      my @dirs = $dir->GetDirectories();
      Console->WriteLine("Directories:");
      foreach my $d (in @dirs)
      {
         Console->WriteLine("   {0}", $d->{Name});
      }
   }
```

```
   else
   {
      Console->WriteLine(
         "The following commands are available:");
      Console->WriteLine("\tcd       -- change directory");
      Console->WriteLine(
         "\tdir      -- show files in directory");
      Console->WriteLine("\tquit     -- exit the program");
   }
   };
   if (!defined $res)
   {
      Console->WriteLine($@);
   }
   $command = GetString(">>");
}
Console->WriteLine("\nGoodbye.");
```

Here is a sample run of the program. Notice that the current directory starts out as the directory containing the program's executable. The sample run also illustrates the exception handling performed by the program. When we enter an illegal directory name **foo**, the program does not bomb out, but prints an error message, and we can continue entering commands. (We discussed exception handling in Chapter 12.)

```
Welcome to Directory Demo
For the list of commands type help
path = C:\OI\NetPerl\Chap13\DirectoryDemo
>>dir
Files:
   directorydemo.exe
   DirectoryDemo.perlproj
   DirectoryDemo.pl
   DirectoryDemo.sln
   DirectoryDemo.suo
   InputWrapper.pl
Directories:
>>cd
path: ..
path = C:\OI\NetPerl\Chap13

>>dir
Files:
Directories:
   DirectoryDemo
   FileDemo
   StockObj
   ThreadDemo
>>cd
path: foo
```

```
System.IO.FileNotFoundException: Could not find file "foo".
File name: "foo"
  at System.IO.__Error.WinIOError(Int32 errorCode, String
str)
  at System.IO.Directory.SetCurrentDirectory(String path)
>>cd
path: FileDemo
path = C:\OI\NetPerl\Chap13\FileDemo

Goodbye.
```

For the most part, this code is very straightforward, making direct calls to .NET Framework classes. You can check out the methods called in the MSDN documentation. Note how terse the Perl code is, relying on the fact that Perl variables are not typed. For example, you do not have to declare **$dir** as a variable of type **DirectoryInfo**. You can just invoke the **Directory::GetCurrentDirectory** method.

Files and Streams

Programming languages have undergone an evolution in how they deal with the important topic of input/output (I/O). Early languages, such as FORTRAN, COBOL, and the original BASIC, had I/O statements built into the language. Later languages have tended not to have I/O built into the language, but instead rely on a standard library for performing I/O, such as the **<stdio.h>** library in C. The library in languages like C works directly with files.

Still later languages, such as C++ and Java, introduced a further abstraction called a *stream*. A stream serves as an intermediary between the program and the file. Read and write operations are done to the stream, which is tied to a file. This architecture is very flexible, because the same kind of read and write operations can apply not only to a file, but to other kinds of I/O, such as network sockets. This added flexibility introduces a slight additional complexity in writing programs, because you have to deal not only with files but also with streams, and there exists a considerable variety of stream classes. But the added complexity is well worth the effort, and the .NET Framework strikes a nice balance, with classes that make performing common operations quite simple.

Code Example

As with directories, the **System.IO** namespace contains two classes for working with files. The **File** class has all static methods, and the **FileInfo** class has instance methods. The program **FileDemo** extends the **DirectoryDemo** example program to illustrate reading and writing text files. The directory commands are retained so that you can easily exercise the program on different directories. The two new commands are **read** and **write**. The **read** command illustrates using the **File** class. The **dir** command, already present in the **DirectoryDemo** program, illustrates using the **FileInfo** class.

Here is the code for the **read** command. The user is prompted for a file name. The static **OpenText** method returns a **StreamReader** object, which is used for the actual reading. There is a **ReadLine** method for reading a line of text, similar to the **ReadLine** method of the **Console** class. A nondefined reference is returned by **ReadLine** when at end of file. Our program simply displays the contents of the file at the console. When done, we close the **StreamReader**.

```perl
...
elsif ($command eq 'read')
    {
        my $fileName = GetString("file name: ");
        my $reader = File->OpenText($fileName);
        my $str = $reader->ReadLine();
        my $null;
        while (defined($str))
        {
            Console->WriteLine($str);
            $str = $reader->ReadLine();
        }
        $reader->Close();
    }
}
...
```

As with the **DirectoryDemo** program, the Perl code is very terse—perhaps even too terse, as the code itself does not show the data type of various variables. For instance, the **File::OpenText** method returns a **StreamReader** object in the object **$reader**, which you can verify by consulting the MSDN documentation.

Here is the code for the **write** command. Again, we prompt for a file name. This time, we also prompt for whether or not to append to the file. There is a special constructor for the **StreamWriter** class that will directly return a **StreamWriter** without first getting a file object. The first parameter is the name of the file, and the second a **bool** flag specifying the append mode. If **true**, the writes will append to the end of an already existing file. If **false**, the writes will overwrite an existing file. In both cases, if a file of the specified name does not exist, a new file will be created.

```perl
...
elsif ($command eq 'write')
{
    my $fileName = GetString("file name: ");
    my $strAppend = GetString("append (yes/no): ");
    my $append;
    if ($strAppend eq "yes")
    {
        $append = PerlNET::true;
```

```
   }
   else
   {
      $append = PerlNET::false;
   }
   my $writer = StreamWriter->new($fileName, $append);
   Console->WriteLine(
      "Enter text, blank line to terminate");
   my $str = GetString(": ");
   while ($str ne "")
   {
      $writer->WriteLine($str);
      $str = GetString(": ");
   }
   $writer->Close();
}
...
```

Here is a sample run of the program. We first obtain a listing of existing files in the current directory. We then create a new text file, **one.txt**, and enter a couple of lines of text data. We again do **dir**, and our new file shows up. We try out the **read** command. You could also open up the file in a text editor to verify that it has been created and has the desired data. Next, we write out another line of text to this same file, this time saying yes for append mode. We conclude by reading the contents of the file.

```
Welcome to File Demo
For the list of commands type help
path = C:\OI\NetPerl\Chap13\FileDemo
>>dir
Files:
   filedemo.exe
   FileDemo.perlproj
   FileDemo.pl
   FileDemo.sln
   InputWrapper.pl
Directories:
>>write
file name: one.txt
append (yes/no): no
Enter text, blank line to terminate
: hello, world
: second line
:

>>dir
Files:
   filedemo.exe
   FileDemo.perlproj
   FileDemo.pl
```

```
      FileDemo.sln
      InputWrapper.pl
      one.txt
Directories:
>>read
file name: one.txt
hello, world
second line

>>write
file name: one.txt
append (yes/no): yes
Enter text, blank line to terminate
: third line
:

>>read
file name: one.txt
hello, world
second line
third line

>>quit

Goodbye.
```

Multiple Thread Programming

Modern programming environments allow you to program with multiple threads. Threads run inside of processes and allow multiple concurrent execution paths. If there are multiple CPUs, you can achieve parallel processing through the use of threads. On a single processor machine, you can often achieve greater efficiency by using multiple threads, because when one thread is blocked, for example, waiting on an I/O completion, another thread can continue execution. Also, the use of multiple threads can make a program more responsive to shorter tasks, such as tasks requiring user responses.

Along with the potential benefit of programming with multiple threads, there is greater program complexity, because you have to manage the issues of starting up threads, controlling their lifetimes, and synchronizing among threads. Since threads are within a common process and share an address space, it is possible for two threads to concurrently access the same data. Such concurrent access, known as a *race condition,* can lead to erroneous results when nonatomic operations are performed.

.NET Threading Model

The .NET Framework provides extensive support for multiple thread programming in the **System.Threading** namespace. The core class is **Thread**, which encapsulates a thread of execution. This class provides methods to start and suspend threads, to sleep, and to perform other thread management functions. The method that will execute for a thread is encapsulated inside a *delegate* of type **ThreadStart**. A delegate can be thought of as an object-oriented function pointer, and can wrap either a static or an instance method. When starting a thread, it is frequently useful to define an associated class, which will contain instance data for the thread, including initialization information. A designated method of this class can be used as the **ThreadStart** delegate method.

USING DELEGATES

Delegates are constructed like any other .NET objects. The first argument to the constructor is an object pointer and the second one is the method name of the callback function:

```
my $handler = System::EventHandler->new($this, "callback");
```

The initial release of PerlNET does not support defining your own delegates, but it is easy to create delegates as called for by methods of .NET classes. We will also see delegates used in connection with event handling in Chapter 14, when we discuss user interface programming.

CONSOLE LOG DEMONSTRATION

Code Example

The **ThreadDemo** solution provides an illustration of this architecture. There are two projects. **ConsoleLog** is a C# class library project, and **ThreadDemo** is a Perl-managed EXE project. The **ConsoleLog** class encapsulates a thread ID and parameters specifying a sleep interval and a count of how many lines of output will be written to the console. It provides the method **ConsoleLog** that writes out logging information to the console, showing the thread ID and number of elapsed (millisecond) ticks.

We implement this class in C# for simplicity, because C# is more concise than Perl for implementing components. If you are not calling Perl code in your component, this approach works well. We have been using C# from time to time in this book, and a quick introduction is provided in the C# Survival Guide in Appendix B, which also contains some references for learning more about C#. Here is the program code:

```
//
// ConsoleLog.cs
//
using System;
using System.Threading;
```

```
public class ConsoleLog
{
   private int delta;
   private int count;
   private int ticks = 0;
   private static int nextThreadId = 1;
   private int threadId;
   public ConsoleLog(int delta, int count)
   {
      this.delta = delta;
      this.count = count;
      this.threadId = nextThreadId++;
   }
   public void ConsoleThread()
   {
      for (int i = 0; i < count; i++)
      {
         Console.WriteLine(
            "Thread {0}: ticks = {1}", threadId, ticks);
         Thread.Sleep(delta);
         ticks += delta;
      }
      Console.WriteLine(
         "Thread {0} is terminating", threadId);
   }
}
```

The basic purpose of this class is to provide the **ConsoleThread** method, which will display a count of ticks at a periodic interval and print a "terminating" message when it is done.

The Perl project **ThreadDemo** is configured with a "slow" thread and a "fast" thread. The slow thread will sleep for 1 second between outputs, and the fast thread will sleep for only 400 milliseconds.

```
#
# ThreadDemo.pl
#

use strict;
use namespace "System";
use namespace "System.Threading";
use PerlNET qw(AUTOCALL);

my $slowLog = ConsoleLog->new(1000,5);
my $fastLog = ConsoleLog->new(400,5);
my $slowStart = ThreadStart->new($slowLog,
   "ConsoleThread");
my $fastStart = ThreadStart->new($fastLog,
   "ConsoleThread");
my $slowThread = Thread->new($slowStart);
```

```
my $fastThread = Thread->new($fastStart);
Console->WriteLine("Starting threads ...");
$slowThread->Start();
$fastThread->Start();
Console->WriteLine("Threads have started");
```

A **ConsoleLog** object is created for each threads, initialized with appropriate parameters. Both will do five lines of output.

Next, appropriate delegates are created of type **ThreadStart**. Notice that we use an instance method, **ConsoleThread**, as the delegate method. Use of an instance method rather than a static method is appropriate in this case, because we want to associate parameter values (sleep interval and output count) with each delegate instance.

We then create and start the threads. We write a message to the console just before and just after starting the threads. When do you think the message "Threads have started" will be displayed, relative to the output from the threads themselves? Here is the output from running the program. You will notice a slight delay as the program executes, reflecting the sleep periods.

```
Starting threads ...
Threads have started
Thread 1: ticks = 0
Thread 2: ticks = 0
Thread 2: ticks = 400
Thread 2: ticks = 800
Thread 1: ticks = 1000
Thread 2: ticks = 1200
Thread 2: ticks = 1600
Thread 1: ticks = 2000
Thread 2 is terminating
Thread 1: ticks = 3000
Thread 1: ticks = 4000
Thread 1 is terminating
```

The "Threads have started" message is displayed immediately, reflecting the asynchronous nature of the two additional threads. The **Start** calls return immediately, and the second message prints. Meanwhile, the other threads get started by the system, which takes a little bit of time, and then they each start producing output.

RACE CONDITIONS

A major issue in concurrency is shared data. If two computations access the same data, different results can be obtained depending on the timing of the different accesses, a situation known as a race condition. Race conditions present a programming challenge because they can occur unpredictably. Careful programming is required to ensure they do not occur.

Race conditions can easily arise in multithreaded applications, because threads belonging to the same process share the same address space and thus can share data. Race conditions can be avoided by serializing access to the shared data. Suppose only one thread at a time is allowed to access the shared data. Then the first thread that starts to access the data will complete the operation before another thread begins to access the data (the second thread will be blocked). In this case, threads synchronize based on accessing data.

The **System.Threading** namespace provides a number of thread synchronization facilities.

Further discussion of multithreading is beyond the scope of this book. For details, you may consult a book on the .NET Framework, such as *Application Development Using C# and .NET*. The book *Introduction to C# Using .NET* provides a more elementary discussion, with several examples, including a pure C# implementation of the **ThreadDemo** example provided in this section.

More About Delegates

Our threading example illustrated using a delegate of type **ThreadStart**. We pass such a delegate to the constructor of the **Thread** class. When we call the **Start** method of the thread, the callback function that is wrapped by the delegate will be called.

A powerful feature of delegates is that you can combine them. Delegates can be *multicast,* in which they have an invocation list of methods. When such a delegate is called, all the methods on the invocation list will be called in turn. The **Delegate.Combine** method can be used to combine the invocation methods of two delegate objects, and **Delegate.Remove** can be used to remove methods.[4]

Code
Example

As a simple illustration of combining delegates, consider the solution in the folder **DelegateDemo**. Like the previous example, there is a C# class library project **ConsoleLog** and a PerlNET-managed EXE project **Thread-Demo**. We have changed the PerlNET project to illustrate combining delegates.

```
#
# DialogDemo.pl
#

use strict;
use namespace "System";
use namespace "System.Threading";
```

4. In C# you can use the overloaded + and − operators to combine and remove delegate methods. In PerlNET you must use the **Combine** and **Remove** methods.

```
use PerlNET qw(AUTOCALL);

my $slowLog = ConsoleLog->new(1000,5);
my $dlgSlow = ThreadStart->new($slowLog, "ConsoleThread");
my $dlgQuick = ThreadStart->new($slowLog, "QuickMethod");
my $dlgCombo = Delegate->Combine($dlgSlow, $dlgQuick);
my $slowThread = Thread->new($dlgCombo);
Console->WriteLine("Starting thread ...");
$slowThread->Start();
Console->WriteLine("Thread has started");
```

Now there is only one thread, but we create a combined delegate **$dlgQuick** with an invocation list of two methods that will get called when the thread starts up. Here is the output from running the program.

```
Starting thread ...
Thread has started
Thread 1: ticks = 0
Thread 1: ticks = 1000
Thread 1: ticks = 2000
Thread 1: ticks = 3000
Thread 1: ticks = 4000
Thread 1 is terminating
QuickMethod called
```

Notice that the first method runs through to completion before the second method gets called.

Summary

This chapter examined a number of important classes in the .NET Framework. We began with a study of the root class **Object** and looked at some methods that should frequently be overridden in your own classes. We then studied garbage collection and finalization and saw some of the relationships between memory management in .NET and in Perl. We looked at directories and files, including the use of streams. We concluded with an introduction to multiple thread programming using .NET and Perl. As part of our architecture for using the .NET thread classes, we saw how to make use of delegates in Perl programs, a topic that will also be important in the next chapter when we study event handling in user interface programs implemented with .NET.

GUI Programming: Windows Forms

*T*he applications we have worked on thus far have had text-based user interfaces. Such interfaces are often the most suitable and easy to use. However, the graphical user interface (GUI) has proved to be very popular and convenient for most users. The .NET Framework offers a wide set of classes that encapsulate windows and graphics functionality, are very easy to use, and are accessible by all .NET-compliant objects. This means that we can use PerlNET to develop graphical applications as easily as we can text-based analogues. First, we discuss the importance of GUI and learn how to create a simple window. Then, we enrich our application with different graphical controls: textboxes, buttons, and so on. Next, we show how to handle user interaction through event-handling mechanisms. Finally, we show how to work with a **ListBox** control to handle lists in a GUI application and develop a GUI for the stock management case study.

GUI and .NET

In the last few years, most users migrated or upgraded to graphical operating systems: Microsoft Windows and UNIX with X-Windows, for example. As a result, most of the tasks of performing configurations, setting up operating systems and components, working with file systems, and many other activities involve a GUI. A great deal of success in modern software engineering lies in correct interface design. Sometimes, the location of a button on the screen may be crucial. Researches continue to look for new and better ways to configure interaction with software users.

The topic of correct GUI design is out of the scope of this book. Our aim is to give you the tools for developing applications that involve user interaction in a graphical environment. .NET makes it easy for us. Hence, it may be a good reason to choose a .NET platform as the default base for our software. Moreover, it may attract beginners as well as experienced programmers, since they do not need to waste too much time in writing code for the presentation layer and its functionality. It is already encapsulated inside numerous .NET Framework classes. Instead, programmers may concentrate on the business logic of their applications. Still, some work should be done.

In the next sections of this chapter, we describe how to create a standard windows application using .NET classes and PerlNET.

Creating a Simple Windows Form

Classes that are responsible for the functionality of windows reside in the **System.Windows.Forms** namespace. Whenever we create a PerlNET application involving a GUI, we must define a new class that extends the **Form** class from this namespace. **Form** handles standard window operations: resizing, moving, closing, and so on. Classes that inherit from **Form** are also referred as **Winforms**. Additionally, we have to declare explicitly the **Main** method for the starting class, which will be the entry point to our program.

Creating a Window

Code
Example

Here is the simple PerlNET window application from the **SimpleWinform** folder:

```perl
#
# SimpleWinform.pl
#
package SimpleWinform;
use strict;
use namespace "System";
use namespace "System.Windows.Forms";
use namespace "System.Drawing";
use PerlNET qw(AUTOCALL);

=for interface
   [extends: Form]
   [STAThread]
   static void Main();
=cut

sub Main
{
   my $app = SimpleWinform->new();
   Application->Run($app);
```

```
}

sub SimpleWinform
{
   my $this = shift;

   $this->{Text} = "Simple Winform",
   $this->{Size} = Size->new(int(300), int(200));
}
```

To compile and build our window application we have to reference **System.Windows.Forms.dll**:

```
plc SimpleWinform.pl -reference=System.Windows.Forms.dll
```

We apply the **[STAThread]** attribute to our **Main** method so that our form will run using the Single Threaded Apartment (STA) model. To examine the behavior of our application without this attribute, you can remove the **[STAThread]** line and build the application. Now run it from the command prompt. You can see that the window was successfully created. However, you can continue working with the command prompt only after you close the window. In order to force our window application to run in its own process, we should return the line that was commented. Optionally, instead of applying the attribute, we may specify a **target** option with the **winexe** value to **plc**, and **plc** will create an executable with the STA model.

```
plc -target=winexe SimpleWinform.pl
-reference=System.Windows.Forms.dll
```

In our **Main** method, we create a new instance of **SimpleWinform** and run an application, passing to the **Run** method the reference to our form, which will be the main window of the application.

Inside the constructor of the **SimpleWinform** class, we set two properties that are inherited from the **Form** class. The **Text** property represents the caption of the window. Through the **Size** property, we set the width and height for our window. In this sample, the caption is "Simple Winform"; the window width is 300 and its height is 200. The window should look like the one shown in Figure 14-1.

The functionality that was inherited from the **Form** class allows us to resize, move, minimize, and maximize our window. However, this is not enough to make the application useful. Our next step is to learn how we output some text information in the client area of our window (the gray region under the caption).

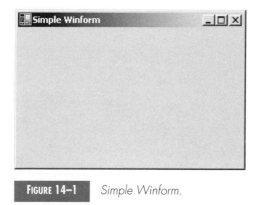

FIGURE 14-1   *Simple Winform.*

Printing Text on a Window

Text output in the window applications is different from in console applications. To be more precise, we should refer to this process as *drawing text*. You should consider the client area of a window as a blank paper sheet on which you would like to place some text fragment. Before actually drawing on paper, you have to decide where to place the text, what font and color to use, and so on. The same logic is applicable for a window application. The painting code should reside in the special virtual method **OnPaint**. We inherit it from the **Form** class, and our responsibility is to provide an implementation if we want to perform some painting in the application window.

Code
Example

WinTime: Step 1

The following program outputs the current time in the middle of the window. We placed its code under the **WinTime\Step1** directory.

```
#
# WinTime.pl
#
package OI::Samples::WinTime;
use strict;
use namespace "OI.Samples";
use namespace "System";
use namespace "System.Windows.Forms";
use namespace "System.Drawing";
use PerlNET qw(AUTOCALL);

=for interface
   [extends: Form]
   [STAThread]
   static void Main();
   protected override void OnPaint(PaintEventArgs e);
=cut
```

```
=for interface
   private field Brush f_Brush;
   private field str f_strTime;
   private field int x;
   private field int y;
=cut
sub Main
{
   my $app = "WinTime"->new();
   Application->Run($app);
}

sub WinTime
{
   my $this = shift;

   $this->{Text} = "WinTime - Step 1";
   $this->{Size} = Size->new(int(300), int(200));
   $this->{x} = 100;
   $this->{y} = 50;
   $this->{f_Brush} = SolidBrush->new(Color->Black);
   my @time = localtime;
   $this->{f_strTime} = sprintf("%02d:%02d:%02d",
                                $time[2], $time[1],
                                        $time[0]);
}

sub OnPaint
{
   my($this, $e) = @_;
   $e->{Graphics}->DrawString($this->{f_strTime},
                              $this->{Font},
                              $this->{f_Brush},
                              $this->{x}, $this->{y});
}
```

We bolded the lines of code that are relevant to drawing. Inside the interface definition, we override the virtual method **OnPaint**. This method gets the **PaintEventArgs** class object as a parameter through which we may access the **Graphics** read-only property of the **Graphics** class.

The **Graphics** class resides in the **System.Drawing** namespace, and it has a rich set of methods for drawing. We chose to use the **DrawString** method, which displays for us the current time in the middle of the client area of our application window. The parameters we have to supply to the **Draw-String** method are

- The string to display
- The font to use

● The brush to paint with

● The location

All the **DrawString** parameters, except the font to use, are initialized inside the **WinTime** constructor, which performs the following tasks:

● Setting values for coordinates

● Constructing a new black **SolidBrush**

● Setting the **f_strTime** field to reflect the current time

We use the default font for the form by specifying the **Font** property of the **Form** class in the call to **DrawString**.

Running the above program will display the window with the current time, as in Figure 14-2.

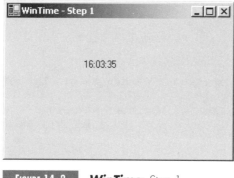

FIGURE 14–2   **WinTime**: Step 1.

Events Handling

One of the most important aspects of GUI applications is interaction with the user. Windows Forms implement it through an event-handling mechanism. We refer to applications that employ such mechanism as *event-driven*. In the case of a GUI, the user issues the events. He or she may move the mouse pointer over the window and click somewhere in the client area. Our task is to provide the code, which will run in response to these events and perform appropriate tasks.

Windows Forms employ the .NET event model, which uses delegates that we discussed in Chapter 13. Using delegates, we bind events to the methods that handle them. The Windows Forms classes use multicast delegates. This means that we may bind the delegate to more than one method. The delegate will call all these methods in response to an event.

MouseDown Event

Every form may accept the **MouseDown** event. To handle it, we should construct an appropriate delegate, passing to its constructor a method that will execute in response to the **MouseDown** event. Then, we should call the **add_MouseDown** method of our form and pass to it the delegate we constructed. This way, we add our method to the **MouseDown** event delegate list. Here are the lines of code that add the **Form_MouseDown** method to the **MouseDown** event:

```
my $evtHandler = MouseEventHandler->new($this,
                                      "Form_MouseDown");
$this->add_MouseDown($evtHandler);
```

$this is the reference to our **form** object. We should declare the **Form_MouseDown** method as follows:

```
void Form_MouseDown(any sender, MouseEventArgs evArgs);
```

Optionally, we may apply some access modifier. Our handler receives **MouseEventArgs** (derived from **EventArgs**) that implements read-only properties to provide information specific to this event:

- **Button** specifies which button was pressed.
- **Clicks** indicates how many times the button was pressed and released.
- **Delta** provides a count of rotations of a mouse wheel.
- **x** and **y** provide the coordinates where the mouse button was pressed.

WinTime: Step 2

We enriched the functionality of our **WinTime** program by adding the **MouseDown** event handling. In response to this event, we output the most current time in the location where the user pressed the mouse button. Please refer to the **WinTime\Step2** folder for the full code.

```
=for interface
   [extends: Form]
   [STAThread]
   static void Main();
   protected override void OnPaint(PaintEventArgs e);
   private void Form_MouseDown(any sender,
                              MouseEventArgs evArgs);
   private void _init();
=cut
. . .
sub _init
{
   my $this = shift;
```

```
    my $evtHandler = MouseEventHandler->new($this,
                                    "Form_MouseDown");
    $this->add_MouseDown($evtHandler);
}
sub WinTime
{
    my $this = shift;

    $this->_init();
    $this->{Text} = "WinTime - Step 2";
    $this->{Size} = Size->new(int(200), int(200));
    $this->{x} = 50;
    $this->{y} = 50;
    $this->{f_Brush} = SolidBrush->new(Color->Black);
    my @time = localtime;
    $this->{f_strTime} = sprintf("%02d:%02d:%02d",
                                    $time[2], $time[1],
                                    $time[0]);
}
. . .
sub Form_MouseDown
{
    my ($this, $sender, $e) = @_;
    my @time = localtime;
    $this->{f_strTime} = sprintf("%02d:%02d:%02d",
                                    $time[2], $time[1],
                                    $time[0]);
    $this->{x} = $e->{X};
    $this->{y} = $e->{Y};
    $this->Invalidate();
}
```

The resulting application window may look like the one shown in Figure 14-3.

FIGURE 14-3   *WinTime*: Step 2.

In order to handle the **MouseDown** event, we added some code to Step 1. We bolded those lines of code that are relevant to the event handling. We expanded our interface definition by adding two methods: **_init** and **Form_MouseDown**. The former is responsible for initializing the **MouseDown** event delegate and adding the **Form_MouseDown** method to the delegate list; the latter is the **MouseDown** event handler. We call the **_init** method from our **WinTime** form constructor and the **Form_MouseDown** method is invoked each time a **MouseDown** event occurs on the form.

Our event handler gets the most current time using the **localtime** function and sets **f_strTime** to reflect it. Additionally, we examine the **MouseEventArgs** object and set our **WinTime** form **x** and **y** fields to the coordinates where the user pressed the mouse button. Finally, we call the **Invalidate** method with no arguments. This way, we instruct our form that it should repaint its client area. As a result, our application window gets the **WM_PAINT** message, which in turn entails the execution of the **OnPaint** method. Applications that are more sophisticated may take an approach of invalidating just a rectangle of the client area for the sake of efficiency.

Handling Left and Right Mouse Buttons

We can distinguish between left and right mouse buttons by using the **Button** property of the **MouseEventArgs** parameter. This property holds one of the values from the **MouseButtons** enumeration. The following code demonstrates possible scenarios of responding to left and right button **MouseDown** events:

```
use PerlNET qw(enum);
. . .
sub Form_MouseDown
{
   my ($this, $sender, $e) = @_;
   if ($e->{Button}==enum("MouseButtons.Left"))
   {
      # Handle Left Button Down
      . . .
   }
   elsif ($e->{Button}==enum("MouseButtons.Right"))
   {
      # Handle Right Button Down
      . . .
   }
}
```

KeyPress Event

If the user presses a key when our form is active, then the form gets the **KeyPress** event. We can handle this event following the regular procedure of writing a handler and using the corresponding delegate.

Code Example

WinTime: Step 3

Step 3 of our demonstration **(WinTime\Step3)** illustrates handling the **MouseDown** and **KeyPress** events. Now, we distinguish right and left buttons. In response to the right button, we clear the time string. The left button causes recalculation and relocation of the time string. If the user presses any key, we output the corresponding character. To extract the character when handling the **KeyPress** event, we access the **KeyChar** property of **KeyPressEventArgs** object, which our event handler accepts as a second argument. Here is the code for the event handlers:

```
use PerlNET qw(AUTOCALL enum);
. . .
sub Form_MouseDown
{
   my ($this, $sender, $e) = @_;
   if ($e->{Button} == enum("MouseButtons.Left"))
   {
       $this->{f_strTime} = "WinTime"->CalculateTime();
       $this->{x} = $e->{X};
       $this->{y} = $e->{Y};
   }
   elsif ($e->{Button} == enum("MouseButtons.Right"))
   {
       $this->{f_strTime} = "";
   }
   $this->Invalidate();
}

sub Form_KeyPress
{
   my ($this, $sender, $e) = @_;
   $this->{f_strTime} =
       "'" . $e->{KeyChar} . "'Was Pressed";
   $this->Invalidate();
}
```

The **CalculateTime** static method returns the current time string. Figure 14-4 shows the Step 3 application window and the response to pressing the *d* character.

FIGURE 14-4   ***WinTime****: Step 3.*

Menus

The important part of modern window-based user interfaces is menus. We implement them in code so that we do not need any additional resource file. We build up an application menu using the **MenuItem** class objects that can contain subitems of the same class. The top-level menu is a **MainMenu** class object. We assign its reference to the **Menu** property of our form. To handle choosing by the user of menu items, we hook a delegate to the **Click** event.

WinTime: Step 4

Code Example

In Step 4, we enrich our **WinTime** application by adding a simple menu (see Figure 14-5). By choosing File | Exit, we can exit our program. The code for this step resides in the **WinTime\Step4** directory.

FIGURE 14-5   ***WinTime****: Step 4.*

MENU CODE

```
#
# WinTime.pl - Step 4
#
. . .
=for interface
   private field MainMenu f_mainMenu;
   private field MenuItem f_menuFile;
   private field MenuItem f_menuExit;
=cut
. . .
sub _init
{
   my $this = shift;

   # Creating Application Menu
   $this->{f_mainMenu} = "MainMenu"->new();
   $this->{f_menuFile} = "MenuItem"->new();
   $this->{f_menuExit} = "MenuItem"->new();
   # f_mainMenu
   $this->{f_mainMenu}->{MenuItems}->AddRange
            ("MenuItem[]"->new($this->{f_menuFile}));
   # f_menuFile
   $this->{f_menuFile}->{Index} = 0;
   $this->{f_menuFile}->{MenuItems}->AddRange
            ("MenuItem[]"->new($this->{f_menuExit}));
   $this->{f_menuFile}->{Text} = "File";
   # f_menuExit
   $this->{f_menuExit}->{Index} = 0;
   $this->{f_menuExit}->{Text} = "Exit";

   $this->{Menu} = $this->{f_mainMenu};
   . . .
}
```

MENU EVENT CODE

We use the **Exit** method of the **Application** class to exit our program.

```
. . .
=for interface
   . . .
   private void MenuExit_Click(any sender, EventArgs e);
   . . .
=cut
. . .
sub _init
{
   . . .
   my $menuHandler = "System.EventHandler"->new($this,
```

```
                                          "MenuExit_Click");
    $this->{f_menuExit}->add_Click($menuHandler);
    . . .
}
. . .
sub MenuExit_Click
{
    Application->Exit();
}
```

Closing Event

You may want to ask the user for a confirmation when he or she chooses to exit the application. To add such behavior to your application, you should handle the **Closing** event, which is raised when a form is about to close. There are several ways to close the window:

- From the "X" at top right of the window
- From the system menu at the top left of the window
- By the keyboard Alt + F4
- From the application menu

To tap into this behavior, in our File | Exit handler we should not exit the application but instead close the main window by calling the **Close** method:

```
sub MenuExit_Click
{
    # Application->Exit();
    my $this = shift;
    $this->Close();
}
```

Here we present **Closing** event handler, which brings a message box to confirm the exit. Notice that we set to **true** the **Cancel** property of the **CancelEventArgs** object if the user chooses not to exit.

```
=for interface
        private void Form_Closing(any sender,
                System.ComponentModel.CancelEventArgs e);
=cut
. . .
sub Form_Closing
{
    my ($this, $sender, $e) = @_;

    my $res = MessageBox->Show("Exit Application?", "Exit",
                    enum("MessageBoxButtons.YesNo"));
    if ($res eq "No")
    {
        $e->{Cancel} = PerlNET::true;
```

```
    }
}
```

To add the event handler we modified the **_init** method as follows.

```
use namespace "System.ComponentModel";
. . .
sub _init
{
   my $this = shift;
   . . .
   my $closeHandler = CancelEventHandler->new($this,
                          "Form_Closing");
   $this->add_Closing($closeHandler);
}
```

Code Example

You should always see the message box shown in Figure 14-6 when the **Closing** event is raised.

The full code for this step resides in the **WinTime\Step5** folder.

FIGURE 14–6   **WinTime**: *Exit confirmation.*

Controls

Many window-based applications contain different user interface controls that were designed to make the work with the application more convenient and easy to use for its users. The most frequently used controls are

- labels
- textboxes
- buttons
- listboxes

We learn in this section how to incorporate these controls into our GUI applications. When we create a new control for our form, we should add it to the controls collection of the form. We can do it by calling the **Add** method on the **Controls** property of the **Form** class.

with Function

When working with controls, we often need to set multiple properties for a single object representing some control. To make it easier, we can use the **with** function exposed by the PerlNET module. Its syntax is similar to Perl hashes' initialization. As a first argument, we pass the reference to an object, and the next arguments are pairs of property name and value to set. For example, to set the **Text** and **TabIndex** properties of the object, reference to which is stored in **$obj**, we would write

```
PerlNET::with($obj,
              Text => "Hello",
              TabIndex => 1);
```

Normally, we would import the **with** function by specifying:

```
use PerlNET qw(with);
```

Labels

Labels are static controls, as the user cannot interact with them. We can use labels to display static text on our form. The only way to change the text displayed by the label is by mutating its **Text** property programmatically. We emphasize that creating a label is not the same as drawing a string, as it may seem at first glance. Whenever we change the **Text** property of our label, we do not have to invalidate the client area, as the form redraws the control for us automatically. We demonstrate changing label text when we learn about our next control, the **TextBox**. Here is the code for creating a label with the text "Hello from PerlNET!"(see Figure 14-7). The code is located in the **ControlsLabel** folder.

```
#
# ControlsLabel.pl
#
package OI::Samples::Controls;
use strict;
use namespace "OI.Samples";
use namespace "System";
use namespace "System.Windows.Forms";
use namespace "System.Drawing";
use PerlNET qw(AUTOCALL with);

=for interface
   [extends: Form]
   [STAThread]
   static void Main();
=cut
sub Main
{
```

```
    my $app = "Controls"->new();
    Application->Run($app);
}

sub Controls
{
    my $this = shift;

    $this->{Text} = "Label Sample";
    $this->{Size} = Size->new(int(300), int(200));

    my $lblGreeting = Label->new();
    my $lblGreeting = Label->new();
    with ($lblGreeting,
          Text => "Hello from PerlNET!",
          Size => Size->new(int(200), int(20)),
          Location => Point->new(80, 10));

    $this->{Controls}->Add($lblGreeting);
}
```

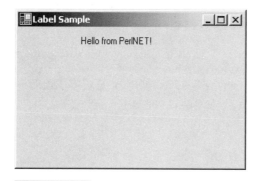

FIGURE 14–7   *Label control sample.*

Textboxes

Often, we require the user of our application to enter some text information, such as name or email address. The **TextBox** control is perfect for this purpose. It has the **Text** property, which we may access to get the user's entered text as the **System.String** object (PerlNET will translate it for us into a Core Perl string). After extracting the text, we can use it as any other string in our program.

TEXTBOX DEMONSTRATION

Our **TextBox** demonstration program asks the user to enter his or her name, and it then displays a greeting to the user. To make this work, we have to trap pressing the Enter key. We do it by handling the **KeyDown** event on the text-box and examining the **KeyCode** property of the **KeyEventArgs** object inside our event handler.

```
if ($e->{KeyCode} == enum("Keys.Enter"))
{
    # Enter Was pressed
    . . .
}
```

Code Example

The following is the code in our program context. We present the code that we added to the previous step to enrich our application user interface with the textbox control. For the full code, look in the **ControlsTextbox** folder under the chapter samples directory.

```
#
# ControlsTextbox.pl
# TextBox step
package OI::Samples::Controls;
. . .
use PerlNET qw(AUTOCALL with enum);

=for interface
    . . .
    private void Greet();
=cut

# Controls fields
=for interface
    private field Label f_lblGreeting;
    private field TextBox f_txtName;
=cut

# Event Handlers
=for interface
    private void txtName_KeyDown(any sender,
                                 KeyEventArgs e);
=cut
. . .
sub Controls
{
    . . .

    my $lblName = Label->new();
    with ($lblName,
          Text => "Your Name:",
          Size => Size->new(int(100), int(20)),
          Location => Point->new(50, 50));

    my $txtName = TextBox->new();
```

```perl
    with ($txtName,
          Size => Size->new(int(100), int(20)),
          Location => Point->new(160, 50));
    my $enterHandler = KeyEventHandler->new($this,
                                    "txtName_KeyDown");
    $txtName->add_KeyDown($enterHandler);

    with ($this,
          Text => "Textbox Sample",
          Size => Size->new(int(300), int(200)),
          f_lblGreeting => $lblGreeting,
          f_txtName => $txtName);

    $this->{Controls}->Add($_) for ($lblGreeting, $lblName,
                                                   $txtName);
}

sub txtName_KeyDown
{
    my ($this, $sender, $e) = @_;
    if ($e->{KeyCode} == enum("Keys.Enter"))
    {
        $this->Greet();
    }
}

sub Greet
{
    my $this = shift;

    my $name = $this->{f_txtName}->{Text};
    if ($name eq "")
    {
        $this->{f_lblGreeting}->{Text} =
                        "Hello from PerlNET!";
    }
    else
    {
        $this->{f_lblGreeting}->{Text} = $name .
                                ", hello from PerlNET!";
    }
}
```

The resulting application window may look like that shown in Figure 14–8.

FIGURE 14-8   *Textbox control sample.*

Buttons

Probably the most often used control is the **Button** control. We use buttons to issue a generic command to our application. As a response to the button click by the user, the application may close the window, display some information, open a new window, and so forth. To program such behavior, we have to add a button control to our form and handle the **Click** event on it.

BUTTON DEMONSTRATION

In this step of our demonstration program, we added the Greeting button. Now, after typing his or her name, the user may either press Enter or click the button to see the greeting. For this purpose, we defined the **btnGreeting_Click** event handler, which calls the **Greet** method from the previous step. The code for this step is in the **ControlsButton** directory.

```
#
# ControlsButton.pl
#
package OI::Samples::Controls;
. . .

# Event Handlers
=for interface
   private void txtName_KeyDown(any sender,
                               KeyEventArgs e);
   private void btnGreeting_Click(any sender,
                                  EventArgs e);
=cut
. . .

sub Controls
{
   . . .
```

```
my $btnGreeting = Button->new();
with ($btnGreeting,
      Text => "Greeting",
      Size => Size->new(int(100), int(30)),
      Location => Point->new(100, 80));

my $btnHandler = EventHandler->new($this,
                      "btnGreeting_Click");
$btnGreeting->add_Click($btnHandler);

with ($this,
      Text => "Button Sample",
      Size => Size->new(int(300), int(200)),
      f_txtName => $txtName,
      f_lblGreeting => $lblGreeting);

$this->{Controls}->Add($_) for ($lblName, $txtName,
                      $lblGreeting, $btnGreeting);
}

sub btnGreeting_Click
{
   my $this = shift;

   $this->Greet();
}
```

. . .

Figure 14-9 shows the possible appearance of our form.

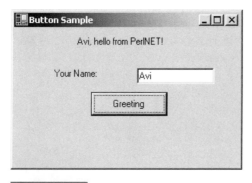

FIGURE 14–9   *Button control sample.*

Listboxes

List controls are another important user interface element. .NET provides the
ListControl class for working with lists. An interesting descendant of this class
is the **ListBox** control, which we may use to display a set of items, add to it
new items, and select or remove existing items. Most of these tasks are performed through the **Items** property, which exposes the collection of items that
currently appears in the list. This means that all methods that we learned when
we discussed collections are relevant here.

POPULATING A LISTBOX

In this step, we add the **ListBox** control to our form. The code for this step is
in the **ControlsListbox** folder. We use it to store the names of people to whom
we displayed a greeting. To make this demonstration a little more ambitious, we
add a new name only if the list does not already contain it. The **Contains**
method of the **Items** collection performs the check for the name containment.
We slightly altered our **Greet** method and added some code, which is responsible for working with the list.

```
#
# ControlsListbox.pl
#
package OI::Samples::Controls;
. . .
#Controls
=for interface
    . . .
   private field ListBox f_lstNames;
=cut
. . .
sub Controls
{
    . . .
   my $lstNames = ListBox->new();
   with ($lstNames,
         Size => Size->new(int(150), int(130)),
         Location => Point->new(75, 130));

   with ($this,
         Text => "Listbox Sample",
         Size => Size->new(int(300), int(300)),
         f_txtName => $txtName,
         f_lblGreeting => $lblGreeting,
         f_lstNames => $lstNames);

   $this->{Controls}->Add($_) for ($lblName, $txtName,
              $lblGreeting, $btnGreeting, $lstNames);
}
```

```
. . .
sub Greet
{
   my $this = shift;

   my $name = $this->{f_txtName}->{Text};
   if ($name eq "")
   {
      $this->{f_lblGreeting}->{Text} =
                  "Hello from PerlNET!";
   }
   else
   {
      $this->{f_lblGreeting}->{Text} = $name .
               ", hello from PerlNET!";
      my $items = $this->{f_lstNames}->{Items};
      if (not $items->Contains($name))
      {
         $items->Add($name);
      }
   }
}
```

SELECTING AN ITEM FROM A LISTBOX

Additionally, we demonstrate how you can handle selecting an item from the **ListBox** control on your form (see Figure 14-10). We do it by defining a handler for the **SelectedIndexChanged** event. You can access the selected item through the **SelectedIndex** and **SelectedItem** properties. If no item is selected, **SelectedIndex** is -1. Here is the code for the event handler of the **SelectedIndexChanged** event.

```
sub lstNames_SelectedIndexChanged
{
   my $this = shift;
   if ($this->{f_lstNames}->{SelectedIndex} != -1)
   {
      my $item = $this->{f_lstNames}->{SelectedItem};
      $this->{f_txtName}->{Text} = $item;
      $this->Greet();
   }
}
```

When the user selects an item from our listbox, we set the **Text** property of the **f_txtName** textbox to reflect the selection and call the **Greet** method.

FIGURE 14-10 *Listbox control sample.*

Stock Management Case Study

In the previous chapters we presented several applications for managing the inventory. In this chapter we created the GUI version of the stock management application. You can view the items that are currently in stock, add new items, and modify the details of the existing items. Figure 14-11 shows the main window of our application.

For this demonstration, we used several back-end components. Some of them we already met in the previous chapters and some we created especially for the study.

- **StockItem** provides the functionality of the item in stock with several properties: **ID**, **Name**, **Price**, **Quantity**.
- **IStock** defines an interface in C# for managing the stock items (adding, removing, modifying).
- **Stock** implements the **IStock** interface and manages the items using the **ArrayList**.

All these components reside inside the case study directory (**StockMgrForm**) in their own folders. Please refer to the **readme.txt** file inside the **StockMgrForm** directory for application building instructions.

The application has two additional forms for adding a new item (**ItemFrm**) and modifying the details of an existing item (**DetailsFrm**). Pressing the "Add New Item…" button will cause the **ItemFrm** dialog to be shown. We may show the form as a dialog box by calling the **ShowDialog** method of

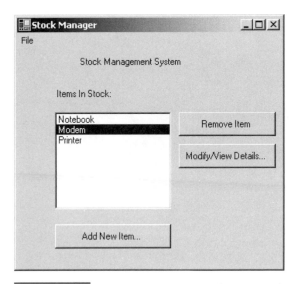

Stock Management application window.

the **Form** class as we did in the handler of the button click event in our **StockMgrForm**:

```
sub btnAddItem_Click
{
   my $this = shift;

   my $dlg = "ItemFrm"->new();
   if ($dlg->ShowDialog() != enum("DialogResult.OK"))
   {
      $dlg->Dispose();
      return;
   }
   my $name = $dlg->{itemName};
   my $price = $dlg->{itemPrice};
   my $qty = $dlg->{itemQuantity};
   $dlg->Dispose();

   my $id = $this->{f_stock}->GenerateID();
   $this->{f_stock}->AddItem("StockItem"->new($id, $name,
                               $price, $qty));
   $this->ShowItems();
}
```

After the user closes the dialog, we examine the return value of **ShowDialog** to check whether the user added a new item or cancelled the action. If the method returns **DialogResult.OK**, the user did not cancel the action and we may read the details of a new item through the **ItemFrm** properties and add this new item to stock.

Figure 14-12 shows the dialog box for adding a new item.

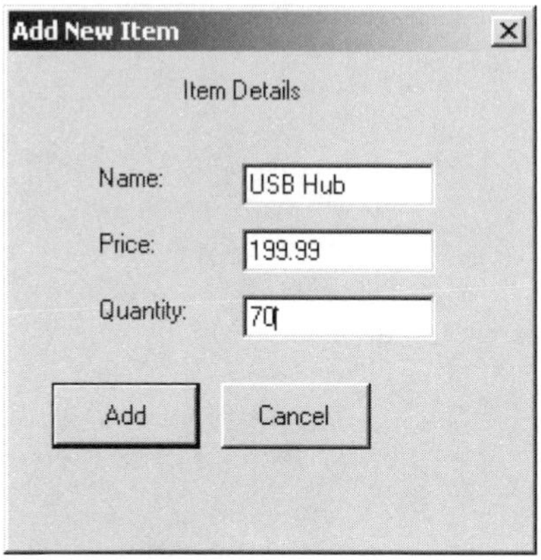

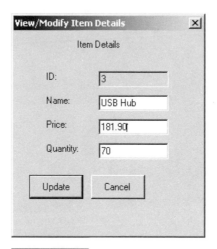

FIGURE 14–12   *Dialog for adding a new item.*

Similarly, we may change the details of an existing item by selecting it inside the listbox and pressing the "Modify/View Details…" button. Figure 14-13 shows the **DetailsFrm** dialog box that we use to edit item details.

FIGURE 14–13   *Dialog for modifying item details.*

To remove an item, simply select it and press the "Remove Item" button. The application will show the confirmation message box and will act according to your response.

In the next chapter, we will present the database version of the Stock Management System application.

Summary

In this chapter we introduced the main concepts of creating GUI applications using .NET Framework classes. Your window class should inherit from the **Form** class, which provides much of the window functionality. The text output on the window is referred to as drawing. All the drawing occurs in the **OnPaint** method of the **Form** class that we may override and provide our version.

Your forms may contain different controls, such as labels, textboxes, and buttons. You add them to the **Controls** collection of your form. In order to interact with the user, we employ the event-handling mechanism and delegates.

The **ListBox** control is useful to treat lists of data. It provides an easy interface for working against its **Items** collection.

We presented the Stock Management System as an illustration of a more complex user interface.

Database Programming with ADO.NET

*M*any modern applications work with different information storages. The ultimate solution for storing large amounts of data is using database engines that provide easy access and high optimizations for different operations on your data. The .NET environment introduces ADO.NET, which represents a set of classes for performing various database operations from your .NET applications. In this chapter we review these classes with emphasis on discussing data providers, working with datasets, and describing different scenarios of working with a database that you may implement in your PerlNET programs.

Data Providers

ADO.NET data providers[1] allow you to execute commands directly against the data source. Functionality is exposed directly without intermediary objects such as an OLE DB (object linking and embedding database) that stand between ADO and the data source. The .NET **DataAdapter** class models a data source as a set of database commands and a connection to that data source. Differences between data sources are not hidden by generic interfaces. The OLE DB data provider allows for nested transactions with data sources that support that functionality; the SQL Server data provider does not.[2]

---

1. .NET data providers are what used to be called in the beta literature *managed providers*. You may still see them referred to by that term.
2. There is a **Begin** method on the **OleDbTransaction** class; the **SqlTransaction** class does not have such a method.

.NET data providers supply data to a dataset or a data reader. A dataset is a memory-resident, lightweight relational database that is not connected to any database (disconnected scenario). You can also obtain a dataset from an XML document or create an XML document from a dataset. This allows you to work, if it makes sense, with your data as relational data or as hierarchical XML data.[3] Data readers model the traditional method of working with a database (connected scenario).

The data access classes that currently ship with the .NET Framework are found in the namespaces: **System.Data**, **System.Data.SqlClient**, **System.Data.OleDb**, **System.Data.Common**, and **System.Data.SqlTypes**. The **SqlClient** and **OleDb** namespaces reflect the SQL Server and OLE DB .NET data providers. An open database connectivity (ODBC) .NET data provider has been written, and additional ones will be written in the future.

To make our examples concrete, we use SQL Server 2000 and the SQL Server data provider.[4] Nonetheless, much of the basic functionality discussed in this chapter applies to the OLE DB data provider as well.

This chapter assumes you have some understanding of database concepts.

Setting Up the Example Databases

This chapter assumes that SQL Server 2000 has been installed using the Local System account, with authentication mode set to Mixed Mode. The user is assumed to be **sa**, with a blank password.

Please refer to the **readme.txt** file in the sample code directory for this chapter for more information about database setup.

.NET Database Classes

The prefix on the database classes and methods indicates the data provider used to access the data source. For example, the **OleDb** prefix applies to the OLE DB data provider. The **Sql** prefix applies to the SQL Server data provider.

The SQL Server data provider uses the native SQL Server wire protocol. The OLE DB data provider goes through the COM interop layer to talk to the

---

3. The many-to-many relations that you can have in a relational database do not automatically map to XML hierarchies, but this is no different from working with the classic object-relational model clash.

4. If you do not have a SQL Server available, you can go to the Microsoft site and download the MSDE, which is a scaled-down version of SQL Server. As of this writing, MSDE is available for free. Microsoft suggests using MSDE instead of Access in the future. Since we use vanilla functionality, you should be able to use the OLE DB data provider against the Access version of the Northwind traders by changing the **Sql** classes to the corresponding **OleDb** classes. We have not yet tested this scenario, however.

various OLE DB providers. For example, you could talk to SQL Server through the OLE DB data provider to the OLE DB provider for SQL Server. Nonetheless, the performance of going through the SQL Server data provider will be superior. The advantage of the OLE DB and the ODBC data providers is that you can work with ADO.NET against most data sources that you work with today.

There are some interfaces that define common functionality and some base classes that can be used to provide common functionality, but there is no requirement for a data provider to fit a specification that does not correspond to the way the underlying data source works.

For example, the **SqlDataAdapter** class and the **OleDbDataAdapter** class both use the abstract base classes **DbDataAdapter** and **DataAdapter** that are found in the **System.Data.Common** namespace. The **OleDbError** class and the **SqlError** class do not resemble each other at all. Server-side cursors are not in the ADO.NET model, because some databases (such as Oracle and DB2) do not have native support for them. Any support for them in the SQL Server data provider would be as an extension.[5]

As Table 15-1 shows, the **Connection**, **Command**, **DataReader**, **DataAdapter**, and **DataParameter** classes of the data providers do have some parallels that are defined by the **IDbConnection**, **IDbCommand**, **IDataReader**, **IDbDataAdapter**, and **IDataParameter** interfaces. Nothing, of course, prevents an implementation of these classes from having additional methods beyond those specified in the interfaces.

TABLE 15–1	Comparison of Parallel Classes in the OLE DB and SQL Server Data Providers	
Interface	**OLE DB**	**SQL Server**
IDbConnection	OleDbConnection	SqlConnection
IDbCommand	OleDbCommand	SqlCommand
IDataReader	OleDbDataReader	SqlDataReader
IDbDataAdapter	OleDbDataAdapter	SqlDataAdapter
IDbTransaction	OleDbTransaction	SqlTransaction
IDataParameter	OleDbParameter	SqlParameter

Classes such as the **DataSet** or the **DataTable**, which are independent of any data provider, do not have any prefix.

In our further discussion we demonstrate the ADO.NET concepts on the SQL data provider classes. You should get the same result when working with

---

5. Besides, server-side cursors are rarely appropriate, so it is not surprising that databases do not support them. Scrolling through the output is usually the result of a user interaction. Holding state on the server while the user interacts with the data is not the way to build a scalable application.

OLE DB (unless we state otherwise) by changing the prefix of the class names accordingly.

The Visual Studio.NET Server Explorer

Visual Studio.NET Server Explorer is a very useful tool for working with databases. While not as powerful as the SQL Server Enterprise Manager, it can give you the basic functionality you need when writing or debugging database applications. It will be very useful when we work with the examples in this chapter.

You may access the Server Explorer through the View | Server Explorer menu item. The Server Explorer is a dockable window that can be moved around as required. Figure 15-1 illustrates the Server Explorer.

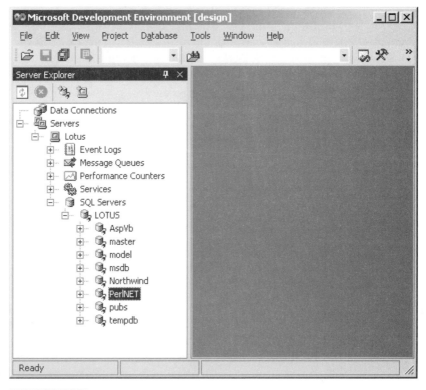

FIGURE 15–1   *Visual Studio.NET Server Explorer window.*

You can find information about all the fields in a table or look at and edit the data in the tables. You can create or edit stored procedures and design tables. We use the Server Explorer in the first few examples to show a little bit of how it can be used.

ADO.NET Connection

In order to obtain access to information stored in a database, we have to connect to our data source. ADO.NET provides special Connection classes for different data providers. These classes encapsulate all the required functionality to establish connection to databases. You just have to make sure you choose the relevant class and supply it with correct connection parameters.

Whenever we need to connect to our database, the **SqlConnection** class will serve this purpose. We instantiate this class in our PerlNET programs as we do every other .NET class. We pass to its constructor the *connection string*. This string contains all the required information for connecting to a database server and/or authentication. The connection string we use is

```
"server=Lotus;uid=sa;pwd=;database=PerlNET"
```

As you can see, we provide the server name, user to connect with, user's password (in our case it is blank), and database name (we have created PerlNET database on the SQL Server). You should edit the string so that it reflects your local settings, like substituting your server's name instead of Lotus. Here is the code fragment of creating a connection object:

```
use namespace "System.Data";
use namespace "System.Data.SqlClient";
. . .
my $connstr = "server=Lotus;uid=sa;pwd=;database=PerlNET";
my $conn = SqlConnection->new($connstr);
```

After we create the **SqlConnection** instance, we have to instruct the .NET Framework to actually connect to the database or, in other words, to open a connection. We do it by calling the **Open** method on the **SqlConnection** object.

```
$conn->Open();
```

If there were no network or other problems, the above line establishes for us a connection to the database. We may now utilize it to do something useful and important (since all our programs are such), such as update data, insert new data, and run various queries, with the information inside the database.

The next sections describe these operations. After we finish all our operations on the data, we close the connection and free this valuable resource:

```
use PerlNET qw (enum);
. . .
if ($conn->{State} == enum("ConnectionState.Open"))
{
    $conn->Close();
}
```

Pay attention, that before closing our connection, we check that it is still opened by examining the **State** property.

Connected Database Scenario

In the previous section, we described establishing and terminating a connection to the database. This section describes what action we may take while we have an open connection to the database. In other words, we show how to work in the connected database scenario.

Command Class

When writing database-oriented applications, we run different commands against our data source. We issue our statements with the help of the **SqlCommand** class. The command class performs the following actions:

- Executes SQL statements
- Executes DDL (Data Definition Language) statements
- Runs stored procedures

We initialize the command object with the command text and connection object. Here is how we create a new command that will query the People table for all its rows (in the following fragment, we just instantiate the **SqlCommand** object without executing it yet).

```
my $connstr = "server=Lotus;uid=sa;pwd=;database=PerlNET";
my $query = "select * from People";
my $conn = SqlConnection->new($connstr);
my $command = SqlCommand->new($query, $conn);
$conn->Open();
```

Notice that we do not have to supply an open connection when instantiating our command object. However, we must open the connection before actually executing the command.

After we have successfully created a command, we have to choose one of the executing methods:[6]

- **ExecuteReader**
- **ExecuteScalar**
- **ExecuteNonQuery**

ExecuteReader

The **ExecuteReader** method returns the **SqlDataReader** class instance, which holds the rows that were retrieved from the database by our command. We then use the simple interface of the **SqlDataReader** class to access the returned rows. Hence, the **ExecuteReader** is most suitable for the **select** SQL statements or for running stored procedures that perform **select** queries.

DATA READERS

Once we run the **ExecuteReader** method on our command object, we obtain the reference to the **SqlDataReader** class. This class represents a forward-only cursor model. We may fetch the row using its **Read** method with no parameters. This method returns **false** if there are no rows to fetch. The analogues in the ADO recordset programming model are calling the **MoveNext** method and checking the **EOF** property. Initially, there are no fetched rows in the **SqlDataReader**. You have to invoke the **Read** method before accessing the columns' values, unlike the ADO recordset that automatically fetches the first row.

```
my $reader = $command->ExecuteReader();
while($reader->Read())
{
   # Access columns
   . . .
}
```

To access the columns' values in the fetched row, the **SqlDataReader** class defines the indexed **Item** property. We may supply an integer zero-based index and obtain the corresponding column value. Optionally, we may access the column using its name as an index. Since PerlNET supports syntactic sugar of square brackets for indexed properties with integer parameters only, we

---

6. These are three methods that are common to the SQL Server and OLE DB data providers. There is an additional executing method for the SQL Server data provider: **ExecuteXmlReader**.

would have to use the **get_Item** method to access the column value by its name. Hence, when working with rows of the People table, the two following statements are identical:

```
print $reader->[0], "\n";
print $reader->get_Item("ID"), "\n";
```

After we finish working with data reader, we should call its **Close** method. We have to do it before closing the connection to the database.

```
if (defined $reader)
{
    $reader->Close();
}
```

SHOWPEOPLE SAMPLE

Let us demonstrate the above explanations with a simple example program, which will query the People table from the PerlNET database and will display the returned information. This example is found in the **Connected\ShowPeople** folder under the chapter samples directory.

```
#
# ShowPeople.pl
#
use strict;
use namespace "System.Data";
use namespace "System.Data.SqlClient";
use PerlNET qw(AUTOCALL enum);

my $connstr = "server=Lotus;uid=sa;pwd=;database=PerlNET";
print "======================\n";
my $query = "select * from people";
my $conn = SqlConnection->new($connstr);
my $command = SqlCommand->new($query, $conn);
$conn->Open();

my $reader = $command->ExecuteReader();
if (defined $reader)
{
    print "ID\tName\n";
    print "--\t----\n";
    while($reader->Read())
    {
        print $reader->get_Item("ID"), "\t",
              $reader->get_Item("Name"), "\n";
    }
}
if (defined $reader)
{
    $reader->Close();
```

```
}
if ($conn->{State} == enum("ConnectionState.Open"))
{
    $conn->Close();
}
print "======================\n";
```

Our program will have the following output:

```
======================
ID      Name
--      ----
1       Elvis
2       John
3       Ringo
======================
```

You may use the Visual Studio.NET Server Explorer to check the results of the program. Select the People table under the PerlNET database explorer and right-click to get a context menu. Select Retrieve Data from Table, and you can retrieve the data associated with the table and compare it with the results of the program. You will see that they are the same. Figure 15–2 shows this.

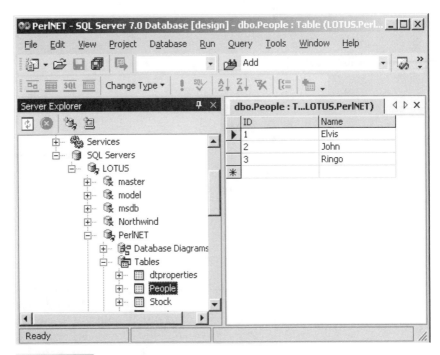

FIGURE 15–2   *Server Explorer showing People table, fields, and data.*

ExecuteScalar

This executing method returns the single value from the query. If the resulting row set has multiple columns or rows, then the return value will be the data from the first row and first column. We use this method if we know a priori that our command should return a single value, like the following **select** statement:

```
select count(*) from People
```

Note that the **ExecuteScalar** method returns an object. PerlNET converts the returned value to the scalar if we deal with a value type object. If the query selects no rows, then the method returns an undefined value. You may test it with the **defined** function.

```
my $query = "select Name from People where ID = 4";
my $command = SqlCommand->new($query, $conn);
my $value = $command->ExecuteScalar();
if (!defined($value))
{
    # Empty query result - No person with ID = 4
}
else
{
    # Do something with $value
}
```

ExecuteNonQuery

The **ExecuteNonQuery** method is useful when running commands that should not return any data from the database. Among such commands may be SQL statements (insert, delete, update), DDL commands (create table, alter table, etc.), or any stored procedure that does not perform a select query. This method returns an integer value indicating the number of rows affected in the case of a SQL statement. For any other commands, it returns 1.

In the following fragment we add a new row to our People table:

```
my $query = 'insert into People(ID, Name) values(4,
                                             "Eric")';
my $command = SqlCommand->new($query, $conn);
$command->ExecuteNonQuery();
```

As we mentioned before, we may utilize the **ExecuteNonQuery** method for executing stored procedures. In the previous example we added a new row to the People table and we had to supply both the ID and name of a new person. It would be more convenient if the ID was generated automatically.

We wrote the stored procedure **sp_NewPerson**, which expects one parameter—a name of a new person. The procedure generates a new ID and inserts the new person into the People table. The script is located in the chapter samples directory in the **sp_NewPerson.sql** file.

```
ALTER PROCEDURE sp_NewPerson
   @PersonName varchar(20) = NULL
AS
   declare @ID int

   if exists(select MAX(ID) from People)
   begin
      set @ID = (select MAX(ID) from People)
      set @ID = @ID + 1
      insert into People(ID, Name)
      values(@ID, @PersonName)
   end
```

To run the stored procedure through the **Command** object, we have to alter some of its properties. We should set the correct **CommandType** and populate the **Parameters** collection, adding to it the new person's name. Here is the code for adding a new person using the **sp_NewPerson** stored procedure (we assume that the connection was already opened).

```
my $command = SqlCommand->new("sp_NewPerson", $conn);
$command->{CommandType} =
    PerlNET::enum("CommandType.StoredProcedure");
my $sqlParam = $command->{Parameters}->Add('@PersonName',
    PerlNET::enum("SqlDbType.NVarChar"), 20);
$sqlParam->{Value} = "Eric";
$command->ExecuteNonQuery();
```

The **Add** of the **Parameters** collection returns a reference to the **SqlParameter** class instance. We set its **Value** property before executing the command. The full version of the program resides in the **Connected\StoredProc** folder.

Code
Example

Connected Database Scenario Summary

We described and demonstrated the connected scenario. The program connects to the database, does the work it needs to do, and then disconnects. You can run through the returned data only in the forward direction. This corresponds to the classic ADO forward-only cursor/recordset. In the connected mode you must open and close the database connection explicitly.

Keeping a connection continually open is not the best way to work in an environment where you want to minimize the resources consumed (connections are expensive) to allow for scalability.

In the next section we describe another option that you may choose when writing .NET database applications: the disconnected scenario using **DataSet**, **DataTable**, and related classes.

The Disconnected Database Scenario

One of the innovations that ADO.NET introduces is working in the disconnected manner. The **DataSet** class implements an in-memory lightweight database. You can fill the **DataSet** with the information from the database to manipulate your data inside the **DataSet** without being connected and propagate the changes to the database server as necessary.

When working with **DataSet**, you populate it with the **DataTable** class objects that represent tables. You may have several tables inside one **DataSet**. This way you may even build in-memory relational databases.

The **DataSet** and **DataTable** classes are independent of any data provider. Therefore, we need an adapter, which will mediate between our **DataSet** objects and database server. The **SqlDataAdapter** class plays the role of such mediator. All the operations that involve both **DataSet** class instances and the database will pass through **SqlDataAdapter**.

You do not have to fill the **DataSet** objects with information from the database. This means that you may create a temporary in-memory database for your PerlNET application if this makes sense.

DataSet and DataTable

The **DataSet** and **DataTable** classes reside in the **System.Data** namespace. As we mentioned before, they are not bound to any data provider. Therefore, we may work with them independently on any data source.

You instantiate **DataSet** objects as any other .NET class objects by calling the **new** method. Normally, you either pass no parameters to the constructor or pass the string with the name that you give to your **DataSet** object.

```
use namespace "System.Data";
. . .
my $ds = DataSet->new();
my $dsWithName = DataSet->new("MyDataset");
```

After you create a new **DataSet** instance, it is a good idea to populate it with some data—after all, this is why we need **DataSet**. We have two options: obtain the data from the database server or work with our own data. For now, we use the latter, as we have not yet learned about the data adapters.

The **DataSet** class exposes the **Tables** property that represents **DataTableCollection**. We may add a new table by calling one of the three versions of the **Add** method on the **Tables** property:

- **DataTable Add()**
- **void Add(DataTable)**
- **DataTable Add(String)**

The first and third versions will create an empty table inside the **DataSet** and return a reference that you may use to alter your table. The difference is that the first version creates the **DataTable** with the automatic name and the third version assigns to the table the name that you pass as a parameter. The second version accepts a **DataTable** reference to add to the **Tables** collection. The code may look like follows.

```
# Create DataSet
my $ds = DataSet->new();
# Add "Emails" Table and obtain reference to it
my $dt = DataSet->{Tables}->Add("Emails");
```

No matter what version we choose, we should know more about working with **DataTable** class objects.

DATATABLE CLASS

As we stated, you obtain a reference to the **DataTable** class either by instantiating a new object with the **new** method or as a return value of the two versions of the **DataTableCollection.Add** method. In any case, we obtain an empty table without defined columns. Before populating our table with rows of data, we have to define the table structure[7]—the list of columns and their types, and optionally keys and constraints, as in any other database environment like SQL Server.

COLUMNS

We alter our table structure by adding new **DataColumn** objects through the **Columns** property, which represents **DataColumnCollection**. The **DataColumn** class has multiple properties that you may set, such as name of the column, its type, and allowance of NULL value. We modify these values according to our application requirements.

The following sample creates a **DataTable** object for storing emails and defines the structure of the table (two columns: ID and Email). The code resides in the **DataTable** folder.

Code
Example

```
#
# DataTable.pl
#
use namespace "System";
use namespace "System.Data";
use PerlNET qw(enum AUTOCALL);

# Create empty table "Emails"
my $dt = DataTable->new("Emails");
```

---

7. We don't have to make such definitions of the table structure when working through data adapters.

```
# Add new column ID to the table
my $colID = $dt->{Columns}->Add("ID");
# Alter ID column type
$colID->{DataType} = Type->GetType("System.Int32");
# Create new column Email
my $colEmail = DataColumn->new("Email");
# Alter Email column type
$colEmail->{DataType}= Type->GetType("System.String");
# Add Email column to the "Emails" table
$dt->{Columns}->Add($colEmail);
```

CONSTRAINTS

There often arises a need to control the data in our tables by enforcing constraints. For example, we may define that our Email column of the Emails table should have unique values for each row. Also, we may want to define a primary key for the whole table. The **DataTable** class exposes the **Constraints** property, which represents the collection of constraints. By default, this collection is empty. We may add new constraints with the **Add** method.

Here is how we may define the ID column as our primary key:

```
$dt->{Constraints}->Add("PK_ID", $colID, PerlNET::true);
```

This statement creates a unique constraint on our table. We specify the constraint name and the column we choose as our key, and the **true** value indicates that this is the primary key constraint. If the last parameter is **false**, then the new constraint will be unique, but not a primary key.

Note that the above form of setting a primary key allows you to choose only one column. There are many cases when the primary key consists of several columns. To resolve this situation, you may directly modify the **PrimaryKey** property of your **DataTable**. You should assign this property with an array of **DataColumn** objects. Suppose that our Emails table's primary key should consist of the ID and Email columns. The following fragment sets both columns to be primary key:

```
my $EmailsPK = "DataColumn[]"->new($colID, $colEmail);
$dt->{PrimaryKey} = $EmailsPK;
```

POPULATING DATATABLE

Now that we know how to define the structure of our table and add constraints, we can fill our tables with some data. We use the **NextRow** method on the **DataTable** object. It returns a reference to the **DataRow** class instance. Then, we may set the values of the columns. The **DataRow** class exposes the indexed property **Item**. We can access it and pass an integer or string value as indexes. In PerlNET we may use square-brackets syntax for integer index only. When working with other types, we call the **set_Item** method explicitly. We demonstrate both ways in the following example:

```
# Obtain DataRow for "Emails" table
my $row = $dt->NewRow();
# Set ID using syntactic sugar
$row->[0] = "1";
# Set Email by calling set_Item method
$row->set_Item("Email", "jeka_books@hotmail.com");
# Add the row
$dt->{Rows}->Add($row);
```

DataSet and DataTable Summary

In the previous subsections you acquired the techniques of working with the **DataSet** and **DataTable** classes. We showed how to fill them with the data that is independent of any external data source. However, the best way to utilize these classes is to work against database servers in the disconnected mode. This is done with the help of **Data Adapters**, discussed next.

Data Adapters

Each data provider (OLE DB, SQL Server, etc.) defines its own data provider class (**OleDbDataAdapter**, **SqlDataAdapter**, etc.) to communicate with data sources. Our samples are SQL Server data provider-oriented. The transition to OLE DB can be made by correcting the appropriate class name's prefixes.

FILLING DATASETS

To retrieve some data from the data source and fill in the dataset, we first create a **SqlDataAdapter** object. Then, we set the **SelectCommand** property, assigning to it the **SqlCommand** object. Finally, we call the **Fill** method on the data adapter, specifying to it the dataset to fill. The code fragment below populates the dataset, selecting all the rows from the People table.

```
my $conn = SqlConnection->new($connstr);
my $pplAdapter = SqlDataAdapter->new();
my $SqlCmd = SqlCommand->new("select * from People",
                                            $conn);
$pplAdapter->{SelectCommand} = $SqlCmd;
my $pplDataset = DataSet->new();
$pplAdapter->Fill($pplDataset, "People");
```

The **SqlDataAdapter** class has properties associated with it for selecting, inserting, updating, and deleting data from a data source. Here the **SqlCommand** instance is associated with the **SelectCommand** property of the **SqlDataAdapter** instead of being executed independently through one of its own execute methods.

The **Fill** method of the **SqlDataAdapter** is then used to execute the **select** command and fill the **DataSet** with information to be put in a table whose name is supplied as an argument. If the database connection was closed when the **Fill** method was executed, it will be opened. When finished, the **Fill** method leaves the connection in the same state as it was before **Fill** was called.

At this point the connection to the database could be closed. You now can work with the **DataSet** and its contained data independently of the connection to the database.

SqlDataAdapter is implemented with the **SqlDataReader** class, so you can expect better performance with the latter. The **SqlDataReader** might also be more memory efficient, depending on how your application is structured. If you do not need the features of the **DataSet**, there is no point incurring the overhead. If you are doing expensive processing, you can free up the database connection by using a **DataSet**. You may get better scalability by loading the data into the **DataSet**, freeing the associated database resources and doing the processing against the **DataSet**.

DataSet Collections

To access the tables that the data adapter stored inside the dataset, you may use the **Tables** collection. Inside a specific table, the data resides in rows and columns as in regular database tables. The **Rows** and **Columns** collections of the **DataTable** class provide the access to the rows and columns of the table respectively.

With the following fragment, we output the table contents that were placed into the dataset, selecting all the rows from the People table in the PerlNET database.

```
my $t = $pplDataset->{Tables}->get_Item("People");
if (!defined $t)
{
   die "Table People was not retrieved";
}

foreach my $c (in $t->{Columns})
{
   print $c->{ColumnName}, "\t";
}
print "\n";
foreach my $r (in $t->{Rows})
{
   for (my $i = 0; $i < $t->{Columns}->{Count}; $i++)
   {
      print $r->[$i], "\t";
   }
   print "\n";
}
print "\n";
```

The **Tables** collection includes all the **DataTable** instances in the **DataSet**. In this particular case there is only one, so there is no need to iterate through that collection. The program iterates through all the columns in the table and sets them up as headers for the data that will be printed out. After the headers have been set up, all the rows in the table are iterated through.

Since the data from the People table resides in the **DataSet** object, we may add new rows to the **Rows** collection exactly in the same manner as we showed in the "Populating DataTable" subsection.

```
my $t = $pplDataset->{Tables}->get_Item("People");
# Obtain DataRow for "People" table
my $row = $t->NewRow();
# Set ID
$row->set_Item("ID", "5");
# Set Name
$row->set_Item("Name", "Alex");
# Add the row
$t->{Rows}->Add($row);
```

Updating DataSources

Changes to the **DataSet** are placed back based on the **InsertCommand**, **UpdateCommand**, and **DeleteCommand** properties of the **SqlDataAdapter** class. Each of these properties takes a **SqlCommand** instance that can be parameterized to relate the variables in the program to the parts of the related SQL statement. We will show how to add a new row to the People table working with the data set.

A **SqlCommand** instance is created to represent the parameterized SQL statement that will be used when the **SqlAdapter.Update** command is invoked to add a new row to the database. At that point, the actual values will be substituted for the parameters.

```
my $cmd = SqlCommand->new(q(insert into People(ID,
                          Name)values (@id, @name)), $conn);
```

We used the **q()** function to enclose the **insert** statement, since in double-quotes the parameter name following the @ character is interpreted as a Perl array name.

The parameters have to be associated with the appropriate columns in a **DataRow**. In the People table, columns were referenced by the column names: ID and Name. Notice how they are related to the SQL statement parameters **@id** and **@name** in the **SqlParameter** constructor. This last argument sets the **Source** property of the **SqlParameter**. The **Source** property sets the **DataSet** column to which the parameter corresponds. The **Add** method places the parameter in the **Parameters** collection associated with the **SqlCommand** instance.

```
my $paramID = SqlParameter->new(q(@id),
enum("SqlDbType.Int"), 9, "ID");
my $paramName = SqlParameter->new(q(@name),
enum("SqlDbType.Char"), 20, "Name");

$cmd->{Parameters}->Add($_) for $paramID, $paramName;
```

Finally, the **SqlAdapter**'s **InsertCommand** property is set to the **SqlCommand** instance. Now this command will be used whenever the adapter has to insert a new row in the database.

```
$pplAdapter->{InsertCommand} = $cmd;
```

The same way, we set the **UpdateCommand** and **DeleteCommand** properties to be used whenever a row has to be updated or deleted. Whatever changes you have made to the rows in the **DataSet** will be propagated to the database when **SqlDataAdapter.Update** is executed.

```
$pplAdapter->Update($pplDataset, "People");
```

Stock Management System Case Study

Code Example

To illustrate the concepts we presented in this chapter, we modified the Stock Management System application from the previous chapter. The case study resides in the **StockMgrForm** folder. The code for the user interface remained intact. We made changes to the **Stock** component, which implements now the **IStock** interface using ADO.NET classes. Here we present the code for the **Stock** constructor, where we fill the dataset with the items from the **Stock** table. Additionally, we initialize the commands for the data adapter used to propagate the changes back to the data base. You should change the server name in the connection string to your local server name.

```
sub Stock
{
   my $this = shift;

   # Change the server name accordingly
   my $connstr =
      "server=Lotus;uid=sa;pwd=;database=PerlNET";
   my $conn = SqlConnection->new($connstr);
   my $stockAdapter = SqlDataAdapter->new();
   my $SelCmd = SqlCommand->new("select * from Stock",
                                               $conn);
   $stockAdapter->{SelectCommand} = $SelCmd;
   $this->{f_dsItems} = DataSet->new();
   $stockAdapter->Fill($this->{f_dsItems}, "Stock");
```

```
# Initialize Insert command
my $InsCmd = SqlCommand->new(q(insert into
   Stock(ID, Name, Price, Quantity) values
        (@ID, @Name, @Price, @Qty)), $conn);
#Initialize Parameters for Insert Command
my $prmID = SqlParameter->new(q(@ID),
        enum("SqlDbType.NChar"), 5, "ID");
my $prmName = SqlParameter->new(q(@Name),
        enum("SqlDbType.Char"), 20, "Name");
my $prmPrice = SqlParameter->new(q(@Price),
        enum("SqlDbType.Decimal"), 8, "Price");
my $prmQty = SqlParameter->new(q(@Qty),
        enum("SqlDbType.NChar"), 5, "Quantity");
my @params = ($prmID, $prmName, $prmPrice, $prmQty);
$InsCmd->{Parameters}->Add($_) for @params;
$stockAdapter->{InsertCommand} = $InsCmd;

# Initialize Delete command
my $DelCmd = SqlCommand->new(q(delete from Stock where
            ID = @rmvID), $conn);
#Initialize Parameters for Delete Command
my $prmRmvID = SqlParameter->new(q(@rmvID),
        enum("SqlDbType.NChar"), 5, "ID");
$prmRmvID->{SourceVersion} =
        enum("DataRowVersion.Original");
$DelCmd->{Parameters}->Add($prmRmvID);
$stockAdapter->{DeleteCommand} = $DelCmd;

# Initialize Update command
my $UpdCmd = SqlCommand->new(q(update Stock
        set Name=@newName, Price=@newPrice,
          Quantity=@newQty
        where ID=@oldID), $conn);

#Initialize Parameters for Update Command
my $prmOldID = SqlParameter->new(q(@oldID),
        enum("SqlDbType.NChar"), 5, "ID");
my $prmNewName = SqlParameter->new(q(@newName),
        enum("SqlDbType.Char"), 20, "Name");
my $prmNewPrice = SqlParameter->new(q(@newPrice),
        enum("SqlDbType.Decimal"), 8, "Price");
my $prmNewQty = SqlParameter->new(q(@newQty),
        enum("SqlDbType.NChar"), 5, "Quantity");
@params = ($prmOldID, $prmNewName, $prmNewPrice,
          $prmNewQty);
$UpdCmd->{Parameters}->Add($_) for @params;
$stockAdapter->{UpdateCommand} = $UpdCmd;
```

```
# Initialize SqlCommands for Generating ID from StockID
# Table
$this->{f_cmdGetID} = SqlCommand->new("Select LastID
                         from StockID" ,$conn);
$this->{f_cmdIncID} = SqlCommand->new("Update StockID
                         set LastID=LastID+1" ,$conn);
$this->{f_adapter} = $stockAdapter;
}
```

As we use the same data adapter for **Insert**, **Delete**, and **Update** commands, we have to give different names to all the commands parameters, which means that we cannot use **@id** for both **Insert** and **Update** commands.

We update the data source once the user makes a change. Here is the code for the **RemoveItem** method, where we first mark the item for deleting in the dataset and then call the **Update** method:

```
sub RemoveItem
{
    my($this, $id) = @_;
    my $ds = $this->{f_dsItems};
    my $t = $ds->{Tables}->get_Item("Stock");
    foreach my $row(in $t->{Rows})
    {
        if ($row->get_Item("ID") == $id)
        {
            $row->Delete();
            $this->{f_adapter}->Update($ds, "Stock");
            return;
        }
    }
}
```

Some of the operations inside the **Stock** component we perform through the execute methods of the **SqlCommand** object. For example, to generate a new ID for an item, we first call the **ExecuteScalar** method of the **f_cmdGetID** command object field we initialized in the constructor and then we invoke the **ExecuteNonQuery** method of the **f_cmdIncID** command object to increment the ID in the **StockID** database table.

```
sub GenerateID
{
    my $this = shift;

    # Obtain ID
    $this->{f_cmdGetID}->{Connection}->Open();
    my $id = int($this->{f_cmdGetID}->ExecuteScalar());
    $this->{f_cmdGetID}->{Connection}->Close();
```

```
# Increment LastID in the table
$this->{f_cmdIncID}->{Connection}->Open();
$this->{f_cmdIncID}->ExecuteNonQuery();
$this->{f_cmdIncID}->{Connection}->Close();

return $id;
}
```

Figure 15-3 shows the main window of the Stock Management System application with the data from the **Stock** table.

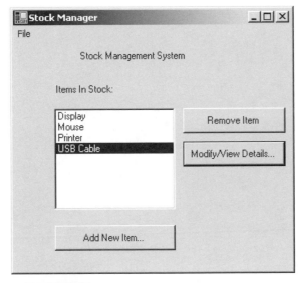

FIGURE 15–3   *Main window of the Stock Management System.*

Summary

This chapter presented the ADO.NET classes and features they provide. We connect to the database using the ADO.NET Connection object of the relevant data provider. We have two options of working with a database: connected mode and disconnected mode. The former represents the classic ADO model. With the latter we may achieve better performance for our database applications, since we may perform the operations on data locally and then propagate changes to the database.

When working in connected mode, we use data readers to fetch the data. In the disconnected mode, the data is placed in the datasets that are independent of any data provider. Data adapters mediate between the database and dataset when transferring data from and to a database.

We presented the database version of the Stock Management System. There we illustrate most of the techniques of working with databases that we acquired in this chapter.

ASP.NET Web Development and PerlASPX

*T*he Microsoft.NET platform consolidates a wide range of tools aimed to serve programmers for various tasks. Web development has one of the highest ratings, according to the number of programmers working in the area. Hence, as part of the vision to provide as complete as possible a set of instruments for the developer, Microsoft has put much effort into building generic, expandable, and convenient technology for Web development. The resulting product is ASP.NET, which is not just another version of classic ASP, but a new way to do things on the Web front. In this chapter, we explain the ASP.NET fundamentals. Using our simple examples of Web applications, we show how you should configure your Internet Information Services (IIS) Web server to run ASP.NET. Then, we introduce Web Forms and Web controls that help to enrich Web UI and ASP.NET functionality. Next, we discuss state management in ASP.NET. Additionally, we show how existing PerlNET components may be incorporated into Web applications and used as a back end.

The second part of this chapter is dedicated to a discussion of Web services. Web services provide tools for rapid development of applications that support remote method invocation utilizing XML-based protocols. We will see how PerlASPX may help us in creating PerlNET Web services.

Prerequisites

Before we start our journey into the exciting world of ASP.NET programming, it is a good idea to check that we have a complete set of prerequisites:

- IIS and .NET
- PerlASPX

349

IIS and .NET

IIS provides the functionality to make the computer where it is installed into a Web server. In other words, it allows other Internet users to browse the Web pages that reside on your computer.

The standard IIS configuration supports classic ASP development. To make your Web server ASP.NET-enabled, it is enough to install the .NET Framework that is probably already installed if you have successfully worked with our PerlNET samples. The standard .NET distribution upgrades and configures your IIS to support ASP.NET development in three .NET-compliant languages:

- C#
- VB.NET
- JScript

To configure the IIS Web server settings, we use the Microsoft Management Console (MMC). It has a user-friendly user interface and allows advanced settings configurations. We present a more detailed explanation of IIS in the next sections of this chapter.

PerlASPX

To add the Perl language to the ASP.NET family, you should install an additional product from ActiveState: PerlASPX. Consult ActiveState for choosing the right version of PerlASPX for your Perl Development Kit.

During the installation process of PerlASPX, you will be asked if you want to install a set of samples. If you answer yes, then a new virtual directory named **PerlASPX** will be created for you, where simple Perl ASP.NET examples will reside. We will explain the notion of a virtual directory shortly.

What Is ASP.NET?

After all the prerequisites are successfully installed, you may start authoring your ASP.NET pages and build Web applications. We begin our exploration of this Web technology with a simple example. Along the way we will establish a testbed for ASP.NET programming, and we will review some of the fundamentals of Web processing. Our little example reveals some of the challenges in developing Web applications, and we can then appreciate the features and benefits of ASP.NET that we will elaborate on in the rest of the chapter.

Web Application Fundamentals

A Web application consists of document and code pages in various formats. The simplest kind of document is a static HTML page, which contains information that will be formatted and displayed by a Web browser. An HTML page may also contain hyperlinks to other HTML pages. A hyperlink (or just *link*) contains an address, or a Uniform Resource Locator (URL), specifying where the target document is located. The resulting combination of content and links is sometimes called *hypertext* and provides easy navigation to a vast amount of information on the World Wide Web.

SETTING UP THE WEB EXAMPLES

As usual, all the example programs for this chapter are in the chapter folder. To run the examples, you must have IIS installed on your system. IIS is installed by default with Windows 2000 Server. You will have to explicitly install it with Windows 2000 Workstation. Once installed, you can access the documentation on IIS through Internet Explorer via the URL **http://localhost**, which will redirect you to the starting IIS documentation page, as illustrated in Figure 16–1.

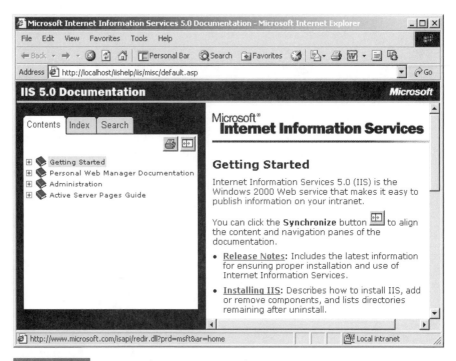

FIGURE 16–1   *Internet Information Services documentation.*

The management tool for IIS is an MMC snap-in, the Internet Services Manager, which you can find under Administrative Tools in the Control Panel. Figure 16–2 shows the main window of the Internet Services Manager. You can start and stop the Web server and perform other tasks by right-clicking on Default Web Site. Choosing Properties from the Context menu will let you perform a number of configurations on the Web server.

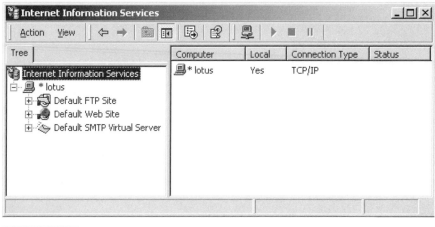

FIGURE 16–2   *Internet Services Manager.*

The default home directory for publishing Web files is **\Inetpub\wwwroot** on the drive where Windows is installed. You can change this home directory using Internet Services Manager. You can access Web pages stored at any location on your hard drive by creating a virtual directory. The easiest way to create one is from Windows Explorer. Right-click over the desired directory, choose Sharing..., select the Web Sharing tab, click on the Add button, and enter the desired alias, which will be the name of the virtual directory. Figure 16–3 illustrates creating an alias **NetPerl**, or virtual directory, for the folder **\OI\NetPerl\Chap16**. You should perform this operation now on your own system in order to follow along as the chapter's examples are discussed.

Once a virtual directory has been created, you can access files in it by including the virtual directory in the path of the URL. In particular, you can access the file **default.htm** using the URL **http://localhost/NetPerl/**. The file **default.htm** contains a home page for all the ASP.NET and Web services example programs for this chapter. See Figure 16–4.

We are sure that you can't wait to see the first examples of ASP.NET pages. Here you go!

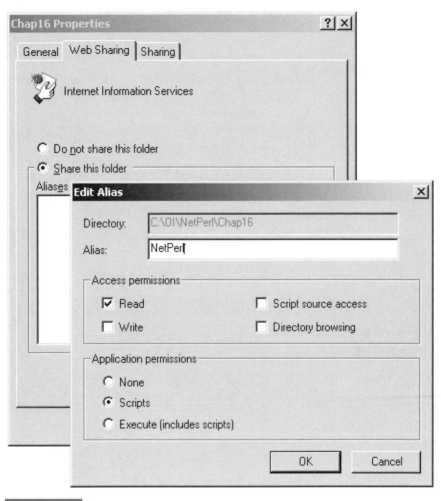

FIGURE 16–3   *Creating a virtual directory.*

A Random Program

Our **Random** example contains a single ASP.NET page. There is a very simple user interaction. The Web page displays a random number between 0 and 36 that will be generated with the help of the **rand** function in response to a button press by the user. The example contains embedded server code. Here is the source code, which consists of HTML along with some PerlNET script code. There are also some special tags for *server controls,* recognized by ASP.NET.

```
<!-- Random.aspx -->
<%@ Page Language="Perl" %>
<HTML>
```

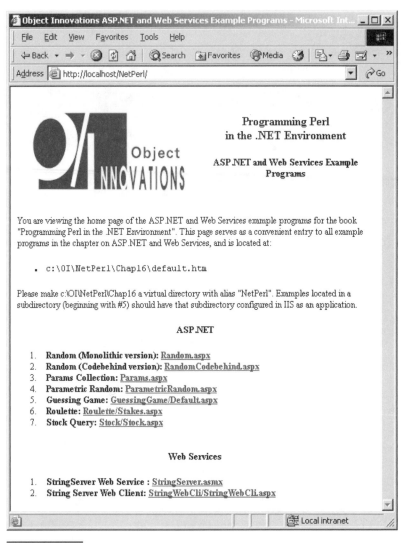

FIGURE 16–4   *Home page for this chapter's example programs.*

```
<BODY>
<CENTER>
<H2>Random Number Generation</H2>

<SCRIPT RUNAT="SERVER">
=for interface
   public void Generate(System.Object source,
                    System.EventArgs e);
=cut
```

```
sub Generate
{
   my $this = shift;

   $this->{lblNum}->{Text} = "Random number is " .
                             int(rand(37));
}
</SCRIPT>

<asp:Label RUNAT="SERVER" id="lblNum"></asp:Label>
<BR>
<FORM RUNAT="SERVER">
<asp:button RUNAT="SERVER" TEXT="Generate New Number"
onClick=Generate tooltip="Click to generate new random
number"></asp:button>
</FORM>
</CENTER>
</BODY>
</HTML>
```

You can run the program using the URL **http://localhost/NetPerl/Random.aspx** or by clicking on the link **Random.aspx** in the home page of the examples programs. The page shows a header and the Generate New Number button. Clicking the button will display a new random number (the **onClick** attribute of **asp:button** makes the **Generate** subroutine into an event handler of the **Click** event). The simple form is again displayed, so you can try to generate other numbers. If you slide the browser's mouse cursor over the button, you will see the tooltip "Click to generate new random number" displayed in a yellow box. Figure 16–5 illustrates a run of this example.

This little program would not be completely trivial to implement with other Web application tools, including ASP. The key user-interface feature of such an application is its thoroughly forms-based nature. The user is presented with a form and interacts with the form. The server does some processing, and the user continues to see the same form. This UI model is second nature in desktop applications but is not so common in Web applications. Typically, the Web server will send back a different page.

This kind of application could certainly be implemented using a technology like ASP, but the code would be a little ugly. The server would need to synthesize a new page that looked like the old page, creating the HTML tags for the original page, plus extra information sent back (such as the random number right after the header of our Web page). A mechanism is needed to remember the current data that is displayed in the controls in the form.

Another feature of this Web application is that it does some client-side processing too—the tooltip displayed in the yellow box is performed by the browser. Such rich client-side processing can be performed by some browsers, such as Internet Explorer, but not others.

FIGURE 16–5   *Running the **Random.aspx** sample.*

As can be seen by the example code, with ASP.NET it is very easy to implement this kind of Web application. We study the code in detail later. For now, just observe how easy it is!

ASP.NET Features

ASP.NET provides a programming model and infrastructure that facilitates developing new classes of Web applications. Part of this infrastructure is the .NET runtime and framework. Server-side code is written in .NET-compliant languages. Two main programming models are supported by ASP.NET.

- Web Forms helps you build form-based Web pages. A WYSIWYG development environment enables you to drag controls onto Web pages. Special server-side controls present the programmer with an event model similar to what is provided by controls in ordinary Windows programming. This chapter discusses Web Forms in detail.

- Web services make it possible for a Web site to expose functionality via an API that can be called remotely by other applications. Data is exchanged using standard Web protocols and formats such as HTTP and XML, which will cross firewalls. We discuss Web services later in this chapter.

Both Web Forms and Web services can take advantage of the facilities provided by .NET, such as the compiled code and .NET runtime. In addition,

ASP.NET itself provides a number of infrastructure services, including state management, security, configuration, caching, and tracing.

COMPILED CODE

Web Forms (and Web services) can be written in any .NET language that runs on top of the CLR, including C#, VB.NET, and C++ with Managed Extensions. Naturally, we will do it using Perl. This code is compiled, and thus offers better performance than ASP pages with code written in an interpreted scripting language such as VBScript. All of the benefits, such as a managed execution environment, are available to this code, and of course the entire .NET Framework class library is available.

SERVER CONTROLS

ASP.NET provides a significant innovation known as server controls. These controls have special tags, such as **<asp:label>**. Server-side code interacts with these controls, and the ASP.NET runtime generates straight HTML that is sent to the Web browser. The result is a programming model that is easy to use and yet produces standard HTML that can run in any browser. In many cases, you will find server controls very similar to WinForms controls that we presented in Chapter 14. This is one of achievements of ASP.NET technology in the front of Web UI.

BROWSER INDEPENDENCE

Although the World Wide Web is built on standards, the unfortunate fact of life is that browsers are not compatible and they have special features. A Web page designer then has the unattractive options of either writing to a lowest common denominator of browser or writing special sniffing code for different browsers. Server controls help remove some of this pain. ASP.NET takes care of browser compatibility issues when it generates code for a server control. If the requesting browser is upscale, the generated HTML can take advantage of these features; otherwise, the generated code will be vanilla HTML. ASP.NET takes care of detecting the type of browser.

SEPARATION OF CODE AND CONTENT

Typical ASP pages have a mixture of scripting code interspersed with HTML elements. In ASP.NET there is a clean separation between code and presentation content. The server code can be isolated within a single **<SCRIPT RUNAT="SERVER"> ... </SCRIPT>** block or, even better, placed within a *code-behind* page. We discuss code-behind pages later in this chapter. If you would like to see an example right away, you can examine the second example program, **RandomCodebehind.aspx**, with code in the file **RandomCodebehind.aspx.pm**. (These files are in the top-level chapter directory.)

Code Example

STATE MANAGEMENT

HTTP is a stateless protocol. Thus, if a user enters information in various controls on a form, and sends this filled-out form to the server, the information will be lost if the form is displayed again, unless the Web application provides special code to preserve this state. ASP.NET makes this kind of state preservation totally transparent. There are also convenient facilities for managing other types of session and application state.

Web Forms

A Web Form consists of two parts:

- The visual content or presentation, typically specified by HTML elements
- Code that contains the logic for interacting with the visual elements.

A Web Form is physically expressed by a file with the extension **.aspx**. Any HTML page could be renamed to have this extension and could be accessed using the new extension with identical results to the original. Thus Web Forms are upwardly compatible with HTML pages. Unlike ASP pages, our ASPX pages won't be interpreted. Instead, they are compiled into .NET classes and executed by the CLR, providing better performance of Web applications.

The way code can be separated from the form is what makes a Web Form special. This code can be either in a separate file (having an extension corresponding to a .NET language, such as **.pm** for Perl) or in the **.aspx** file within a **<SCRIPT RUNAT="SERVER"> ... </SCRIPT>** block. When your page is run in the Web server, the user interface code runs and dynamically generates the output for the page.

Code-Behind Feature

We can understand the architecture of a Web Form most clearly by looking at the code-behind version of our **Random** example. The visual content is specified by the **.aspx** file **RandomCodebehind.aspx**.

```
<!-- RandomCodebehind.aspx -->
<%@ Page Language="Perl" Src="RandomCodebehind.aspx.pm"
Inherits=MyWebPage %>
<HTML>
<BODY>
<CENTER>
<H2>Random Number Generation</H2>

<asp:Label RUNAT="SERVER" id="lblNum"></asp:Label>
```

```
<BR>
<FORM RUNAT="SERVER">
<asp:button RUNAT="SERVER" TEXT="Generate New Number"
onClick=Generate tooltip="Click to generate new random
number"></asp:button>
</FORM>
</CENTER>
</BODY>
</HTML>
```

The user interface code is in the file **RandomCodebehind.aspx.pm**.

```
#
# RandomCodebehind.aspx.pm
#

package MyWebPage;

use namespace "System";
use namespace "System.Web";
use namespace "System.Web.UI";
use namespace "System.Web.UI.WebControls";

=for interface
   [extends: System.Web.UI.Page]
   public void Generate(System.Object source,
                        System.EventArgs e);
   protected field Label lblNum;
=cut

sub Generate
{
   my $this = shift;

   $this->{lblNum}->{Text} = "Random number is " .
                                   int(rand(37));
}
```

Page Class

The key namespace for Web Forms and Web services is **System.Web**. Support for Web Forms is in the namespace **System.Web.UI**. Support for server controls such as text boxes and buttons is in the namespace **System.Web.UI.WebControls**. The classes that dynamically generate the output for an **.aspx** page are the **Page** class (in the **System.Web.UI** namespace) and classes derived from **Page**, as illustrated in the code-behind page in the previous example.

The **$this** reference we use in our **Generate** subroutine is the **Page** class reference. Through **$this** we access our controls as regular properties and fields. Unlike with WinForms controls, we do not have to add ASP.NET controls to any collection. In the code-behind scenario we just declare the appropriate field for the control. The name of the field should be the same as **id** of the control inside **.aspx** file.

```
protected field Label lblNum;
```

In the case of the **<SCRIPT RUNAT="SERVER">** blocks, we do not have to perform any field declarations for the controls.

INHERITING FROM PAGE CLASS

The elements in the **.aspx** file, the code in the code-behind file (or script block), and the base **Page** class work together to generate the page output. This cooperation is achieved by ASP.NET's dynamically creating a class for the **.aspx** file, which is derived from the code-behind class, which in turn is derived from **Page**. This relationship is created by the Inherits attribute in the **.aspx** file. Figure 16–6 illustrates the inheritance hierarchy. We implement the **MyWebPage** class, which is derived from **Page**.

Page

MyWebPage

My .aspx Page

FIGURE 16–6   *Hierarchy of page classes.*

The most derived page class, shown as My .aspx Page in Figure 16–6, is dynamically created by the ASP.NET runtime. This class extends the **Page** class, shown as MyWebPage in the figure, to incorporate the controls and HTML text on the Web Form. This class is compiled into an executable, which is run when the page is requested from a browser. The executable code creates the HTML that is sent to the browser.

Page Directives

An **.aspx** file may contain a *page directive* defining various attributes that can control how ASP.NET processes the page. A page directive contains one or more attribute/value pairs of the form

```
attribute="value"
```

within the page directive syntax

```
<@ Page ... @>
```

Our example program, **RandomCodebehind.aspx**, illustrates an **.aspx** page that does not have any code within it. The code-behind file **Random-Codebehind.aspx.pm** that has the code is specified using the **Src** attribute.

```
<!-- RandomCodebehind.aspx -->
<%@ Page Language="Perl" Src="RandomCodebehind.aspx.pm"
Inherits=MyWebPage %>
...
```

SRC

The **Src** attribute identifies the code-behind file.

LANGUAGE

The **Language** attribute specifies the language used for the page. The code in this language may be in either a code-behind file or a SCRIPT block within the same file. Values can be any .NET-supported language, including C# and VB.NET.

INHERITS

The **Inherits** directive specifies the page class from which the **.aspx** page class will inherit.

DEBUG

The **Debug** attribute indicates whether the page should be compiled with debug information. If **true**, debug information is enabled, and the browser can provide detailed information about compile errors. The default is **false**.

ERRORPAGE

The **ErrorPage** attribute specifies a target URL to which the browser will be redirected in the event that an unhandled exception occurs on the page.

TRACE

The **Trace** attribute indicates whether tracing is enabled. A value of **true** turns tracing on. The default is **false**.

We present additional page directives later in this chapter.

Response and Request Handling

The server control architecture is built on top of a more fundamental process-ing architecture, which may be called request/response. Understanding request/response is important to solidify our overall grasp of ASP.NET. Also, in certain programming situations request/response is the natural approach. The **HttpRequest** objects handles the information that the Web server receives from the client, and the **HttpResponse** object is responsible for the informa-tion that is sent back to the client.

HttpRequest Class

The **System.Web** namespace contains a useful class, **HttpRequest**, that can be used to read the various HTTP values sent by a client during a Web request. These HTTP values would be used by a classical CGI program in acting upon a Web request, and they are the foundation upon which higher level processing is built. Table 16–1 shows some of the public instance properties of **HttpRe-quest**. If you are familiar with HTTP, the meaning of these various properties should be largely self-explanatory. Refer to the .NET Framework documentation of the **HttpRequest** class for full details about these and other properties.

TABLE 16–1	*Public Instance Properties of HttpRequest*
Property	**Meaning**
AcceptTypes	String array of client-supported MIME accept types
Browser	Information about client's browser capabilities
ContentLength	Length in bytes of content sent by the client
Cookies	Collection of cookies sent by the client
Form	Collection of form variables
Headers	Collection of HTTP headers
HttpMethod	HTTP transfer method used by client (e.g., GET or POST)
Params	Combined collection of QueryString, Form, ServerVariables, and Cookies items
Path	Virtual request of the current path
QueryString	Collection of HTTP query string variables
ServerVariables	Collection of Web server variables

The **Request** property of the **Page** class returns an **HttpRequest** object. You may then extract whatever information you need, using the properties of **HttpRequest**. For example, the following code determines the length in bytes of content sent by the client and writes that information to the **Response** object.

```
my $request  = $this->{Request};
my $response = $this->{Response};
my $length = $request->{ContentLength};
$response->Write("ContentLength = " . $length . "<br>");
```

COLLECTIONS

A number of useful collections are exposed as properties of **HttpRequest**. The collections are of type **NamedValueCollection** (in **System.Collections.-Specialized** namespace). You can access a value from a string key. For example, the **Form** collection can be used to extract the control values. You could use the value of the **REQUEST_METHOD** server variable (GET or POST) to determine which collection to use (the **QueryString** collection in the case of GET and the **Form** collection in the case of POST).

Another important collection that is widely used is **ServerVariables**. It provides the information about the Web server, such as the server name and the port that is used (usually 80).

With ASP.NET you don't have to worry about which HTTP method was used in the request. ASP.NET provides a **Params** collection, which is a combination (union in the mathematical sense) of the **ServerVariables**, **QueryString**, **Form**, and **Cookies** collections. In our example we iterate through **Params** and output all the **name = value** pairs of this **NameValueCollection**.

EXAMPLE PROGRAM

Code
Example

Params.aspx page contains the code for displaying all the **name = value** pairs from the **Params** collection. Figure 16-7 shows the partial results of running **Params.aspx**.

Here is the code for **Params.aspx**.

```
<!-- Params.aspx -->
<%@ Page Language="Perl" %>
<HTML>
<BODY>
<CENTER>
<H2>Server Variables</H2>
</CENTER>
<%
use PerlNET qw(in);
my $request  = $this->{Request};
my $response = $this->{Response};
my $params = $request->{Params};

# Obtain Keys of NameValueCollection
my $keys = $params->{AllKeys};
```

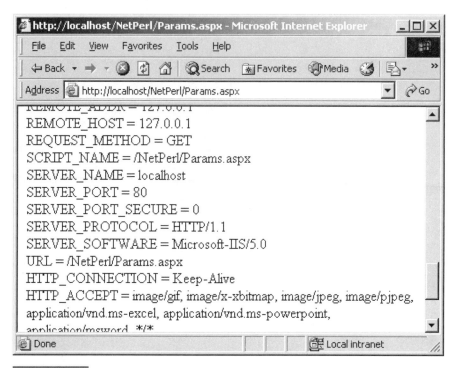

FIGURE 16–7   *Information displayed by **Params.aspx**.*

```
# Iterate through Params collections
# and output the value for each key
foreach my $key(in $keys)
{
   my $value = $params->get_Item($key);
   $response->Write($key . " = " . $value . "<BR>");
}
%>

</BODY>
</HTML>
```

We use **<% … %>** blocks to inject Perl server-side code. Note that we may use the pragmas in these blocks, as we did in regular PerlNET programs. In this case, we import the **in** helper function from the PerlNET module. **$this** holds the reference to the **Page** object that represents our **Params.aspx** Web page.

We obtain the collection of all keys for **Params**.

```
my $keys = $params->{AllKeys};
```

Next, we iterate through **$keys** and extract the values from the **Params** collection for each key and output it using the **HttpResponse** object.

```
foreach my $key(in $keys)
{
   my $value = $params->get_Item($key);
   $response->Write($key . " = " . $value . "<BR>");
}
```

HttpResponse Class

The **HttpResponse** class encapsulates HTTP response information that is built as part of an ASP.NET operation. The .NET Framework uses this class when it creates a response that includes writing server controls back to the client. Your own server code may also use the **Write** method of the **Response** object to write data to the output stream that will be sent to the client. We have already seen many illustrations of **Response.Write**.

REDIRECT

The **HttpResponse** class has a useful method, **Redirect**, which enables server code to redirect an HTTP request to a different URL. A simple redirection without passing any data is trivial—you need only call the **Redirect** method and pass the URL. An example of such usage would be a reorganization of a Web site, where a certain page is no longer valid and the content has been moved to a new location. You can keep the old page live by simply redirecting traffic to the new location.

It should be noted that redirection always involves an HTTP GET request, like following a simple link to a URL. (POST arises as an option when submitting form data, where the action can be specified as GET or POST.) The following code redirects the client to **NewPage.aspx** (we provide a relative path, which means that **NewPage.aspx** is located in the same directory as the Web page with the **Redirect** statement).

```
$this->{Response}->Redirect("NewPage.aspx");
```

HTML Representation of Web Forms

One of the key concepts of ASP.NET technology is to provide a comfortable way to define a Web GUI and yet not require from existing browsers any extra features. ASP.NET equips programmers with a set of Web controls that run on the server and produce plain HTML output that is sent to a client's browser. We may create event handlers that run on the server and are invoked as a result of user client-side events. For the purpose of processing such events on the server, there occurs form submission, and then the event handler runs and new HTML is produced that is delivered to the client. In our **Random.aspx** sample the **Generate** function represents an event handler of the Generate New Number button **Click** event.

Generated HTML Example

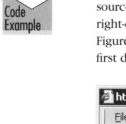

To understand the ASP.NET concepts, let's look at the HTML code that our **.aspx** pages generate. We enrich the **Random.aspx** page with the **TextBox** control. The user enters a number to define the upper bound of the random number generated (the lower bound remains 0). We then use the new version, **ParametricRandom.aspx**, for our explanations. To examine the HTML source, you may access **http://localhost/NetPerl/ParametricRandom.aspx**, right-click on the page, and choose View Source from the displayed menu. In Figure 16–8 we show how this Web page looks in the Internet Explorer when it first displayed.

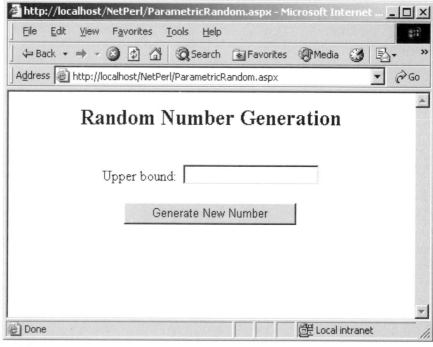

FIGURE 16–8 *ParametricRandom.aspx* in the Internet Explorer.

Here are the ASPX and HTML codes. The ASPX code is presented first.

```
<!-- ParametricRandom.aspx -->
<%@ Page Language="Perl" %>
<HTML>
<BODY>
<CENTER>
<H2>Random Number Generation</H2>

<SCRIPT RUNAT="SERVER">
=for interface
   public void Generate(System.Object source,
                        System.EventArgs e);
=cut

sub Generate
{
   my $this = shift;

   my $ubound = int($this->{txtUpBound}->{Text});
   $this->{lblNum}->{Text} = "Random number is " .
                             int(rand($ubound+1));
}
</SCRIPT>

<asp:Label RUNAT="SERVER" id="lblNum"></asp:Label>
<BR>
<FORM RUNAT="SERVER">
Upper bound: 
<asp:TextBox RUNAT="SERVER" id="txtUpBound"></asp:TextBox>
<BR><BR>
<asp:button RUNAT="SERVER" TEXT="Generate New Number"
onClick=Generate tooltip="Click to generate new random
number"></asp:button>
</FORM>
</CENTER>
</BODY>
</HTML>
```

We bolded the lines of code that we added to the original **Random.aspx** version. The HTML code that was generated for our **ParametricRandom.aspx** page is next.

```
<HTML>
<BODY>
<CENTER>
<H2>Random Number Generation</H2>

<span id="lblNum"></span>
<BR>
<form name="_ctl0" method="post"
```

```
action="ParametricRandom.aspx" id="_ctl0">
<input type="hidden" name="__VIEWSTATE"
value="dDwtNjIxOTc5MzA1Ozs+82xl1/2YosblMLM18uloqrZcHFE=" />

Upper bound: 
<input name="txtUpBound" type="text" id="txtUpBound" />
<BR><BR>
<input type="submit" name="_ctl1" value="Generate New
Number" title="Click to generate new random number" />
</form>
</CENTER>
</BODY>
</HTML>
```

You may see that the HTML code we placed in **Parametric-Random.aspx** remained intact. The script block is not present. The **<asp:Label>** control produced the following line:

```
<span id="lblNum"></span>
```

If we press the Generate New Number button, then the HTML output of the **Label** control may look like the following, depending on the upper bound we set and the random number generated.

```
<span id="lblNum">Random number is 23</span>
```

The next thing that catches our eye is the **<form>** tag:

```
<form name="_ctl0" method="post"
action="ParametricRandom.aspx" id="_ctl0">
```

In our **.aspx** page we enclosed our **TextBox** and **Button** controls within the **<FORM RUNAT=SERVER> ... </FORM>** tags. When delivering the page to the client's browser, ASP.NET substitutes the required attributes of the HTML **<FORM>** tag for us. For example, the **action** attribute of the form is given the **ParametricRandom.aspx** value. In fact, this is the form that the browser will submit as a result of the user pressing the Generate New Number button, which is actually the Submit button of the form in the generated HTML:

```
<input type="submit" name="_ctl1" value="Generate New
Number" title="Click to generate new random number" />
```

The **TextBox** control is converted to a regular **<INPUT>** HTML control with **text** type

```
<input name="txtUpBound" type="text" id="txtUpBound" />
```

When the page is first displayed, this textbox is empty. Once we set the upper bound, it will be reflected in the value attribute of this input control. If we set the upper bound to 15, then the generated HTML tag will look as follows after we generate the new number.

```
<input name="txtUpBound" type="text" value="15"
id="txtUpBound" />
```

Figure 16-9 illustrates the **ParametricRandom.aspx** page after random number generation.

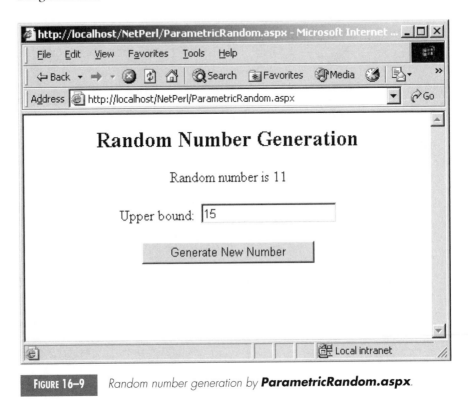

FIGURE 16-9   *Random number generation by **ParametricRandom.aspx**.*

VIEW-STATE

You may see that the value that we entered for the upper bound is persisted after submission. In ASP, we had to program such behavior explicitly. ASP.NET does it for us implicitly. In other words, ASP.NET preserves the *view-state* of our controls. The view-state information is stored in the hidden input control that you might have already noticed in the generated HTML:

```
<input type="hidden" name="__VIEWSTATE"
value="dDwtNjIxOTc5MzA1Ozs+82xl1/2YosblMLM18uloqrZcHFE=" />
```

The value of this hidden control changes accordingly after each submission. It doesn't provide us with any useful information. However, ASP.NET modules successfully encode and decode its value string and in this way preserve the view-state for us.

ASP.NET Applications

Until now, we examined single-paged Web Forms. However, when programming more ambitious Web systems, developers divide the functionality
between several Web Forms that are responsible for different aspects of interacting with the user or performing other tasks. In other words, the code
resides in multiple **.aspx** pages that are related. Such Web pages are unified
under a *Web application*. You may create a Web application using IIS by right-
clicking on the directory, choosing Properties, and clicking on the Create button on the displayed dialog box (see Figure 16–10). All the Web pages under the
chosen directory will be considered as belonging to the newly created Web
application.

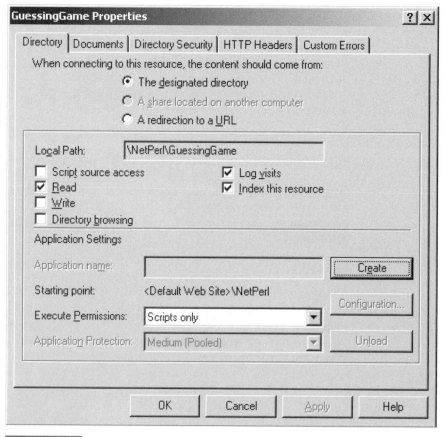

FIGURE 16–10   *Creating a Web application with IIS for the **GuessingGame** sample.*

There are many advantages of unifying a set of pages under the same Web application. You may share values among the application pages using **Session** or **Application** scopes. We illustrate this on the **GuessingGame** sample that resides in the NetPerl virtual directory. To work with the sample, you must create for it a Web application, as explained above. In this sample you first choose the upper bound for the game. Then the computer generates a random integer number between 1 and the number you provided in the upper bound. Your task is to guess the number and not to exceed the maximum attempts number. After each guess, the program indicates whether your guess was greater or less than the correct number. In the case of a successful guess you will be redirected to the **WellDone.aspx** page, and if you run out of attempts, you will be sent to the **GameOver.aspx** page.

Sessions

To appreciate the Web application support provided by ASP.NET, we need to understand the concept of a Web *session*. HTTP is a stateless protocol. This means that there is no direct way for a Web browser to know whether a sequence of requests is from the same client or from different clients. A Web server such as IIS can provide a mechanism to classify requests coming from a single client into a logical session. ASP.NET makes it very easy to work with sessions.

Global.asax

An ASP.NET application can optionally contain a file **Global.asax**, which contains code for responding to application-level events raised by ASP.NET. This file resides in the root directory of the application. If you do not have a **Global.asax** file in your application, ASP.NET will assume you have not defined any handlers for application-level events.

Global.asax is compiled into a dynamically generated .NET Framework class derived from **HttpApplication**.

Here is the **Global.asax** file for our **GuessingGame** sample.

```
<SCRIPT language="Perl" runat="server">

=for interface
    void Application_Start(any sender,
                    System.EventArgs e);
    void Session_Start(any sender, System.EventArgs e);
=cut

sub Application_Start
{
    my $this = shift;
```

```
    # Set Maximum number of guesses allowed
    $this->{Application}->set_Item("MaxAttempts", 10);
}

sub Session_Start
{
    my $this = shift;

    # Redirect use to the start page
    $this->{Response}->Redirect("Default.aspx");
}

</SCRIPT>
```

The most common application-level events are shown in this code. The typical life cycle of a Web application consists of these events:

- **Application_Start** is raised only once during an application's lifetime, on the first instance of **HttpApplication**. An application starts the first time it is run by IIS for the first user. In your event handler you can initialize a state that is shared by the entire application.
- **Session_Start** is raised at the start of each session. Here you can initialize session variables.
- **Application_BeginRequest** is raised at the start of an individual request. Normally, you can do your request processing in the **Page** class.
- **Application_EndRequest** is raised at the end of a request.
- **Session_End** is raised at the end of each session. Normally, you do not need to do cleanup of data initialized in **Session_Start**, because garbage collection will take care of normal cleanup for you. However, if you have opened an expensive resource, such as a database connection, you may wish to call the **Dispose** method here.
- **Application_End** is raised at the very end of an application's lifetime, when the last instance of **HttpApplication** is torn down.

For each event, you may declare an event handler in the same manner as we did for **Application_Start** and **Session_Start**.

In our sample, we set the maximum number of attempts for our guessing game in **Application_OnStart**. We store it as *application variable*.

```
$this->{Application}->set_Item("MaxAttempts", 10);
```

Its value may be then retrieved in the Web pages of our application.

In the **Session_Start** event handler we redirect the user to the **Default.aspx** page.

```
$this->{Response}->Redirect("Default.aspx");
```

It is a useful technique when you want all the users to start browsing your application from a certain page (like log-in page) at the beginning of the session. Figure 16–11 shows the start page of the guessing game.

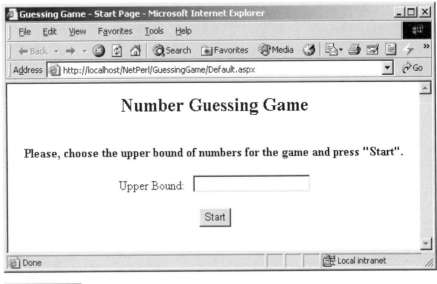

FIGURE 16–11   *Start page of the guessing game application.*

State Management in ASP.NET Applications

Preserving state across HTTP requests is a major problem in Web programming, and ASP.NET provides several facilities that are convenient to use. There are two main types of state to be preserved.

- **Application state** is global information that is shared across all users of a Web application.
- **Session state** is used to store data for a particular user across multiple requests to a Web application.

APPLICATION OBJECT

You can store global application information in the built-in **Application** object, an instance of the class **HttpApplicationState**. You can conveniently access this object through the **Application** property of the **Page** class. The **HttpApplicationState** class provides a key-value dictionary that you can use for storing both objects and scalar values.

In our **GuessingGame** sample we stored the **MaxAttempts** variable inside the **Application** object. We used this value to check whether a player exceeded the maximum number of attempts guessing the number. Here is the fragment from the code-behind **Guess.aspx.pm** file for the **Guess.aspx** Web form:

```
if ($attempt_num >=
  int($this->{Application}->get_Item("MaxAttempts")))
{
    $this->{Response}->Redirect("GameOver.aspx");
}
```

Additionally, we display the current number of attempts and total number of allowed attempts at the bottom of the page (see Figure 16-12).

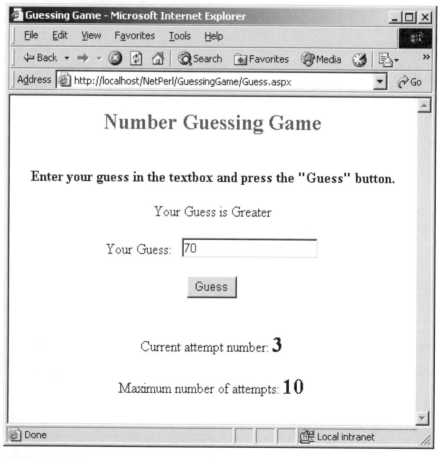

SESSION OBJECT

You can store session information for individual users in the built-in **Session** object, an instance of the class **HttpSessionState**. You can conveniently access this object through the **Session** property of the **Page** class. The **HttpSession-State** class provides a key-value dictionary that you can use for storing both objects and scalar values, in exactly the same manner employed by **HttpApplicationState**.

In our guessing game Web application, we store the player's attempt number and number to guess inside the **Session** object. We initialize the **AttemptNum** session variable in the code for **Default.aspx** Web Form as a response to pressing the Start button:

```
sub btnStart_Click
{
   my $this = shift;
   my $ubound = int($this->{txtUbound}->{Text});
   if ($ubound > 0)
   {
      my $session = $this->{Session};
      my $num = int(rand($ubound))+1;
      $session->set_Item("Number", $num);
      $session->set_Item("AttemptNum", 1);
      $this->{Response}->Redirect("Guess.aspx");
   }
}
```

Guessing Game

Most of the interesting things in this sample go on inside **Guess.aspx** Web Form and its **Guess.aspx.pm** code-behind file. Here is the full code for both files. If you followed our explanations, the code should be self-explanatory for you.

```
<!-- Guess.aspx -->
<%@ Page Language="Perl" SRC="Guess.aspx.pm"
Inherits=GuessPage %>
<HTML>
<HEAD>
<TITLE>Guessing Game</TITLE>
</HEAD>
<BODY>
<CENTER>
<H2>
<FONT color="red">
```

```
Number Guessing Game
</FONT>
</H2>
<BR>
<P>
<B>
Enter your guess in the textbox and press the "Guess"
button.
</B>
</P>
<P>
<asp:Label RUNAT="SERVER" id=lblMsg></asp:Label>
</P>
<FORM RUNAT="SERVER">
Your Guess:  
<asp:TextBox RUNAT="SERVER" id=txtGuess></asp:TextBox>
<BR>
<BR>
<asp:Button RUNAT="SERVER" id=btnGuess Text="Guess"
onClick=btnGuess_Click></asp:Button>
</FORM>
<BR>
<P>
Current attempt number:
<FONT size="5">
<B><%= $this->{Session}->get_Item("AttemptNum") %></B>
</FONT>
</P>
<P>
Maximum number of attempts:
<FONT size="5">
<B><%= $this->{Application}->get_Item("MaxAttempts")  %>
</B>
</FONT>
</P>
</CENTER>
</BODY>
</HTML>
```

Note that we used <%= … %> ASP.NET tags (bolded in the code) for displaying **Session** and **Application** variables. The expression within these tags is evaluated on the server, and its value is displayed in the resulting HTML.

Here is the code-behind.

```
#
# Guess.aspx.pm
#

package GuessPage;
```

```
use namespace "System";
use namespace "System.Web";
use namespace "System.Web.UI";
use namespace "System.Web.UI.WebControls";

=for interface
   [extends: System.Web.UI.Page]
   void btnGuess_Click(any sender, System.EventArgs e);
   protected field Label lblMsg;
   protected field TextBox txtGuess;
=cut

sub btnGuess_Click
{
   my $this = shift;

   # get the Answer number
   my $number = int($this->{Session}->get_Item("Number"));
   # get the guessed number
   my $guess = int($this->{txtGuess}->{Text});
   # get the current attempt number
   my $attempt_num = int($this->
                  {Session}->get_Item("AttemptNum"));
   if ($guess > $number)
   {
      if ($attempt_num >= int($this->{Application}->
                          get_Item("MaxAttempts")))
      {
         $this->{Response}->Redirect("GameOver.aspx");
      }
      $this->{lblMsg}->{Text} = "Your Guess is Greater";
   }
   elsif ($guess < $number)
   {
      if ($attempt_num >= int($this->{Application}->
                          get_Item("MaxAttempts")))
      {
         $this->{Response}->Redirect("GameOver.aspx");
      }
      $this->{lblMsg}->{Text} = "Your Guess is Less";
   }
   else
   {
      $this->{Response}->Redirect("WellDone.aspx");
   }
   $attempt_num++;
   $this->{Session}->set_Item("AttemptNum", $attempt_num);

}
```

All the code is executed in response to the user pressing the Guess button. We compare the guess with the correct answer stored in the **Session** variable and act accordingly.

Using PerlNET Components in ASP.NET

We saw the power of ASP.NET in conjunction with PerlASPX when authoring Web Forms and providing the server code in Perl for these forms. However, the ability of using existing PerlNET components as back-end in ASP.NET makes this platform perfect for authoring robust Web applications by putting the business logic in separate, independent .NET assemblies.

Roulette Component

We demonstrate this concept using the **Roulette** component we presented in Chapter 12. We altered its functionality to be suitable for more general use. The full code resides in the **RouletteBackend** folder under this chapter's samples. Here we present the fragments with major changes.

```
#
# Roulette.pm - ASP.NET Back-end
#

package OI::Samples::Roulette;
use namespace "OI.Samples";
use strict;

# Define Mixed type
=for interface
    [interface: mixed]
=cut

# Implements IResettable interface
=for interface
    [implements: IResettable]
    void Reset();
=cut

# Methods
=for interface
    # Add new stake
    void AddStake(int guess, num stake);
    # Roll the roulette - generate the result
    int Roll();
    # Update prizes for all gamblers
```

```perl
    private void UpdatePrizes(int result);
    # Obtain all Stakes
    wantarray! str[] GetStakes();
    # Obtain all Prizes
    wantarray! num[] GetPrizes();
=cut


# Private Data Member: Last Gambler ID
=for interface
    private field int f_LastGambler;
=cut

sub Roulette
{
    my ($this, $self) = @_;
    $this->{f_LastGambler} = 0;
    $self->{Stakes} = [];
    $self->{Prizes} = [];
}
. . .

sub Roll
{
    # We do not retrieve $self since we do not need it
    my $this = shift;

    my $result = int(rand(37));
    $this->UpdatePrizes($result);

    return $result;
}

sub UpdatePrizes
{
    my ($this, $self, $result) = @_;

    $self->{Prizes} = [];
    my ($guess, $stake, $prize);
    for (my $i = 0; $i < $this->{f_LastGambler}; $i++)
    {
        $guess = $self->{Stakes}->[$i][0];
        $stake = $self->{Stakes}->[$i][1];
        $prize = ($result == $guess ? 36*$stake : 0);
        $self->{Prizes}->[$i] = $prize;
    }
}

sub GetStakes
{
```

```perl
    my ($this, $self) = @_;

    my @stakes;
    for (my $i = 0; $i < $this->{f_LastGambler}; $i++)
    {
        my $str = "Gambler " . int($i+1) . ": ";
        $str = $str . "Guess = " .
                $self->{Stakes}->[$i][0] . "; ";
        $str = $str . "Stake = " .
                $self->{Stakes}->[$i][1];
        $stakes[$i] = $str;
    }
    return (@stakes);
}

sub GetPrizes
{
    my ($this, $self) = @_;

    my $prizes = $self->{Prizes};
    return(@$prizes);
}
. . .
```

The main changes are the addition of two methods—**GetStakes** and **Get-Prizes**—that return arrays of gamblers' stakes and the gamblers' prizes respectively. We may then use these arrays for displaying the relevant information.

Roulette Web Application

Under this chapter's samples, you should create a new Web application for the **Roulette** folder. In this folder is an empty **bin** folder, where assemblies for the PerlNET components we are going to use in our ASP.NET application should reside. We prepared the **build.bat** script, which will compile and place all the required assemblies into the **bin** directory.

After creating a Web application in IIS and running **build.bat**, you may run **Roulette** by opening the **http://localhost/NetPerl/Roulette/Stakes.aspx** URL. Figure 16-13 shows the Web page you should see in your browser.

You may add new stakes, reset them, and roll the roulette to obtain the results of the round. All the work behind the scenes is done by the **Roulette** component.

GLOBAL.ASAX FOR ROULETTE APPLICATION

We instantiate a new **Roulette** object for each user session. The most suitable place for this instantiation code is **Global.asax**. In this sample we created the

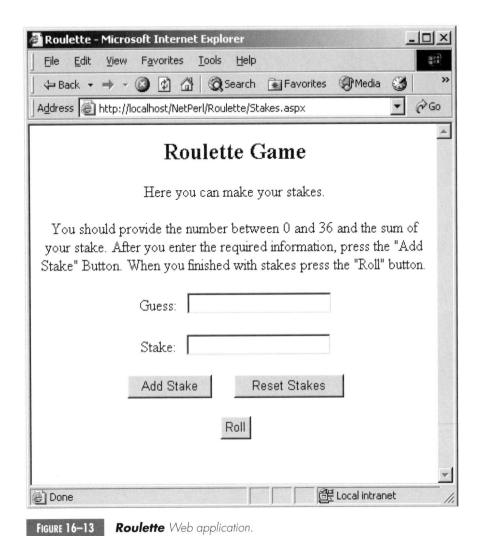

FIGURE 16–13 *Roulette* *Web application.*

code-behind file **Global.asax.pm**. Inside **Global.asax** we reference it with the following directive:

```
<%@ Application SRC="Global.asax.pm" Inherits="Global" %>
```

In addition, we reference two required assemblies using the following directives:

```
<%@ Assembly Name="roulette" %>
<%@ Assembly Name="IResettable" %>
```

ASP.NET looks for the referenced assemblies in the **bin** folder of our Web application. In the code-behind we declare the **Global** class, which inherits from the **System.Web.HttpApplication** class. We handle the **Session_Start** event, where we create a new **Roulette** instance and store it as a session variable (the bolded lines in the code below). Here is the code for **Global.asax.pm**.

```
#
# Global.asax.pm
#

use namespace "System";
use namespace "System.Collections";
use namespace "System.ComponentModel";
use namespace "System.Web";
use namespace "System.Web.SessionState";
use namespace "OI.Samples";

package Global;

=for interface
   [extends: System.Web.HttpApplication]
   protected void Session_Start(any sender, EventArgs e);
=cut

sub Session_Start
{
   my $this = shift;

   $this->{Session}->set_Item("Roulette",
               "OI.Samples.Roulette"->new());
}
```

STAKES.ASPX

Here is the PerlNET **=for interface** block definition for the code-behind of **Stakes.aspx**.

```
#
# Stakes.aspx.pm
#

package StakesPage;

use namespace "System";
use namespace "System.Collections";
use namespace "System.Web";
use namespace "System.Web.UI";
use namespace "System.Web.UI.WebControls";
use namespace "System.Data";
use namespace "OI.Samples";

use PerlNET qw(AUTOCALL int double in);
```

```
=for interface
   [extends: System.Web.UI.Page]
   protected override void OnLoad(EventArgs e);
   void btnAddStake_Click(any source, EventArgs e);
   void btnRoll_Click(any source, EventArgs e);
   void btnReset_Click(any source, EventArgs e);
   protected void BindControls();
   protected ICollection CreateDataSource(str name,
                                          any array);
   protected field Label lblMsg;
   protected field TextBox txtGuess;
   protected field TextBox txtStake;
   protected field Label lblResult;
   protected field DataGrid dgStakes;
   protected field DataGrid dgPrizes;
=cut
```

In the code-behind file of the **Stakes.aspx** Web Form, which defines the **StakesPage** class, we retrieve the **Roulette** session variable (the reference to the **Roulette** class) and invoke the appropriate methods. For example, in response to the user pressing the Add Stake button, the following code will be executed:

```
sub btnAddStake_Click
{
   my $this = shift;

   my $roulette = $this->{Session}->get_Item("Roulette");

   my $guess = int($this->{txtGuess}->{Text});
   my $stake = double($this->{txtStake}->{Text});
   $roulette->AddStake($guess, $stake);

   . . .
}
```

The bolded lines show the work with our **Roulette** component.

BINDING LIST CONTROLS TO DATA SOURCES

In the code of **Stakes.aspx** we used the **DataGrid** controls to display the data about gamblers' stakes and their prizes (**dgStakes** and **dgPrizes**). For example, here is the ASP.NET code for the stakes **DataGrid**.

```
<asp:DataGrid id="dgStakes" RUNAT="SERVER"
      BorderColor="black"
      BorderWidth="1"
      GridLines="Both"
      CellPadding="3"
      CellSpacing="0"
      HeaderStyle-BackColor="#aaaadd"/>
```

These controls can be bound to certain data sources and display the data in tabular form. We should set the **DataSource** property for such controls and call the **DataBind** method to bring the data into control. The requirement of **DataSource** is implementing the **IEnumerable** interface.

We bind the controls inside our **BindControls** method of the **StakesPage** class:

```
sub BindControls
{
   my $this = shift;

   my $roulette = $this->{Session}->get_Item("Roulette");

   my $stakes = $roulette->GetStakes();
   my $ds = $this->CreateDataSource("Stakes", $stakes);
   $this->{dgStakes}->{DataSource} = $ds;
   $this->{dgStakes}->DataBind();

   my $prizes = $roulette->GetPrizes();
   $ds = $this->CreateDataSource("Prizes", $prizes);
   $this->{dgPrizes}->{DataSource} = $ds;
   $this->{dgPrizes}->DataBind();
}
```

We call the appropriate methods on the **$roulette** reference to obtain the **Stakes** and **Prizes** arrays. Then we create the data source with the help of the **CreateDataSource** method, passing to it the name string and the array with data. This method creates the **DataTable** and fills it in with the data from the provided array. The name for the single column of the data table is determined by the first argument of this method. Then the **DataView** based on the **DataTable** object is created and returned by **CreateDataSource**.

```
sub CreateDataSource
{
   my ($this, $name, $array) = @_;

   if (!defined $array)
   {
      return;
   }
   my $dt = "DataTable"->new();
   $dt->{Columns}->Add("DataColumn"->new($name,
           "Type"->GetType("System.String")));
   foreach my $item(in $array)
   {
      my $dr = $dt->NewRow();
      $dr->[0] = $item;
```

```
        $dt->{Rows}->Add($dr);
    }

    return("DataView"->new($dt));
}
```

The data view is bound to the appropriate control and the data is displayed on Web page. Figure 16-14 shows **Stakes.aspx** with stakes and prizes data inside **DataGrid** controls, which are displayed as regular HTML tables.

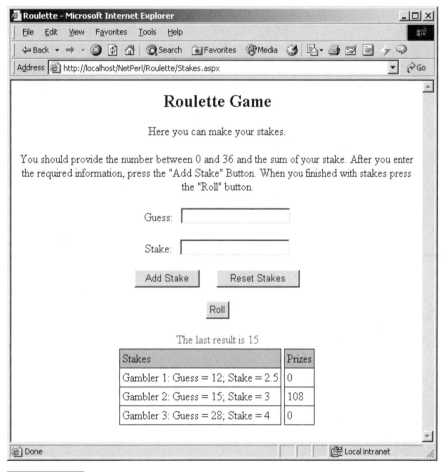

Stakes.aspx *with gambling and prizes data.*

Note that along the way we work with the **Roulette** component in ASP.NET as we do in a regular PerlNET client program.

Stock Query

To demonstrate additional techniques of data binding we present the **Stock\Stock.aspx** page for showing the read-only query of items in stock. We use the **Stock** component from the previous chapter. This component implements the **IStock** interface and works against the **Stock** table in our database. We reference the relevant assemblies in the **Stock.aspx** file:

```
<%@ Assembly Name="StockItem" %>
<%@ Assembly Name="IStock" %>
<%@ Assembly Name="Stock" %>
```

Please refer to the **readme.txt** file in the **Stock** sample folder for the instructions on building the assemblies. Figure 16–15 shows the results of running the stock query.

Stock query.

To run this sample you should create a Web application for the **Stock** folder.

We modified the **GetItems** method of the **Stock** component to return a **DataView** object instead of **ArrayList**. We bind this object to the **Repeater** server control. This control allows defining the HTML template for rendering the items in the bound collection. We enclose this template by the **<ItemTemplate>** tags inside the **Repeater** control. Additionally, you may define the template for header and footer placing them in the **<HeaderTemplate>** and **<FooterTemplate>** tags respectively.

```
<asp:repeater runat="server" id="rptItems">
<HeaderTemplate>
<table align="center" width="95%" style="font:
      8pt verdana">
<tr style="background-color:DFA894">
    <th>
    ID
    </th>
    <th>
    Name
    </th>
    <th>
    Price
    </th>
    <th>
    Quantity
    </th>
</tr>

</HeaderTemplate>

<ItemTemplate>
<tr style="background-color:FFCCAA">
    <td align="center">
    <%# PerlNET::call("System.Web.UI.DataBinder.Eval",
                $Container, "DataItem.ID", "{0}") %>
    </td>
    <td align="center">
    <%# PerlNET::call("System.Web.UI.DataBinder.Eval",
                $Container, "DataItem.Name", "{0}") %>
    </td>
    <td align="center">
    <%# PerlNET::call("System.Web.UI.DataBinder.Eval",
                $Container, "DataItem.Price", "{0}") %>
    </td>
    <td align="center">
    <%# PerlNET::call("System.Web.UI.DataBinder.Eval",
                $Container, "DataItem.Quantity", "{0}") %>
    </td>
</tr>
</ItemTemplate>
<FooterTemplate>
```

```
</table>
```

```
</FooterTemplate>
```

```
</asp:repeater>
```

To specify the data item to display we use the special binding syntax inside the **<ItemTemplate>** tags. The following code shows the ID of an item from the **Stock** table:

```
<%# PerlNET::call("System.Web.UI.DataBinder.Eval",
                  $Container, "DataItem.ID", "{0}") %>
```

Notice that we enclose the binding code by the **<%# . . . %>** tags. We call the **DataBinder.Eval** method to evaluate the data item inside the bound collection of **$Container**. The **$Container** holds the reference to the **Repeater** control object. The last argument is optional and we may use it for formatting the output through the placeholders like in the **Console.WriteLine** method.

We bind the **Repeater** control to the data source in the **BindControls** method, which we invoke in the **OnLoad** event handler in the code-behind file.

```
#
# Stock.aspx.pm
#

package StockPage;

use namespace "System";
use namespace "System.Collections";
use namespace "System.Web";
use namespace "System.Web.UI";
use namespace "System.Web.UI.WebControls";
use namespace "System.Data";
use namespace "OI.Samples";

use PerlNET qw(AUTOCALL int decimal in);

=for interface
    [extends: System.Web.UI.Page]
    protected override void OnLoad(EventArgs e);
    protected void BindControls();
    protected field Repeater rptItems;
=cut

sub OnLoad
{
    my $this = shift;
```

```
    $this->BindControls();
}

sub BindControls
{
    my $this = shift;

    my $stock = "Stock"->new();

    my $items = $stock->GetItems();
    $this->{rptItems}->{DataSource} = $items;
    $this->{rptItems}->DataBind();

}
```

You may run the Stock Management System application from the previous chapter and examine how the results of the stock query reflect the changes
you make through the Windows Forms application.

Web Services

As part of ASP.NET support, PerlASPX provides developers with additional facility besides creating ASP.NET Web pages: creating Web services. Web services are
much like the PerlNET components that we created throughout this book. You
declare the class with methods that may then be invoked by the Web service
clients. The major difference is that Web services run on the Web server and the
methods are called remotely through the network. Hence, the infrastructure
for Web services differs from one for regular PerlNET components.

By exposing Web services to the developers, the Web sites become
"smarter." Suppose you want to perform some orders through the Internet on a
regular basis. You will either do it manually each time or you may create a very
complicated application that will perform the HTTP connection, parse the
HTML files, fill in the forms, and finally submit them. The second option is very
challenging and interesting (I once did it!), but it is time consuming and is
bound to the structure of the Web site and its HTML files that may change. It is
a lot more convenient to create the same order by remotely invoking a couple
of methods on the Web site like on the regular local object. This is what the
Web services are about.

Web services rely on certain network protocols to perform the method
invocation through the network. In the heart of these protocols lies XML,
which helps to describe Web services definitions (methods, types of parameters, return values, and so on) to the clients on different platforms.

Creating Web Services

The code for Web services is placed on the Web server (like **.aspx** pages) in the file with an **.asmx** extension. You can test Web services using Internet Explorer simply by referring to the URL of the **.asmx** file.

Our first sample represents simple Web service with one method, which concatenates two strings passed to it as parameters. Here is the code for the **StringServer.asmx** Web service (it resides under the chapter samples folder).

```
<%@ WebService class="StringServer" Language="perl" %>

package StringServer;

=for interface
   [System.Web.Services.WebMethod]
   str Concat(str str1, str str2);
=cut

sub Concat
{
   my ($this, $str1, $str2) = @_;

   return($str1 . $str2);
}
```

We start our Web service declaration with the ASP.NET **WebService** directive in the first line of the **.asmx** file. We define the class name and the language to use. Then we follow the regular procedure of defining a PerlNET component by defining the **=for interface** block and supplying the code for method's subroutine. Note that the methods you want to be accessible by the clients as part of the Web services API should be marked with the **WebMethod** attribute that resides in the **System.Web.Services** namespace.

Now, let us test our first Web service by navigating to its URL (**http://localhost/NetPerl/StringServer.asmx**) with Internet Explorer. Figure 16-16 shows the page that is displayed for our Web service.

For each method of a Web service, there is a link on its Web page. In our case, there is only one **Concat** link, which we will follow. On the displayed page (Figure 16-17) we may fill in the parameters for the **Concat** method of our **StringServer** Web service and press the Invoke button.

The result is displayed inside a new browser window in the XML format

```
<?xml version="1.0" encoding="utf-8" ?>
<string xmlns="http://tempuri.org/">Have a nice day
</string>
```

FIGURE 16-16   *The Web page for the **StringServer** Web service.*

Web Service Client Program

It is nice to test our Web service inside the Web browser. However, the more ambitious task is to write our own client program for Web service. This program will call the Web methods in the same way as other .NET methods are called.

To create client programs for certain Web service, we first write a *proxy class* that will handle all the infrastructure of passing parameters to the Web service and extracting the return values from the XML. Fortunately, there is an automatic tool that generates such proxy class: **wsdl**. This tool reads the XML description of the Web service. The description is written in WSDL (Web Service Definition Language). The **wsdl** tool extracts all the required information and generates the code for the proxy class. The default language of **wsdl** is C#.

To create a proxy file for our **StringServer** Web service, we run **wsdl** from the command line with the following parameters:

```
wsdl /out:StringProxy.cs
        http://localhost/NetPerl/StringServer.asmx?WSDL
```

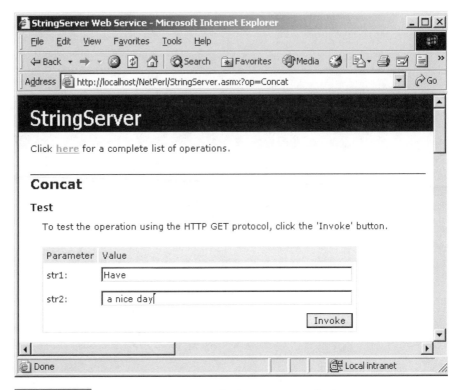

The **http://localhost/NetPerl/StringServer.asmx?WSDL** URL returns the **WSDL** XML file for the **StringServer** Web service. The generated proxy is placed in the **StringProxy.cs** file. This file defines the **StringServer** class with the **Concat** method (along with other auxiliary methods).

```
. . .
public class StringServer :
System.Web.Services.Protocols.SoapHttpClientProtocol {

    /// <remarks/>
    public StringServer() {
       this.Url =
       "http://localhost/NetPerl/StringServer.asmx";
    }

    /// <remarks/>
    . . .
    public string Concat(string str1, string str2) {
       object[] results = this.Invoke("Concat",
```

```
        new object[] {str1,str2});
          return ((string)(results[0]));
      }
       . . .
```

We may compile this class into a DLL and then reference it in our PerlNET client program. Here is the simple testing PerlNET client for **StringServer** (we placed it in the **StringServerCli** folder along with the generated C# proxy class file).

```
#
# StringServerCli.pl
#

my $str_svr = StringServer->new();
my $str = $str_svr->Concat("Good", " Luck!");
print $str, "\n";
```

First, we compile the proxy class.

```
csc /target:library StringProxy.cs
```

Then we may build our client program.

```
plc -reference="StringProxy.dll" StringServerCli.pl
```

Both compilation commands are inside the **build.bat** file in the sample directory. As a result of running **StringServerCli.exe**, we obtain the following output:

```
Good Luck!
```

Creating a Web Client

After we generate the proxy class, we may reference it in ASP.NET pages and create the Web client. The **StringWebCli.aspx** Web page from the **StringWebCli** folder implements such a client, providing the user with a simple form to supply parameters for the **StringServer** Web service. Pressing the Concatenate button will display the result returned by the **Concat** method of our Web service. Figure 16–18 demonstrates our Web client.

Since we create a Web client, we have to be cautious when displaying special characters, such as '<' and '>', that may occur in strings we concatenate. Hence, we use the **HtmlEncode** method of the **HttpServerUtility** class to display the resulting string correctly.

To keep it simple, we placed all the code inside the **StringWebCli.aspx** page without using the code-behind. Here is this code.

```
<!-- StringWebCli.aspx -->
<%@ Assembly Name="StringProxy" %>
```

FIGURE 16–18   *The Web client for the* **StringServer** *Web service.*

```
<%@ Page Language="Perl" %>
<HTML>
<BODY>
<CENTER>
<H2>String Server Web Client</H2>

<SCRIPT RUNAT="SERVER">
=for interface
   public void btnConcat_Click(System.Object source,
                              System.EventArgs e);
=cut

sub btnConcat_Click
{
   my $this = shift;

   my $str1 = $this->{txtStr1}->{Text};
   my $str2 = $this->{txtStr2}->{Text};
   my $str_svr = "StringServer"->new();

   my $result = $str_svr->Concat($str1, $str2);
   my $writer = "System.IO.StringWriter"->new();
   $this->{Server}->HtmlEncode($result, $writer);
```

```
    $this->{lblResult}->{Text} = $writer->ToString();
}
</SCRIPT>

<BR>
<FORM RUNAT="SERVER">
<TABLE border=0>
<TR>
    <TD>
    First String:
    </TD>
    <TD>
    <asp:TextBox RUNAT="SERVER" id="txtStr1"/>
    </TD>
</TR>
<TR>
    <TD>
    Second String:
    </TD>
    <TD>
    <asp:TextBox RUNAT="SERVER" id="txtStr2"/>
    </TD>
</TR>
</TABLE>
<BR>
<asp:button RUNAT="SERVER" TEXT="Concatenate" id=btnConcat
onClick=btnConcat_Click/>
</FORM>
<BR>
<B><asp:Label RUNAT="SERVER" id="lblResult"/></B>
</CENTER>
</BODY>
</HTML>
```

Please run the **build.bat** script to compile the proxy class and create the Web application using IIS for the sample folder before running the sample.

Web Services Summary

We demonstrated the main concepts and principles of developing Web services in Perl using simple examples. We are sure that you will be able to extrapolate our samples and explanation and build powerful and useful applications based on Web services and ASP.NET technologies.

Summary

In this chapter we sampled ASP.NET technology and demonstrated the development with PerlASPX. We learned how to create simple ASP.NET pages with server Web controls. We presented the code-behind scenario where the presentation is separated from the code. We demonstrated the event handling in ASP.NET, which is somewhat similar to WinForms. ASP.NET pages may be unified under a Web application. This enables us to store the values in the **Session** and **Application** scopes. PerlNET components may be used as a back-end for Web applications. Certain controls may be bound to data sources and display the data in tabular form.

ASP.NET and PerlASPX allow us to develop Web services written in Perl. Such Web services expose Web methods that may be invoked across the Internet in various client programs and Web applications.

Visual Studio .NET and Visual Perl

*A*lthough it is possible to program .NET using only the command-line compiler, it is much easier and more enjoyable to use Visual Studio .NET. You can program straight Perl using any text editor and the Perl interpreter, but again it is easier to use an integrated development environment. Visual Perl, an add-on to Visual Studio .NET, provides such an IDE.

This appendix covers the basics of using Visual Studio to edit, compile, run, and debug programs. We introduce additional features of Visual Studio throughout the book as we encounter a need. Visual Studio is a very elaborate Windows application that is highly configurable, and you may encounter variations in the exact layout of windows, what is shown by default, and so on. As you work with Visual Studio, a good attitude is to see yourself as an explorer discovering a rich and varied new country.

Overview of Visual Studio .NET

Open up Microsoft Visual Studio .NET and you will see a starting window similar to that shown in Figure A–1.

What you see on default startup is the main window with an HTML page that can help you navigate among various resources, open or create projects, and change your profile information. (If you close the start page, you can get it back anytime from the menu Help | Show Start Page.) Clicking on **My Profile** will bring up a profile page on which you can change various settings. There is a standard profile for "typical" work in Visual Studio (Visual Studio Developer profile) and special ones for various languages. Since Visual Studio .NET is the unification of many development environments, programmers used to one

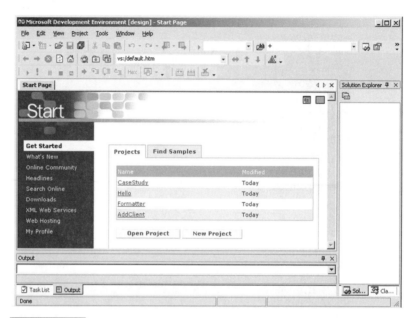

FIGURE A-1 *Visual Studio .NET main window.*

particular previous environment may prefer a particular keyboard scheme, window layout, and so on. For example, if you choose the profile Visual Basic Developer, you will get the Visual Basic 6 keyboard scheme. In this book we use all the defaults, so go back to the profile Visual Studio Developer if you made any changes. See Figure A–2.

Code Example

To gain an appreciation of some of the diverse features in Visual Studio .NET, open up the **TestInputWrapper** solution in this chapter (File | Open Solution..., navigate to the **TestInputWrapper** directory, and open the file **TestInputWrapper.sln**). You will see quite an elaborate set of windows. See Figure A–3.

Starting from the left is the main window area, which currently is just a gray area. Underneath the main window is the Output Window, which shows the results of builds and so on. Continuing our tour, on the top right is the Solution Explorer, which enables you to conveniently see all the files in a solution, which may consist of several projects. On the bottom right is the Properties window, which lets you conveniently edit properties on forms for Windows applications. The Properties window is very similar to the Properties Window in Visual Basic.

From the Solution Explorer you can navigate to files in the projects. In turn, double-click on each of **InputWrapper.pl** and **TestInputWrapper.pl**, the two source files in the **TestInputWrapper** project. Text editor windows

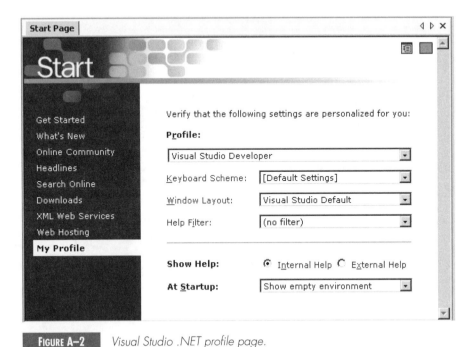

FIGURE A–2   *Visual Studio .NET profile page.*

will be brought up in the main window area. Across the top of the main window are horizontal tabs to quickly select any of the open windows. Visual Studio .NET is a Multiple Document Interface (MDI) application, and you can also select the window to show from the Windows menu. Figure A–4 shows the open source files with the horizontal tabs.

Toolbars

Visual Studio comes with many different toolbars. You can configure which toolbars you wish displayed, and you can drag toolbars to position them to where you find them most convenient. You can also customize toolbars by adding or deleting buttons that correspond to different commands.

To specify which toolbars are displayed, bring up the menu View | Toolbars. You can also right-click in any empty area of a toolbar. There will be a checkmark next to the toolbars that are currently displayed. By clicking on an item on this menu, you can make the corresponding toolbar button appear or disappear. For your work in this book, add the toolbars

- Build
- Debug

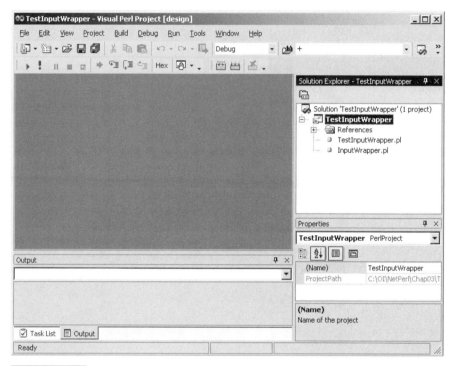

A managed Exe project in Visual Studio .NET.

CUSTOMIZING A TOOLBAR

We want to make sure that the Start Without Debugging command is available on the Debug toolbar. If it is not already on your Debug toolbar (it is a red exclamation point), you can add it by the following procedure, which can be used to add other commands to toolbars.

1. Select menu Tools | Customize... to bring up the Customize dialog.
2. Select the Commands tab.
3. In Categories, select Debug, and in Commands select Start Without Debugging. See Figure A–5.
4. Drag the selected command onto the Debug toolbar, positioning it where you desire. Place it to the immediate right of the wedge shaped Start ▶ button.
5. Close the Customize dialog.

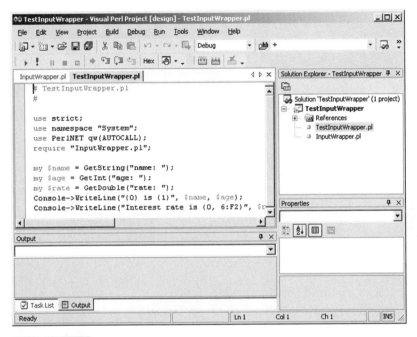

FIGURE A–4   *Horizontal tabs for open source files.*

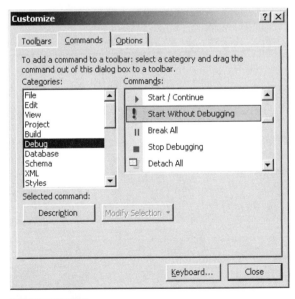

FIGURE A–5   *Adding a new command to a toolbar.*

Creating a Managed Exe Application

As our first exercise in using Visual Studio, we create a simple Managed Exe application. Our program **Echo** will prompt the user for her name and then display a personalized greeting. If you want to follow along on your PC as you read, you can use the **Demos** directory for this chapter. A final version can be found in the **Echo** directory.

Code
Example

Creating a Visual Perl Project

When you install Visual Perl, you will be able to create Visual Perl projects in Visual Studio as well as in Visual C#, Visual Basic .NET, and Visual C++ projects. There are different kinds of Visual Perl projects. We will illustrate with a Managed Exe project, which will build an executable file consisting of IL instructions, as discussed in Chapter 1.

1. From Visual Studio main menu choose File | New | Project.... This will bring up the New Project dialog.
2. For Project Types choose Visual Perl Projects and for Templates choose Managed Exe Project.
3. Click the Browse button, navigate to **Demos**, and click Open.
4. In the Name field, type **Echo**. See Figure A-6. Click OK.

Building the Starter Project

At this point you will have a Visual Perl project that has some starter code. You can examine the code file **Echo.pl**, as illustrated in Figure A-7. You will see code for using PerlNET followed by code to print out the message "Hello, World."

You can build the project by using one of the following:

● Menu Build | Build
● Toolbar 🖽
● Keyboard shortcut Ctrl + Shift + B

Running the Program

You can run the program by using one of the following:

● Menu Debug | Start Without Debugging
● Toolbar ❗
● Keyboard shortcut Ctrl + F5

You will see output displayed in a special Run window that opens up, as illustrated in Figure A-8. When you are done inspecting the output, you can close this window in the usual way (click on the "x" at the top-right). If you run

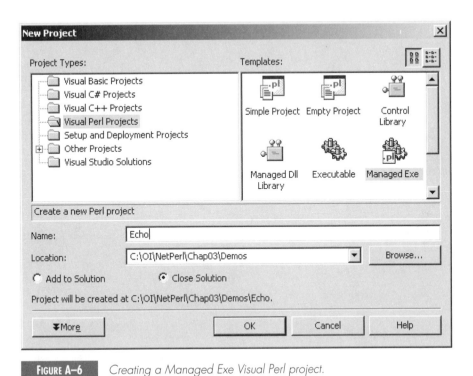

FIGURE A–6   *Creating a Managed Exe Visual Perl project.*

the project again, you will see the Run window displayed again, showing both the previous run and the current run.

Adding a File

The starter program prints out a fixed greeting message. We want to create a program that will prompt a user for her name, and then echo back her name in a greeting message. We could of course just write a little code inline to prompt for the name and read it in. But we want to illustrate a simple project with more than one source file, so we use the **InputWrapper.pl** file illustrated earlier.

1. Copy the file **InputWrapper.pl** from **TestInputWrapper** to **Demos\Echo**.
2. In Solution Explorer, right-click over Echo and choose Add | Add Existing Item from the context menu.
3. In the dialog that comes up, navigate to the file you want to add. (Because of the copy you did in Step 1, the desired file **InputWrapper.pl** should be immediately available. Double-click on the file to add it to the project.

You should now see the second file in Solution Explorer.

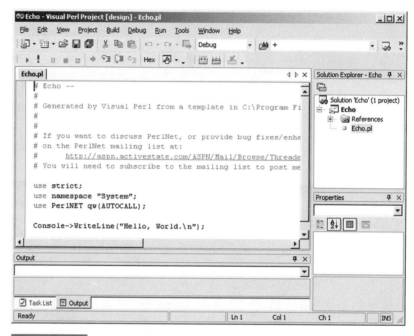

FIGURE A-7   *A Visual Perl starter project.*

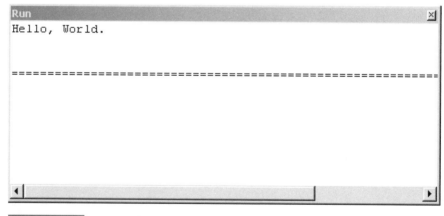

FIGURE A-8   *Run window shows output from a Visual Perl program.*

Using the Visual Studio Text Editor

In Solution Explorer double-click on **Echo.pl**. This will open up the generated file **Echo.pl** in the Visual Studio text editor. Type in the lines shown in bold, and notice things like color syntax highlighting as you type. (We have deleted some of the comments in the generated code, and we show the file name as the first comment.)

```
# Echo.pl
#

use strict;
use namespace "System";
use PerlNET qw(AUTOCALL);
require "InputWrapper.pl";

Console->WriteLine("Hello, World.\n");
my $name = GetString("Your name: ");
Console->WriteLine("Hello, {0}", $name);
```

Besides the color syntax highlighting, other features include automatic indenting and putting in a closing right curly brace to match the left curly brace you type. All in all, you should find the Visual Studio editor friendly and easy to use. If you run the program, you should see output in the Run window that is similar to what is shown:

```
Hello, World.

Your name: Jill
Hello, Jill
```

==

Debugging in Visual Studio and Visual Perl

Visual Studio comes with great debugging features, and Visual Perl enables you to use these debugging features with standard Perl scripts. At the time of this writing, interactive IDE debugging of managed PerlNET executables was not supported, so we will illustrate with a standard Perl script.

SimpleBytes Program – Step 1

Code Example

The **SimpleBytes\Step1** program calculates how many bytes there are in a kilobyte, a megabyte, a gigabyte, and a terabyte. It then goes on to prompt the user for an exponent and prints out a table of powers of 1,024 up to the exponent supplied by the user.

```
# SimpleBytes.pl - Step 1

use strict;
```

```perl
my $kilo = 1024;
print "kilo = $kilo \n";
my $mega = $kilo * 1024;
print "mega = $mega \n";
my $giga = $mega * 1024;
print "giga = $giga \n";
my $tera = $giga * 1024;
print "tera = $tera \n";

print "exponent: ";
my $exponent = <STDIN>;
my $bytes = $kilo;
for (my $i = 1; $i <= $exponent; $i++)
{
   print "$i    $bytes \n";
   $bytes = $bytes * $kilo;
}

print "Press Enter to exit\n";
my $line = <STDIN>;
```

The idea of the program is to try to induce some kind of bug so that we can practice the debugging features of Visual Studio. There is a similar C# program in Appendix B, where an exception is thrown on the line that tries to calculate a terabyte. Perl calculates a terabyte like a champ, and then goes on to use floating-point numbers for larger values. It is not easy to make this program misbehave! The following run illustrates the user entering an exponent of 8.

```
kilo = 1024
mega = 1048576
giga = 1073741824
tera = 1099511627776
exponent: 8
1    1024
2    1048576
3    1073741824
4    1099511627776
5    1.12589990684262e+015
6    1.15292150460685e+018
7    1.18059162071741e+021
8    1.20892581961463e+024
Press enter to exit
```

Note the statements at the end of the program to prompt the user for some input. Without these statements, when you run the program from inside Visual Studio you will see a console window open briefly and then close. You can try this behavior out by commenting out the last two statements in the program.

Floating-point can hold very large numbers, but eventually you should get an overflow. A little experimentation shows that overflow occurs for an exponent of 103. Perl will print out "INF" but not crash!

```
. . .
100    1.07150860718627e+301
101    1.09722481375874e+304
102    1.12355820928895e+307
103    1.#INF
104    1.#INF
105    1.#INF
. . .
```

SimpleBytes Program – Step 2

Code Example

Continuing our quest for a bug, we put in some code that at some point will do a divide by zero. See **SimpleBytes\Step2**.

```
# SimpleBytes.pl - Step 2

. . .

print "exponent: ";
my $exponent = <STDIN>;
my $bytes = $kilo;
for (my $i = 1; $i <= $exponent; $i++)
{
    my $x = 1 / ($bytes - $tera);
    print "$i    $bytes    $x \n";
    $bytes = $bytes * $kilo;
}

print "Press Enter to exit\n";
my $line = <STDIN>;
```

Running the Program in the Debugger

You can run the program in the debugger by using one of the following:

- Menu Debug | Start
- Toolbar ▶
- Keyboard shortcut F5

A console window will briefly open up and then immediately close. If you want the window to stay open, you must explicitly program for it, for example, by asking for input (like we illustrated in the **SimpleBytes** program).

Run **SimpleBytes\Step2** and enter the value 8 for the exponent (any value of 4 or greater will do). Despite the explicit code at the end of the program to prompt the user for input, the program shuts down immediately. At last, a bug!

Breakpoints

The way you typically do standard debugging is to set a breakpoint and then run using the debugger. As an example, set a breakpoint at the line where a divide takes place.

```
my $x = 1 / ($bytes - $tera);
```

The easiest way to set a breakpoint is by clicking in the gray bar to the left of the source code window. You can also set the cursor on the desired line and click the "hand" toolbar button ✋ to toggle a breakpoint (set if not set, and remove if a breakpoint is set). Now you can run under the debugger, and the breakpoint should be hit. A yellow arrow over the red dot of the breakpoint shows where the breakpoint has been hit. See Figure A–9.

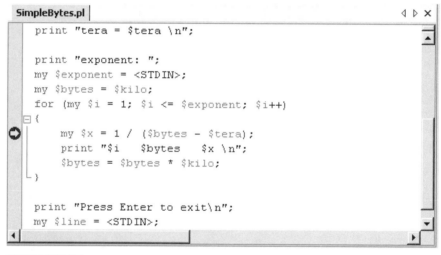

FIGURE A–9   *A breakpoint has been hit.*

When you are done with a breakpoint, you can remove it by clicking again in the gray bar or by toggling with the hand toolbar button. If you want to remove all breakpoints, you can use the menu Debug | Clear All Breakpoints, or you can use the toolbar button 🐾.

WATCHING VARIABLES

At this point you can inspect variables. The easiest way is to slide the mouse over the variable you are interested in, and the value will be shown as a yellow tool tip. You can also right-click over a variable and choose Quick Watch (or use the eyeglasses toolbar button 👓). Figure A-10 shows a typical Quick Watch window. You can also change the value of a variable from this window.

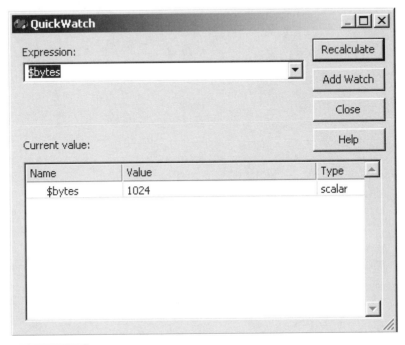

FIGURE A-10   *Quick Watch window shows a variable, and you can change it.*

When you are stopped in the debugger, you can add a variable to the Watch window by right-clicking over it and choosing Add Watch. The Watch window can show a number of variables, and the Watch window stays open as the program executes. When a variable changes value, the new value is shown in red.

The Locals window shows all the local variables automatically. As with a Watch window, when a variable changes value, the new value is shown in red. Figure A-11 shows the Locals window at the occurrence of the first breakpoint.

DEBUGGER OPTIONS

You can change debugger options from the menu Tools | Options, and select Debugging from the list. Figure A-12 illustrates setting a hexadecimal display. If you then go back to a Watch window or a Locals window, you will see a hex value such as **0x400** displayed.

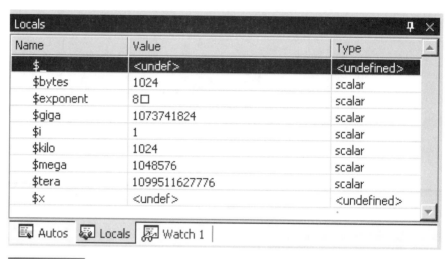

FIGURE A–11   *Visual Studio Locals window.*

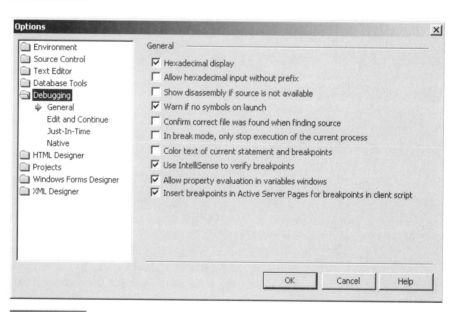

FIGURE A–12   *Setting hexadecimal display in Debugging Options.*

SINGLE STEPPING

When you are stopped in the debugger, you can *single step*. You can also begin execution by single stepping. There are a number of single step buttons ⤵ ⤷ ⤴ . The most common are (in the order shown on the toolbar):

- Step Into
- Step Over
- Step Out

There is also a Run to Cursor button ⤴ .

With Step Into you will step into a function if the cursor is positioned on a call to a function. With Step Over you will step to the next line (or statement or instruction, depending on the selection in the dropdown next to the step buttons `Line ▾`). To illustrate Step Into, build the **SimpleBytes\Step3** project, where the multiplication by 1,024 has been replaced by a function call to the function **OneK**. Set a breakpoint at the function call, and then Step Into. The result is illustrated in Figure A-13. Note the red dot at the breakpoint and the yellow arrow in the function.

```
SimpleBytes.pl                                        ◁ ▷ ✕

    sub OneK
⊟  {
⇨      my $args = @_;
        my $num = $_[0];
        return $num * 1024;
    }


    print "exponent: ";
    my $exponent = <STDIN>;
    my $bytes = 1024;
    for (my $i = 1; $i <= $exponent; $i++)
⊟  {
        print "$i   $bytes \n";
●       $bytes = OneK($bytes);
    }
```

FIGURE A-13   *Stepping into a function.*

When debugging, Visual Studio maintains a Call Stack. In our simple example the Call Stack is just two deep. See Figure A-14.

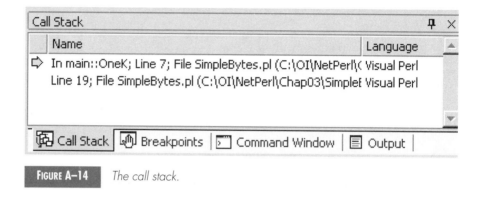

FIGURE A-14   *The call stack.*

Summary

Visual Studio .NET is a very rich integrated development environment (IDE), with many features to make programming more enjoyable. Visual Perl is an add-on that enables you to work with Perl in the Visual Studio environment. In this chapter we covered the basics of using Visual Studio to edit, compile, run, and debug programs so that you will be equipped to use Visual Studio in the rest of the book. .NET has a vast array of features for building database applications, Web applications, components, and many other kinds of projects. It supports many different languages. In this book we use only a tiny fraction of the capabilities of this powerful tool, but the simple features we employ are very useful, and will certainly make your life as a Perl programmer easier.

C# Survival Guide
for PerlNET Programmers

*A*lthough .NET was designed to work effectively with many programming languages, the new C# language plays a special role, designed from the ground up along with the .NET Framework. Thus C# enjoys the best match with the facilities of .NET. C# is an especially good language for the PerlNET programmer's toolkit, because its C-like syntax will be comfortable for Perl programmers, and PerlNET data types have been designed to match the C# data types. Also, since the current release of PerlNET does not allow you to do everything in Perl (for example, create your own interface), you will sometimes find it convenient to create C# components to work with your PerlNET programs.

This appendix is intended to get you up to speed on C# quickly. Naturally, we can provide only a basic introduction, and for more details you can consult any of the many books on C#. We especially recommend two titles from The Integrated .NET Series:

- *Introduction to C# Using .NET* for an introductory book focused on the C# language.
- *Application Development Using C# and .NET* for an intermediate book with a concise but quite complete treatment of C# and emphasis on the .NET Framework.

Hello, World in C# (Object-Oriented Version)

We begin with the traditional "Hello, world" program made popular beginning at least with the first edition of *The C Programming Language* by Kernighan and Ritchie. We already presented a version of this program in C# in Chapter 9. In this section we provide an object-oriented version and also introduce

413

building components from C# that can be called from PerlNET. Along the way we cover basic input/output (I/O) and arrays.

The Hello Class

It has been suggested that the traditional "Hello, world" program is harmful to students.[1] They start thinking in terms of a monolithic program, and this habit is hard to shake. As Perl programmers, we can have the same problem ourselves, as Perl makes it so easy to create sophisticated scripts as monolithic code. In learning C# and .NET, which are so thoroughly object-oriented, it will be very helpful to us to start "thinking in objects" from the beginning. If you already have experience with an object-oriented language such as C++ or Java, you can breeze through this first section, paying attention only to the syntax of C#.

We begin with an object-oriented version that supports encapsulation. The implementation of an abstraction should be hidden from the rest of the system, or encapsulated, as shown in Figure B-1.

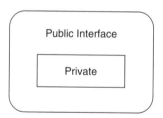

FIGURE B-1   *An abstraction presents a public interface to a private implementation.*

We define a class **Hello** with a public interface supporting

- The *method* **SayHello()**
- The *property* **Greeting**

There is a private implementation:

- The string **m_greeting**

The C# code for this class is contained in the file **Hello.cs** in the folder **Hello\Step1** in the folder **AppB** that is provided for this appendix.

```
// Hello.cs

using System;

public class Hello
```

---

1. Ralph Westfall, "Hello, World Considered Harmful," *Communications of the ACM*, October, 2001, p. 129.

```
{
   private string m_greeting = "Hello, world";
   public Hello()
   {
   }
   public Hello(string greeting)
   {
      m_greeting = greeting;
   }
   public void SayHello()
   {
      Console.WriteLine(m_greeting);
   }
   public string Greeting
   {
      get
      {
         return m_greeting;
      }
      set
      {
         m_greeting = value;
      }
   }
}
```

A test program for this class is provided in the file **TestHello.cs** in the same folder.

```
// TestHello.cs

public class TestHello
{
   public static int Main(string[] args)
   {
      Hello obj;
      obj = new Hello();
      obj.SayHello();
      obj = new Hello("Goodbye, world");
      obj.SayHello();
      obj.Greeting = "Brave New World";
      System.Console.WriteLine(obj.Greeting);
      return 0;
   }
}
```

A Visual Studio solution is provided, which you can build as described in Appendix A, and run (use menu Debug | Start Without Debugging or keyboard Ctrl + F5). Alternatively, you can run the batch file **build.bat** at the command line and run the program by simply typing the name of the EXE file **Test-Hello.exe**. You will see the following output:

```
Hello, world
Goodbye, world
Brave New World
```

Classes and Objects

The most basic concept in this program is that of *class*, which represents a type of data. A class can be thought of as a template from which individual instances can be created. An instance of a class is called an *object*.

In C# a class is defined using the keyword **class**. A C# class can contain several kinds of elements. The **Hello** class includes the following elements:

- The private data member **m_greeting**. Each object instance will have its own value for this data member. A default value of "Hello, world" is defined.
- Constructors, which can be used to provide initialization at the time an object instance is created. This class has two constructors. A constructor has the same name as the class and can take a parameter list. The first constructor has no parameters and is called the *default constructor*. The second constructor takes a string parameter, which is used to assign a nondefault value to **m_greeting**.
- The method **SayHello**, which is used to implement behavior, in this case printing out a greeting message.
- The property **Greeting**, which exposes data outside the class.

In C# an object instance is created using the **new** keyword, as illustrated in the **TestHello.cs** program.

```
obj = new Hello();
...
obj = new Hello("Goodbye, world");
```

The first line invokes the default constructor, and the second line invokes the constructor with a string parameter.

Access Control

C# provides language features so that the programmer can enforce access rules for a class and its members. (Not all languages that provide classes and objects have support for access control. For example, Perl expects programmers to play by the rules, but does not have an enforcement mechanism.)

C# has two means for controlling accessibility of class members. Access can be controlled at both the class level and the member level.

CLASS ACCESSIBILITY

An access modifier can be placed in front of the **class** keyword to control who can get at the class at all. Access can be further restricted by member accessibility, discussed in the next subsection.

- The most common access modifier of a class is **public**, which makes the class available to everyone.
- The **internal** modifier makes a class available within the current *assembly,* which can be thought of as a logical EXE or DLL. (We discuss assemblies later in this appendix.) If you leave out an access modifier in front of a class, **internal** will be assumed.

MEMBER ACCESSIBILITY

Access to individual class members can be controlled by placing an access modifier such as **public** or **private** in front of the member. Member access can only further restrict access to a class, not widen it. Thus if you have a class with **internal** accessibility, making a member **public** will not make it accessible from outside the assembly.

- A **public** member can be accessed from outside the class.
- A **private** member can be accessed only from within the class (but not from derived classes).
- Inheritance introduces a third kind of accessibility, **protected**. A protected member can be accessed from within the class and from within any derived classes. (We discuss inheritance in C# later in this appendix.)
- An **internal** member can be accessed from within classes in the same assembly but not from classes outside the assembly.
- An **internal protected** member can be accessed from within the assembly and from outside the assembly by a derived class.

Methods

Typically, a class will specify behavior as well as data. A class encapsulates data and behavior in a single entity. A method specifies the behavior and consists of

- An access specifier, typically **public** or **private**
- A return type (can be **void** if the method does not return data)
- A method name, which can be any legal C# identifier
- A parameter list, enclosed by parentheses, which specifies data that is passed to the method (can be empty if no data is passed)
- A method body, enclosed by curly braces, which contains the C# code that the method will execute

```
public void SayHello()
{
    Console.WriteLine(m_greeting);
}
```

Fields

In C# data members of a class are referred to as *fields*. Fields may be assigned access modifiers like other members of a class. In the Step1 version of the **Hello** example, the greeting data is stored in a private field **m_greeting**. Although not usually recommended, you can also have public fields, as illustrated in **Hello\Step1F.**

```
// Hello.cs

using System;

public class Hello
{
   public string Greeting = "Hello, world";
   public Hello()
   {
   }
   public Hello(string greeting)
   {
      Greeting = greeting;
   }
   public void SayHello()
   {
      Console.WriteLine(Greeting);
   }
}
```

This version of the **Hello** class presents exactly the same interface to the outside world as the original version, so the test program does not have to be changed. Notice that variables in C# are case-sensitive, so we may have both the data field **Greeting** and the parameter **greeting**.

Properties

Although exposing internal data of a class to the outside world is generally a bad idea, the data interface is rather convenient for users of the class. Thus in the test program we can read and write the data by simple assignments, without having to invoke any special methods.

```
   ...
   obj.Greeting = "Brave New World";
   System.Console.WriteLine(obj.Greeting);
```

It is easy to understand how this notation works with the Step1F version, where there is a public data member **Greeting**. But it also works in the Step1 version, where a *property* is defined, using the following C# code. Note that in this case the property is read-write (both get and set are provided). It is also possible to implement read-only (just get) and write-only (just set) properties.

```
public string Greeting
{
    get
    {
        return m_greeting;
    }
    set
    {
        m_greeting = value;
    }
}
```

Here **value** is a special C# keyword that is used for implementing properties. There are several advantages to using properties in place of public fields. The basic advantage is encapsulation. We can change the data representation without breaking the rest of the program, and client programs cannot directly access private data, possibly causing damage. Another advantage is that code can be provided as part of the data access. For example, in a read-property the value could be calculated or obtained from some real-time sensor and not actually stored as data at all. In a write-property some validation could be performed before actually making the assignment.

System.Console

The **System.Console** class provides convenient methods for input and output. The **Hello** example illustrates only one of these methods, **WriteLine**, for performing output. It writes a string followed by a new line.

```
System.Console.WriteLine(obj.Greeting);
```

In later programs we will see illustrations of other methods, such as **Write**, which writes a string without the new line, and **ReadLine**, which reads a string from the console.

Namespaces

Much standard functionality in C# is provided through many classes in the .NET Framework. Related classes are grouped into *namespaces*. Many useful classes, such as **Console**, are in the **System** namespace. The fully qualified name of a class is specified by the namespace followed by a dot followed by a class name.

```
System.Console
```

A **using** statement allows a class to be referred to by its class name alone. Whereas in the **TestHello** class we use the fully qualified name, in the **Hello** class we rely on the **using** statement.

```
// Hello.cs

using System;

public class Hello
{
   ...
   public void SayHello()
   {
      Console.WriteLine(m_greeting);
   }
   ...
```

Main Method

The **TestHello** class has a distinguished method called **Main**, which is the entry point to the program. It is a *static* method, which means that no object instance of the **TestHello** class need be created in order to call the method. The **Main** method is called by the runtime environment, and the method may return an integer code when it exits. (Alternatively, the method may be declared as **void**, with no return value.) The **Main** method has an array of strings as an argument, which will receive the command line arguments from invoking the program.

```
// TestHello.cs

public class TestHello
{
   public static int Main(string[] args)
   {
      Hello obj;
      obj = new Hello();
      obj.SayHello();
      ...
```

Every method in C# has one or more *statements*. A statement is terminated by a semicolon. A statement may be spread out over several lines. Variables in C# must be declared.

```
      Hello obj;
```

Unlike in C++, this statement does not cause a **Hello** object to be constructed; only a reference is created. The following line instantiates the object via the **new** operator, and then a method is invoked on the object.

```
        obj = new Hello();
        obj.SayHello();
```

Command-Line Arguments

The **Hello** program does not do anything with command-line arguments. The **ShowArgs** program illustrates retrieving the command-line arguments. It shows them on one line, separated by commas. It also maintains a count of the total number of characters in these arguments. Note the syntax for working with arrays, and the **Length** property. The **for** loop is also like its counterpart in C.

```
// ShowArgs.cs

using System;

class ShowArgs
{
    static void Main(string[] args)
    {
        int numChars = 0;
        for (int i = 0; i < args.Length; i++)
        {
            numChars += args[i].Length;
            Console.Write("{0}, ", args[i]);
        }
        Console.WriteLine();
        Console.WriteLine("{0} arguments", args.Length);
        Console.WriteLine("{0} characters", numChars);
    }
}
```

If you run the program at the command line, you can simply enter the arguments when you invoke the program. Here is a sample run.

```
>showargs one two three
one, two, three,
3 arguments
11 characters
```

If you are building the project in Visual Studio, you can set the command-line arguments using project properties. In Solution Explorer right-click on the project and choose Properties from the context menu. Choose Debugging from the Configuration Properties. You can then set command-line arguments under the Start Options, as illustrated in Figure B–2.

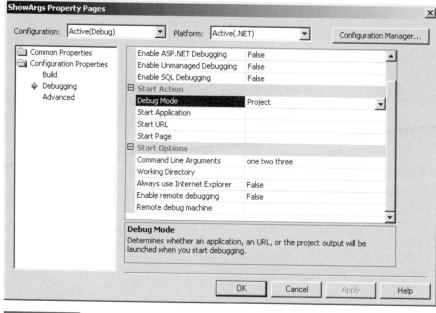

Setting command-line arguments in Visual Studio.

Hello, World (Component Version)

In terms of object-oriented programming, C# and the other .NET languages are nice, but the real innovation of .NET comes from the ease with which *components* can be created. A component can be thought of as a piece of black-box functionality, and different components can be hooked together as long as the proper external interfaces are observed. Components of a stereo system are a good example. You can plug in different speakers, and they will still work, provided the speakers use the standard interface.

In software there have been a number of different component architectures. Before .NET the leading component architecture on Microsoft systems was the Component Object Model (COM), which did indeed provide black-box reusability of software modules written in different languages. But COM requires either the program (in languages like C++) or the programming environment (in languages like Visual Basic) to implement the plumbing code required for interoperability. COM is complex and places a substantial burden on the programmer.

The beauty of .NET is that the .NET Framework itself transparently provides all the needed plumbing, and creating a .NET component out of a class is as easy as compiling as a special kind of project, a class library. Once built, other programs can call this class library merely by obtaining a reference to it. These other programs can be in any .NET language, including PerlNET.

Hello, World Class Library

As an example of creating a class library in C#, we will create a component version of our **Hello** class. A completed solution is in **HelloLib**. The source files are identical. We just compile them in a different way. To build the class library **Hello.dll** at the command line, use the **/t:library** switch (short for **/target:library**).

```
csc /t:library Hello.cs
```

To use the class library, you need to obtain a reference to it, which you can do when you build the EXE program by using the **/r** switch (short for **/reference**).

```
csc /out:TestHello.exe /r:Hello.dll TestHello.cs
```

These two compile commands are provided in the batch file **build.bat**.

A PERL CLIENT PROGRAM

You can easily create a client program **TestHello.pl** that uses this class library. See the folder **HelloPerl**. For convenience we have the C# class source file **Hello.cs** and the Perl file **TestHello.pl** together in the same folder, along with a batch file **build.bat** that builds both. (We also provide a Visual Studio solution.) Here is the Perl script.

```
#
# HelloPerl.pl
#

use strict;
use namespace "System";
use PerlNET qw(AUTOCALL);

my $obj = Hello->new();
$obj->SayHello();
$obj = Hello->new("Goodbye, world");
$obj->SayHello();
$obj->{Greeting} = "Brave New World";
Console->WriteLine($obj->{Greeting});
```

You may wish to review the Chapter 10 discussion of using .NET components in PerlNET programs.

In the rest of this appendix we will stick strictly to C# programs. As an exercise, you may wish to rebuild the C# classes as class libraries and create PerlNET programs to exercise them.

Performing Calculations in C#

Our "Hello, World" program illustrated the basic structure of a C# program and introduced classes and components, but we need a slightly more elaborate example to show the use of other basic programming constructs, such as variables, expressions, and control structures. Our next example is a simple calculator for a savings account. The user is prompted for annual contribution, interest rate, and number of years. We calculate the accumulation of deposits two ways:

- In a loop, year by year, accumulating a total as we go
- Using a formula

The example program is in the folder **Savings**.

```
// Savings.cs

using System;

class Savings
{
    public static void Main(string[] args)
    {
        InputWrapper iw = new InputWrapper();
        decimal amount;    // annual deposit amount
        decimal rate;      // interest rate
        int years;         // number of years
        decimal total;     // total accumulation
        decimal interest;  // interest in a year
        Console.Write("amount: ");
        string data = Console.ReadLine();
        amount = Convert.ToDecimal(data);
        rate = iw.getDecimal("rate: ");
        years = iw.getInt("years: ");
        total = 0m;
        Console.WriteLine("{0,4} {1,12} {2,12} {3,12}",
            "Year", "Amount", "Interest", "Total");
        for (int i = 1; i <= years; i++)
        {
            interest = total * rate;
            total += amount + interest;
            Console.WriteLine(
                "{0, -4} {1, 12:C} {2, 12:C} {3, 12:C}",
                i, amount, interest, total);
        }
        Console.WriteLine("\nTotal using formula = {0}",
            Total(years, (double) rate, (double) amount));
    }
    private static double Total(int years, double rate,
```

```
    double amount)
{
    double total =
        amount * (Math.Pow(1 + rate, years) - 1) / rate;
    long total_in_cents = (long) Math.Round(total * 100);
    total = total_in_cents /100.0;
    return total;
}
}
```

If you compile and run it, you will see this output:

```
amount: 1000
rate: .05
years: 10
Year        Amount       Interest         Total
1        $1,000.00         $0.00      $1,000.00
2        $1,000.00        $50.00      $2,050.00
3        $1,000.00       $102.50      $3,152.50
4        $1,000.00       $157.63      $4,310.13
5        $1,000.00       $215.51      $5,525.63
6        $1,000.00       $276.28      $6,801.91
7        $1,000.00       $340.10      $8,142.01
8        $1,000.00       $407.10      $9,549.11
9        $1,000.00       $477.46     $11,026.56
10       $1,000.00       $551.33     $12,577.89
```

Variables

In C# variables are of a specific data type. Some common types are **int** for integers and **double** for floating-point numbers. C# has the **decimal** data type, which has a high degree of precision, suitable for monetary calculations.

You must declare and initialize variables before you can use them.

```
int years = 10;          // reserves space and assigns
                         // an initial value
decimal interest;        // reserves space but does
                         // not initialize it to any value
```

If an initial value is not specified in the declaration, the variable must be initialized in code before it can be used. We discuss initialization later in the appendix.

Variables must be either local within a method or members of a class. There are no global variables in C#.

Literals

A *literal* is used when you explicitly write a value for a variable in a program. An integer literal is represented by either an ordinary decimal integer or a hexadecimal integer. A floating-point or decimal literal is represented by a number with a decimal point or by exponential notation. You may influence the type that is used for storing a literal by a suffix. The suffix **f** or **F** indicates single precision floating point. The suffix **d** or **D** indicates double-precision floating point. The suffix **m** or **M** indicates decimal (think money).

```
decimal rate = 0.06m;
decimal amount = 2000M;
```

There are two forms for string literals. Escape sequences are not processed for string literals that are prefixed with **@**.

```
string file1 ="c:\\test1.txt";
string file2 = @"c:\test2.txt";
```

C# Operators and Expressions

You can combine variables and literals via operators to form expressions. The C# operators are similar to those in C and C++, having similar precedence and associativity rules. There are three kinds of operators:

- *Unary* operators take one operand and use prefix notation (e.g., **–a**) or postfix notation (e.g., **a++**).
- *Binary* operators take two operands and use infix notation (e.g., **a + b**).
- The one *ternary* operator **?:** takes three operands and uses infix notation (e.g., **expr ? x : y**).

Operators are applied in the precedence order shown in Table B–1. For operators of the same precedence, order is determined by associativity.

- The assignment operator is right-associative (operations are performed from right to left).
- All other binary operators are left-associative (operations are performed from left to right).

Precedence and associativity can be controlled by parentheses; what is done first is shown as the primary operator **(x)** in the precedence table.

TABLE B–1	Operator Precedence in C#
Category	**Operators**
Primary	(x) x.y f(x) a[x] x++ x-- new typeof sizeof checked unchecked
Unary	+ - ! ~ ++x --x (T)x
Multiplicative	* / %
Additive	+ -
Shift	<< >>

TABLE B—1	*Operator Precedence in C# (continued)*
Category	**Operators**
Relational	`<  >  <=  >=  is  as`
Equality	`==  !=`
Logical AND	`&`
Logical XOR	`^`
Logical OR	`|`
Conditional AND	`&&`
Conditional OR	`||`
Conditional	`?:`
Assignment	`=  *=  /=  %=  +=  -=  <<=  >>=  &=  ^=  |=`

Output and Formatting

The **Console** class in the **System** namespace supports two simple methods for performing output:

- **WriteLine** writes out a string followed by a new line.
- **Write** writes out just the string without the new line.

You can write out other data types by relying on the **ToString** method of **System.Object**, which will provide a string representation of any data type. We discussed the root class **System.Object** in Chapter 13, where we also saw how to override **ToString** for your own custom data type. You can use the string concatenation operator + to build up an output string.

```
int x = 24;
int y = 5;
int z = x * y;
Console.Write("Product of " + x + " and " + y);
Console.WriteLine(" is " + z);
```

The output is all on one line:

```
Product of 24 and 5 is 120
```

PLACEHOLDERS

A more convenient way to build up an output string is to use *placeholders:* {0}, {1}, and so on. An equivalent way to do the output shown above is

```
Console.WriteLine("Product of {0} and {1} is {2}", x,y,z);
```

The program **OutputDemo** illustrates the output operations just discussed.

Code Example

We will generally use placeholders for our output from now on. Placeholders can be combined with formatting characters to control output format.

FORMAT STRINGS

C# has extensive formatting capabilities, which you can control through place-holders and format strings.

- Simple placeholders: {n}, where n is 0, 1, 2, … , indicating which variable to insert
- Control width: {n,w}, where w is the width (positive for right justified and negative for left justified) of the inserted variable
- Format string: {n:S}, where S is a format string indicating how to display the variable
- Width and format string: {n,w:S}

A format string consists of a format character followed by an optional precision specifier. Table B–2 shows the available format characters. (These format characters are defined in the .NET Framework, and thus can be used in other .NET languages, including PerlNET.)

TABLE B–2	.NET Format Characters
Format Character	**Meaning**
C	Currency (locale specific)
D	Decimal integer
E	Exponential (scientific)
F	Fixed point
G	General (E or F)
N	Number with embedded commas
X	Hexadecimal

SAMPLE FORMATTING CODE

Our sample program **Savings** provides an illustration. The header uses width specifiers, and the output inside the loop uses width specifiers and the currency format character.

```
...
Console.WriteLine("{0,4} {1,12} {2,12} {3,12}",
   "Year", "Amount", "Interest", "Total");
for (int i = 1; i <= years; i++)
{
   interest = total * rate;
   total += amount + interest;
   Console.WriteLine(
      "{0, -4} {1, 12:C} {2, 12:C} {3, 12:C}",
      i, amount, interest, total);
}
...
```

Control Structures

The preceding code fragment illustrates a **for** loop. The C# control structures include the familiar control structures of the C family of languages,

- if
- while
- do
- for
- switch
- break
- continue
- return
- goto

These all have standard semantics, except for *switch*, which is less error prone in C#. There are several other control statements in C#:

- There is a **foreach** loop, which we discuss later in connection with arrays and collections.
- The **throw** statement is used with exceptions. We discuss exceptions later in this appendix.
- The **lock** statement can be used to enforce synchronization in multi-threading situations.

SWITCH STATEMENT

In C#, after a particular case statement is executed, control does not automatically continue to the next statement. You must explicitly specify the next statement, typically by a **break** or **goto** *label*. (As in C and C++, you may call for identical handling of several cases by having empty statements for all the case labels except the last one.) In C# you may also switch on a **string** data type. The program **SwitchDemo** illustrates use of the **switch** statement in C#.

Code Example

```
...
switch(scores[i])
{
    case 1:
        Console.Write("Very ");
        goto case 2;  // cannot fall through
    case 2:
        Console.WriteLine("Low");
        break;
    case 3:
        Console.WriteLine("Medium");
        break;
    case 4:
    case 5:
        Console.WriteLine("High");
```

```
                    break;
            default:
                Console.WriteLine("Special Case");
                break;
        }
    . . .
```

Methods

Our **Savings** example program has a method **Total** for computing the total accumulation by use of a formula. In C# *every* function is a method of some class; there are no freestanding functions. If the method does not refer to any instance variables of the class, the method can be *static*. We discuss instance data of a class later in this appendix. Since the method is accessed only from within the class, it is designated as *private*.

Note the use of the **Pow** and **Round** methods of the **Math** class, which is another class in the **System** namespace. These methods are static methods. To call a static method from outside the class in which it is defined, place the name of the class followed by a period before the method name. In C# you cannot employ the alternative C++ style of using an instance name to qualify a static method.

```
  . . .
  private static double Total(int years, double rate,
      double amount)
  {
      double total² =
          amount * (Math.Pow(1 + rate, years) - 1) / rate;
      long total_in_cents = (long) Math.Round(total * 100);
      total = total_in_cents /100.0;
      return total;
  }
  . . .
```

Console Input in C#

An easy, uniform way to do input for various data types is to read the data as a string and then convert to the desired data type. Use the **ReadLine** method of the **System.Console** class to read in a string. Use the **ToXxxx** methods of the **System.Convert** class to convert the data to the type you need.

```
Console.Write("amount: ");
string data = Console.ReadLine();
amount = Convert.ToDecimal(data);
```

---

2. Note that identifiers in C# are case-sensitive, so the variable **total** is different from the method **Total**. Such usage is not recommended but is permissible.

Although console input in C# is fairly simple, we can make it even easier using object-oriented programming. We can encapsulate the details of input in an easy-to-use wrapper class, **InputWrapper** (which is not part of the .NET Framework class library).

USING THE INPUTWRAPPER CLASS

In C# you instantiate a class by using the **new** keyword.

```
InputWrapper iw = new InputWrapper();
```

This code creates the object instance **iw** of the **InputWrapper** class.

The **InputWrapper** class wraps interactive input for several basic data types. The supported data types are **int**, **double**, **decimal**, and **string**. Methods **getInt**, **getDouble**, **getDecimal**, and **getString** are provided to read those types from the command line. A prompt string is passed as an input parameter. For convenience, we provide the file **InputWrapper.cs** in each project where we use it.

You can use the **InputWrapper** class without knowing its implementation. With such encapsulation, complex functionality can be hidden by an easy-to-use interface.

C# Type System

In C# there is a fundamental distinction between *value* types and *reference* types. Value types have storage allocated immediately on the stack when the variable is declared. Reference types have storage allocated on the heap, and the variable is only a reference to the actual data, which can be allocated later.

We looked at classes in the first section. A class defines a reference type. In this section we survey the entire C# type system, including simple types such as **int** and **decimal**. In C# a **struct** has many similarities to a **class** but is a value type. Another important kind of value type in C# is an **enum**. All types in C# are rooted in a fundamental base class called **object**.[3] In C# "everything is an object," and value types are transparently converted to object references as needed through a process known as *boxing*. The inverse process, *unboxing*, returns an object to the value type from which it came.

Value Types

Value types directly contain their data. Each variable of a value type has its own copy of the data. Value types typically are allocated on the stack and are

---

3. The C# keyword **object** is just another name for the .NET class **System.Object**.

automatically destroyed when the variable goes out of scope. Value types include the simple types like **int** and **decimal**, structures, and enumeration types.

SIMPLE TYPES

The simple data types are general-purpose value data types, including numeric, character, and Boolean.

- The **sbyte** data type is an 8-bit signed integer.
- The **byte** data type is an 8-bit unsigned integer.
- The **short** data type is a 16-bit signed integer.
- The **ushort** data type is a 16-bit unsigned integer.
- The **int** data type is a 32-bit signed integer.
- The **uint** data type is a 32-bit unsigned integer.
- The **long** data type is a 64-bit signed integer.
- The **ulong** data type is a 64-bit unsigned integer.
- The **char** data type is a Unicode character (16 bits).
- The **float** data type is a single-precision floating point.
- The **double** data type is a double-precision floating point.
- The **bool** data type is a Boolean (**true** or **false**).
- The **decimal** data type is a decimal type with 28 significant digits (typically used for financial purposes).

STRUCTURES

A **struct** is a value type that can group heterogeneous types together. It can also have constructors and methods. In C++ the concepts of **class** and **struct** are very close. In C++ a class has default visibility of **private** and a struct has default visibility of **public**, and that is the *only* difference. There is a more fundamental difference in C#.

In C# the key difference between a class and a struct is that a class is a *reference* type and a struct is a *value* type. A class must be instantiated explicitly using **new**. The new instance is created on the heap, and memory is managed by the system through a garbage-collection process. Since a default constructor will be created for a struct if none is defined, a struct declared on the stack will be initialized. You may also use **new**. A new instance of a struct is created on the stack, and the instance will be deallocated when it goes out of scope.

There are different semantics for assignment, whether done explicitly or via call by value mechanism in a method call. For a class, you will get a second object reference, and both object references refer to the same data. For a struct, you will get a completely independent copy of the data in the struct.

ENUMERATION TYPES

The final kind of value type is an *enumeration* type. An enumeration type is a distinct type with named constants. Every enumeration type has an underlying type, which is one of the following.

- byte
- short
- int
- long

An enumeration type is defined through an **enum** declaration.

```
public enum ItemStatus :  byte
{
   NotFound,    // 0 implicitly
   NotEnough,   // 1 implicitly
   Ok = 5       // explicit value
}
```

If the type is not specified, **int** is used. By default, the first **enum** member is assigned the value 0, the second member 1, and so on. Constant values can be explicitly assigned.

You can make use of an enumeration type by declaring a variable of the type indicated in the **enum** declaration (e.g., **BookingStatus**). You can refer to the enumerated values by using the dot notation. Here is some illustrative code:

```
ItemStatus status = inven.BuyItem(id, qty, out avail);
if (status == ItemStatus.NotFound)
   Console.WriteLine("Item not found");
...
```

REFERENCE TYPES

Reference types do not contain data directly but only refer to data. Variables of reference types store references to data, called objects. Two different variables can reference the same object. Reference types are allocated on the *managed heap* and eventually get destroyed through a process known as *garbage collection*. Reference types include **string**, **object**, class types, array types, interfaces, and delegates.

Reference types have a special value **null**, which indicates the absence of an instance.

Two classes in the .NET Framework class library are so important that they have C#-reserved words as aliases for them: **object** and **string**.

OBJECT

The **object** class type is the ultimate base type for all types in C#. Every C# type derives directly or indirectly from **object**. The **object** keyword in C# is an alias for the predefined **System.Object** class. **System.Object** has methods such as **ToString**, **Equals**, and **Finalize**, which we will study later.

STRING

The **string** class encapsulates a Unicode character string. The **string** keyword is an alias for the predefined **System.String** class. The string type is a *sealed* class. (A sealed class is one that cannot be used as the base class for any other classes.)

The **string** class inherits directly from the root **object** class. String literals are defined using double quotes. There are useful built-in methods for **string**. For now, note that the **Equals** method can be used to test for equality of strings.

```
string a = "hello";
if (a.Equals("hello"))
    Console.WriteLine("equal");
else
    Console.WriteLine("not equal");
```

There are also overloaded operators:

```
if (a == "hello")
    ...
```

Boxing and Unboxing

One of the strong features of C# is that it has a unified type system. Every type, including the simple built-in types such as **int**, derive from **System.Object**. In C# "everything is an object."

A language such as Smalltalk also has such a feature but pays the price of inefficiency for simple types. Languages such as C++ and Java treat simple built-in types differently from objects, thus obtaining efficiency but at the cost of a non-unified type system.

C# enjoys the best of both worlds through a process known as *boxing*. Boxing converts a value type such as **int** or a **struct** to an object reference and is done implicitly. *Unboxing* converts a boxed value type (stored on the heap) back to an unboxed simple value (stored on the stack). Unboxing is done through a type cast.

```
int x = 5;
object o = x;        // boxing
x = (int) o;         // unboxing
```

Inheritance in C#

C# supports a single inheritance model. Thus a class may derive from a single base class, and not from more than one. (In fact, as we saw earlier in the appendix, every class in C# ultimately derives from the root class **System.Object**. In C# we may use the alias **object** for this root class.) This single inheritance model is simple and avoids the complexities and ambiguities associated with multiple inheritance in C++. Although a C# class can inherit only from a single base *class*, it may inherit from several *interfaces*, a topic we will discuss later.

Inheritance Fundamentals

With inheritance, you factor the abstractions in your object model and put the more reusable abstractions in a high-level base class. You can add or change features in more specialized derived classes, which "inherit" the standard behavior from the base class. Inheritance facilitates code reuse and extensibility.

As an example, consider a class **Item** that models rather generic items that may be stocked. A special kind of item is **Book**, which we can model as a class that derives from **Item**. Since every class derives from **object**, we have the simple inheritance hierarchy shown in Figure B–3.

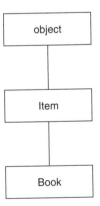

FIGURE B–3   *A three-level inheritance hierarchy ultimately deriving from **object**.*

The two attributes of an **Item** are **Id** and **Name**, which are implemented as properties. There is also a method **GetItem**, which returns a string representation of the item. The class is defined in the file **Item.cs** in the folder **Test-Book**.

Code
Example

```
// Item.cs

public class Item
```

```
{
   private int m_id;
   private string m_name;
   public Item(int id, string name)
   {
      m_id = id;
      m_name = name;
   }
   public int Id
   {
      get
      {
         return m_id;
      }
   }
   public string Name
   {
      get
      {
         return m_name;
      }
      set
      {
         m_name = value;
      }
   }
   public virtual string GetItem()
   {
      return m_id + " " + m_name;
   }
}
```

You should be familiar with the syntax in this class from our earlier **Hello** example, including definition of properties. The only new feature is the use of the keyword **virtual** in the **GetItem** method. We discuss **virtual** shortly.

C# INHERITANCE SYNTAX

You implement inheritance in C# by specifying the derived class in the **class** statement with a colon followed by the base class. The file **Book.cs** in the **Test-Book** folder illustrates deriving a new class **Book** from the class **Item**.

```
// Book.cs

public class Book : Item
{
   private string m_author;
   public Book(int id, string name, string author)
      : base(id, name)
   {
```

```
        m_author = author;
   }
   public override string GetItem()
   {
      return base.GetItem() + " " + m_author;
   }
   public string Author
   {
      set
      {
         m_author = value;
      }
   }
}
```

The class **Book** automatically has all the members of **Item**, and in addition has the write-only property **Author**. The derived class also has a new constructor, and it overrides the method **GetItem**.

INVOKING BASE CLASS CONSTRUCTORS AND METHODS

If your derived class has a constructor with parameters, you may wish to pass some of these parameters along to a base class constructor. In C# you can conveniently invoke a base class constructor by using a colon followed by the **base** keyword and a parameter list.

```
   public Book(int id, string name, string author)
      : base(id, name)
   {
      m_author = author;
   }
```

Note that the syntax allows you to explicitly invoke a constructor only of an immediate base class. There is no notation that allows you to directly invoke a constructor higher up the inheritance hierarchy.

The **base** keyword can also be used to invoke a method of the base class.

```
   public override string GetItem()
   {
      return base.GetItem() + " " + m_author;
   }
```

VIRTUAL METHODS AND OVERRIDING

The **GetString** method in the base class uses the keyword **virtual** in its definition. This makes binding to the method dynamic so that if several classes in a class hierarchy all implement the same virtual method, the method selected will be determined at runtime by the class of the invoking object. We call this ability to determine the method at runtime *polymorphism*.

In some languages such as C++ the use of the **virtual** keyword is the complete story, and methods in derived classes that have the same name and signature will automatically override the method. This behavior can give rise to a subtle problem known as the *fragile base class problem*. You may derive a class from some base class in a third-party class library and provide an ordinary method that does not exist in the base class. Then an update to the class library provides a new virtual method that happens to have the same name and signature. Now the behavior of the program may be changed, as in some cases your method may wind up being invoked rather than the new method in the class library.

C# provides a safeguard against this potential difficulty by requiring the use of the **override** keyword in a derived class if you want to override a method in a base class.

```
public override string GetItem()
{
    return base.GetItem() + " " + m_author;
}
```

TEST PROGRAM

The test program **TestBook.cs** illustrates using objects of both the base class and derived class. Note in particular the last part of the program where we create a heterogeneous array of **Item** objects, where in fact the actual objects in the array may be instances of any class in the hierarchy, in our case **Item** or **Book**. When we call the virtual method **GetItem**, the proper method is invoked.

```
// TestBook.cs

using System;

public class TestBook
{
    public static void Main()
    {
        Item itm = new Item(1, "Notebook");
        Console.WriteLine(itm.GetItem());
        Book bk = new Book(2, "Moby Dick", "Walt Whitman");
        Console.WriteLine(bk.GetItem());
        Console.WriteLine("OOPS!!!");
        bk.Author = "Herman Melville";
        Item[] items = new Item[] {itm, bk};
        foreach (Item item in items)
        {
            Console.WriteLine(item.GetItem());
        }
    }
}
```

Here is the output:

```
1 Notebook
2 Moby Dick Walt Whitman
OOPS!!!
1 Notebook
2 Moby Dick Herman Melville
```

Case Study

We conclude this survival guide with a somewhat larger example that illustrates the concepts we have already discussed and also introduces a few additional features of C#. Our example is a version of the Stock Management System that we have used as a case study throughout the second part of this book. The sample code is in the folder **StockManager**.

StockDefs.cs

The file **StockDefs.cs** defines an enumeration, a structure, and an interface that are used in the system.

```csharp
// StockDefs.cs

using System.Collections;

public enum ItemStatus :  byte
{
    NotFound,     // 0 implicitly
    NotEnough,    // 1 implicitly
    Ok = 5        // explicit value
}

public struct StockItemStruct
{
    public int Id;
    public string Name;
    public int Count;
}

public interface IStock
{
    int AddItem(string name, int count);
    void DeleteItem(int id);
    void RestockItem(int id, int qty);
    ArrayList GetItems(int id);
    ItemStatus BuyItem(int id, int qty, out int avail);
}
```

INTERFACES

We define an *interface* **IStock** that specifies a *contract* for our Stock Management System, independently of its implementation. Our class **Inventory** will implement this interface, and it must do so completely and precisely—it must support all the methods of the interface, and each method must have an exact match of the signature.

A class indicates that it implements an interface by using a colon notation, similar to the notation for inheritance.

```
public class Inventory : IStock
{
    . . .
```

But while a class can inherit from only a single base class, it can implement multiple interfaces. If a class inherits both from a class and from one or more interfaces, the class is shown first.

```
public class BookInventory : Inventory, IStock, IAccount
{
    . . .
```

Interfaces are very important in the .NET Framework, which defines many standard interfaces that you can optionally implement in your own classes. Chapter 12 provides an illustration of implementing the .NET interface **IComparable** using Perl. While you can implement existing interfaces in Perl, at present you cannot define new interfaces using PerlNET. In C# you can both define and implement interfaces.

REF AND *OUT* PARAMETERS

The standard parameter-passing mechanism in C# is *call-by-value* (as it is in C and in Perl). This means that a copy is made of arguments to method calls, and if you change an argument in the called method, the change will not be reflected in the method that made the call.

C# supports two other parameter-passing mechanisms. The keyword **ref** indicates a *reference* parameter, in which case the parameter inside the method and the corresponding actual argument refer to the same argument. The keyword **out** refers to an *output* parameter, which is the same as a reference parameter, except that on the calling side, the parameter need not be assigned prior to the call.

Normally, you can return a value simply as the return value of a method call. But if you want to pass back two or more values, a **ref** or **out** parameter is useful. Note that you must use the keyword in the method call as well as in the method definition.

```
int avail;
ItemStatus status = inven.BuyItem(id, qty, out avail);
```

```
if (status == ItemStatus.NotFound)
   Console.WriteLine("Item not found");
...
```

StockItem.cs

The file **StockItem.cs** contains the definition of the **StockItem** class. This class
is very similar to other versions of **StockItem** that we have used elsewhere in
the book. It defines the attributes **Id**, **Name**, and **Count**, implemented as public properties with private data members.

```
// StockItem.cs

public class StockItem
{
   private int m_id;
   private string m_name;
   private int m_count;
   static private int m_nextId = 1;
   public StockItem(string name, int count)
   {
      m_id = m_nextId++;
      m_name = name;
      m_count = count;
   }
   public StockItem(int id)
   {
      m_id = id;
      m_name = "";
      m_count = 0;
   }
   public override bool Equals(object obj)
   {
      StockItem item = (StockItem) obj;
      return (item.m_id == m_id);
   }
   public override int GetHashCode()
   {
      return m_id;
   }
   public override string ToString()
   {
      return m_id + " " + m_name + m_count ;
   }
   public int Id
   {
      get
      {
         return m_id;
      }
```

```
    }
    public string Name
    {
       get
       {
          return m_name;
       }
    }
    public int Count
    {
       get
       {
          return m_count;
       }
       set
       {
          m_count = value;
       }
    }
}
```

STATIC DATA MEMBERS

Ordinary data members of a class have unique data for each object instance. Sometimes it is useful to have a *static* data member that is shared by all object instances. In the **StockItem** class we maintain the static variable **m_nextId** that can be used to automatically generate a new ID every time a new stock item is constructed.

```
static private int m_nextId = 1;
public StockItem(string name, int count)
{
   m_id = m_nextId++;
   m_name = name;
   m_count = count;
}
...
```

OVERRIDING METHODS OF OBJECT

In order to make your class well behaved in the .NET Framework, you should normally override certain methods of the **object** root class. **ToString** will return a reasonable string representation of your object instance (default behavior is to return the name of the class). **Equals** will perform a test of equality of two objects (default behavior is to test for reference equality—which means that two different references that refer to objects with identical data will test out as not equal). **GetHashCode** calculates an integer hash for your object instance. The C# compiler will issue a warning if you override **Equals** but not if you override **GetHashCode**.

We rely on the override of **Equals** in our code for removing an item from a collection. This topic is discussed more completely in Chapter 13.

Inventory.cs

The file **Inventory.cs** contains the implementation of the **Inventory** class, which is a collection of **StockItem** instances.

```
// Inventory.cs

using System;
using System.Collections;

public class Inventory : IStock
{
    private ArrayList items;
    public Inventory()
    {
        items = new ArrayList();
        AddItem("Notebook", 10);
        AddItem("Monitor", 20);
    }
    public int AddItem(string name, int count)
    {
        StockItem item = new StockItem(name, count);
        items.Add(item);
        return item.Id;
    }
    public void DeleteItem(int id)
    {
        StockItem item = new StockItem(id);
        items.Remove(item);
    }
    public void RestockItem(int id, int qty)
    {
        StockItem item = FindItem(id);
        if (item != null)
            item.Count += qty;
    }
    public ArrayList GetItems(int id)
    {
        StockItemStruct sitem;
        ArrayList list = new ArrayList();
        if (!CheckId(id) && id != -1)
            return null;
        foreach (StockItem item in items)
        {
            if (id == -1 || id == item.Id)
            {
                sitem.Id = item.Id;
```

```
            sitem.Name = item.Name;
            sitem.Count = item.Count;
            list.Add(sitem);
        }
    }
    return list;
}
public ItemStatus BuyItem(int id, int qty,
    out int avail)
{
    avail = 0;
    StockItem item = FindItem(id);
    if (item == null)
        return ItemStatus.NotFound;
    else if (qty <= item.Count)
    {
        item.Count -= qty;
        return ItemStatus.Ok;
    }
    else
    {
        avail = item.Count;
        return ItemStatus.NotEnough;
    }
}
private bool CheckId(int id)
{
    StockItem item = new StockItem(id);
    return items.Contains(item);
}
private StockItem FindItem(int id)
{
    foreach (StockItem item in items)
    {
        if (item.Id == id)
            return item;
    }
    return null;
}
}
```

The .NET Framework defines a number of useful collection classes in the namespace **System.Collections**. A particularly useful class is **ArrayList**, which is a list of items stored like an array. An array list can be dynamically sized and will grow as necessary to accommodate new elements being added. Collection classes are made up of instances of type **object** and thus can be used to store any kind of data. Our **Inventory** class uses an array list to store a list of **StockItem** instances. The C# **foreach** loop is a convenient control structure for iterating through the items in a collection.

StockManager.cs

The file **StockManager.cs** contains code for exercising the **Inventory** class. It uses the **InputWrapper** class to simplify console input. By this time the code in this class should be quite understandable. The one new feature is using exceptions in C#.

```csharp
// StockManager.cs

using System;
using System.Collections;

public class StockManager
{
    public static void Main()
    {
        Inventory inven = new Inventory();
        InputWrapper iw = new InputWrapper();
        string cmd;
        Console.WriteLine(
            "Welcome to Stock Management System");
        Console.WriteLine(
            "For the list of commands type help");
        cmd = iw.getString(">>");
        while (! cmd.Equals("quit"))
        {
            try
            {
                if (cmd.Equals("show"))
                {
                    int id = iw.getInt("id (-1 for all): ");
                    ShowItemList(inven.GetItems(id));
                }
                else if (cmd.Equals("all"))
                {
                    ShowItemList(inven.GetItems(-1));
                }
                else if (cmd.Equals("add"))
                {
                    string name = iw.getString("name: ");
                    int count = iw.getInt("count: ");
                    int id = inven.AddItem(name, count);
                    Console.WriteLine("id = {0}", id);
                }
                else if (cmd.Equals("rmv"))
                {
                    int id = iw.getInt("id: ");
                    inven.DeleteItem(id);
                }
                else if (cmd.Equals("buy"))
```

```csharp
        {
            int id = iw.getInt("id: ");
            int qty = iw.getInt("quantity: ");
            int avail;
            ItemStatus status =
                inven.BuyItem(id, qty, out avail);
            if (status == ItemStatus.NotFound)
                Console.WriteLine("Item not found");
            else if (status == ItemStatus.NotEnough)
            {
                Console.WriteLine("Order not filled");
                Console.WriteLine(
                    "Only {0} items available", avail);
            }
        }
        else
            help();
    }
    catch (Exception e)
    {
        Console.WriteLine("Exception: {0}", e.Message);
    }
    cmd = iw.getString(">> ");
    }
}
private static void help()
{
    Console.WriteLine(
        "The following commands are available:");
    Console.WriteLine(
        "\tshow        show selected item(s)");
    Console.WriteLine("\tall         show all items");
    Console.WriteLine("\tadd         add an item");
    Console.WriteLine("\trmv         remove an item");
    Console.WriteLine("\tquit        exit the program");
}
private static void ShowItemList(ArrayList list)
{
    foreach (StockItemStruct sitem in list)
    {
        string strid = sitem.Id.ToString().PadLeft(4);
        string name = sitem.Name.PadRight(12);
        string strcount =
            sitem.Count.ToString().PadLeft(4);
        string str =
            strid + "    " + name + "    " + strcount;
        Console.WriteLine(str);
    }
}
}
```

Here is a sample run, illustrating both some normal operations and some exceptional conditions.

```
Welcome to Stock Management System
For the list of commands type help
>>all
   1    Notebook          10
   2    Monitor           20
>> add
name: Phone
count: 30
id = 3
>> all
   1    Notebook          10
   2    Monitor           20
   3    Phone             30
>> buy
id: 2
quantity: 5
>> buy
id: 2
quantity: 16
Order not filled
Only 15 items available
>> all
   1    Notebook          10
   2    Monitor           15
   3    Phone             30
>> buy
id: 2
quantity: 1x
Exception: Input string was not in a correct format.
>> buy
id: 2
quantity: 15
>> all
   1    Notebook          10
   2    Monitor            0
   3    Phone             30
>> rmv
id: 2
>> all
   1    Notebook          10
   3    Phone             30
>>
```

EXCEPTIONS

An inevitable part of programming is dealing with error conditions of various sorts. Our program illustrates the exception-handling mechanism of C#. You enclose a code that may encounter an exception in a **try** block. You handle the exception in a **catch** block. Although not shown in our example, you can raise exceptions by a **throw** statement. The .NET class library provides an **Exception** class, which you can use to pass information about an exception that occurred. To further specify your exception and to pass additional information, you can derive your own class from **Exception**. When handling an exception, you may want to throw a new exception. In such a case you can use the "inner exception" feature of the **Exception** class to pass the original exception on with your new exception.

As discussed in Chapter 12, you can work with exceptions in PerlNET through the **eval** block and the **die** function. This chapter also illustrates C# exceptions.

Summary

This concludes our C# survival guide. C# is a language that is object-oriented from the ground up, and we began our exploration of C# with an object-oriented version of the famous "Hello, World" program. C# provides the class mechanism for creating abstractions, and through access specifiers such as **private** you can achieve encapsulation of your data. C# has standard C-like control structures. C# has a wealth of data types. Value types store the data itself, and reference types store a reference to the data. C# supports a single inheritance model. With C# you can also define and use interfaces. C# supports exception handling. We provided an implementation of our Stock Management System as a case study, illustrating a number of features of this new programming language. We hope you enjoyed it!

INDEX

▼ Q

▼ R

▼ S

DEVELOPER TRAINING

OBJECT INNOVATIONS offers training course materials in fundamental software technologies used in developing applications in modern computing environments. We emphasize object-oriented techniques, with a focus on Microsoft® technologies, XML, Java™, and Linux®. Our courses have been used by businesses, training companies, and universities throughout North America. End clients include Microsoft, IBM®, HP®, Dell®, Compaq®, FedEx®, UPS®, AOL®, U.S. Bank®, Mellon Bank®, and NASA. Our courses are frequently updated to reflect feedback from classroom use. We aggressively track new technologies and endeavor to keep our courseware up-to-date.

Founded in 1993, Object Innovations has a long record of firsts in courseware. Our Visual C++ course was released before Microsoft's, we introduced one of the first courses in JavaServer Pages, and our Linux Internals 2.4 kernel course came out several months before Red Hat's course. Now we are leading the development of comprehensive developer training in Microsoft's .NET technology.

.NET DEVELOPER TRAINING

OBJECT INNOVATIONS is writing the premier book series on .NET for Prentice Hall PTR. These authoritative books are the foundation of our curriculum and are an ideal supplement to .NET training courses. We provide both comprehensive 5-day courses and also shorter courses focused on specific aspects of .NET technology. Our curriculum is evolving, so please check our Web site *www.objectinnovations.com* for current information. The following is a representative list of our courses.

401	Introduction to .NET for Developers (1 day)
402	.NET Overview (1 day)
410	Object Oriented Programming in C# (5 days)
411	C# Essentials (2 days)
414	Application Development Using C# and .NET (5 days)
415	.NET Framework Using C# (3 days)
416	ASP.NET Using C# (3 days)
420	Introduction to Programming Visual Basic Using .NET (5 days)
421	VB.NET Essentials (2 days)
424	Application Development Using Visual Basic and .NET (5 days)
425	.NET Framework Using VB.NET (3 days)
426	ASP.NET Using VB.NET (3 days)
434	.NET Architecture and Programming Using Visual C++ (5 days)
451	Web Services Using Microsoft .NET and C# (5 days)

MICROSOFT DEVELOPER TRAINING

Our Microsoft curriculum is very extensive, with introductory and advanced courses on MFC, COM/DCOM, OLE, COM+, and advanced topics in Visual Basic™. Selected courses include:

    123   Programming COM and DCOM Using ATL (5 days)
    127   Programming COM and OLE Using MFC (5 days)
    149   Distributed COM+ Programming (5 days)
    133   Distributed COM+ Programming Using Visual Basic (5 days)
    145   MFC Windows Programming for C++ Programmers (5 days)

XML AND WEB SERVICES DEVELOPER TRAINING

Our XML curriculum covers the broad range of XML technology. We offer courses in "pure" XML—all discussions and exercises based entirely on W3C recommended standards—as well as training in the use of XML through today's dominant enterprise platforms, .NET and Java. We offer Web services training using both .NET and Java. Selected courses include:

    511   XML for the Enterprise (5 days)
    514   Powering Web Sites Using XML (4 days)
    542   XML Programming Using Java (3 days)
    562   Fundamentals of Java Web-Service Development (3 days)
    451   Web Services Using Microsoft .NET and C# (5 days)

JAVA DEVELOPER TRAINING

Java training courses span the spectrum from beginning to advanced and provide extensive coverage of both client-side and server-side technologies. We emphasize distributed application development using Java. Selected courses include:

    103   Java Programming (5 days)
    105   Using and Developing JavaBeans (4 days)
    106   CORBA Architecture and Programming Using Java (4 days)
    109   JavaServer Pages (2 days)
    163   Enterprise JavaBeans (4 days)
    172   Java Foundation Classes (5 days)

LINUX AND PERL COURSES

Linux courses range from fundamentals and system administration to advanced courses in internals, device drivers and networking. We offer introductory and advanced courses in Perl. Selected courses include:

    135   Fundamentals of Linux (4 days)
    310   Linux Internals (5 days)
    314   Linux Network Drivers Development (3 days)
    158   Programming in Perl (5 days)
    159   Advanced Perl Programming (4 days)

See our Web site for complete course listings: www.objectinnovations.com

OBJECT INNOVATIONS .NET TRAINING PARTNERS

For information about .NET training using OBJECT INNOVATIONS courseware,
please check with our .NET Training Partners.

ANEW TECHNOLOGY CORPORATION   www.Anew.net

Specialized in IT consulting, training, mentoring, and development, Anew Technology has been serving many satisfied clients. Our business mission is threefold: to stay at the forefront of IT technologies, to satisfy client needs by applying these technologies, and to provide the best service in our industry. Anew Technology is a business partner with Object Innovations in operations and courseware development.

COMPUTER HORIZONS   www.ComputerHorizons.com/Training

For over sixteen years Computer Horizons Education Division (CHED) has been providing on-site, instructor-led IT training and customized workshops for organizations nationwide. We have developed extensive curriculum offerings in Web Technologies, Relational Databases, Reporting Tools, Process Improvement, UNIX® and LINUX®, Client/Server, Mainframe & Legacy Systems, Windows® 2000, and much more. CHED will design, develop and deliver a training solution tailored to each client's training requirements.

COMPUWORKS SYSTEMS, INC.   www.CompuWorks.com

CompuWorks Systems, Inc. is an IT solutions company whose aim is to provide our clients with customized training, support and development services. We are committed to building long term partnerships with our clients in an effort to meet their individual needs. Cutting-edge solutions are our specialty.

CUSTOM TRAINING INSTITUTE   www.CustomTraining.com

Custom Training Institute is a provider of high quality High-End training since 1989. Along with our full line of "off-the-shelf" classes, we excel at providing customized Solutions—from technical needs assessment through course development and delivery. We specialize in Legacy Skill Transformation, Oracle, UNIX, C++, Java™ and other subjects for computer professionals.

DB BASICS   www.DBBasics.com

DBBasics, founded in 1988 as a Microsoft® solution development company, has developed and delivered Microsoft technology training since its inception. DBBasics specializes in delivering database and developer technology training to corporate customers. Our vast development experience, coupled with the requirement for instructors to consistently provide hands-on consulting to our customers, enables DBBasics to provide best of breed instruction in the classroom. In addition to instructor-led training, DBBasics also develops customized eLearning solutions and provides database technology consulting.

DEVCOM   www.dev-cominc.com

Devcom Corporation offers a full line of courses and seminars for software developers and engineers. Currently Devcom provides technical courses and seminars around the country for Hewlett-Packard®, Compaq® Computer, Informix® Software, Silicon Graphics®, Quantum/Maxtor® and Gateway® Inc. Our senior .NET/C# instructor is currently working in conjunction with Microsoft to provide .NET training to their internal technical staff.

FOCAL POINT   www.FocalPoint-Inc.com

Focal Point specializes in providing optimum instructor-led Information Technology training for our corporate clients on either an onsite basis, or in regional public courses. All of our course curricula is either developed by our staff of "World Class Instructors" or upon careful evaluation and scrutiny is adopted and acquired from our training partners who are similarly focused. Our course offerings pay special attention to Real World issues. Our classes are targeted toward topical areas that will ensure immediate productivity upon course completion.

OBJECT INNOVATIONS .NET TRAINING PARTNERS

For information about .NET training using OBJECT INNOVATIONS courseware,
please check with our .NET Training Partners.

I/SRG   www.isrg.com

The I/S RESOURCE GROUP helps organizations to understand, plan for and implement emerging I/S technologies and methodologies. By combining education, training, briefings and consulting, we assist our clients to effectively apply I/S technologies to achieve business benefits. Our eBusiness Application Bootcamp is an integrated set of courses that prepares learners to utilize XML, OOAD, Java™, JSP, EJB, ASP, CORBA and .NET to build eBusiness applications. Our eBusiness Briefings pinpoint emerging technologies and methodologies.

RELIABLE SOFTWARE   www.ReliableSoftware.com

Reliable Software, Inc. uses Microsoft technology to quickly develop cost-effective software solutions for the small to mid-size business or business unit. We use state-of-the-art techniques to allow business rules, database models and the user interface to evolve as your business needs evolve. We can provide design and implementation consulting, or training.

SKILLBRIDGE TRAINING   www.SkillBridgeTraining.com

SkillBridge is a leading provider of blended training solutions. The company's service offerings are designed to meet a wide variety of client requirements. Offering an integration of instructor-led training, e-learning and mentoring programs, SkillBridge delivers high value solutions in a cost-effective manner. SkillBridge's technology focus includes, among others, programming languages, operating systems, databases, and internet and web technologies.

/TRAINING/ETC INC.   www.trainingetc.com

A training company dedicated to delivering quality technical training, courseware development, and consulting in a variety of subject matter areas, including Programming Languages and Design (including C, C++, OOAD/UML, Perl, and Java), a complete UNIX curriculum (from UNIX Fundamentals to System Administration), the Internet (including HTML/CGI, XML and JavaScript Programming) and RDBMS (including Oracle and Sybase).

WATERMARK LEARNING   www.WatermarkLearning.com

Watermark Learning provides a wide range of IT skill development training and mentoring services to a variety of industries, software/consulting firms and government. We provide flexible options for delivery: onsite, consortium and public classes in three major areas: project management, requirements analysis and software development, including e-Commerce. Our instructors are seasoned, knowledgeable practitioners, who use their industry experience along with our highly-rated courseware to effectively build technical skills relevant to your business need.

informIT